FREEING CHINA'S FARMERS RURAL RESTRUCTURING IN THE REFORM ERA

SOCIALISM AND
★ SOCIAL MOVEMENTS ★

Series Editor: Mark Selden

FREEING CHINA'S FARMERS
Rural Restructuring in the Reform Era
David Zweig

DANWEI
The Changing Chinese Workplace in
Historical and Comparative Perspective
Edited by Xiaobo Lü and Elizabeth J. Perry

**COOPERATIVE AND COLLECTIVE IN
CHINA'S RURAL DEVELOPMENT**
Between State and Private Interests
*Edited by Eduard Vermeer, Frank N. Pieke,
and Woei Lien Chong*

**THE DISTRIBUTION OF WEALTH IN
RURAL CHINA**
Terry McKinley

CHINA AFTER SOCIALISM
In the Footsteps of Eastern Europe
or East Asia?
*Edited by Barrett L. McCormick
and Jonathan Unger*

CHINA IN REVOLUTION
The Yenan Way Revisited
Mark Selden

DILEMMAS OF REFORM IN CHINA
Political Conflict and Economic Debate
Joseph Fewsmith

THE HIGHLANDERS OF CENTRAL CHINA
A History, 1895-1937
Jerome Ch'en

CHINA'S TRANSITION FROM SOCIALISM
Statist Legacies and Market Reform,
1980-1990
Dorothy J. Solinger

BUKHARIN IN RETROSPECT
*Edited by Theodor Bergmann,
Gert Schaefer, and Mark Selden
Introduction by Moshe Lewin*

REINVENTING REVOLUTION
New Social Movements and
the Socialist Tradition in India
Gail Omvedt

**THE POLITICAL ECONOMY OF
CHINESE DEVELOPMENT**
Mark Selden

**THE CHINESE STATE IN
THE ERA OF ECONOMIC REFORM**
Edited by Gordon White

**MARXISM AND THE
CHINESE EXPERIENCE**
Issues in Contemporary Chinese Socialism
Edited by Arlif Dirlik and Maurice Meisner

**STALINISM AND THE SEEDS OF
SOVIET REFORM**
The Debates of the 1960s
Moshe Lewin

★ *Socialism and Social Movements* ★

FREEING CHINA'S FARMERS RURAL RESTRUCTURING IN THE REFORM ERA

DAVID ZWEIG

An East Gate Book

M.E. Sharpe
Armonk, New York
London, England

An East Gate Book

Library of Congress Cataloging-in-Publication Data

Zweig, David.
Freeing China's farmers : rural restructuring in the reform era /
David Zweig.
p. cm.
"An East Gate book"
Includes bibliographical references and index.
ISBN 1-56324-837-9 (cloth : alk. paper). — ISBN 1-56324-838-7
1. China—Rural conditions.
2. Rural development—China.
3. Land reform—China.
I. Title.
II. Series.
HN733.5.Z94   1997
307.72′0951—dc21
97-16303
CIP

Printed in the United States of America

The paper used in this publication meets the minimum requirements of the
American National Standard for Information Sciences—
Permanence of Paper for Printed Library Materials,
ANSI Z 39.48-1984.

BM (c)   10   9   8   7   6   5   4   3   2   1
BM (p)   10   9   8   7   6   5   4   3   2   1

To Mike Oksenberg, who set me on the path of the study of rural China, and to Xie Naikang and the late Ji Xiaolin, who kept the door to rural China open for me

Contents

Publication Acknowledgments

Many chapters in this book first appeared in scholarly journals and edited volumes. I thank all the publishers who granted permission to use those articles in this book.

Chapter 1 was originally published in *Asian Survey* 23 (July 1983): 879–900.

Chapter 2 was originally published in David M. Lampton, ed., *Policy Implementation in the Post-Mao Era* (Berkeley: University of California Press, 1987), pp. 255–283.

Chapter 3 was originally entitled "Peasants, Ideology, and New Incentive Systems: Jiangsu Province, 1978–1981," and appeared in William L. Parish, ed., *Chinese Rural Development: The Great Transformation* (Armonk, N.Y.: M.E. Sharpe, 1985), pp. 141–164.

Chapter 4 was originally published in *The China Quarterly,* no. 105 (March 1986): 1–18.

Chapter 5 was originally entitled "Struggling over Land in China: Villager Resistance after Collectivization, 1966–1986," and appeared in Forrest D. Colburn, ed., *Everyday Forms of Peasant Resistance* (Armonk, N.Y.: M.E. Sharpe, 1989), pp. 151–174.

Chapter 6 was originally entitled "Law, Contracts, and Economic Modernization: Recent Lessons from Chinese Rural Reforms," and appeared in the *Stanford Journal of International Law* 23 (Summer 1987): 319–364.

Chapter 7 was originally published in *International Regional Science Review,* no. 11 (1987): 43–58.

Chapter 8 was originally published in Bruce R. Reynolds, ed., *Chinese Economic Policy: Reform at Midstream* (New York: Paragon Publishers, 1989), pp. 13–40.

Chapter 9 was originally published in David M. Lampton and Kenneth G. Lieberthal, eds., *Bureaucracy, Politics, and Decision Making in Post-Mao China* (Berkeley: University of California Press, 1992), pp. 334–363.

Chapter 10 was originally entitled "Rural Industry: Constraining the Leading Growth Sector in China's Economy," and appeared in the Joint Economic Committee, Congress of the United States, *China's Dilemmas in the 1990s: The Problems of Reforms, Modernization and Interdependence* (Washington, D.C.: U.S. Government Printing Office, 1991), pp. 418–436.

Chapter 11 was originally presented at the Nineteenth Sino-American Conference on Mainland China, June 12–14, 1989, Taipei, Taiwan, and was published in *The China Quarterly,* no. 128 (December 1991): 716–741.

Chapter 12 was originally published in *Comparative Politics* 27 (April 1995): 253–274.

Preface and Acknowledgments

During fifteen years of research on rural China, one runs up many debts. At the outset, I want to thank those who have helped me through this long-term project. No doubt, as scholars, we need money for research; but, more important, we need access to often closed rural communities. The most important of the organizations that helped me gain access to areas necessary for my field research were the Office of Foreign Students and Scholars and the Economics Department at Nanjing University. Since 1980, when I went to Nanda to do my dissertation field research, I have relied on the leaders and staff of those two organizations, and they have never let me down. No wonder Nanjing University has retained such a strong reputation for facilitating scholarly research on China. My friends at Nanjing University include Xie Naikang, Zhao Shuming, Zhou Haixu, Zhou Sandou, Chai Ping, and Zhang Rongcun. In Beijing, the late Ji Xiaolin was always supportive; I miss him terribly. In Nanjing, I met several times with officials from the Nanjing Rural Work Department and the Jiangsu provincial Department of Foreign Trade and Investment.

Governments often help their citizens do research in foreign countries and despite the burden I have imposed on them, the Canadian government and its cultural officials in Beijing and Ottawa enthusiastically arranged my long research trips in 1980–1981 and 1986. Particular thanks go to Don Waterfall, Mary Sun, Diana Lary, Ruth Hayhoe, and other members of the Department of Foreign Affairs and International Trade.

The most important source of funding for this research came from the Social Science and Humanities Research Council of Canada (SSHRC), which supported my 1986 research trip to China to study the changing nature of urban–rural relations. That 1986 trip provided the data for Parts II and III of this book. The council also provided funds in 1992–1994 for my study of Canadian aid to China. At SSHRC, Hilda Nantais, Diane Trembley, and Les McDonald have been supportive over the years. I have also benefited from my years as a resident of the United States and as an American academic. The Rackham School at The University of Michigan supported my early research on decollectivization. As codirector of a rural development project funded by the Henry Luce Foundation and administered through Harvard University's Fairbank Center for East Asian Research, I visited Wuxi County. I also established close ties to and learned much about rural China from colleagues in the former Research Centre for Rural Development under the Chinese State Council. Both the Sackler Foundation and the Kearney Foundation (Merle Henrichs) paid for my visits to Wujiang County. Finally, the Committee on Scholarly Communication with China supplied a research grant and helped arrange the research for chapter 12. Particular thanks go to Bob Geyer, Pam Pierce, Keith Clemenger, Kathlin Smith, Megan Close, and Ellen Catz.

Persons to whom I owe my many intellectual debts include Bernie Frolic, Mike Oksenberg, Dan Tretiak, Marc Blecher, Tom Bernstein, Marty Whyte, Woody Watson, Rod MacFarquhar, Andrew Walder, Dorie Solinger, Lucian Pye, Norma Diamond, Wang Zhenyao, Bai Nansheng, Mike Lampton, Ken Lieberthal, Kate Hartford, Jim Feinerman, Deng Jianxu, Pei Ping, Lu Mai, Luo Xiaopeng, Zhao Yang, Greg Guldin, Zhong Weitong, Zhang Mingquan, Han Zhun, Terry Lautz, Nick Lardy, Li Kang, Ramon Myers, Anthony Ody, William Parish, Jean Oi, Dwight Perkins, Margaret Pearson, Louis Putterman, Denis Fred Simon, James Scott, Forrest Colburn, Yang Shun, Nina Halpern, James Tong, Mark Rosenberg, Doak Barnett, Ann Anagnost, David Bachman, Penny Prime, Kevin Kramer, David Shambaugh, Bernard Gallin, Huang Shumin, Richard Baum, Merle Goldman, Morris Mottalle, Deborah Brautigam, Donald Klein, Sonny Lo, Christine Wong, Roger Bolton, David Powell, Ed Tower, Dirck Stryker, Bruce Reynolds, Janet Cady, Jean Hong, Yok-shiu Lee, and Fan Conglai.

My work was facilitated by the research and graphic efforts of Alexis Feringa Thurman, Mulatu Wirtu, Xu Ziwang, Merritt Maddux, Zachary Abuza, John Auerbach, Dia Warren, Chan Housun, Howard Yao, Li Yuan, Mike Moynihan, Yu Wing Yat, and Karen Cheung. Nancy Hearst was always there with citations, and her library supplied me with much important data. Administrative support came from Carol Irving at the Joint Centre for Asia–Pacific Studies at York University—University of Toronto; the Department of Political Science at the University of Waterloo; the Fletcher School of Law and Diplomacy at Tufts University; and my new home, the Department of Social Science at the Hong Kong University of Science and Technology.

As for the overall manuscript, two people deserve enormous thanks. Mark Selden gave me very extensive and enormously helpful comments on each and every chapter and supported this project from start to finish. My debt to him is the deepest. Connie Moynihan, the best secretary a scholar ever had, helped whip the first draft into shape. At M.E. Sharpe, particular thanks go to my two editors, Mai Cota and Angela Piliouras, whose patience and energy saw this project through to completion. Thanks, too, to Doug Merwin at M.E. Sharpe who believed in the project.

Finally, my thanks to my wife, Joy, who pushed me to finish this project as quickly as possible so that I could move on to the next book, and to my daughter, Rachel, who saw a little less of me than she might have because Daddy was often in his "office."

Tables and Figures

Tables

Figures

Freeing China's Farmers Rural Restructuring in the Reform Era

Introduction

Scholarly Debates and Rural Development as the Countryside Moves into the Twenty-First Century

One of five people in the world lives in rural China. Given the magnitude of China's population, what happens to China's farmers has tremendous implications, not just for urban China or China's ambitious reform program, but for the entire world. Global commodity prices, political and economic stability in East Asia, and China's foreign trade competitiveness will all be affected by outcomes in rural China.[1] For 18 years, China's rural inhabitants have undergone one of the most dramatic transformations in world history: restructuring the economic, political, social, and transnational institutions extant at the end of the Maoist era. New, expanded freedoms have been granted to China's farmers by the state, while they themselves have fought for other political rights and economic opportunities. The enormity of these events cannot be overstated. Since I first lived in rural China in 1981, I have observed these ongoing changes. The chapters that follow, written over 15 years, reflect the core themes in my work which touch on the socioeconomic and political transition still under way in rural China.

Rural reform began with a major adjustment to property rights in land, machinery, and property. While formal ownership remained with the collective, by 1983, farmers' property rights over land had become quasi-private. In most of rural China, small strips of land were divided among rural households that suddenly possessed the legal right to decide how to use that land. Clearly, farmers' rights over land have remained limited; they cannot sell their land, the state can expropriate or redistribute it, and many farmers are still forced by state agents to grow crops according to central and local plans and quotas. Caution must be exercised when using terms such as "privatization" to describe decollectivization and the current state of rural ownership rights over land.[2] Still, if property rights are defined as a "bundle" of rights that can be disaggregated,[3] the farmers' rights to allocate land, labor, and agricultural outputs reflect important aspects of private property rights.

The reform of the rural marketing system and increased competitiveness challenged formerly placid, monopolistic state companies and brought rural markets, commerce, and the moribund, rural service sector to life.[4] Under Mao, state bureaucrats controlled agricultural inputs and outputs, and during the Cultural Revolution decade proponents of "agrarian radicalism" had suppressed private rural markets, drying up a critical social and economic institution which had brought prosperity and cultural richness to rural China through the mid-1950s and into the mid-1960s.[5] Social services were collectivized and, by the mid-1970s, it was difficult to find a simple repairman. By the mid-1980s, significant marketization reestablished regional comparative advantage, enlivened the rural economy, and increased output. A new breed of private merchants emerged in the countryside, challenging the local state's former monopsony and improving the delivery of goods and services.[6] The share of commercial sales controlled by "designated" state commercial agencies dropped between 1978 and 1992 from 70 to 35 percent.[7] In response, county and township officials altered their roles and the roles of their former bureaucratic organizations,[8] entering the fray of market competition while maintaining their organizations' corporate nature. Yet, the partial nature of the rural reforms—including lingering social responsibilities and vestiges of the planned economy—severely constrained the ability of these local state agents to respond flexibly to new market opportunities.

Decollectivization transformed authority relations between local cadres and farmers, the nexus by which the state influenced political and economic activity and agricultural production. Under Mao, local cadres had used the material incentives inherent in the collective ownership system,[9] the moral authority of Maoist egalitarianism,[10] and coercion,[11] to limit or suppress autonomous villager activity and insure that farmers followed central and local directives. Market-oriented reforms transformed these relationships, leaving cadres with fewer collective resources to use as incentives to gain compliance with state agricultural plans.[12] The critique of Maoism and delegitimization of the regular use of coercion have forced local officials to impose new unauthorized taxes to accumulate capital for public welfare functions.

What will be the new balance of power between farmers and local officials? Cadres, finding that their political authority can be used to increase their wealth, have become quite rapacious. Can the state restructure these relationships before widespread rebellions emerge in response to cadre malfeasance? Can law and the courts establish new institutional relations between citizens and state agents? As farmers become less passive and respond to egregious cadre behavior with angry protests, resistance, and sporadic anti-state violence,[13] will the state find a peaceful means to ameliorate these conflicts?[14]

The "great wall" erected by Maoism between urban and rural China, which for Potter carried all the psychological, economic, and physical weight of apartheid,[15] has been punctured by the emancipation of Mao's "serf-like" rural residents.[16] Beginning in 1955, the state differentiated between "urban" and "rural" "resident permits" (*hukou*), and, in 1960, it carved these divisions into stone, strictly regulating the farmers' access to grain in urban settings, cutting the natural urban-rural interactions characteristic of precommunist China. Similarly, the state used the urban-rural divide to soak resources out of the countryside to subsidize urban industrial expansion. First, in 1953, it imposed compulsory grain sales on China's villagers, and then, after locking farmers onto the land, the state imposed an invisible tax based on the mythical category of "surplus grain" to extract rural wealth to subsidize urban living standards.[17] As has happened in other developing countries, farmers paid to stabilize state power in the urban sector.[18]

But, the reforms have changed all that; the weakening of the *hukou* system has allowed farmers to flock to cities and towns in the tens of millions, searching for the good life.[19] Some have become merchants, marketing rural produce to earn profits previously reserved for state trading firms and other state agents. I will never forget the jealousy and contempt in the eyes of Nanjing residents observing unkempt farmers in 1986, who were spending their newfound profits on a large meal in the Sichuan Restaurant. Such animosity reflects the depth of rural-urban hostility and the enormity of the social transformation triggered by this changing rural-urban gap. Other farmers, however, still face exploitative working conditions in urban factories run by Chinese and foreigners.

Polyani's *Great Transformation* has come to significant parts of rural China.[20] Rural industrialization and the shift from an agricultural society, a process that took centuries in the West, has occurred in parts of suburban and coastal China in a matter of years. No doubt, the seeds of rural industry can be found in the efforts of rural collective leaders from 1958 to 1978. But, for most of that period, township and village enterprises (TVEs) were seen as an ancillary sector of the rural economy (see chapter 10).[21] Today, TVEs play a crucial role in China's overall economy, transferring wealth and influence from the urban to the rural areas and thereby challenging urban economic and political interests by shifting power and resources to lower levels of the state hierarchy.[22] And, through TVE exports and joint ventures between TVEs and foreign investors, the countryside has gone out to meet the world. While in the mid-1980s rural China played a minimal role in China's export-led growth strategy, by 1993 one of every two *yuan* of merchandise bought for exports came from rural factories.[23] For many small foreign investors, rural enterprises became the partners of choice.

The Prereform Era

Initially, I went to the Chinese countryside in 1980–1981 to study policy making and implementation of radical-leftist agricultural policies introduced in the 1960s and 1970s.[24] Drawing their ideological roots from the Great Leap Forward's effort to eradicate private initiative and move property rights to higher levels of the collective system, some central leaders used informal policy channels—what I called "policy winds"—to inculcate China's villagers with a communist ethos.[25]

Under this radical policy regime, rural health care delivery improved significantly, raising life expectancy, although today some would assert that state propaganda overstated the reach of rural medical clinics. Rural education also improved under collectivized agriculture. The integrative force of Maoist ideology and the lessons of Maoist campaigns, especially the Four Cleans campaign (1964–1966), limited corrupt activities by rural officials. Rural industry grew out of the strengthened collective economies of the 1970s. Finally, mass mobilization of rural labor for field and water conservation projects, which increased agricultural output and the amount of high-yield arable land in the countryside, stabilized agriculture and created economic rents that were reaped during the reform era.

But the radical strategy had very serious negative consequences which become evident when one compares rates of growth in crop output and per capita income, nonagricultural job formation, quality of life, and food consumption during the reforms to rural life during the later Maoist era. Marginal returns to labor and capital had been declining, while agricultural output was increasing only slowly. Within collectives, an intrinsic anti-incentivism undermined labor enthusiasm.[26] Much of rural China lived in a world of collective subsistence, in which farmers hesitated to increase output beyond their own consumption levels. Suppression of economic crops and an overemphasis on grain devastated comparative advantage, impoverishing parts of Guangdong, Fujian, and Shandong provinces. Restrictions on interregional trade, due to the Maoist emphasis on local economic self-reliance or cellularity, slowed economic growth. Ecological damage resulted from unscientific efforts to turn lakes into paddy fields. Farmer-cadre relations suffered as well, as the decreased usefulness of normative incentives, and the absence of material ones, forced cadres to resort increasingly to coercion. Restricting sideline production and using a payment method that made household income totally reliant on the number of laborers working in the collective made the dependency ratio—the ratio of laborers to non-laborers in each household—the key determinant of intra-village, household income inequality. And, despite Maoist rhetoric glorifying the rural areas, urban-rural inequalities expanded as urban women entered urban collective enterprises, while surplus rural laborers were forbidden to seek urban or rural off-farm employment. The impressive growth in output and incomes after 1978 shows both the enormity of the wasted opportunity costs under the radical developmental strategy and that an alternative one was more productive and efficient.[27] Although the radical strategy had created opportunities for prosperity, only removing its institutional fetters allowed rural incomes and production to rise dramatically.

My Research Agenda

My research focus has been threefold. First, I wanted to understand the relationship between national policy and local implementation, hypothesizing that local interests, and the ecological, political, and socioeconomic characteristics of villages and bureaucrats, ultimately determined the final form of policy implementation. Those decisions, however—and the freedom of choice among villagers and local officials—existed within the political and ideological context of central and regional politics and policy.

Second, I focused on the relationship among material resources, power, and social conflict. Power in rural China is based on a person's control of the allocation of resources—capital, labor, crops, technology, information, and raw materials—and ability to establish rules and norms that enhance control over those resources.[28] This explains why decollectivization, which transferred land use rights, was initially such a challenge to local cadres and such a liberating force for China's farmers. Mao's adage of political power growing out of the barrel of a gun must be rewritten in a rural context; since the 1970s, political power in the Chinese countryside has grown out of the barrel of a smokestack. The battle over those resources, between villagers and local officials, between state and society, and among various levels of the state hierarchy, is the source of much of the social conflict extant in rural China. The trick for farmers is to maximize their share of those resources, expand their freedoms to create others, and prevent officials and the state from using their control over those resources to maintain unfair patterns of dominance.

Finally, my interest shifted to the effect of exogenous resources and opportunities—extant in the international realm—on these same domestic institutions and relations in rural China. I wanted to assess how the introduction of a new development strategy, based on export-led growth, affected the distribution of wealth, power, and status among farmers, local governments, and the central state.

The Local and Regional Context of My Research

My field research came in three major periods. In 1980–1981, I lived in the countryside and, while investigating agrarian radicalism, observed decollectivization first hand in a suburban commune in Nanjing, and in Jiangpu and Jiangying counties (see map). In 1986–1989, I returned to two of these three localities, and also visited Wujiang County to document the second phase of rural reform—market liberalization, privatization of the service sector, expanded urban-rural exchanges, and rural urbanization. Finally, beginning in 1988 and culminating with field research in 1991–1992 in Zhangjiagang, in southern Jiangsu, Nantong Municipality and Nantong County, as well as Kunshan County, within Suzhou Municipality, I collected data on the impact of export-led growth on rural and urban centers in the lower Yangzi River delta.[29] My research, therefore, occurred primarily in southern, western, and northern Jiangsu Province.

Jiangsu Province has several characteristics that have influenced my findings. It has been in the forefront of rural industrialization based largely on the spillover from Shanghai's state-owned enterprises (SOEs). And, although it is not geographically situated next to any external territory (as compared to Guangdong's links to Hong Kong or Dalian's proximity to Japan), which would give it even greater advantages in foreign trade,[30] the strength of its collective institutions and local governments, the quality of its products, and the skills of its rural workforce have made it the leader in rural industry and rural industrial exports (see Table I.1 on pages 10–11).

As for decollectivization, Jiangsu was a laggard province. Because Jiangsu possesses a strong collective economy that has facilitated irrigation and industrialization, its provincial leaders, local cadres, and many farmers resisted initial pressures to dismantle the commune system. Yet, that opposition gives us insight into the entire process of decollectivization, supplying a window onto interest-based resistance to institutional change.

Finally, Jiangsu Province, while commercially rich and wealthier than most of rural China, has significant regional variations and three distinct economic zones: (1) the wealthy *Sunan,* including the cities of Suzhou, Wuxi, and Changzhou (also called Suxichang); (2) the poorer *Subei,* comprised of Xuzhou, Huaiyin, and Lianyungang; and (3) a middle zone, sometimes referred to as *Suzhong,* including Nanjing, Yangzhou, and Zhenjiang in the west, and Yancheng and Nantong in the east (see map, opposite page). Significant differences exist among these three zones in terms of industrial versus agricultural output, per capita income, foreign investment, and the types of economic linkages that exist within other regions of the country. *Sunan,* where Zhangjiagang is located (see chapters 10 and 12), is one of the fastest growing areas in all of China. *Suzhong,* where Nanjing and Nantong are located, is a middle-income region in the province that has done well under the reforms. Finally, *Subei* on the Huadong (East China) Plain remains significantly poorer than the rest of the province.[31] In fact, even within Nanjing Municipality one finds rich agricultural communities, industrialized rural suburbs, and poorer communities such as Jiangpu County on the north side of the Yangzi, which have benefited little from the boom in the rural economy.

Since it is only through comparison that we can really test our explanations, Jiangsu, despite its relative wealth, has served as a rich laboratory for both intra-

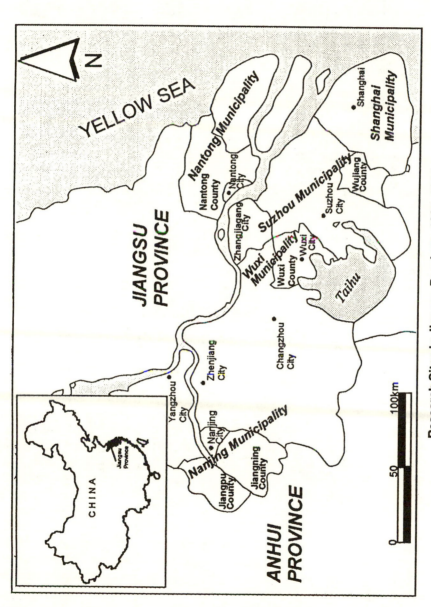

Research Sites in Jiangsu Province, 1981–1992

Table I-1

Industrial Output, TVE Exports by Sector and Province, 1987–1994[1] (in 100 mil. *RMB*)

	Jiangsu	Guangdong	Zhejiang	Shandong
I. Gross Industrial Output Value by sector[a]				
1990				
SOEs	948.56 (17%)	765.43 (26%)	447.65 (14%)	911.88 (36%)
Urban collectives	3,260.43 (59%)	1,228.36 (42%)	1,886.29 (60%)	710.17 (28%)
TVEs	1,131.32 (29%)	432.88 (15%)	664.10 (21%)	756.00 (30%)
Private	107.04 (2%)	91.19 (3%)	93.80 (3%)	158.41 (6%)
Other (FFEs)[2]	104.66 (2%)	385.98 (13%)	30.53 (1%)	14.37 (0.6%)
1994				
SOEs	1,959.99 (13%)	1,562.24 (19%)	936.01 (11%)	2,012.72 (17%)
Urban collectives	5,654.41 (37%)	1,888.02 (22%)	1,395.14 (17%)	3,107.72 (26%)
TVEs	6,078.78 (40%)	1,679.29 (20%)	4,476.73 (53%)	5,051.35 (43%)
Private	476.39 (3%)	524.04 (6%)	1,030.01 (12%)	1,041.81 (9%)
Other (FFEs)	1,206.25 (8%)	2,712.19 (32%)	577.84 (7%)	658.26 (6%)
II. Value of TVE Products Purchased Domestically for Export by Province[b, 3]				
1987	32.53 (20%)[4]	24.89 (15%)	16.47 (10%)	10.90 (7%)
1989	78.57 (21%)	38.81 (10%)	44.62 (12%)	33.78 (9%)
1991	166.45 (23%)	74.50 (10%)	109.83 (15%)	67.13 (9%)
1992	367.93 (31%)	105.05 (9%)	155.63 (13%)	98.62 (8%)
III. Total Value of Domestic Commodities Purchased for Exports by Province[c]				
1987	75.93 (43%)	179.42 (14%)	50.30 (32%)	89.30 (12%)
1989	87.85 (89%)	212.45 (18%)	109.38 (41%)	100.30 (34%)
1991	270.88 (60%)	293.98 (25%)[4]	174.38 (63%)	152.60 (44%)
1992	511.22 (72%)	358.81 (29%)[4]	228.81 (68%)	175.72 (56%)
IV. Provincial TVE Exports as a Percentage of National TVE Exports				
1987	20%	15%	10%	7%
1989	21%	10%	12%	9%
1991	23%	10%	15%	9%
1992	31%	9%	13%	8%

V. Export Purchases from TVEs as a Percentage of Total Export Purchases in the Province[5]

Year				
1987	43%	14%	32%	12%
1989	89%	18%	41%	34%
1991	60%	25%	63%	44%
1992	72%	29%	68%	46%

Sources:

[a]Data from *Chinese Statistical Yearbook, 1991* (Beijing: State Statistical Bureau, 1991), *Chinese Statistical Yearbook, 1995* (Beijing: State Statistical Bureau, 1995), *TVE Statistical Yearbook, 1991* (Beijing: Ministry of Agriculture, 1991), and *TVE Statistical Yearbook, 1995* (Beijing: Ministry of Agriculture, 1995). Data supplied by Dr. Daniel Tretiak, The Second Line Ltd., Hong Kong.

[b]TVE exports from *TVE Yearbook, 1978–1987*, p. 616, *TVE Yearbook, 1990*, p. 168, and 1991 and 1992 data are from *Zhongguo xiangzhen qiye*, no. 5 (1993): 38, in *Renda baokan fuyin ziliao* (People's University Journal Reference Materials), no. 6 (1993).

[c]Ministry of Foreign Economic Relations and Trade, *Foreign Economic and Trade Yearbook (Duiwai jingji maoyi nianjian)*, various years.

Notes:

[1]These values are not adjusted for inflation.

[2]FFEs refers to foreign funded enterprises.

[3]TVE Export Purchases refers to goods purchased domestically by foreign trade companies in *RMB* for export. In Chinese, the term is *wai mao shougou e*. I use this measure to show how much TVE production actually goes into the export sector. By 1994, foreign trade companies bought over half of their export commodities from TVEs. See chapter 11.

[4]Using domestic purchases of exported goods grossly understates the export volume from Guangdong Province as it does not include exports by joint ventures. Total exports for Guangdong by some calculations are actually 7–10 times those of Jiangsu. Also, export data published in the *MOFERT Yearbooks* for Guangdong Province is significantly lower than data reported in the *Chinese Statistical Yearbook*. For example, in 1991, while the *MOFERT Yearbook* reported total foreign trade as $US22.198 billion, the *Chinese State Statistical Yearbook* reported it as over $US50 billion.

[5]This value is inflated since total export purchases do not include exports by FFEs, a fact which affects Guangdong Province's results in particular as many rural factories in Guangdong are joint ventures by the late 1980s.

and inter-provincial comparisons. My early observations of decollectivization (1980–1981) were centered on Nanjing Municipality, where farmers and cadres in Jiangpu and Jiangning counties, as well as suburban Nanjing, responded differently to decollectivization. My fieldwork on privatization, marketization, changes in urban-rural relations, and rural urbanization, carried out in 1986–88, took place in both Jiangpu and Wujiang counties (the latter under Suzhou Municipality), and while the former county is quite rural, the latter reflects the integrated urban-rural economy (or *desakota*) for which southern Jiangsu is famous. Finally, my study on rural internationalization took me to Zhangjiagang (in Suzhou Municipality) and Nantong County (under Nantong Municipality), areas which again responded differently to China's export-led growth strategy.

Decollectivization

Who dismantled the communes? The peasants? The state? Was it a secret, silent revolution from below, an organized centrally planned and executed reform, or a mix of the two? This is an enormously salient question as decollectivization, and the emancipation of rural farmers from the institutional constraints of collectivism, heralded the redistribution of power and authority in rural China. In 1978, deep in the bowels of Anhui Province, a few farmers, driven by hunger, drought, and poverty, risked the wrath of the Chinese Communist Party (CCP) and divided the land among households in their villages. But did that single spark start a prairie fire that could not be smothered?[32] Or, did the state employ a heavy hand and force localities to decollectivize?[33] As is often the case with China, the truth is more complex, lying somewhere between these two extremes; any simple explanation, given the enormous diversity in the country, can only distort local reality.

Two authors in particular emphasize the spontaneous and local role of farmers in decollectivization, arguing that farmers imposed their own preference for decollectivization, despite central opposition. According to Kelliher, China's leaders lost control of the rural reform process, making decollectivization an unplanned manifestation of peasant power despite the presence of an otherwise strong state.[34] In fact, because state power and collectivization placed all farmers within the same institutional constraints, self-actualized action by individual farmers seeking to escape the confines of the collective took on the manner and force of collective action, crystallizing into a popular movement that overthrew the collective system.[35] For Kate Zhou, too, decollectivization was a bottom-up process where provincial cadres did little more than provide an umbrella under which farmers dismantled the collective through what she calls a "spontaneous, unorganized, leaderless, nonideological, apolitical movement." For Zhou, the farmers accomplished this earth-shaking transformation because "officials were looking the other way."[36]

Chapters 1 through 3 present my perspective on the balance among mass spontaneity; cadre interests and resistance; radical reformers' views, activities, and signaling;[37] and central policy disputes, all of which are necessary components for a full explanation of decollectivization. While chapter 1 discusses the roots of resistance to decollectivization, and chapter 3 compares the pattern of decollectivization in three parts of rural Nanjing Municipality, chapter 2 presents a nationwide portrait of the entire process. Although I strongly believe that farmers and the localities were the driving force behind decollectivization,[38] I disagree with Kelliher and Zhou's overemphasis on the farmers' autonomous activity and their efforts to at best downplay (Zhou) or actually reject (Kelliher) the important role of radical reformers, such as Wan Li and Zhao Ziyang, in the process of decollectivization. In localities where "household production contracts" (*baochan daohu*) were introduced early on, without central approval, China's farmers flexed their "power." Transforming institutions and dismantling Mao's collective property on their own were remarkable feats for a rural population that was long viewed by many as passive, disorganized, a veritable "sack of potatoes" in regard to an imposing state authority. Any explanation must recognize that farmers pushed for decollectivization; this was no orchestrated plan that sprang from the mind of Deng Xiaoping, Zhao Ziyang, or Wan Li.

However, a model that relies totally on "peasant" power is only a partial explanation, in that it cannot incorporate the regional variation that occurred. Farmers' economic and institutional conditions are absolutely critical to understanding local actions and attitudes towards decollectivization. In fact, chapter 3 shows that even in rural Nanjing Municipality, significant variations in the response to the responsibility system can be explained by diverse factors such as income; attitudes of cadres; level of mechanization and industrialization; and ecological factors, such as irrigation or cropping patterns. Similarly, variation in the influence of market-oriented reformers and their allies across different provinces explains when and why different provinces or areas within provinces instituted and pressed for decollectivization.[39] An alliance between, on the one hand, farmers, who, in small groups and based on their own economic, ecological, geographic, and political conditions, sought to escape the institutional confines of collective poverty and lost opportunity costs, and, on the other hand, reformers, who protected the farmers as they tested the waters of decollectivization, and pushed the process forward to its destination: the decollectivization of the Chinese countryside.

Let us turn to these issues. Overemphasizing farmer power understates the role of market-oriented reformist leaders and factionalism in the process of decollectivization and presents an overly totalitarian or unified view of China's leaders. True, decollectivization could not have succeeded without the spontaneous actions of Chinese farmers who dismantled the collectives in various locations. On this point Kelliher and Zhou are correct. But China's farmers could not have gone forward without the acquiescence and support of market-oriented reformers in the top elite, particularly Wan Li and even Zhao Ziyang, who dissented from the more general leadership line whose policy pronouncements opposed household farming. Had these leaders wanted to stop decollectivization, they could have. According to Kate Zhou, Zhao admitted that his criticism of household production contracts in 1980 slowed the pace of decollectivization. No doubt, as Kelliher asserts, had central elites cracked down and tried to put all the household genies back in the collective bottle, agricultural output would have stagnated, if not crashed, as farmers' enthusiasm for production would have nose-dived. However, the highest levels of the Party, armed with the power to crack down on reform, chose to let the process work itself out.[40]

Wan Li, for example, skillfully created a conducive climate for dividing the land, within which farmers pushed for complete decollectivization, when he decided to monitor the progress of decollectivation carefully, all the while preventing official party declarations prohibiting household contracting from stopping the farmers from experimenting with it.[41]

> Wan Li watched carefully the appearance of contracting production to individual households. . . . He did not let the explicit provisions of the provincial CPC Committee's Six Articles "not permitting the contracting of production to individual households, and not permitting the figuring of compensation according to output" to tie [sic] his hands. Instead, he let mass practice enrich and readjust itself."[42]

He called on his adviser on agriculture to investigate and study decollectivization carefully, but not to take a public position on it. "Let it develop; when the time comes it can always be restudied again. Otherwise, the enthusiasm of the masses will be stifled." In this way he kept decollectivization under wraps, prevented a conservative backlash, and let it ripen to a point where it could not be stopped. According to Wan, "It should not be publicized, it should not be promoted, and it should not appear in newspapers. Let practice demonstrate whether or not it is correct." Clearly, Wan tacitly supported decollectivization and played an important political role in making it a *fait accompli,* and without his efforts farmers in Anhui Province would not have felt capable of pushing for decollectivization on such a massive scale. Moreover, he regularly informed Deng of the progress of decollectivization.

Kate Zhou, indeed, makes an impassioned case that China's farmers decollectivized on their own, despite the opposition of the central leadership. Based on interviews with Chen Yizi, who was working for the reformers in Beijing, she suggests that as late as June 1980, when some poor localities had shifted to *baochan daohu,* Zhao Ziyang opposed non-collective forms of the household responsibility system and called for a retrenchment. At one point she even argues that market-oriented reformers "were ready to crush any radical departure from the collective structure."[43] To this extent, the farmers clearly pushed beyond the guidelines set even by the reformers.[44]

However, while her writing forces us to recognize the enormous role that China's farmers played in transforming the world around them, her description of these events does not challenge the argument that, without reform leadership support, decollectivization could not have occurred. Despite Zhao's apparent opposition, in fall 1980 he and Wan Li, overriding the protests of many provincial leaders, pushed through a new policy on *baochan daohu* in poorer areas.[45] A fuller explanation, therefore, must recognize the critical alliance that emerged between farmers, who in small groups sought to escape collective poverty, and market-oriented reformers, who, if not actively promoting decollectivization, protected the farmers as they pushed the process forward.

Second, stark variations in the level and pace of decollectivization across provinces demonstrate that there was more at work here than simple villager power or initiative. If, as Kelliher asserts, decollectivization resulted because all farmers, confronting the same institutional constraints and economic deprivations, simultaneously pushed forward on their own initiative, then all poor areas should have shifted to *baochan daohu* at the same approximate time. But, if peasants were so strong, why were farmers in poorer areas in certain provinces blocked by officials from decollectivizing in earlier stages of this process? Kelliher's own data show that, while farmers in poor areas in provinces run by market-oriented reformers—Anhui and Sichuan—were successful in promoting decollectivization, farmers in poor areas of conservative provinces, such as Hubei Province, where Kelliher did his fieldwork, or in parts of Jiangsu Province where I did my research, were prevented from doing so.

Where the state tried to constrain farmers' behavior, as in Hubei Province, the farmers could not decollectivize, despite their desire to do so. All they could do was adapt or twist the policy somewhat, as they have been wont to do since the 1950s (if not from time immemorial). Therefore, if poor farmers in Anhui and Hubei and Jiangsu provinces all wanted to introduce family farming, but the policy occurred in only one of three provinces, then the key explanatory variable does not lie with the farmers' interests or inherent power—whose desires and efforts did not vary—but with some factor manifested at the provincial or subprovincial level that did vary. In fact, according to Chung, attitudes of provincial leaders is the key variable to determining the pace of decollectivation.[46] And since the reforms moved fastest in provinces led by reformers and did not succeed in provinces where conservative leaders stopped them, the actions of provincial and central reformers must be a critical part of any explanation of decollectivization. Without their support, this change simply could not have occurred.[47]

Farmer-Cadre Relations under the Reforms

Under collective agriculture, cadres were caught in a pincer. State demands for policy conformity pressed down from above, even as farmers demanded that

cadres, as members of the local community, take local characteristics and interests into consideration when devising local policies.[48] To insure policy compliance, cadres could employ a wide assortment of political tools including material
incentives (work points), moral suasion and ideology, and coercive strategies,
such as "killing the chickens to scare the monkeys."[49] They also used a variety of
evasive strategies.[50] The approximately 10 percent of farmers who established
clientelist ties with village cadres to advance their political careers could be
counted on to support state or local policies.[51] Yet, throughout the collective era,
self-interested local cadres at the brigade, commune, or even county-level expropriated peasant labor, grain, or cash to expand the enterprises, bureaucratic posts,
and funds under their administrative controls.[52]

Decollectivization threatened the cadres' world,[53] and the positional power
they wielded under the administrative system.[54] Would this distinct rightist policy shift be followed by a subsequent leftist backlash? As wealth shifted out of
the redistributive economy and onto the market, scholars such as Nee initially
suggested that cadre influence would wane accordingly.[55] Therefore, it is not
surprising to find them opposing decollectivization. And in fact, after
decollectivization, cadres in poorer areas lacked the resources to persuade farmers to comply with central government policies.[56] Therefore, to forestall cadre
opposition to reform, China's reform-minded elites created an image of rural
development that portrayed local cadres as the primary beneficiaries of the commercialization of the rural economy and structured economic benefits in ways
that helped woo reluctant cadres over to reform.[57]

Other Western scholars, however, have shown that under the rural reforms
cadres still wielded enormous influence through administrative controls over a
growing economy,[58] through the allocation of agricultural inputs,[59] by becoming
hybrid cadre-entrepreneurs,[60] or, as chapter 4 shows, by imposing arbitrary taxes
and expropriating wealth from successful rural entrepreneurs. Under decollectivization, cadres bought collective property for a song and used their power
and networks to control valuable resources.[61] In a Sichuan village where there
was only one major enterprise, cadres grabbed the majority of shares and used
the dividends to keep their incomes high and their control over entry to the
factory to maintain their political authority.[62] Chapter 5 also shows that, as land
became a valuable commodity, cadres, in some localities, used personal ties and
administrative power to carry out a significant land grab.

A cadre's ability to manipulate the emerging system to personal advantage
was in part the result of a normative ambiguity over who had the rights to the
spoils of the new wealth. As chapter 6 shows, the initial wealth that cadres
grabbed consisted of the "extranormal profits" that could be earned when individuals with incentives to maximize profits, and the ability to do so, took control
of formerly collective endeavors. The true value of collective property (and the
level of income this property could generate) was hard to estimate since the
"rents" invested by collective labor had not materialized due to poor collective

management. Thus, disbursed property was undervalued, giving those who were subcontractors of collective property a one-time extranormal profit. In addition, manufacturers of new products with enormous demand but limited supply also reaped short-term extranormal profits. However, as entrepreneurs recognized these opportunities and entered the expanding market, the cadres' comparative advantage and large profits disappeared.

The extent to which cadres suppressed long-term competition remains problematic. Chapter 8 shows that collective cadres who controlled local commercial organizations were threatened by the emerging private sector. And, while directors of these organizations called on their comrades running the industrial and commercial bureaus (ICBs) to suppress new entrepreneurs, some ICB officials took their responsibility to promote a regulated market seriously and guided but also protected the new entrepreneurs.[63] In addition, while cadres may have transformed their political authority into entrepreneurial opportunities in the early 1980s, by the late 1980s some studies found little correlation between former cadre status and income.[64] Similarly, while initially cadres became entrepreneurs more easily than non-cadres did, Odegaard found that the percentage of cadres among successful entrepreneurs was relatively small, especially for small- and medium-sized businesses. Cadres dominated only large enterprises, where personal ties were most important.[65]

While cadres have become more openly rapacious under the reforms,[66] the work of Odegaard, Li, and O'Brien and some of the chapters in this volume show that farmers have fought back.[67] Farmers have responded in four ways: becoming entrepreneurs, becoming politically active, adopting "everyday forms" of passive resistance, or simply succumbing to cadre pressures and abuse. Many of their choices, however, were framed by national or regional policy. First, buoyed by the second stage of rural reform (1984–1988), which legalized private activity in the commercial sector, farmers, rural youth, and ex–factory workers became entrepreneurs and competed directly with former officials.[68] Second, they turned to various types of protest and protestation. The relatively quiescent peasant of the Maoist era has been replaced by the farmer who, while still fearful of cadre authority, is far more assertive in protecting his or her rights. Chapter 5 shows how farmers fought more openly to protect their land from rapacious cadres than they had under the Maoist era.[69] In some cases, this assertive behavior has taken the form of collective violence.[70] Li and O'Brien described what they call "policy based resistance," in which farmers, whom villagers call "shrewd and unyielding people" (diaomin), cite laws and government policies established to protect them from oppressive cadres when they demand just treatment from officials or call for those officials to be replaced.[71] These diaomin are particularly nettlesome for local officials who frequently sidestep or ignore national policies as a means to fulfill their own local agendas.[72]

Third, some farmers, who remain more cautious and fearful of cadre retribution, resort to what Scott calls "everyday forms of peasant resistance." Silently, and perhaps quite invisibly, they undermine cadre authority and challenge local cadre and state behavior. I recall quite vividly an incident in 1981 when a team leader hosted me for lunch with collective funds. During the meal, farmers walked by at various points and grumbled that we were eating quite well. The criticism clearly got through. Chapter 5 looks at how farmers have employed these strategies to protect their claims to land. Finally, many farmers choose the path of least resistance. These "compliant villagers" have not organized, lack information, and believe the costs of open resistance outweigh the potential benefits. As a result, they fail to act individually or collectively.[73]

In the case of farmers who do take action, however, the state facilitates increased activism, participation, and resistance. First, the state has tried to restructure farmer-cadre relations by introducing new legal institutions, in particular legal reform and contract law. The goal (as outlined in chapter 6) has been to limit the impact of the market fluctuations on economic exchanges, prevent breach of contract by jealous cadres when farmers suddenly earned extranormal profits through hard work and entrepreneurship, and maintain farmer enthusiasm for agricultural and sideline investment. While the state still hoped to use contracts to increase the predictability of the farmers' delivery of agricultural produce, it let farmers use the legal system to protect their own economic interests vis-à-vis local state political and economic units. As a result, legal claims by farmers against local cadres increased in the late 1980s (see chapter 6). Li and O'Brien's *diaomin* clearly rely on state policies introduced to curb cadre malfeasance. Similarly, the entire ethos and nature of the state's hegemonic ideology changed with the passing of "agrarian radicalism," legitimizing greater farmer activism (see chapter 5). Yet, even as the state introduced a degree of fairness in adjudicating disputes among cadres and farmers, it asserted that the interests of local governments and administrative organs might take precedence over formal contracts signed by farmers.[74]

Despite refusing to grant farmers formal political representation at the center,[75] the state introduced villager committees and free elections to reestablish local authority and fill the political vacuum that emerged after decollectivization undermined the CCP's legitimacy and power. Rural citizens, who view most taxes with great suspicion,[76] have refused to invest in public goods, such as roads, schools, and development projects, all of which are necessary for economic development. However, when CCP leaders sought a solution to this loss of legitimacy, they came up with a surprising conclusion: let farmers elect their own local officials. Beginning in the mid-1980s, and especially after 1987, conservative and reformist leaders in China have launched rural China on a transition toward democracy unheralded in recent Chinese history.[77] Through the election of villager committees and direct elections for village and township leaders, organized by the Ministry of Civil Affairs, China's farmers have reportedly expanded their influence over the selection of local leaders.[78] Although the true impact of these policies remains to be evaluated, tentative findings suggest that, at a minimum, localities instituting such elections have been more willing to invest in public works and follow some party policies. However, in areas where elections have not been held, cadre efforts to withdraw funds for public works projects have faced strong resistance, because they are viewed as expropriative and reminiscent of the Maoist era.[79]

Transforming Urban-Rural Relations

The increased flow of people, goods, and services across previously sacrosanct boundaries separating urban and rural China has altered urban-rural relations. Chapters 7 through 9 focus specifically on the political economy of this aspect of rural reform.

As chapter 7 outlines, Maoism, with its stress on rural self-sufficiency, imposed a hermetic seal on the countryside; through the household registration system, "residency permits" (*hukou*) divided all Chinese into "urban" (*chengshi*) or "rural" (*nongcun*) residents.[80] This division, which prevented unregulated rural migration for those in search of job opportunities and a better life, was the most fundamental one separating winners and losers in Maoist China.[81] Welfare benefits, allocated through urban, state-run work units, had no rural counterparts, as the real benefits of rural collectives were limited to improved education and health-care delivery. Similarly, upward mobility and life chance opportunities, income and consumption levels, and cultural consciousness all varied along these urban-rural lines.[82] Estimates of the rural-urban income gap suggest that it grew from a 2 to 1 ratio in the 1950s to perhaps a 3 to 1 ratio by the 1970s.[83] Under the planned economy, all produce and capital goods transfers were allocated by administrative decisions; the resulting "price scissors" allowed the urban areas to grow by extracting resources from the rural areas, creating apartheid-like conditions,[84] with discrete urban and rural castes, and an "economic dualism" of stagnant rural life and expanding urban incomes.[85]

But the expansion of the household responsibility system between 1981 and 1983, the weakening of state control over cropping patterns, and the commercialization of marketing and transportation under the "second stage" of the rural reforms (1984–1988) allowed farmers to flock to the cities in search of markets, jobs, and permanent residency. The benefits of this rural influx for urban residents was clear; one of the most striking changes I found when I returned to China in 1985 after a four-year absence was that the quality and quantity of fresh food available in urban markets had undergone a revolutionary improvement. Suddenly, Chinese friends could treat their guests proudly. For a food conscious culture, for health and welfare, too, this was a transformation of historic proportions.

Moreover, chapter 8 shows that, as farmers flocked to Nanjing with this increased produce, they undermined the local state's monopoly on the marketing of rural produce in the urban areas. For some products, such as fresh fish, the influx of rural merchants destroyed the state-owned companies altogether. I also found that, in smaller rural centers and in the towns that were the seats of the county government, farmers who moved to town challenged local state companies, such as the supply and marketing cooperatives, department stores, hotels, and restaurants created in the 1950s, by the socialization of then private businesses. Rural construction teams brought hundreds of thousands of male farmers to town, increasing their wages and their rural households' economic efficiency,[86] even as this development contributed to the increased feminization of agricultural labor. These rural construction teams competed successfully with urban companies and helped transfer wealth created by China's urban infrastructure boom back to the rural areas in the hinterland.

Chapter 9 focuses on another major demographic change and a shift in urban-rural relations: the buildup of small rural towns through industrial development and the reemergence of rural markets. The policy begun in 1982 to develop small towns and promote rural urbanization was an effort to limit mass migration to large cities, all the while bringing the benefits of modernization and urban life to the countryside. Moving to these towns allowed farmers to increase their incomes, living standards, and quality of life, while gaining a tentative foothold in the lower echelons of urban settlement through which they could improve their opportunities and those of the next generation. But, as chapter 5 shows, many of the first migrants to some small towns under this policy were local cadres who used their administrative power to expropriate farmland for their own new homes in the suburbs of these growing population centers.[87]

The question remains whether accelerated rural-to-urban migration has meant a wholesale restructuring of rural-urban relations, such that China no longer suffers from a major urban bias. Chapter 7, written in 1986, focuses on the ways the reforms narrowed, rather than expanded, the urban-rural gap.[88] Nevertheless, although increased rural-to-urban flows, as well as the increased price paid by the state for crops, initially lessened urban-rural income differences dramatically, after 1987, the direction of change shifted. By the mid-1990s, the gap had returned to prereform levels. Urban inflation increased the price scissors effect, while rapid urbanization, commercialization, and internationalization raised urban salaries.[89] Income gaps between coastal and inland residents grew as well.[90] China's health-care delivery system, one of Maoism's true successes, has deteriorated; and while increased nutrition has ameliorated the expected rural health care crisis, the health gap between rural and urban residents has increased.[91] Similarly, a very significant gap between access and attendance to middle schools between urban and rural youths has emerged.[92]

As chapter 9 argues, in wealthier parts of rural China, where resources remain ensconced in the rural administrative hierarchy and rural industry is controlled by the local state, the distribution of power and authority between local state agents and society has changed less dramatically than in regions where economic development has shifted into private hands. State policy continues to channel the flow of permanent rural resettlement into smaller towns and cities, despite an increased level of "urbanization from below,"[93] protecting larger urban centers from the shantytowns characteristic of most developing states. Holders of rural residency permits who live in cities can neither easily become urban residents, and thus gain access to urban welfare benefits, nor shed their stigmatized lower status.[94] Moreover, modernization and the increased incorporation of urban China into the world economy, combined with the reemergence of pre-socialist Chinese culture in the countryside, has "contributed to increased divergence between urban and rural customs."[95]

Thus, while urban-to-rural flows may have increased, and the rigid boundaries between the two worlds of urban and rural China weakened, the rural reforms alone have not ended the long-standing urban bias that has underpinned development in the People's Republic of China. Knowing that political order depends primarily on satisfying urban residents, China's elites pour billions of *yuan* into SOEs as insurance against urban disorder. But long-term disregard of farmers' interests generates its own form of instability. During the Ninth Five Year Plan (1996–2000), the CCP is trying to shift its focus toward the country-side (see Epilogue). Given China's history of rural unrest and the expansion of the rural-urban gap, such a policy shift cannot come too soon.

The Partial Nature of the Rural Reform

State efforts to maintain regulatory controls over aspects of urban-rural relations reflect a core characteristic of the rural reform program—its partial nature.[96] Fearful that a "big bang" strategy would seriously disrupt economic and political stability, China's leaders chose a strategy of "segmented deregulation" or "reform by exemption," whereby they deregulated or exempted certain economic or industrial sectors or regions of the country from the control of the planned economy, all the while maintaining regulatory controls over other sectors.[97] As new markets and new growth opportunities emerged under economic liberalization, the deregulated sectors or regions were better able to respond flexibly to new market opportunities and incentives. Those sectors that had been coddled under the plan, had benefited from the administrative allocation of resources, and now existed under greater spatial or administrative monitoring and control, found that these continuing relationships, and the welfare functions they were forced to perform for the state, had become fetters on their ability to respond to market opportunities.

Under the responsibility system, only poorer areas were to shift from collective farming, although, in the end, demand for more rapid and extreme decollectivization propelled the process much further than the reformers had anticipated. In other sectors, China liberalized less essential sectors of the economy that were not critical to the state plan or to state welfare services, all the while maintaining controls over more critical sectors. Thus, rural industries (as well as private and foreign firms) have thrived in the emerging market economy at the expense of more regulated SOEs, which still shoulder heavy welfare and fiscal functions. Competition between the two sectors and their incentives, constraints, and behaviors were all deeply affected by the relatively different level of state regulation they faced.[98]

As chapter 8 outlines, not all service sector firms were deregulated at the same pace or forced to confront the same institutional constraints. This created a state-imposed inequality. Even as the state allowed farmers to enter the towns and small cities to open small shops, hotels, and restaurants, it maintained a more rigorous, regulatory regime over local state firms that labored under greater economic constraints. Therefore, partial reform had a differentiated impact on private, as compared with local state, firms.[99] For example, supply and marketing cooperatives still had the welfare burden of supporting hundreds of retirees, even as private merchants and marketeers who challenged them for market share carried no similar economic burden. Even salaries, working hours, and rules of management for restaurants and shops varied depending on whether they were privately or publicly owned. Under these conditions, private firms flourished while managers of local state firms, whom I interviewed in 1986, loudly denounced the constraints imposed on their ability to respond to market opportunities.

Partial reform affected the pace and success of the internationalization of the TVE sector. While restricted from competing with the SOEs in exports and foreign direct investment until 1987, the TVE sector was encouraged under Zhao Ziyang's "Coastal Development Strategy" to engage in international trade. As chapter 12 shows, their flexible ownership rights, greater work discipline, and weaker supralocal administrative interference[100]—that is, weaker regulatory controls by administrative superiors—allowed TVEs to compete successfully in international trade and surpass the SOEs. Thus, Zhangjiagang, with its coterie of TVEs, responded quickly to international market demands, while Nantong Municipality, with its large SOE sector, was "path dependent,"[101] and had greater difficulty responding to the new international economic opportunities that came with China's "open policy." In addition, rather than promote its TVEs to compete internationally, Nantong channeled foreign investors away from the countryside, even as its SOEs proved inflexible due in part to administrative and managerial constraints. The result was that, while Nantong established few joint ventures with its TVEs and experienced slower growth in foreign trade overall, Zhangjiagang boomed.

Our proclivities in the West lead us to sympathize with private entrepreneurs who confront or challenge state monopolists. These monopolists have throughout the 1980s used their bureaucratic networks to stifle private market competition. At a time when they succeeded, consumers, no doubt, suffered. Nevertheless, the rapaciousness and callousness of the market does necessitate more than a modicum of state intervention to create the necessary institutions that can create an efficient market economy. Moreover, if we want to understand the dynamic of rural reform and the people's response to it, we must be sensitive to how partial reform can generate distortions in market opportunities and create administrative constraints for actors in similar industries or industrial sectors that limit their ability to grow and develop.

Rural Industry and "Political Dualism" in Rural China

Since 1984, rural China has undergone phenomenal industrialization. From 1983 to 1993, TVE workers as a percentage of all rural laborers increased from 9.4 to 27.8 percent. While TVE production was 24.7 percent of total rural output in 1983, it had reached 66 percent by 1992.[102] The changes in these industries reflect a national shift in the structure of labor and the economy from agriculture to industry—constituting a major transformation in urban-rural relations—and a restructuring of local power in rural China.[103]

As chapter 12 shows, rural industry has strengthened the local state, the CCP, and party officials whose control over the allocation of resources, job opportunities, and capital (more than their ideological and coercive power or their control over information)[104] is key to the everyday power of local state officials. By controlling these resources, local cadres have expanded their networks, incorporating rural industrial workers into the local state-run economy. Rural industrialization and local economic growth further shifted power from the center to the localities; as local wealth increased, cadres had fewer economic incentives to move upward, somewhat weakening a key vehicle of influence for the party hierarchy.[105] For these political and economic reasons, the local state and its agents have had enormous incentives to industrialize.[106] Cadres also have had private incentives, since industrialization is "the vehicle through which the personal income of village leaders can most easily and dramatically be raised."[107] Yet, for political scientists, the key issue is the impact economic development has had on local political power and the more general political consequences of rural industrialization.

One can look at the political implications of rural industrialization along several dimensions. To a certain extent, TVEs have undermined the state's legitimacy and political stability in urban China. Once the state eased its monopoly over various industries and TVEs grabbed market share from subsidized urban enterprises and their pampered urban workers, these less competitive SOEs could no longer insure the state a budgetary surplus.[108] By forcing the state to cut its subsidies, TVEs threatened the CCP's urban-focused welfare regime and its ability to insure SOE workers cradle-to-grave security, which had formed part of the informal social contract between urban workers and the state.[109] Similarly, as outlined in chapters 11 and 12, following the 1987 Coastal Development Strategy, TVEs increased their light industrial exports and, combined with joint ventures, replaced the SOEs as the engine of China's export-led growth strategy. Moreover, as chapter 10 argues, while many analysts have underestimated the significance of the rural industrial sector in Chinese politics, rural industry has deflected numerous attacks on it by central economic interests and political elites, making it an important player in China's evolving political economy.[110]

Rural industry's success has also challenged the assumption that privatization is the only feasible path away from state-directed socialism. Analysts such as Sachs and Woo initially underestimated the incentives inherent in rural industrialization for local state officials, arguing that only a big bang strategy, as in Poland, and a clear demarcation of property rights could successfully trigger a transition to market socialism.[111] They also asserted that decollectivization was, in fact, a form of privatization that has boosted rural output. However, while the jury is still out on this assertion, a rich literature is emerging that proposes that rural industry, with its less than clear ownership rights, may offer an effective and reasonably efficient way to make a less shocking transition to a more market-oriented and competitive economy.[112]

As for state-society ties, according to Oi, TVEs form the economic basis for "local state corporatism."[113] The "fiscal responsibility system" introduced in the mid-1980s bestowed on local governments a fixed tax burden to pass up to the next administrative level. Any above-quota profit became the property of the local government, making TVEs and the income they generated a new opportunity for expanding the income and wealth of the local government.[114] In Oi's portrait of rural China, she shows that local governments at the county and township level are structured in ways more similar to corporations than to a coterie of private firms. For example, local governments manage several businesses or factories and transfer funds among them. In this picture, too, the role of the local party is salient only to the extent that it is an important economic player. Moreover, as one moves further down the hierarchy, these local corporations face harder and harder budget constraints, making them more efficient and competitive.[115] These incentives and the resultant jump in industrialization empowered local governments, allowing them to carve out an autonomous domain between the central state and society.

Nan Lin dissents from a view which argues that TVEs strengthen formal state power at the local level, maintaining instead that TVEs abet the reemergence of traditional society and traditional state-society relations.[116] According to Lin, the local state may be based less on formal government structures and more on traditional social networks. Therefore, TVE growth, rather than building Nee's "market socialism" or Oi's "local state corporatism," reinforces traditional structures, creating what Lin calls "local market socialism." The outcome is a more factionalized or highly personalized dictatorship, in which family links, and not formal political positions, become the key to economic and political power.

However, because both Oi and Lin focus on areas with highly developed industrial economies and do not compare these successful cases to less successful ones, they cannot fully explain the source of the industrialization; they also cannot focus on the national political impact of highly differentiated levels of industrial development. Thus, while Oi shows the enormous incentives generated by the central state's tax policy for industrialization, she does not explain why cadres in other localities, facing similar tax incentives and economic institutions, fail to industrialize. But if everyone has the same institutional incentives, and outcomes still vary, then the incentives under the fiscal responsibility system themselves are not a sufficient explanation for growth. The incentives she cites clearly explain the widespread desire to industrialize, and therein lies the strength of her study; but, without looking at areas that tried to industrialize but failed, or areas that never industrialized at all, she cannot explain why the same incentives lead to different outcomes in different locations.[117]

Regional variations, including comparative advantages in location (proximity to the coast, harbors, or large cities, such as Shanghai) and the quality of local leaders, go a long way toward explaining variations in the level of industrialization in rural China.[118] In the mid-1980s, the major centers of rural industry were near big cities as SOEs, which sought to evade many of the constraints imposed by state regulations, subcontracted production to TVEs in the near and more distant suburbs.[119] Rural industrial growth has remained uneven and a source of expanding intrarural inequality, with the core regions of rural industrialization still in the suburbs of big cities or in rural areas along the coast.[120] Within provinces, too, significant differences in rural incomes have been due primarily to the emergence of (or lack of) opportunities for nonagricultural labor afforded by TVEs.[121] No doubt, it is in the wealthier localities that we find local state corporatism or local market socialism, both of which are institutional arrangements more characteristic of newly industrializing economies.[122]

However, as a result of the uneven growth of rural industry and modernization, a form of "political dualism" may be emerging in rural China. Thus, while we do find local state corporatism or local market socialism, with formidable statist or traditional institutions bringing stability to local polities in wealthy areas, significant parts of rural China lack the political institutions or party authority to maintain a stable political order.[123] First, because poorer areas have weaker industrial bases, are almost totally dependent on agriculture, and have weaker party structures, their officials have few economic and political incentives with which to insure policy conformity from the local community.[124] Officials in these localities cannot establish a local *redistributive economy,* which in the more industrialized areas garners support for local political authorities. Also, without the resources for collective goods, such as public works projects, they can generate little public support. Second, less industry also increases out-migration of cheap labor into the cities and rural factories of coastal China. Even though cadres organize some of these labor contracts, they wield less control over the out-migrants than officials who are granting farmers employment opportunities in TVEs. Third, with smaller public coffers, these localities offer fewer private benefits to local cadres who, in wealthier areas, can supplement their incomes through the perquisites of public office or various forms of pay-offs. Poorer locations may have great difficulty developing or maintaining a coterie of talented leaders, and those leaders that do emerge will probably be more rapacious, frequently employing coercion or unofficial levies to gain access to private resources for public welfare or private graft that would otherwise remain outside the purview of local government officials.[125]

The central state is clearly aware of these issues and has introduced several policies to resolve this political dualism. Economically, it has pushed coastal areas to help inland or hinterland rural localities promote TVEs and introduced a national five-year plan to support rural industrialization in inland areas.[126] Politically attempts have been made to reconstruct the political institutions in these localities by opening up and democratizing the procedures by which local officials are chosen. Advocates of local elections believe that farmers will pay for public works projects if they are consulted or if it is their elected representatives who propose such projects. By empowering the farmers and allowing them to "throw the bums out," these political reformers believe they can both limit the power of exploitative cadres and increase political stability in the countryside. They also hope that political and economic stability will increase economic development in these localities. Time will tell, however, whether localities with low levels of economic development and industrialization will be able to consolidate these kinds of local political reforms.[127] Preliminary findings suggest that it is in areas of moderate wealth, rather than in the rich or poor areas, that democracy is planting the deepest rural roots.

Internationalization: The Impact of Foreign Forces on Rural China

International markets can profoundly affect rural political economies. Dependency analysts would predict a growing income gap between an urban "core" that processes rural produce and a rural periphery supplying raw materials which faces increased immiseration.[128] With trade policy made by a new class of urban internationalists, who sell out the state to advance their own and global interests, rural areas have little opportunity to protect or advance their own interests.[129] Greater susceptibility to global market forces and fluctuations in global markets could trigger rural unrest, if not revolution.[130] More optimistic, neomercantilist models predict that a globally oriented, rural economy, using comparative advantage in the production and export of light industrial and agricultural products, could grow rapidly and fuel an economic takeoff.[131] On the other hand, a strong socialist state with powerful bureaucracies monitoring (if not controlling) the linkage points between external markets and domestic producers might protect the rural areas from external price fluctuations.[132] In fact, foreign direct investment may strengthen, not weaken, the state.[133] Moreover, as in Taiwan, internationalization may narrow the urban-rural gap.[134] Finally, even shifts in international relative prices should prompt domestic actors with a comparative advantage in exports to advocate further trade liberalization, which would deepen internationalization and increase economic growth.[135]

For decades, China protected the countryside from international market forces. Despite the establishment of "agricultural export bases" (*nongcun chukou chanpin jidi*) in the 1960s,[136] China's autarkic trade policy, introduced in the Cultural Revolution, effectively shielded rural China from fluctuations in the international economy that could have directly affected cropping patterns and farmers' incomes.[137] A powerful trade bureaucracy served as a transnational buffer between the domestic and international economies, determining domestic market prices for exportable products that had little relationship to their international price.[138] Even if changes in international prices favored rural producers, outside the few export bases, cropping patterns were not based on shifting global demand and changes in international relative prices of agricultural crops; farmers were not allowed to respond to such price signals. As a result, China under Maoist autarky had forgone the potential benefits of its comparative advantage in labor intensive production, a strategy which would have favored rural over urban China. Since 1987, rural China's role in China's export boom has shown the scale of those lost opportunity costs, not just to the countryside but to the entire nation.

As I show in chapters 11 and 12, however, since 1978, and particularly after 1987, the opening of the countryside to foreign trade, foreign investment, and technology transfers with the global economy has deeply affected communities in coastal China. No doubt, no strong lobby advocating rural internationalization emerged at the grass roots; outside an inner core of elites and their advisers, few political forces in Beijing advocated linking the countryside with the international marketplace.[139] Nevertheless, individuals and localities did pursue their economic interests and alter the trade regime that impeded export-led growth in rural China. Decentralization of China's foreign trade regime in 1987, and the liberalization of domestic and global markets, let farmers and local communities with comparative advantages in foreign trade challenge the monopoly of the foreign trade bureaucracy which had manipulated the domestic prices of exportable commodities to earn large rents. They have extracted a greater share of the benefits of foreign trade, weakening the state's control over China's transnational relations. But, as chapter 11 shows, farmers' dependence on state agents is a two-sided affair. While farmers resented the regulatory machinations of the foreign trade bureaucracy and its manipulation of prices, payments, and information, as soon as export markets dried up, farmers wanted bureaucrats to protect them from the vagaries of the international market and demanded that the state buy their export products.

Nevertheless, some negative predictions may hold true. Foreign trade expands regional inequalities. China's state policy of "segmented deregulation" which sequentially internationalized parts of rural coastal China before opening the inland areas, allowed those areas to establish preferred market positions.[140] Similarly, rural communities with long historical links to overseas Chinese communities along the coast, as well as communities with greater numbers of rural

enterprises, became home to FDI,[141] while localities lacking such overseas linkages had more difficulties establishing export production and undergoing an
economic takeoff.[142] This policy advantage, combined with the natural advantages of trade, geography, and rural industry, opened an economic gap between
coastal and inland areas that has been hard to narrow.

Contrary to expectations, however, greater foreign penetration increases,
rather than decreases, the power of the local party-state. As chapter 12 suggests,
because local governments are partners or allies in many joint ventures, this rural
elite has a strong incentive to help foreign investors gain access to the formerly
protected domestic market.[143] Such "developmental communities" along the
coast, which combine strong CCP mobilization for export-oriented growth and a
powerful TVE sector with a highly disciplined rural industrial workforce, further
strengthen the local party-state, not only *vis-à-vis* rural society but also in its
relations to the central government. Other studies concur with such findings. The
Xiamen CCP's efforts to use United Front organizations to control foreigners
apparently failed, because local elites proved more interested in placating foreign
investors than in responding to central party demands.[144] Also, overseas Chinese
from one Guangdong provincial village invested in schools and government-run
firms, and infrastructure, improving the local government's ability to service the
needs of the rural community.[145] In this way, foreign investment stabilized the
countryside and the party's control, rather than challenged it.

Conclusion

China's reformist policies restructured Maoist economic and political institutions
that over time had become rather brittle and economically counterproductive.
The results have been a far more fluid, ever-changing rural scene, replete with
newly emerging economic, social, and political forces that have allowed China's
farmers and their local communities the freedom to challenge state controls in
many locations and in a wide array of sectors. Evolving property rights over land
and enterprises affect the authority relations among farmers and local state
agents. Township and village enterprises have posed an enormous challenge to
SOEs, just as global competition has undermined these long-pampered vestiges
of the Stalinist model of development. Increased urban-rural interactions have
added new meaning to the Maoist concept of the "countryside surrounding the
city," creating a new invasionary force of millions of unemployed farmers who
have flooded the urban labor market and who now serve as a new channel for the
flow of urban capital and technology back into the countryside. According to
some reports, these migrant farmers have also threatened the urban social order
that long was the pride of China's leadership. Finally, increased market competition in an environment with weak legal norms and evolving market institutions
has meant that administrative power can still wield enormous influence in the
allocation of goods and services in China's mixed rural economy. All these

reforms have transformed the countryside and its relations to the surrounding economic and political environment.

It is possible to characterize the rural reforms as the farmers' efforts to free themselves from state oppression and exploitation based on enforced rural residency and a price scissors that transferred rural wealth from farmers to urban residents and the central state. This effort, however, could not have occurred without a reformist leadership that initiated these liberalizing policies: encouraging TVEs, rewarding farmers who produced higher value-added or exportable commodities, bestowing on farmers quasi-ownership rights over land, supporting a private sector and economic competition, and granting farmers the freedom to move to urban centers and dream of social mobility. But, as the Maoist fetters fell away, farmers pushed the system further and faster than reformers had anticipated, which resulted in increased urban-rural, farmer-worker, and central-local competition and forced the government in Beijing to respond to a new set of local demands.

However, the reforms also weakened the state's capacity to respond to those demands, control rural inhabitants, determine agricultural output, and limit cadre rapaciousness. Local communities have struggled successfully to advance their own interests, which have not always been consonant with national ones. While the results have been enormous growth and rising standards of living, there have also been increased conflicts over the fruits of the new prosperity.

The challenges facing the leadership of the CCP are enormous. The history of the past 18 years breeds both optimism and pessimism: although the changes have been great, the strains on the social, political, and economic fabric of rural China cannot be overstated. Rural China was the base that brought the CCP to power, but under Mao promises made in the heat of the revolution gave way to utopianism and a set of political priorities that severely constrained rural economic development. Today, farmers and their communities have used the reforms to challenge the central state and many of those policies; should the state fail to deal effectively with the countryside, it may ultimately be the force that brings the CCP down.

Notes

1. For global implications of the rural reforms, see Lester R. Brown, *Who Will Feed China: Wake-up Call for a Small Planet* (New York: W.W. Norton, 1995); Ross Garnaut, Guo Shutian, and Ma Guonan, eds., *The Third Revolution in the Chinese Countryside* (Cambridge, England: Cambridge University Press, 1996); and chapters 11 and 12 in this book.

2. Kelliher quite controversially called decollectivization "the largest privatization in world history." See Daniel Kelliher, *Peasant Power in China: The Era of Rural Reform, 1979–1989* (New Haven: Yale University Press, 1992).

3. Louis Putterman, "The Role of Ownership and Property Rights in China's Economic Transition," *The China Quarterly*, no. 144 (1995): 1047–1064. For an argument that

ownership rights are actually a bundle of rights including the right to allocate profits, to allocate labor within the firm, and to sell the firm itself, see Janos Kornai, *The Socialist System: The Political Economy of Communism* (Princeton: Princeton University Press, 1992), pp. 64–67. Thus, while farmers may not be able to sell the land they till, they have many rights that could be seen as granting them ownership over the land.

4. Terry Sicular, "China's Agricultural Policy during the Reform Period," in Joint Economic Committee of the U.S. Congress, *China's Economic Dilemmas in the 1990s: The Problems of Reforms, Modernization, and Interdependence* (Armonk, N.Y.: M.E. Sharpe, 1993), pp. 340–364.

5. See Thomas Lyons, *Economic Integration and Planning in Maoist China* (New York: Columbia University Press, 1987). See also Nicholas R. Lardy, *Agriculture in China's Modern Economic Development* (Cambridge, England: Cambridge University Press, 1983).

6. See Dorothy J. Solinger, *Chinese Business Under Socialism: The Politics of Domestic Commerce, 1949–1980* (Berkeley: University of California Press, 1984); and Dorothy J. Solinger, "Commerce: The Petty Private Sector and the Three Lines in the Early 1980s," in Dorothy J. Solinger, ed., *Three Visions of Chinese Socialism* (Boulder, Colo.: Westview Press, 1984), pp. 73–111.

7. Terry Sicular, "China's Reforms in Agricultural Commerce," *The China Quarterly*, no. 144 (1995): 1031.

8. Jean C. Oi, "Commercializing China's Rural Cadres," *Problems of Communism*, no. 25 (1986): 1–15.

9. Jean Oi, "Communism and Clientelism," *World Politics* 37 (January 1985): 238–266.

10. Richard Madsen, *Morality and Power in a Chinese Village* (Berkeley: University of California Press, 1984).

11. David Zweig, *Agrarian Radicalism in China, 1968–1981* (Cambridge: Harvard University Press, 1989).

12. Scott Rozelle, "Decision-Making in China's Rural Economy: The Linkage Between Village Leaders and Farm Households," *The China Quarterly*, no. 137 (1994): 99–124.

13. See chapters 4 and 5 in this book; Kevin J. O'Brien, "Rightful Resistance," *World Politics* 49 (October 1986): 31–55; Forrest Colbura, ed., *Everyday Forms of Peasant Resistance* (Armonk, N.Y.: M.E. Sharpe); James C. Scott, *Weapons of the Weak* (New Haven: Yale University Press, 1985); and Elizabeth J. Perry, "Rural Collective Violence: The Fruits of Recent Reforms," in Elizabeth J. Perry and Christine Wong, eds., *The Political Economy of Reform in Post-Mao China* (Cambridge: Harvard Contemporary China Series, 1985), pp. 175–192.

14. See chapter 6 in this book.

15. Sulamith Heins Potter, "The Position of Peasants in Modern China's Social Order," *Modern China*, vol. 9, no. 4 (1983): 465–499. See also Edward Friedman, Paul G. Pickowicz, Mark Selden, and Kay Johnson, *Chinese Village, Socialist State* (New Haven: Yale University Press, 1991); Kam Wing Chan, *Cities without Walls* (Hong Kong: Oxford University Press, 1995); Mark Selden, "City Versus Countryside? The Social Consequences of Developmental Choices in China," in Mark Selden, *The Political Economy of Chinese Development* (Armonk, N.Y.: M.E. Sharpe, 1993), chapter 6; and Tiejun Cheng and Mark Selden, "The Origins and Social Consequences of China's Hukou System," *The China Quarterly*, no. 139 (1994): 644–668.

16. Throughout this book I use the terms "farmers," "villagers," or "rural residents" to refer to a population commonly called in the China field "peasants." Peasant is a pejora-

tive term, inappropriate for the freeholding farmers that emerged from decollectivization. For a further discussion of this issue, see Myron L. Cohen, "Cultural and Political Inventions in Modern China: The Case of the Chinese 'Peasant,' " *Daedalus* 122 (1993): 151–170.

17. Jean C. Oi, *State and Peasant in Contemporary China: The Political Economy of Village Government* (Berkeley: University of California Press, 1989).

18. Michael Lipton, *Why Poor People Stay Poor: Urban Bias in World Development* (Cambridge: Harvard University Press, 1976).

19. The work of Dorothy Solinger is particularly useful on this point. See Dorothy J. Solinger, "The Impact of the Floating Population on the Danwei: Shifts in the Pattern of Labor Mobility Control and Entitlement Provision," in Lü Xiaobo and Elizabeth J. Perry, eds., *The Danwei: The Changing Chinese Workplace in Historical and Comparative Perspectives* (Armonk, N.Y.: M.E. Sharpe, 1997). See also Kam Wing Chan, ed., *Internal Migration in China*, a special issue of *Chinese Environment and Development* (Spring/Summer 1996).

20. Karl Polyani, *The Great Transformation* (Boston: Beacon Press, 1985).

21. There is some confusion as to the appropriate title for these rural industries. The standard term used in English is "TVE" or "township and village enterprise." In Chinese this would be translated as "*xiang cun qiye*." However, the standard Chinese term is *xiang zhen qiye*, which would be interpreted in English as "township and town enterprises" (TTE). In fact, these enterprises are found in villages (*cun*), townships (*xiang*) and towns (*zhen*) with the latter a legal term for rural townships which have been formally "designated" by the Chinese State Council as part of the urban hierarchy of places (see chapter 9). In fact, having a higher level of industrial output is one of the criteria for switching from a rural "township" to an urban "town," so many of the localities hosting these enterprises are in fact "designated towns." However, in this book I have consistently referred to them as TVEs. I also refer to them as "township and village enterprises" rather than "township and village industries" because as the data in chapter 10 shows, most of these enterprises are not involved in industrial production; many are restaurants, hotels, transport or construction companies. Similarly, if one looks at the labor structure of the employees, only a minority (55 of 120 million) are industrial workers. Therefore, it is more appropriate to refer to the entire category as enterprises, with industries forming a subcategory of TVEs.

22. See chapter 12.

23. See Table 11.1.

24. Zweig, *Agrarian Radicalism*.

25. David Zweig, "Strategies of Policy Implementation: Policy 'Winds' and Brigade Accounting in Rural China, 1968-1978," *World Politics* 37 (January 1985): 267–293.

26. Louis Putterman, "Extrinsic versus Intrinsic Problems of Agricultural Cooperation: Anti-Incentivism in Tanzania and China," *Journal of Development Studies* 21 (1985): 175–204.

27. David Zweig, "Agrarian Radicalism as a Rural Development Strategy," in William A. Joseph, Christine Wong, and David Zweig, eds., *New Perspectives on China's Cultural Revolution* (Cambridge: Harvard Contemporary China Series, 1991), pp. 63–81.

28. I would not, however, ignore the role of coercion in forcing farmers to abide by the Communist Party's policies.

29. See, inter alia, David Zweig, "Institutional Constraints, Path Dependence, and Entrepreneurship: Comparing Zhangjiagang and Nantong, 1984–1994," unpublished paper; David Zweig, "Controlling the Opening: Enmeshment, Organizational Capacity, and the Limits on Overseas Development Assistance in China," presented at the Annual

Meeting of the American Political Science National Convention, Washington, D.C., September 2–5, 1993; Chen Changgui and David Zweig, "The Impact of the Open Policy on Higher Education in China," presented at the Annual Meeting of the Association for Asian Studies, Los Angeles, Calif., March 1993; and "Explaining China's Internationalization: Domestic/External Linkages in the Evolution of China's Open Policy," presented to the Workshop on International Relations Theory and Chinese Foreign Policy, American Council of Learned Societies—China Committee, Center for International Affairs, Harvard University, April 21–22, 1995. All these papers form the core of my current book project, tentatively entitled, "Linking China to the World: The Political Economy of the Open Policy."

30. For a fascinating study of provincial variations in foreign trade, see Brantly Womack and Guangzhi Zhao, "The Many Worlds of China's Provinces: Foreign Trade and Diversification," in David S. G. Goodman and Gerald Segal, eds., *China Deconstructs: Politics, Trade and Regionalism* (New York: Routledge, 1994), pp. 131–176.

31. Initial divisions of the province put Nantong and Yancheng within *Subei,* but growth rates there since the mid-1980s have been significantly different from those of counties in northern *Subei,* reflecting in part the influence of Shanghai, *Sunan,* and foreign trade opportunities. Thus, when people in Shanghai think of *Subei* people, they often have in mind people from the Nantong region.

32. Advocates of the "single spark" approach are Kelliher, *Peasant Power in China,* and Kate Xiao Zhou, *How the Farmers Changed China: Power of the People* (Boulder, Colo.: Westview Press, 1996).

33. Unger and Hartford propound the "heavy hand of the state" scenario. See Kathleen Hartford, "Socialist Agriculture Is Dead; Long Live Socialist Agriculture! Organizational Transformations in Rural China," in Elizabeth J. Perry and Christine Wong, eds., *The Political Economy of Reform in Post-Mao China* (Cambridge: Harvard Contemporary China Series, 1985); and Jonathan Unger, "The Decollectivization of the Chinese Countryside: A Survey of Twenty-Eight Villages," *Pacific Affairs,* no. 58 (Winter 1985–1986).

34. Kelliher, *Peasant Power in China,* chapter 3.

35. For a similar argument for the anti-Rightist Campaign, see Zhou Xueguang, "Unorganized Interests and Collective Action in Communist China," *American Sociological Review* 58 (February 1993): 54–73. In chapter 12 of this book, I show how individual collectivities undermined the bureaucratic constraints that limited transnational linkages, expanding their ability to export freely and establish joint ventures.

36. Zhou, *How the Farmers Changed China,* p. 8.

37. For the difference among radical reformers, bureaucrats, and leftists among top elites, see Carol Lee Hamrin, "Competing 'Policy Packages' in Post-Mao China," *Asian Survey* 29 (January 1984): 487–518.

38. Kelliher cites me as an advocate of the argument that the localities were the primary driving force of decollectivization, always keeping one step ahead of central policy. See Kelliher, *Peasant Power in China,* p. 235.

39. A strong advocate of the role of regional factors, particularly political and economic variations at the provincial and subprovincial levels, is Jae Ho Chung, "The Politics of Policy Implementation in Post-Mao China: Central Control and Provincial Autonomy Under Decentralization" (The University of Michigan, unpublished dissertation, 1993).

40. One insider to the rural reform process, Chinese economist Yang Shun, argued that in 1981 when Wan Li reported to Deng Xiaoping that farmers were decollectivizing in Anhui Province, Deng told him to keep quiet and let the process go forward. In this sense, this was a conscious decision.

41. See Wang Lixin, *The Years After Mao Zedong, 1978–1980: An On-the-Spot Re-*

port from Rural Anhui, in *Kunlun,* no. 6, 1989, in Joint Publication Research Service-CAR-89–079 (July 28, 1989): 1–65.

42. Wang, *The Years After Mao Zedong,* p. 28.

43. Zhou, *How the Farmers Changed China,* p. 64.

44. Chen Yizi has his own political agenda and his account of events must be seen within that context.

45. Surveys in summer 1980 by Chen Yizi, Lu Xueyi, and others showed that many localities were successfully implementing *baochan daohu.* See Chen Yizi, "The Bright Sunrise of the Countryside, the Future of China" (*"Nongcun de shuguang, Zhongguo de xiwang"*), in Problems in Rural Development Research Group (*Zhongguo nongcun fazhan wenti yanjiu zu*), eds., "Countryside, Economics, Society" (*Nongcun, jingji, shehui*) (Beijing: zhishi chubanshe, 1985), pp. 33–53. In the same volume, see the paper by Lu Xueyi and Wang Xiaoqiang, "The Return of Household Contracting and Its Future Development" (*Baochan daohu de youlai he jin hou de fazhan*). Lu is the current director of the Sociology Institute at the Chinese Academy of Social Sciences.

46. Jae-Ho Chung, "The Politics of Policy Implementation."

47. For a longer critique of Kelliher's excellent book, see my review in *The Australian Journal of Chinese Affairs,* no. 32 (Spring 1994): 185–189.

48. The classis locus on this is Thomas P. Bernstein, "Problems of Village Leadership After Land Reform," *The China Quarterly,* no. 36 (1968): 1–22.

49. Zweig, *Agrarian Radicalism in China,* pp. 44–45.

50. David Zweig, "Form and Essence in Policy Evasion," presented at the conference on New Perspectives on the Cultural Revolution, Harvard University, 1987.

51. Jean C. Oi, *Peasant and State in Contemporary China* (Berkeley: University of California Press, 1989).

52. In June 1978, the "Movement to Study the Xiangxiang Experience" called on local officials to "lighten the peasants' burden," and return to them property the collectives had expropriated. See Zweig, *Agrarian Radicalism,* p. 171. That concern gets raised all the time, as of this writing most recently in December 1996 on CCTV as a document from the State Council.

53. Richard J. Latham, "The Implications of Rural Reforms for Grass-Roots Cadres," in Perry and Wong, eds., *The Political Economy of Reform,* pp. 157–174.

54. For an analysis of official authority under socialism as based on administrative power, see Ivan Szelenyi, *Urban Inequalities under State Socialism* (London: Oxford University Press, 1983).

55. See Victor Nee, "A Theory of Market Transition: From Redistribution to Markets in State Socialism," *American Sociological Review* 54 (October 1989): 663–681.

56. Rozelle, "Decision Making in China's Rural Economy." See also chapter 2 of this book.

57. See Wan Li, *People's Daily,* December 23, 1982, p. 1. This case was probably chosen because cadres in this locality had been doing well and had been able to become successful entrepreneurs. For an analysis of that report, see Melanie Manion, "Survey Research in the Study of Contemporary China: Learning from Local Samples," *The China Quarterly,* no. 139 (1994): 741–765. Manion argues that this study was in no way representative of conditions in the rest of China.

58. Jean C. Oi, "The Fate of the Collective after the Commune," in Deborah Davis and Ezra F. Vogel, eds., *Chinese Society on the Eve of Tiananmen: The Impact of Reform* (Cambridge: Harvard Contemporary China Series, 1990), pp. 15–36.

59. Oi, "Commercializing China's Rural Cadres."

60. Victor Nee, "Social Inequalities in Reforming State Socialism: Between Redistri-

bution and Markets in China," *American Sociological Review* 56 (June 1991): 267–282.

61. See chapters 4 and 6 in this book, and Anita Chan, Jonathan Unger, and Richard Madsen, *Chen Village Under Mao and Deng* (Berkeley: University of California Press, 1992) , pp. 277–282.

62. Minchuan Yang, "Reshaping Peasant Culture and Community: Rural Industrialization in a Chinese Village," *Modern China* 20 (April 1994): 157–179.

63. Susan Young's findings confirm my findings in chapter 8. She found that the ICB and the Self-Employed Labor Association became advocates of private entrepreneurs in their competition with the local state-owned companies. See Susan Young, "Private Entrepreneurs and Evolutionary Change," in David S. Goodman and Beverly Hooper, eds., *China's Quiet Revolution: New Interactions Between State and Society* (New York: St. Martin's Press, 1994), pp. 105–125.

64. While Nee initially felt that cadres would lose out in the market transition, he changed his view, arguing that even over the middle term, the advantages accruing to administrative status and networks allowed cadres to maintain their advantages. See Nee, "Social Inequalities in Reforming State Socialism."

65. Ole Odegaard, "Entrepreneurs and Elite Formation in Rural China," *Australian Journal of Chinese Affairs,* no. 28 (1992): 89–108.

66. Li Xiwen, "A Tentative Analysis of the Tense Cadre-mass Relations in the Countryside" (*Shixi dangqian nongcun ganqun guanxi jinzhang wenti*), presented at the National Conference on Basic Level Political Power Construction, 1989. For a study of more institutionalized corruption by government agencies, which helped trigger the IOU crisis of 1992, see Andrew Wedeman, "Stealing from the Farmers: Institutional Corruption and the 1992 IOU Crisis," presented at the 1996 Association for Asian Studies Annual Meeting, Honolulu, Hawaii.

67. The most important and prolific study of farmer resistance and protest currently under way is based on the collaborative work of Kevin O'Brien and Li Lianjiang. See *inter alia,* Li Lianjiang and Kevin J. O'Brien, "Villagers and Popular Resistance in Contemporary China," *Modern China* 22 (January 1996): 28–61; and Kevin J. O'Brien and Lianjiang Li, "The Politics of Lodging Complaints in Rural China," *The China Quarterly,* no. 143 (1995): 756–783.

68. See Odegaard, "Entrepreneurs and Elite Formation," and chapter 8 of this book.

69. For a comparison of farmer political activity before and after the reforms, see David Zweig, "Evaluating China's Rural Policies: 1949-1989," *The Fletcher Forum of World Affairs* 14 (Winter 1990): 18-29.

70. See Perry, "Rural Collective Violence: The Fruits of Recent Reforms"; and Sung Kuo-cheng, "Peasant Unrest in Szechwan and Mainland China's Rural Problems," *Issues and Studies* 29 (July 1993): 129–132.

71. Li and O'Brien, "Villagers and Popular Resistance," p. 31.

72. Li and O'Brien, "Villagers and Popular Resistance, p. 32.

73. Li and O'Brien, "Villagers and Popular Resistance," pp. 32–33.

74. Phyllis L. Chang, "Deciding Disputes: Factors that Guide Chinese Courts in the Adjudication of Rural Responsibility Contract Disputes," *Law and Contemporary Problems* 52 (Spring and Summer 1989): 101–142.

75. Thomas P. Bernstein, "Proposals for a National Voice for Agricultural Interests: A Farmer's Association," prepared for the Conference on Rural China: Emerging Issues in Development, East Asian Institute, Columbia University, March 31 through April 1, 1995.

76. Farmers oppose the "*san luan,*" that is, unpredictable fees, fines and apportionments. Written communication from Tom Bernstein, November 7, 1996. See Thomas B. Bernstein and Dorothy J. Solinger, "The Peasant Question for the Future: Citizenship,

Integration, and Political Institutions," presented at the Conference on China and World Affairs in 2010, sponsored by the Institute for International Studies, Stanford University, Stanford, Calif., April 25–26, 1996.

77. Kevin J. O'Brien, "Implementing Political Reform in China's Villages," *Australian Journal of Chinese Affairs,* no. 32 (July 1994): 33–59.

78. China Basic Power Organs Research Association (*Zhongguo jiceng zheng chuan jianshe yanjiuhui*), ed., *The System for Changing and Electing China's Rural Villager Assemblies* (*Zhongguo nongcun cunmin weiyuanhui huanju xuanju zhidu*) (Beijing: China Social Publishing House, 1993); and Zhongguo jiceng zheng quan jianshe yanjiuhui, ed., Discussion draft on establishing a system of rural village assemblies in China (*Zhongguo nongcun cunmin daibiao huiyi zhidu* [*taolun gao*]), June 30, 1994.

79. Interview with Wang Zhenyao, Cambridge, Mass., 1994.

80. For a critique of the Maoist policies on urban-rural relations, see Selden, "City Versus Countryside?"

81. Cheng and Selden, "The Origins and Social Consequences of China's *Hukou* System."

82. See Martin King Whyte, "City Versus Countryside in China's Development," *Problems of Post-Communism* (January/February 1996): 9–22.

83. While Parish estimates the gap to have reached 3 to 1, Rawski argues that it may have reached 6 to 1. See William L. Parish, "Egalitarianism in Chinese Society," *Problems of Communism,* no. 1 (1981): 37–53; and Thomas Rawski, "The Simple Arithmetic of Chinese Income Distribution," *Economic Research* (*Keizai kenkyu*) 33, no. 1 (1982): 12–26. For more on this issue, see chapter 13 of this book.

84. Potter, "The Position of Peasants," p. 466.

85. On economic "dualism" see Louis Putterman, "Dualism and Reform in China," *Economic Development and Cultural Change* 40 (April 1992): 467–493.

86. Denise Hare, "Efficiency Considerations of Out Migration from Rural China," presented at the 1996 Association of Asian Studies National Convention, Honolulu, 1996.

87. More data on the growth of these towns will become available due to the current study on small towns by Kam Wing Chan, Clifton Pannell, and Laurence Ma, in collaboration with Professor Cui Gonghao of Nanjing University's Geography Department, funded by the Luce Foundation.

88. Whyte also challenges the assumption that reforms increased the rural-urban gap. See Martin K. Whyte, "Social Trends in China: The Triumph of Inequality?" in A. Doak Barnett and Ralph Clough, eds., *Modernizing China* (Boulder, Colo.: Westview Press, 1986), pp. 103–123.

89. Still, the urban reforms significantly decreased the benefits that accrued to urban residents from the enormous subsidies given to them by the state.

90. Scott Rozelle, "Stagnation without Equity: Patterns of Growth and Inequality in China's Rural Economy," *The China Journal,* no. 35 (1996): 63–92.

91. William C. Hsiao, "Transformation of Health Care in China," *New England Journal of Medicine* (October 1984): 932–936; and Gail Henderson, "Increased Inequality in Health Care," in Davis and Vogel, eds., *Chinese Society on the Eve of Tiananmen,* pp. 263–282.

92. See Whyte, "City Versus Countryside," p. 11.

93. Using the 1987 1 percent population sample, Ma and Fan found that, in terms of permanent migration to towns, the 1987 national survey showed that only 0.58 percent of the nation's people were involved in permanent migration. Laurence J.C. Ma and Ming Fan, "Urbanization from Below: The Growth of Towns in Jiangsu, China," *Urban Studies* 31, no. 10 (1994): 1625–1645. By 1996, however, the per-

centage of the population involved in permanent resettlement had undoubtedly increased.

94. Dorothy Solinger, lecture at Hong Kong University of Science and Technology, October 26, 1996. According to Mark Selden, there are many reports that the price of an urban *hukou* for Shanghai, Beijing, and other major cities runs as high as US$25,000.

95. Whyte, "City Versus Countryside," pp. 15–16.

96. See chapter 8 in this book. Partial reforms involved the coexistence of plan and market, continued bureaucratic interference, mixed property rights, and "soft budget constraints" for firms. Decentralization shifted control to lower levels of the bureaucracy, not to production units. See Janos Kornai, "Hard and Soft Budget Constraints," in Janos Kornai, ed., *Contradictions and Dilemmas: Studies on the Socialist Economy and Society* (Cambridge: MIT Press, 1986); Christine P.W. Wong, "Between Plan and Market: The Role of the Local Sector in Post-Mao China," *Journal of Comparative Economics,* vol. 11 (1987): 385–398. Also, the vestiges of the plan increased the role of personal relations in facilitating transactions and exchanges. See Dorothy J. Solinger, *China's Transition from Socialism* (Armonk, N.Y.: M.E. Sharpe, 1993), pp. 107–126.

97. Shirk calls this process of favoring certain sectors or localities "particularistic contracting," and sees it as the result of negotiations between central and provincial leaders for political support. See Susan L. Shirk, *The Political Logic of Economic Reform* (Berkeley: University of California Press, 1992). My own concept of "segmented deregulation" or "reform by exemption" asserts that the state's strategy was to open areas or sectors that were not directly linked to the state plan or key state goals, for example, allowing poorer areas to experiment with household contracting; allowing TVEs to develop in the market economy; allowing private firms to enter the service industry; or deregulating second or third category prices, keeping first category prices under tighter control. In some ways it is similar to Naughton's explanation for the reforms success. See Barry Naughton, *Growing Out of the Plan: Chinese Economic Reform, 1978–1993* (New York: Cambridge University Press, 1995). For a comparison of Naughton and Shirk, see Dali Yang, "Governing China's Transition to the Market: Institutional Incentives, Politicians' Choices, and Unintended Outcomes," *World Politics* 48 (April 1996): 424–452.

98. See my unpublished paper, "Explaining China's Internationalization: Global Markets and/or Domestic Institutions," presented at the Center for Asian Studies, Cornell University, Ithaca, N.Y., November 1995.

99. For a study of how partial reform deeply affected incentives in the wool industry, turning China from an exporter to an importer, see Andrew Watson, Christopher Findlay, and Du Yintang, "Who Won the 'Wool War'?: A Case Study of Rural Product Marketing in China," *The China Quarterly,* no. 118 (1989): 213–241.

100. Anthony Leeds, "Locality Power in Relation to Supralocal Power Institutions," in Aidan Southall, ed., *Urban Anthropology: Cross-Cultural Studies of Urbanization* (New York: Oxford University Press, 1973), pp. 15–41. For an application to China, see Dorothy J. Solinger, "The Place of the Central City in China's Economic Reform: From Hierarchy to Network?" in Dorothy J. Solinger, *China's Transition from Socialism: Statist Legacies and Market Reforms, 1980–1990* (Armonk, N.Y.: M.E. Sharpe, 1993), pp. 205–222.

101. David Stark, "Path Dependence and Privatization Strategies in East-central Europe," *East European Politics and Societies* 6 (Spring 1992): 17–54.

102. Data from "Extracts of Statistics on China's Rural Industries (*Zhongguo xiangzhen qiye tongji zhaiyao*) and *China Statistical Yearbook (Zhongguo tongji nianjian*), cited in Yan Shanping, "Export-Oriented Rural Enterprises," *JETRO China Newsletter,* no. 118 (1995): 8–23.

103. Samuel P.S. Ho, "Rural Non-Agricultural Development in Post-Reform China: Growth, Development Patterns, and Issues," *Pacific Affairs* 68 (Fall 1995): 360–391.

104. For an analysis of the importance of control over information as a key to cadre power, see Elizabeth Croll, *From Heaven to Earth: Images and Experiences of Development in China* (London: Routledge, 1994), chapter 5.

105. Luo refers to the dichotomy between wealth and political eminence, arguing that there was an inverse relationship between income and position in China's administrative hierarchy. See Luo Xiaopeng, "Rural Reform and the Rise of Localism," in Jia Hao and Lin Zhimin, eds., *Changing Central-Local Relations in China: Reform and State Capacity* (Boulder, Colo.: Westview Press, 1994), p. 122.

106. See William A. Byrd and Alan Gelb, "Why Industrialize? The Incentives for Rural Community Governments," in William A. Byrd and Lin Qingsong, eds., *China's Rural Industry: Structure, Development, and Reform* (New York: Oxford University Press, 1990), pp. 358–387. See also Jean C. Oi, *Rural China Takes Off: Incentives for Rural Industrialization* (Berkeley: University of California Press, forthcoming).

107. Rozelle, "Decision-Making in China's Rural Economy," p. 116.

108. See Barry Naughton, "Implications of the State Monopoly over Industry and Its Relaxation," *Modern China*, no. 18 (1992): 14–41; and Yingyi Qian and Chenggang Xu, "Why China's Economic Reforms Differ: the M-form Hierarchy and Entry/Expansion of the Non-State Sector," *Economics of Transition* 1, no. 2 (1993): 135–170.

109. For a discussion of the concept of social contracts between communist states and their state workers see Peter Hauslohner, "Gorbachev's Social Contract," *Soviet Economy* 3, no. 1 (1987): 54–89; and Linda J. Cook, *The Soviet Social Contract and Why It Failed: Welfare Policies and Worker's Politics from Brezhnev to Yeltsin* (Cambridge: Harvard University Press, 1993).

110. The most recent effort to "restructure" rural industry is being put forward by the National People's Congress, which is debating a new law to control its activity. See Wang Xiangwei, "Stricter Controls Planned to Tame Rural Industries," *South China Morning Post,* China Business Review section, September 12, 1996, p. 2.

111. Jeffrey Sachs and Wing Thye Woo, "Understanding the Reform Experience of China, Eastern Europe and Russia," in Chung H. Lee and Helmut Reisen, eds., *From Reform to Growth: China and Other Countries in Transition in Asia and Central and Eastern Europe* (Paris: Organization for Economic Cooperation and Development, 1993), pp. 23–48.

112. Thomas G. Rawski, "Progress Without Privatization: The Reform of China's State Industries," in Vedat Milor, ed., *Changing Political Economies: Privatization in Post-Communist and Reforming Communist States* (Boulder: Lynne Reinner, 1994), pp. 27–52.

113. Jean C. Oi, "Fiscal Reform and the Economic Foundations of Local State Corporatism in China," *World Politics* 45, no. 1 (1992): 99–126.

114. Oi, *Rural China Takes Off*.

115. Andrew G. Walder, "Local Governments as Industrial Firms: An Organizational Analysis of China's Transitional Economy," *American Journal of Sociology* 101 (September 1995): 263–301.

116. Nan Lin, "Local Market Socialism: Local Corporatism in Action in Rural China," *Theory and Society* 24 (1995): 301–354.

117. Herein lies the strength of the Byrd and Lin volume in that they looked at four different localities with very different economic conditions *and* different economic and political outcomes. See Byrd and Lin, eds., *China's Rural Industry*. The most interesting case in their study documented the unsuccessful attempts to bring about industrialization

in Jiangxi Province, where rapacious cadres, hungry for capital, taxed incipient entrepreneurs so highly that they did not have the funds to expand their businesses. For a similar study that shows how rapacious cadres, acting as tax maximizers, can prevent the emergence of a local industrial base, see Yali Peng, "The Politics of Tobacco: Relations Between Farmers and Local Governments in China's Southwest," *The China Journal,* no. 36 (1996): 67–82.

118. One study found that industrialization was related mostly to the previous level of industrialization. See John Knight and Lina Song, "The Spatial Contribution to Income Inequality in Rural China," cited in Luo, "Rural Reform and the Rise of Localism," note 27.

119. Dwight H. Perkins, "The Influence of Economic Reforms on China's Urbanization," in R. Yin-Wang Kwok, William L. Parish, and Anthony Gar-On Yeh, eds., *Chinese Urban Reform: What Model Now?* (Armonk, N.Y.: M.E. Sharpe, 1990), pp. 78–108.

120. Rozelle, "Stagnation without Equity," and Kai Yuen Tsai, "China's Regional Inequality, 1952–1985," *Journal of Comparative Economics* 15 (1991): 1–21.

121. Using data in the 1994 Jiangsu Provincial Yearbook, I found that, within Jiangsu Province, the best explanation of the level of foreign direct investment (FDI) in a county was the level of TVE development, which explained over 70 percent of the variation in the level of FDI. Thus, foreign investment is only one more contributor to unequal growth within and across rural areas in provinces.

122. For a comparison of rural industrialization to Asia's new industrializing economies, see Jean C. Oi, "The Role of the Local State in China's Transitional Economy," *The China Quarterly,* no. 144 (1995): 1132–1149. For a study comparing local governments to export-oriented, new industrializing economies, see chapter 12 of this book.

123. The number of local protests and rebellions in rural China has grown significantly since the mid-1980s, and rural China was rocked by local rebellions in 1992–1993. For reports of these protests, see Chuan Hsun-che, "Secret Report on 'Disturbances' on Mainland Last Year," *Chengming,* no. 198 (1994): 21, in FBIS-CHI-94-062 (March 31, 1994): 28–29; and Sung, "Peasant Unrest in Szechwan," pp. 129–132. See also Bernstein and Solinger, "The Peasant Question for the Future."

124. One might argue against such a simple dichotomy. For example, the level of state penetration into a local community may be a key variable, along with the strength of collective institutions, affecting the nature of local political authority and may be used to differentiate among different types of local political arrangements. For such an analysis, see Michelle S. Mood, "The Political Economy of Township and Village Enterprises in China," presented at the 1996 Association for Asian Studies Annual Convention, Honolulu, Hawaii, April 1996. However, the most significant and stark difference may be between localities that have political order and those which do not. The single most important explanation for this variation may be the level of industrialization and economic development.

125. Local government efforts to extract private funds for public projects (and for government investment in the fast-growing coastal economy) are offered as one explanation for the political tumult that hit Renshou County in Sichuan Province in 1994. For a study of cadre efforts to extract taxes from private entrepreneurs in Renshou County, see Ole Odgaard, "Collective Control of Income Distribution: A Case Study of Private Enterprises in Sichuan Province," in Jorgen Delman, Clemens Stubbe Ostergaard, and Flemming Christiansen, eds., *Remaking Peasant China: Problems of Rural Development and Institutions at the Start of the 1990s* (Aarhus, Denmark: Aarhus University Press, 1990): 106–121.

126. State Council Document No. 10 (1993), entitled "Resolution on Accelerating the

Development of Rural Enterprises in Central and Western China," was to help resolve this problem, as was a 1995 document put out by the Ministry of Agriculture and transmitted nationwide by the General Office of the State Council, entitled "Model Projects Plan for the Cooperation Between Western and Eastern Rural Enterprises." See *Farmers' Daily* (*Nongmin ribao*), November 16, 1995, p. 1, in FBIS-CHI-96–020 (January 30, 1996), pp. 28–31. A demonstration program on East-West cooperation among provinces was proposed in September 1993 and approved in February 1995, involving over three hundred projects and 3.37 billion *RMB*. Of a total of ten billion *yuan* set aside by the central government for assisting TVEs in the central and western parts of the country, 5 percent has been set aside for these cooperation projects. See *Renmin ribao,* April 25, 1995, p. 1, in FBIS-CHI-95–086 (May 4, 1995): 45–46.

127. For example, in poorer areas it is difficult to organize elections as the funds for democratic procedures, such as ballot boxes, are lacking.

128. See Andre Gunder Frank, "The Development of Underdevelopment," *Monthly Review,* no. 18 (1966): 17–31; and Fernando H. Cardoso and Enzo Faletto, *Dependency and Development in Latin America* (Berkeley: University of California Press, 1978).

129. Robin Broad, *Unequal Alliance: The World Bank, the International Monetary Fund, and the Philippines* (Berkeley: University of California Press, 1988).

130. James Scott, *The Moral Economy of the Peasantry: Rebellion and Subsistence in Southeast Asia* (New Haven: Yale University Press, 1976).

131. World Bank, *The East Asian Miracle: Economic Growth and Public Policy* (New York: Oxford University Press, 1993).

132. Evangelista asserts that communist-style trade bureaucracies shelter domestic economies from the impact of foreign prices, preventing even those who have comparative advantage from their participation in the global economy from knowing what their interests are. See Matthew Evangelista, "Stalin's Revenge: Institutional Barriers to Internationalization in the Soviet Union," in Robert Keohane and Helen Milner, eds., *Internationalization and Domestic Politics* (New York: Cambridge University Press, 1996).

133. Peter B. Evans, "Transnational Linkages and the Economic Role of the State: An Analysis of Developing and Industrialized Nations in the Post-World War II Period," in Peter B. Evans, Dietrich Rueschemeyer, and Theda Skocpol, eds., *Bringing the State Back In* (Cambridge, Mass.: Cambridge University Press, 1985), pp. 192–226.

134. Alden Speare, Jr., "Taiwan's Rural Populace: Brought In or Left Out of the Economic Miracle," in Denis Fred Simon and Michael Y.M. Kau, eds., *Taiwan: Beyond the Economic Miracle* (Armonk, N.Y.: M.E. Sharpe, 1992), pp. 211–233.

135. Jeffrey A. Frieden and Ronald Rogowski, "The Impact of the International Economy on National Policies: An Analytical Overview," in Keohane and Milner, eds., *Internationalization and Domestic Politics*

136. Lawrence C. Reardon, trans. and ed., "China's Coastal Development Strategy, 1979–1984 (I)," *Chinese Law and Government,* no. 27 (1994).

137. Nicholas R. Lardy, *Foreign Trade and Economic Reform in China, 1978–1990* (Cambridge, Mass.: Cambridge University Press, 1992).

138. Shirk argued that domestic prices in China were sheltered from global price fluctuations. Susan Shirk, "Opening China to the World Economy: Communist Institutions and Foreign Economic Policy Reforms," in Keohane and Milner, eds., *Internationalization and Domestic Politics,* pp. 186–206.

139. See Joseph Fewsmith, *Dilemmas of Reform in China* (Armonk, N.Y.: M.E. Sharpe, 1994).

140. For a discussion of *segmented deregulation,* see David Zweig, "Resources, Policy, Institutions and the Emergence of a Transnational Sector," unpublished paper. For

Chinese documents on the opening, see *Collection of documents concerning the laws, regulations, and standardization of the opening of the coastal, riverine, and border regions (Yanhai, yanjiang, yanbian kaifang falu fagui ji guifanxing wenjian huibian)* (Beijing: Falu chubanshe, 1992). See also Jude Howell, *China Opens Its Door: The Politics of Economic Transition* (Boulder, Colo.: Lynne Reinner Publishers, 1993).

141. Constance Lever-Tracy, David Ip, and Noel Tracy, *The Chinese Diaspora and Mainland China: An Emerging Economic Synergy* (Basingstoke, Hampshire: MacMillan Press, 1996).

142. Graham E. Johnson, "Open for Business, Open to the World: Consequences of Global Incorporation in Guangdong and the Pearl River Delta," in Thomas P. Lyons and Victor Nee, eds., *The Economic Transformation of South China* (Ithaca: Cornell East Asia Program, 1994), pp. 55–88.

143. David Zweig, "Reaping Rural Rewards: China's Town and Village Enterprises Can Make Good Investment Partners," *China Business Review* (November-December 1992): 12–17.

144. Kuo Cheng-Tian, "The PRC and Taiwan: Fujian's Faltering United Front," *Asian Survey* 32 (August 1992): 683–695.

145. Yuen-Fong Woon, "International Links and the Socioeconomic Development of Rural China: An Emigrant Community in Guangdong," *Modern China* 16 (April 1990): 139–172.

Part I

Restructuring Property Rights and Decollectivization

1

Opposition to Change in Rural China

Following the second rehabilitation of Deng Xiaoping in July 1977, rural China's organizational structure and its property rights regime were transformed. Land, while nominally still collectively owned, was distributed among individual households that received legal usufruct or use rights to the farmland, with the term of control set for fifteen years or longer. The organizational or administrative structure that had supported collective land ownership and management was also readjusted. Central to this was the dismantling of the production team, which had organized all farmers' labor, giving farmers relative autonomy in economic decision making. Although support for these reforms was extensive, opposition and differences of opinion existed as well. This chapter explores the motivations of those who resisted these changes and the problems that arose during the implementation of the policy.*

The Historical Development of the System of Responsibility

The major initial reform in the rural sector was the institution of the "responsibility system." The Chinese used this concept to refer to any process of remuneration which created a certain level of accountability by linking the task performed and the income received. In the early 1980s, the term was applied to anything from task rates to independent farming by households on collective land (see appendix to this chapter).

The idea of instituting a responsibility system was advocated in the 1950s by

---

*This chapter was written in 1982, before full-scale decollectivization had occurred. It reflects the trends in opposition to and support for the responsibility system as of 1981–1982. The next chapter takes us through to 1983 and complete decollectivization. Most revisions of this chapter involved changing the tense of the discussion.

the head of the Party's Rural Work Department, Deng Zihui, to make production teams and formal work groups responsible to the Agricultural Producers Cooperatives that were developing at that time.[1] The idea reemerged in 1960 after the millennial Great Leap Forward collapsed. In some locations, particularly Anhui and Fujian provinces, groups of farmers or individual households contracted with production teams to meet an output quota for which the farmers received a set amount of work points. These points were cashed in for money at the end of the year, and any above-quota agricultural produce remained their own. First criticized at the 7000 Cadres Conference of January 1962, these policies were the target of harsh invectives during the Cultural Revolution as part of "Liu Shaoqui's revisionist line."[2]

The advocates of agrarian radicalism in China[3] opposed material incentives and supported instead the evaluation system used in Dazhai, the national model brigade. Through their procedure of self-assessment and public discussion, farmers there reportedly developed strong inner-group cohesion and moral work incentives. Yet even though this policy was maintained in some localities from 1968 until 1980,[4] it failed to motivate the Chinese farmer to work hard.[5] Since everyone tended to get similar amounts of points, income differentials between strong and weak villagers narrowed and strong workers lost their incentive to work harder. Therefore, in 1978, when Wan Li, then first party secretary of Anhui Province, called for the establishment of a responsibility system in agriculture, he was advocating replacing Dazhai's egalitarian method of remuneration with task rates, whereby farmers would perform a job for a predetermined number of work points. With this system, farmers who worked slowly would find that their individual incomes would suffer.[6]

Since 1978, the Chinese leadership has authorized a vast array of responsibility systems. Though complex, these systems can be clarified by recognizing that they are based on three interrelated factors: the nature of the link between work and income, the size of the work unit at which income is determined, and the type of work performed. But, as the Chinese changed their position on these three facets of the responsibility system, they called into question accepted ideological premises concerning the nature of socialist labor organization in agriculture and expanded the types of labor organization that were still deemed socialist. These challenges to accepted doctrine made certain points in the decision-making process about the responsibility system major thresholds in the policy debate. The following two sections trace the historical transitions from 1977 through 1982, and outline the major issues and debates that ensued.[7]

Remuneration Systems

The Link between Work and Income

The first threshold involved replacing the moral incentives of the Dazhai system with task rates. In August 1977, the *People's Daily* advocated task rates for the first time since 1972. But haste makes waste and, as farmers worked faster, the quality of work suffered. Therefore, some locations added a quality standard to the job. If the team leader found the quality of work wanting, farmers either had to redo the work or had to accept fewer work points for their efforts.

The key threshold regarding the remuneration system concerned whether the level of output, rather than the quality of work, would determine income. From a Maoist perspective, linking income and output was the ultimate in material incentives and, therefore, was revisionist. But, in December 1978, the Third Plenum's authorization of a bonus for work groups that surpassed the output quota broke this barrier.[8] Income from then on was partially determined by how much one produced. In the early stages, farmers received extra work points as a bonus, but eventually they began to keep the excess produce instead. The final stage in the process was reached when the contracting unit no longer had to turn over any fixed agricultural quota to the collective (*bao gan*). Responsible only for meeting the state agricultural tax, the "compulsory sale" (*zheng gou*), and making a donation to the collective, the contracting unit was free to dispose of the remaining produce and income as it pleased.[9]

The Size of the Unit of Account

The second issue reflected the size of the work unit at which income was determined. Since 1962, the production team had been the basic accounting unit in over 90 percent of rural China.[10] The team's net income, divided by the number of work points distributed to its members each year, determined the basic work point value. The total number of work points each villager accumulated by year's end determined his or her share of the collective's year-end distribution. However, because the production team was too large a unit to establish effective labor accountability, in 1977-1978, some places made the "work group" (*gongzuo zu*) the unit of account.[11] Though criticized at first, the usefulness of the smaller unit of remuneration was recognized by the Third Plenum of December 1978. The next transition, which established individual responsibility under team administration for a strip of land, was not a major point of conflict. Once the link between income and output was accepted, individual accountability under unified team management differed only marginally from collective farming.

However, because the household reflected traditional family farming, its establishment became the major threshold in deciding the unit's appropriate size. The Third Plenum had rejected "household quotas" (*bao chan dao hu*), but when the two documents on agriculture put forth at that plenum were authorized by the Fourth Plenum nine months later, the absolute prohibition on household quotas had been deleted. Single households in remote poor areas became an acceptable unit of account. This decision opened the door on household contracts, and from this point on their use expanded steadily.

The Type of Work

Because of the initial opposition to linking income and agricultural output, the first jobs placed under the responsibility system were field construction tasks, such as digging ditches, or parts of the planting process, such as transplanting rice or harvesting grain. But, in early 1978, quotas were established for sideline work, such as fishing, forestry, and animal husbandry. Although this policy linked output and income, sideline work involved fewer people than cereal production and seemed ideologically less sensitive. Similarly, in late 1977 and early 1978, output quotas for the entire production process were first established for economic crops, such as cotton, rapeseed, and hemp, because such crops were secondary to grains and vegetables.

The major threshold for this issue was linking output and income for cereal production, but a breakthrough eventually occurred in dry field cultivation. And, although potential conflicts in the irrigation process complicated the use of output quotas for paddy fields, the findings of investigative groups sent in the summer of 1980 to Hebei, Henan, Shanxi, and Shaanxi provinces, and reports from Zhao Ziyang's travels to Hunan, Hubei, and Shandong provinces, convinced the leadership in Beijing by the spring of 1981 to accept officially individual and household quotas for paddy fields.[12]

Support for and Opposition to the Responsibility System

Reforms precipitate a redistribution of economic resources, political authority, and political power, and always result in winners and losers. Therefore, we should not be surprised to find that interviews in China and press reports showed that differences of opinion concerning the responsibility system existed at all levels of the political and bureaucratic system. These divisions existed among national elites, among intellectuals, between wealthier provinces and the party's center, between rich and poor regions, between rural bureaucrats and farmers, and among farmers in different localities. The different attitudes this chapter presents were based primarily on the differential effects of the new reforms on the political and economic interests of the political elites who make policy, and on the different sectors of Chinese rural society that implement policy. Nonetheless, some persons who opposed the responsibility system were truly concerned about the changes it might bring to the basic egalitarianism in the Chinese countryside.

The Forces of Reform

Why was the responsibility system successful? How was it that rural bureaucrats, who in most localities opposed the policies, were unable to stem the tide of rural reform? The pressure for change came from two levels. Reformers in the party were pushing these changes consistently after 1977, with the first experiments occurring in Anhui and Sichuan provinces. In 1977, Wan Li, a first vice premier of China and the member of the Party Secretariat responsible for agriculture, was then first party secretary of Anhui Province; Zhao Ziyang was running Sichuan Province. Closely aligned with Deng Xiaoping, both were advocating and experimenting with these reforms long before they became national policy. Also, these policies were extremely popular with villagers in poorer areas who carried them out in spite of local opposition. In fact, they were probably the most popular policies in the poorer areas since land reform. Press reports from 1979 to 1980 described how villagers sometimes confronted county and commune officials with *faits accomplis* which cadres could overturn only at the price of a great deal of conflict. In such localities, pressure from above meshed with support from below, squeezing the middle-level bureaucrats who opposed the policy. Unlike other movements for change in the countryside, where the center's goals were anathema to villager interests, the responsibility system relied on an unofficial coalition between central reformers and villagers from the poor areas. Caught in this vise, middle level cadres could do little but accept the changes. They stalled, but after the reform faction gained control in Beijing and the Party Secretariat authorized Central Document No. 75 in September 1980, the pressures on local officials increased greatly.

The rural reform movement went faster than anyone expected. In early 1980, Yao Yilin suggested that 10 percent of rural China would have household quotas. By the end of that year, the *People's Daily* predicted that the number would hit 20 percent. But the "rush to freedom" of impoverished Chinese farmers continued unabated. An August 1981 conference in Kunming on the responsibility system admitted that 45 percent of the teams in China had both types of household quotas, and by the summer of 1982, the number had reached 50 percent.[13] In essence we have witnessed the unbridled pursuit of villager political and economic interests. As middle- and local-level opposition collapsed, farmers in the poorer areas went their own way. According to information from the press, the poorer provinces definitely moved quickly in implementing the more extreme forms of the household farming system, and in wealthier provinces some localities moved faster than the provincial leadership.[14]

Nonetheless, opposition existed and, by 1982, different localities were willing to accept only certain forms of the responsibility system. Finding the proper system for each area was a difficult problem, particularly given the rural bureaucrats' penchant for enforcing a uniform policy, a phenomenon the Chinese call "one knife to cut all" (*yi dao qie*). What follows is a look at the problems China confronted in popularizing this new policy and the sources of opposition at the national, regional, and local levels.

Fear of Polarization

Villagers possess a dual nature. On the one hand, they want to get rich, while on the other hand, they get jealous and frightened when others get rich more quickly.[15] Therefore, one of the major difficulties in getting farmers and rural officials (prefecture, county, and commune) who rose from the ranks of the rural inhabitants to use the new policy was their "fear of polarization" (*liang ji fenhua*). Interviews with both cadres and farmers showed that at this critical stage in the transformation of rural property rights, some individuals believed if people were to prosper at different rates, the basically egalitarian rural balance would be upset and class inequality could return. One county official who went to the countryside in 1974 to restrict all avenues for personal enrichment admitted that, at that time,

> The work team was afraid that the gap between the rich and the poor would expand, capitalism would be restored and a new bourgeois class would be established in the countryside. So they were definitely interested in limiting the bourgeois tendencies in the countryside to protect the poorer people and the ones who did not do private endeavors well. . . . They were really afraid of a small group getting rich and the gap increasing as Marx said it would. . . . So when they saw farmers getting rich they wanted to cut back on that. . . . Cadres from the middle level on down had this attitude.[16]

These bureaucrats believed that the responsibility system not only would allow some villagers to get rich first, but would make the poor even poorer, creating the extreme polarization Marx predicted for capitalist societies. For them, the responsibility system opened the door to the eventual reintroduction of capitalism and class exploitation into the Chinese countryside.[17]

This fear of polarization was one of the strongest forces restricting the wholesale adoption of the new incentive systems. In January 1980, *Sichuan Daily* admitted that some officials "fear that polarization will occur and that a new bourgeoisie will arise."[18] And, although the press downplayed the potential for polarization due to the responsibility system, some cadres remained unconvinced. In the summer of 1981 outside Fuzhou, Fujian Province, I hitched a ride on a bus with officials returning from a county-level meeting at a suburban test point for individual quotas. In general, these cadres were supportive of the responsibility system. However, as one commune official got off the bus, he asked, "Do you think that the policy will lead to polarization between rich and poor?" His tone suggested that he feared it would.[19] No doubt, under the responsibility system farmers were getting richer, but the gap between the rich and poor was not necessarily growing. Nor were the poor necessarily getting poorer.[20] But even as of September 25, 1982, *Guangming Daily* admitted that "some people think that the responsibility system has enlarged the gap between the wealthy and the poor. They even confuse the situation with polarization."[21] Wan Li, in a speech published in *Red Flag* and reprinted in *China Daily* on January 19, 1983, suggested that Communist Party members and local cadres were still afraid of letting some people get rich. "Why should the Communist Party be afraid of people prospering? . . . The Communist Party should be adept at leading the people to create wealth while avoiding polarization." Five years after the reforms had begun, rural party officials still resisted the changes out of fear of class polarization.

Some farmers feared other possible outcomes of the responsibility system. The poorest team in a wealthy brigade south of Nanjing turned down the chance to establish household quotas in the spring of 1981. They even rejected group quotas because they feared that, once the first division took place, it was just a question of time until private farming returned to China. A farmer in a neighboring team who confronted the prospect of linking his income to his own output expressed similar fears.

> Before we were so poor and now the economic work is done well. The new policy is a backward retreat. If you divide the land you will have polarization. Landlords and capitalists will return. The collective system is good. Chairman Mao is good. We do not want to move off Chairman Mao's road.[22]

Intellectuals, too, expressed varied opinions, with some concerned about the possibility of increasing polarization if the collective system were to be dismantled. Two schools existed as to the proper perspective on household quotas. Some, who were more concerned about polarization, supported the system of "three fixes and one bonus," but they opposed "the system of total responsibility" because it weakened the collective economy. Others, whose main concern was boosting rural production, favored anything that worked as long as land remained collectively owned. One agricultural economist, an older professor in his fifties, who supported "household quotas under unified management," suggested that "household quotas with total responsibility" could lead to a restoration of class exploitation in the countryside.

> Of all policies put forward, "the system of total responsibility" (*da baogan*) is the most backward in terms of moving away from the collective economy. It is basically the same as "private farming" (*dan gan*). Under this system the team maintains no real control and its relationship with the households is very weak. One major problem with this is that in some parts of Anhui Province where family labor power is weak, such that they cannot meet the task given to them, they must hire labor to help them. The system of exploitation and hired labor may regrow out of this. This is a step back to the time before Land Reform.[23]

Reports show that this situation did occur even in the early 1980s. A letter to the *People's Daily,* dated April 4, 1981, complained about the resurrection of hired labor in the countryside.

However, other intellectuals, such as Yu Guoyao, a leading economist in Beijing, were more concerned about promoting production than the revival of exploitation or the weakening of socialist institutions. While he accepted that unified leadership by the team was necessary to maintain the collective system, he also subtly endorsed household quotas with total responsibility for the very poor areas of China, because this policy would stimulate farmers there to work harder. Only after production had developed, he argued, would poor localities be ready to establish stronger collectives.[24] Nonetheless, the major determinant of the ebb and flow of this policy has been its effect on the economic and political interests of villagers, middle-level bureaucrats, and central elites.

Interests and the Responsibility System

Central leaders did not present a unified front on the issue of interests and the responsibility system. The legitimacy of China's reformers depends on fulfilling the goals of the "four modernizations" and raising living standards. Thus they had to increase agricultural production, but this increase could not come from financial investment. The towering budget deficit of 1979–1980 was a shocking reminder of the financial costs of modernization. China's reformers were forced once again to rely on institutional changes and shifts in incentive structures, rather than capital investment, to increase agricultural production. This stress on material incentives, however, brought the reform faction into conflict with Hua Guofeng and the "whatever faction" that favored Dazhai-type moral incentives. The defeat of the "whatever faction" at the February 1980 Fifth Plenum did not end Hua Guofeng's opposition. Not only did he never publicly support the responsibility system, but Central Document No. 75, the first formal policy document on this issue, was not drafted and promulgated by the Politburo but by the Party Secretariat, of which Hua was not a member and which the reformist faction controlled. One month after this meeting, Hua reportedly offered to resign from the chairmanship of the Communist Party.

A second issue was the amount of freedom farmers and the local units might possess without undermining the state plan. After farmers failed to meet their grain quotas in 1981, Chen Yun, one of China's top leaders, reasserted at a 1982 Chinese New Year's tea party the importance of following the plan. A spate of speeches stressing the farmers' contractual obligations to sell grain to the state appeared in the spring of 1982.[25] Thus, differences of opinion existed between the groups around Chen Yun and Deng Xiaoping regarding the degree of decentralization to be allowed under the responsibility system.

The People's Liberation Army was also unhappy with this new policy because it disrupted the troops.[26] In November 1980, the first political commissar of the Wuhan Military District admitted that "the new rural policy has caused consternation in the ranks."[27] Soldiers were growing restive and wanted to return home to plow the land with their families. In areas where household or individual quotas were being implemented, having a son in the army placed a farming family at a distinct economic disadvantage vis-à-vis its neighbors and involved serious lost opportunity costs. Having fewer laborers meant that the family got less land to cultivate. Moreover, strong young sons could suddenly make more money after the reforms than they could when labor was performed collectively. To remedy this situation, in the fall of 1982 some communes gave farmers work points as compensation for lost labor. After making these distributions, production teams notified the soldiers concerned and their units.[28]

Richer provinces, such as Jiangsu, Zhejiang, and Liaoning, expressed their reservations about the more individualistic responsibility system, particularly with regard to household quotas,[29] while poorer provinces, such as Anhui and Shaanxi, supported "the system of total responsibility."[30] Jiangsu Province, which typified the pattern of opposition among these rich localities, dragged its feet from the start, hoping that the reforms would not go very far.

Jiangsu Province's agricultural success was based primarily on large-scale water conservation and field construction projects, high grain output combined with above-quota sales to the state, and commune- and brigade-run enterprises whose profits were reinvested in agriculture. The household system of farming directly threatened all these factors. The end of the production team's organizational authority meant that the mobilization of villagers for construction projects would be based on contracts and not on administrative commands, and farmers would be free to refuse to participate. With households now in control of the land, above-quota sales became difficult to arrange. In contrast to production teams that could be easily cajoled by higher levels of the rural administration into selling surplus grain to the state, rural households were likely to take their surplus grain to the free market where prices would be higher. Finally, the weakening of the production team diluted its accumulation fund, complicating further development of collectively owned enterprises. Because the responsibility system threatened Jiangsu's successful, collectivized agricultural system, Xu Jiatun, first party secretary of Jiangsu Province, opposed any link between income and output. Only after he was criticized by Zhao Ziyang or Hu Yaobang in late 1980 did Xu call an expanded provincial conference to discuss the responsibility system. According to a well informed source in Nanjing, Xu was publicly self-critical at that meeting. As long as the provincial leadership continued its opposition, lower-level bureaucrats in wealthier parts of Jiangsu Province were able to resist the national trend. Thus, in 1980, commune officials in Nanjing's Jiangpu County rolled back household quotas that had been in use in some villages for two years.

Yet, as support from the Party center for the responsibility system intensified in spring 1981, middle-level bureaucrats, ever concerned about their political future, swung full circle. Not only did they begin to call for the implementation of the responsibility system, but, because any manifestation of opposition to the responsibility system within their domain threatened them politically, they pressured lower level cadres in all locations to establish a link between income and output. Areas which, according to Central Document No. 75, should have been free to use task rates came under strong pressure "to link individual income and output" (*lian chan dao lao*). The impressions I obtained at this time through conversations with local leaders in Shanxi, Jiangsu, and Fujian provinces[31] were substantiated when, on September 22, 1981, the *People's Daily* criticized bureaucrats who forced policy uniformity on unwilling local leaders.[32] Commune and brigade leaders in wealthy areas resented this pressure. An official responsible for irrigation work outside Nanjing feared that household quotas would dilute the collective strength necessary for these projects.

> The upper levels are pushing this policy hard now but it doesn't go down well here (*chi bu xia*). You can't do water conservation projects. How will you use the sprinklers and the machinery? They are really going back. After so many years of building the collective system, they are taking it apart. There is strength in the collective system because the numbers are big. In Anhui the policy they are using now is not good for us. We do not want it here.[33]

Officials interviewed in Dazhai expressed similar concerns about their sprinkler system if individual production quotas were to be established. Even though this opposition occurred mostly in wealthy localities where the collective economy performed a useful function, it was not an isolated phenomenon. A commune official in one of the richest grain growing areas of Jiangsu Province had similar misgivings about the policy:

> Presently, output in our commune is very high for the country. Our technical level is also high. Our rice output is especially high. So on this basis we recently began to say that if the masses want production quotas to the household or the laborer it could affect per capita output. But the masses in the whole commune are not willing to have production quotas to the household or the laborer for paddy fields. They do not have this desire. They still want to do it on the same basis and in this way increase production and mechanization.[34]

In addition, brigade officials in Xiamen's suburbs swore that they would resist all policies that did not fit their prosperous economic conditions.

Local organizations, such as rural banks and marketing cooperatives, opposed these policies as well. Banks were accustomed to dealing with collectives and not with individual rural families. The new policy placed them in unfamiliar business situations. In response to these new conditions, the Gansu Agricultural Bank refused loans to people who used household quotas with full responsibility.[35] Supply and marketing cooperatives were also accustomed to monopolizing the procurement process, but with household quotas their jobs, too, became more difficult.[36] Levels of economic wealth and development directly affected the villagers' response to the responsibility system. In wealthy areas some villagers feared the new policies because they threatened their economic interests. In the early 1980s, in some locations, profits from brigade enterprises were used to supplement the incomes of all members of the collective, not just factory workers.[37] In one team in which the brigade's economy greatly influenced per capita income, the team leader attributed villager enthusiasm for the collective to the brigade enterprises.

> The peasants here work hard. They do their work quickly. If I give them one day to do all the work they do it in day. So, if the people want to work on their private plots, they can. But most prefer to work on the collective fields. This year our income from sidelines increased by 7,000 *RMB* mostly because we sent more people to the brigade enterprises. Last year we had 21 people in the factories and now we have 16 more. *The collective income will increase and the peasants know this. They can calculate. They know the collective income will increase* (emphasis added).

In this wealthy brigade, mechanization was also liberating farmers from the drudgery of farm labor. Convinced that household quotas would complicate the use of their machinery, villagers lamented future developments. As of 1981, villager support had stopped short of the system of total responsibility in localities of average wealth. One brigade in Jiangsu Province had a per capita income from the collective of 100 *RMB,* about the national average. Although in 1981 they used household quotas for cotton, rapeseed, and dry field wheat, the poorest team in the brigade, which had relied on state financial and material support for 20 years, balked at the chance to establish household quotas with total responsibility in 1982. The team leader explained why:

> Most people oppose the policy because there would be no collective economy. People fear "total responsibility" (*da baogan*). They like the collective method (*san bao yi jiang*) because they get fertilizer, insecticide, and points for managing the fields, all from the team. If they get sick and can't plant, the team plants for them. Also, they will still get their grain ration. They will lose their work points but they can borrow money to buy their work points share of "collective grain" (*gong liang*) and pay back the money when they can.[38]

Thus, according to this team leader, when the collective supports the economic interest of the villagers, they support the collective.

More individualistic forms of household quotas developed most rapidly in the poorer parts of China. In these areas the collective, by using political threats to maintain collective production and foreclose private initiative, had served as a fetter on peasant enrichment. Such localities enthusiastically welcomed these new freedoms from bureaucratic control. In 1982, a visitor to Yan'an District in Shaanxi Province found that, in the ten years since she left the area, the villagers' living standards had not improved. In 1982, they dissolved the collective and each household farmed on its own.

Conclusion: The Limits to Reform

This chapter has shown rural China in transition, before the long arm of the central state enforced complete decollectivization on the entire rural sector.

While the next chapter traces the whole history of decollectivization, this chapter has highlighted the forces in the countryside, among farmers, cadres, and China's elites, who resisted the dismantling of an organizational structure that had sat astride rural China for twenty years. Not surprisingly, this institutional arrangement, with its collective property rights, pattern of income and power distribution, and capacity both for organizing rural labor and for extracting grain for urban dwellers from farmers at enforced low prices, created interests, norms, and incentives that supported its continuation.

In wealthier locations, where the collective had contributed to an improved standard of living through the creation of rural enterprises and rising agricultural production, villagers appeared risk averse: Why dismantle an institution which, despite its flaws and unpopularity twenty-five years ago, now ensured a reasonable and growing standard of living? The devil you know is far better than the one you don't. In these richer locations, such as southern Jiangsu Province or southern Zhejiang Province, northern resistance to decollectivization emerged as cadres and farmers hesitated to redistribute the means of production and property, particularly land. Rather than take dramatic first steps towards transforming the property rights regime, they preferred instead to adopt systems of responsibility that improved monitoring efficiency and production without linking income and output.

But outside these areas, where collective property rights undermined prosperity, villagers demonstrated great exuberance for dismantling collective organizations and ignoring obligations imposed by the state. During late 1981 and early 1982, farmers in some areas divided public property, distributed orchards, stripped collective factories, and expropriated collective land for a housing construction boom.[39] Grain quotas were not met, a glut of tobacco flowed onto the market, and farmers sold inferior produce to the state and superior goods on the free market. In late 1981, vegetable marketing companies in many major cities could not supply the urban population; good vegetables, too, had moved to the free market.

For local officials, politics and ideology formed the contours of resistance. No doubt, fear of being on the wrong side of the political spectrum caused cadres to stutter-step before rushing to support what clearly was a rightist policy. Memories of political recriminations towards those who introduced the system of total responsibility back in the early 1960s, plus three decades of rural political campaigns, taught cadres that it is "safer to be on the left than the right (*ning zuo wu you*). Leftism, translated as support for collectivism, enhanced cadre power, and simplified the fulfillment of state imposed responsibilities, such as rendering to the state its share of the harvest. Again, in wealthier areas, where industry and effective irrigation had been the fruits of collective ownership, cadres supported rural institutional arrangements. Cadres, too, may have internalized Maoist and rural norms of egalitarianism and feared that undermining collective property would automatically and rapidly lead to income polarization. Or, perhaps expressed concern about polarization and capitalist restoration reflected bureaucratic efforts to stifle assertions favoring decollectivization in wealthier areas that had been characterized by relatively high intravillage or intraregional equality.

Finally, as will be apparent in the next chapter, these local concerns and interests influenced the central debate over policy reform. Villager and cadre resistance reinforced central opponents of decollectivization. Similarly, villagers' autonomous efforts to surpass official guidelines for the responsibility system, dismantle collective organizations, and ignore state-imposed production tasks, in the short run, strengthened the hand of those who feared that restructuring rural institutions would trigger economic chaos and a loss of control over rural grain production. But by 1983, as we will see, support among inhabitants in poorer parts of rural China, combined with central reformers' beliefs that the collective had outlived its usefulness, became a driving force that would transform the relationship among farmers, their land, and the state.

Appendix

A Few Popular Responsibility Systems

In the late 1970s and early 1980s, the following responsibility systems became the most acceptable and popular forms in rural China.

1. *Short-term task rates* (*xiao duan bao gong*). With the system of short-term task rates, fixed amounts of work points were awarded for a set job. Tasks, varying from field construction to grain harvesting, were given to work groups, individuals, or households. In spring 1981, this system, the only acceptable one that does not link income to output, appeared to lose the support of leaders in Beijing precisely because it did not make that link.[40] But, in November 1981, Du Runsheng, then vice-minister of the State Agricultural Commission, only "encouraged" all advanced units to link remuneration to output, and, as of summer 1982, some localities still publicly supported short-term task rates.[41]

2. *Specialized fixed tasks* (*zhuanye chengbao*). Used primarily for sideline production such as fishery, forestry, and animal husbandry, for which special skills are required, this system involved signing contracts with individuals, households, or "specialized work groups" (*zuoye zu)*. Farmers received a fixed number of work points for meeting a production quota; for surpassing it, a bonus comprising extra work points and some or all of the surplus was awarded. This responsibility system did not exist in the 1960s, but was discovered in Shanxi Province by Zhao Ziyang in 1978 and popularized first in Sichuan Province. It suited the needs of wealthy or densely populated localities where narrow divisions of labor benefit production. When some wealthy localities divided up all

their jobs and linked income to output, crop production was also included as one of the specialized tasks.

3. *Linking output to the group or to the individual (lian chan dao zu, dao lao).* Under the system linking output to the group or individual, the team divided its fields into strips, and individuals or groups contracted to meet fixed production quotas. Farmers were paid in work points and bonuses, and fines were administered depending on the output. For the work groups, the work points paid to the group were further divided among the members of the group depending on their personal labor contributions. The team retained the authority for administering many aspects of the production process, including planning and the use of animals, machinery, pesticides, fertilizer, and irrigation. The most common was the five unified (*wuge tongyi*) system. Because the team's gross income still determined the farmers' collective income, this system was considered to be under "unified distribution" (*tongyi fenpei*). Used also in fairly wealthy areas, it was seen as a precursor to a transition to a finer division of labor under "specialized fixed tasks."

4. *Household contracts (bao chan dao hu).* There were two types of household contracts. The first occurred under unified team management and involved fixed investment, work points, and output levels, in addition to a bonus; hence, it was called "three fixes and one bonus" (*san bao yi jiang*). This was the name used for household contracts in the 1960s. It was similar to the system of "linking output to the individual," except that the team divided all the land among households that contracted to meet the fixed quota.

5. *Household contracts with full responsibility (bao gan dao hu or da baogan).* Although some people viewed *bao chan dao hu* as capitalist farming because it was done on a household basis, the system entitled "household contracts with full responsibility"[42] or the system of total responsibility, resembled private farming much more closely.[43] Under this system, land was divided among households that agreed to fulfill obligations previously belonging to the production team. Households paid the state agricultural tax, turned over the minimal compulsory sale, and contributed money to a fund for needy villagers. In some localities farmers also gave money to the production team for developing collective enterprises.[44] Otherwise, all produce was theirs to sell or consume, and the household became the primary unit of account and accumulation. The only socialist aspect of this system was that land remained collective property; farmers used it but could not sell it.

6. *Dazhai work points (Dazhai gong fen).* The main remuneration system that was not part of the responsibility system was "Dazhai work points," under which the number of work points each farmer received was based both on their labor contribution and on a subjective evaluation of their political attitude towards work and the collaborative. Villagers were expected to meet regularly in open meetings to discuss each other's contribution, a process which led to a great deal of levelling in individual work point scores.

Notes

1. *People's Daily,* February 23, 1982, p. 5.
2. According to Fredrick Crook, the policy was implemented even as late as 1964, but it is hard to know just how widely it was used. See Fredrick W. Crook, "Chinese Communist Agricultural Systems and the Labor Productive Contracts to Households: 1956-1965," *Asian Survey* 13 (May 1973): 470-481. In 1962, Mao attacked the party secretary of Anhui Province, Zeng Xisheng, for introducing this policy, which must have chilled most provincial leaders.
3. See David Zweig, *Agrarian Radicalism in China: 1968-1978* (Cambridge: Harvard University Press, 1989).
4. In Jiangsu Province, one production team used the Dazhai work point system until the brigade forced them to change in 1980. The team leader argued that, because he had too few people and too much land, he could save time by using this method.
5. See Martin R. Whyte, "The Dazhai Brigade and Incentives for the Peasants," *Current Scene* 13 (August 15, 1969): 1–12, and Jonathan Unger, "Remuneration, Ideology and Peasant Interests in a Chinese Village, 1960–1980," in William L. Parish, ed., *Chinese Rural Development: The Great Transformation* (Armonk, N.Y.: M.E. Sharpe, 1985), pp. 117–140.
6. See Red Flag (*Hongqi*) (March 1978): 92–97.
7. For a more in-depth analysis of the historical trends, see chapter 2 of this book. See also Tang Tsou et al., "The Responsibility System in Agriculture: Its Implementation in Xiyang and Dazhai," *Modern China* 8 (January 1982): 44-52, and Jurgen Domes, "Rural Societal Structures in China, 1976-1981," *Journal of Asian Studies* 41 (February 1982): 253-267.
8. See "Decision on Some Questions Concerning the Acceleration of Agricultural Development (draft)," Zhongfa No. 4 (1979), in *Issues and Studies* 15, no. 7 (1979): 102-119, and no. 8 (1979): 91-99.
9. In early 1981, Zhao Ziyang began to advocate this type of system for the poorest areas of China. See "Time to Consider 800 Million Peasants," *People's Daily,* May 20, 1981, p. 1, 4, which supplies much information on decisions concerning the responsibility system made from the summer of 1980 through the spring of 1981.
10. According to a lecture at the Economics Department of Nanjing University, 66,700 brigades or 9 percent of all brigades in China made up the official unit of account in 1978. By 1979, that number had dropped 2 percent to 51,767. See Chinese Agricultural Yearbook (*Zhongguo nongye nianjian*) (Beijing: Agricultural Publishing House, 1981), p. 6. On brigade accounting see also Zweig, *Agrarian Radicalism,* chapter 5.
11. See *Hebei Daily,* October 11, 1978, p. 1.
12. "Time to Consider 800 Million Peasants," p. 1. According to a commune official in Jiangsu Province, Zhao Ziyang advocated first trying this policy in the rice-growing areas of southern China. This official's position corresponds with "Time to Consider," which stated that after the 1981 New Year's Day tea-party, Zhao Ziyang went south to check on the successes of the responsibility system there.
13. *Foreign Broadcast Information Service* (hereafter cited as *FBIS*) (August 23, 1982): R 7.
14. *Hebei Daily* admitted that "sometimes we have lagged behind the masses and reality." See *FBIS* (October 20, 1981): P 2-4.
15. For the general argument anticipating this problem, see George Foster, "Peasant Society and the Image of the Limited Good," in Jack M. Potter, Mary N. Diaz, and George M. Foster, eds., *Peasant Society: A Reader* (Boston: Little, Brown & Co., 1967), pp. 300–323.

16. Interview DSZ-LBL-1 (November 23, 1980).

17. It is also likely that rural officials, who had experienced enormous flip-flops in rural policy and who subsequently suffered political recriminations and persecutions for following the policy shifts, were simply afraid to support a policy that was obviously rightist. The smart cadre "prefers leftism to rightism" (*ning zuo wu you*) as the most low-risk option.

18. *FBIS* (January 8, 1980): Q 2-3.

19. The author was hitchhiking back to Fuzhou from a suburban temple when given a ride on this bus. The above information was derived from the conversation that ensued.

20. For an excellent discussion arguing that, in the initial years of the rural reform inequality was not increasing, see Mark Selden, "Income Inequality and the State," in Parish, ed., *Chinese Rural Development,* p. 211. See also the discussion on this issue in the next chapter.

21. *FBIS* (October 5, 1982): 11–13.

22. Interview LFNZT, 1981. One woman expressed her concern that younger, more energetic farmers would use the new opportunities to cultivate larger tracts of land to get rich, while she, an older woman, wanted to rest and just earn her collective income. No doubt she feared that a weaker collective would be less able to support her in her old age.

23. Interview EPHXZ. This professor did work in Jiangsu Province, where as we will see, support for the collective economy was, and still remains, very strong.

24. See Yu Guoyao, "How to View Household Production Quotas," *Red Flag (Hongqi),* no. 20 (1980): 12-15.

25. See Zhang Jingfu's speech in *Beijing Review* (March 22, 1982): 18-22.

26. Opposition in the villages to rural policies has always had an immediate impact on the People's Liberation Army (PLA). The *Work Bulletin of the PLA (Gong zuo tong xun),* smuggled out in the 1960s, showed that in the post–Great Leap Forward famine, soldiers visiting home had to be escorted by officers or else they would not return. This unrest in the PLA caused by the Great Leap Forward probably prompted Marshal Peng Dehuai to criticize it.

27. See *People's Daily,* November 13, 1980, cited in Domes, "Rural Societal Structures in China," p. 264.

28. *FBIS* (October 21, 1981): O 15.

29. A circular published in Liaoning Province in December 1981 stated that very poor areas could use household quotas only under "unified team management." *FBIS* (February 1, 1982): S 1-2. In Zhejiang Province, in August 1982, a Xinhua article stressed the importance of maintaining the collective's strength. The article emphasized the right of local areas to choose their own systems in a manner so adamant as to suggest that the province felt pressured to shift away from what it called "the collective responsibility system." *FBIS* (August 23, 1982): K 10-12.

30. For Anhui Province, see *FBIS* (August 23, 1982): R 8–9, and *People's Daily,* June 9, 1981, which first introduced Fengyang County, the national model for the system of total responsibility. In 1981, 2,000 people were visiting the county each day to learn from its experience. For Shaanxi Province, see *People's Daily,* April 23, 1981, p. 1, which tells how the provincial party committee changed the leadership in Zhidan County in the summer of 1978 because of its continued support of agrarian radicalism and the Dazhai movement. In the winter of 1979, the new county leadership established the system of total responsibility in the group and the household in 90 percent of the teams in the county.

31. See David Zweig, "Chinese Agriculture: Pragmatism Gone Too Far?" *The Asian Wall Street Journal* (Op-Ed) (August 12, 1981).

32. This propensity to demand uniformity of implementation persists. *People's Daily,* February 6, 1982 criticized this leadership style, as did *Shaanxi Daily,* July 24, 1982.

33. Interview COYCZ, 1981.

34. Interview CMJQL, 1981.

35. Joint Publication Research Service, *Chinese Agriculture* (December 24, 1981): 2.

36. *People's Daily*, September 1, 1981.

37. In one brigade of twenty-six production teams outside Nanjing, which had highly developed brigade industries, workers were paid in work points, not salaries; their salaries instead went into their respective production team's collective coffers. Therefore, in this brigade a strong statistical relationship existed between changes in the salaries paid to the workers and changes in per capita income for *all* members of the production teams. This strategy was introduced during the years of agrarian radicalism to prevent an income gap between farmers and rural factory workers and to build political support for brigade-owned industries among those who still tilled the land in the production teams.

38. Interview CMJQL, 1981.

39. For several examples of the farmers' exuberance for distributing collective property, see *People's Daily* (editorial) in *FBIS* (October 9, 1981): K 15-17; *Shanxi Daily* in *FBIS* (October 22, 1981): T 2-3; *Guizhou Daily* in *FBIS* (November 25, 1981): Q 1; and *People's Daily* (February 6, 1982).

40. Short-term task rates were not mentioned in an important commentary in the *People's Daily* (March 2, 1981), p. 1, entitled "Summarize Experiences, Perfect and Stabilize the Agricultural Responsibility System." Some local leaders in suburban Nanjing tried to give the impression that they were implementing more privatized responsibility systems, while avoiding the link between income and output, by establishing what they called "long-term task rates" (*da duan bao gong*). Although this system included responsibility for the entire agricultural process from planting to harvesting, income was not linked to output.

41. *FBIS* (August 23, 1982): R 10-12.

42. Greg O'Leary and Andrew Watson refer to this system as "contracting land to households." See "The Production Responsibility System and the Future of Collective Farming," *The Australian Journal of Chinese Affairs*, no. 8 (1982): 1-34.

43. Another name for this is *da baogan*, but, because *bao gan dao hu* sounds more like *bao chan dao hu*, while *da baogan* sounds more like *dan gan* ("going it alone," or private farming), the Chinese leadership probably preferred *bao gan dao hu*. This way the change appeared to be only quantitative rather than qualitative. But, by summer 1982, China's press began to refer to *da baogan*, suggesting that another shift in the debate had taken place. See *People's Daily*, July 20, 1982, p. 1. See chapter 2 for the subsequent nationwide shift to *bao gan dao hu*, which meant the decollectivization of agriculture.

44. Initially, under "the system of total responsibility," farmers contributed money only to the welfare fund. But in Fengyang County, Anhui Province, where this system began as early as 1978, the peasants agreed in their contract to supply the team money to expand collective production. See *FBIS* (August 23, 1982): K 9-10.

2

Decollectivization in China, 1977–1983

Dynamics Between Context and
Content in Policy Implementation

Much of the literature on policy implementation focuses on policies that have failed. Whether the analysis has been of policy in the United States or in Third World countries,[1] such disappointing findings suggest that "great expectations in Beijing" should have been "dashed at the grass roots." By summer 1983, however, decollectivization and the shift to household farming with collective land ownership had been almost universally implemented in rural China.[2] If successful implementation of significant reforms is difficult for governments and *failure* has been common elsewhere,[3] how do we explain the Chinese government's *"success"* in decollectivizing agriculture?[4] What did the reform group around Deng Xiaoping do right?

According to Grindle, policy implementation "is an ongoing process of decision making by a variety of actors, the ultimate outcome of which is determined by the content of the program being pursued and by the interaction of the decision makers within a given political administrative context."[5] Borrowing from this framework, *"successful"* implementation of household contracts resulted from the fact that, through long-term sustained attention, the reform group was able both to reengineer the external environment and alter the policy's content, thereby creating continual convergence between policy context and content. Moreover, given most villagers' preferences for household control over agricultural production, the policy's deregulatory character made it almost self-implementing in localities where central or local pressures undermined bureaucratic resistance.

60

Mutually Reinforcing Changes in Policy
Content and Context

Socialist systems generally can control the political environment to a greater degree than pluralist or authoritarian regimes can. In post-Mao China, the defeat of Hua Guofeng and Maoist opposition in early 1980 allowed the reform group to move forward rather rapidly with the responsibility system.[6] Also, by continually undermining lingering central opposition after 1980, the reform group had the time and flexibility to respond to unintended consequences of decollectivization, which in the heat of an intense factional struggle could have seriously undermined policy implementation. Although opposition to decollectivization persisted throughout the political system, and although villager exuberance for dismantling collective property and shifting away from grain cultivation temporarily strengthened the opponents of agrarian reform, the reformers used the economic success of each policy shift to quell opposition and push for even greater changes in the policy's content. Although it is difficult to determine the extent to which the good harvests of 1981-1984 resulted from the responsibility system, incentives inherent in the responsibility system probably helped increase yields; in addition, lifting restrictions on household sidelines surely boosted rural incomes. Buoyed by increasing productivity and rising incomes, the reformers pressed on, leaving the opposition little ground on which to attack the policy.

The changing content of the policy was due in part to the evolving perceptions of the elites. Through experiments in Anhui, Sichuan, and Gansu Provinces, the reformers constantly tested new responsibility systems that had yet to receive official sanction. Central policy documents and editorials in the national press trailed behind these experiments and the regional reports carried in both the *People's Daily* and the provincial press. Once the central political context changed, however, the reform group seized the initiative and promoted these "successful" local experiments.

Moreover, the deregulatory character of the responsibility system was critical. Decollectivization freed farmers whose initiatives propelled the policy in directions unanticipated even by the reformers. Research teams gathered information on farmers' preferences and successful local innovations, which the reformers then incorporated into the evolving policy content. Concisely, the evolving policy content resulted partly from local actions; the reformers, following the best traditions of Yan'an and the "mass line," adjusted the policy's content in response to mass demands.

Other rural reforms also affected the content of the responsibility system. The diversification of agriculture and the expansion of household sidelines were particularly important. Both were trends that could not have occurred without weakening the commune structure. Had farmers remained tied to the collective economy, they would have been unable to follow their own economic logic and seek the most profitable and productive forms of horizontal cooperation. As the leadership came to believe in 1982 that commercialized farming, based on increased lateral trade among households and newly emerging associations, offered the best future for Chinese agriculture, the reformers adopted household contracts with fixed levies and comprehensive contracts as the policy's final content.[7]

Responsibility System: Introduction and Spread from October 1977 to July 1981

In 1977, some of China's more pragmatic leaders recognized that, without a closer link between work performed and remuneration received, Chinese farmers would not work hard and agriculture would continue to grow at a sluggish pace. Indeed, there had been virtually no change in per capita grain production between 1956 and 1977. Following Deng Xiaoping's July rehabilitation and the Eleventh Party Congress of August 1977, reformers called for the reintroduction of material incentives in the rural areas.[8] In November 1977, top provincial secretaries and agricultural experts discussed agricultural problems in Beijing.[9] Some advocated "payment according to labor," whereas others resisted material incentives and supported the Dazhai work-point system (see the appendix to chapter 1, p. 56). In December 1977, the Party's Agricultural and Forestry Department held a management and administrative symposium with cadres from provincial agricultural departments, calling for the reversal of many radical policies of the 1960s and 1970s and the implementation of the 1962 Sixty Articles, which had formed the core of the post–Great Leap Forward consensus on rural institutional arrangements. A *People's Daily* editorial supported these changes, and although "the leading member of the CC-CCP in charge of agriculture" rejected the meeting's eight suggestions and the *People's Daily* editorial, provincial meetings from December through the spring advocated introducing "payment for work."[10]

In March 1978, Wan Li, party secretary of Anhui Province, called for a "responsibility system" for managing rural labor under which "task rates" would replace Dazhai work points, which beginning in 1968 had been popularized throughout the nation.[11] Although Anhui farmers were experimenting with "household quotas," Wan Li prohibited their use for the official record. Given the strength at that time of the "whatever" group in the Politburo,[12] the minimal position—an official shift from Dazhai work points to task rates—would do. The maximum position—a return to household quotas—could come later. During the fall of 1978 national and provincial officials voiced support for these reforms. At a work conference on rural income distribution convened in October 1978 by the Chinese Academy of Social Sciences in Beijing, two leading economists, Yu Guangyuan and Xue Muqiao, publicly criticized Dazhai work points.[13]

At the same time, provinces began to lobby for fixed quotas that linked income to output.[14] In October and November 1978, *Hebei Daily*[15] and *Henan*

Daily[16] revealed that some farmers in their provinces had been using individual or group contracts for cotton since the fall of 1977. Cash bonuses for any above-quota surplus ranged from 15 to 30 percent. Although the term they employed—"fixed quota management system with a bonus for surplus" (*ding e guanli, chao e jiangli*)—differed only in name from "group contracts" (*bao chan dao zu*), names in Chinese politics mean a great deal. The term "quota" (*ding e*) was becoming acceptable as a form of the responsibility system, while the idea of production contracts (*bao chan*) hearkened back to policies from the early 1960s criticized during the Cultural Revolution. By using the term "quota" and merely adding a bonus, the policy would meet less opposition than if the term "contract" were used.[17]

An epistemological debate at this time over the basis of "truth" changed the context of implementation for the responsibility system by altering the criterion of policy evaluation.[18] Unlike the "whatever" group, which insisted that truth be based on Mao's words and his political line, the reformers, resurrecting Mao's slogan of "seeking truth from facts" (*shi shi qiu shi*), denied that truth was based on any *a priori* political line; only a policy's effects could determine its validity. Units, therefore, could not resist reforms on ideological grounds. Also by making economic outcomes, not political orientation, the key criterion of policy evaluation, the reformers circumvented the responsibility system's political content, which, because of its criticism during the Cultural Revolution, remained a sensitive issue.[19]

The issue of linking income to output came to a head at the end of 1978. Although the *People's Daily*, before the December 1978 Third Plenum, failed to support endorsements of output quotas by provincial newspapers such as the *Hebei Daily* and *Henan Daily* cited above, that same Plenum's two draft documents on agriculture accepted that payment based on output with bonuses for overproduction was within the new and expanding parameters of the responsibility system.[20] However, the document stated that "fixing output quotas based on the individual household and distributing land to the individual are both prohibited."[21]

After the historic Third Plenum, the reformers established pilot projects for household contracts, and farmers in Anhui's Qu County began to use the more decentralized household contracts with fixed levies.[22] These and other experiments triggered a dispute in the national press over how to organize spring planting. If new remunerative and organizational structures were to be introduced, they needed to be decided on before the harvest began. On March 1, 1979, the *People's Daily* editor supported a letter from Guangdong Province criticizing group contracts, arguing that such a policy was not in accordance with the Third Plenum documents and threatened the collective economy. Six days later, on March 7, the *People's Daily* presented the opposing view, thereby supporting villager efforts to surpass official policy guidelines. In 1978, a team in Qu County, Anhui Province, had established group contracts with individual responsibility—in essence, individual contracts (*lian chan dao lao*). Although county leaders opposed this, the commune secretary, buoyed by villager support, had refused to change. Thus, while the major national-level effort of 1979 was popularizing group contracts and linking income to output, the responsibility system's content continued to change locally in the direction of individual and even household contracts.

From spring 1979 to spring 1980, important changes propelled this evolution forward. First, Deng Xiaoping is reported to have supported individual, group, and household contracts at a conference that probably took place between the Third and Fourth Plenums.[23] Second, in September 1979, when the Fourth Plenum ratified the Third Plenum documents, the prohibition against household contracts disappeared; household contracts were officially authorized for remote areas.[24] The removal of the "whatever" group from office at the Fifth Plenum in February 1980 further weakened central opposition to decollectivization. In February 1980, Wan Li, the force behind Anhui's experiments, was given responsibility for nationwide agricultural policy, and Zhao Ziyang, the reformer from Sichuan, as well as Hu Yaobang, joined the Politburo's Standing Committee. Hu also was placed in charge of the revived Secretariat, which increasingly became the locus of all policy making in the Party, displacing the Politburo, where more conservative leaders could still exert influence.

These changes in the political context facilitated further alterations in the responsibility policy.[25] Soon after the Fifth Plenum, "specialized contracts" (zhuanye chengbao) for groups and households, reportedly discovered in Shaanxi Province by Zhao Ziyang and introduced into Sichuan Province after the Fourth Plenum, were introduced to the nation.[26] Since a major problem for the reform group would be persuading wealthy units to link income and output at the household level,[27] specialized contracts, whereby farmers with special expertise accepted responsibility for a quota within a particular field of endeavor, were an important innovation. Adaptable to areas with little land, many people, and a fine division of labor, specialized contracts were particularly appropriate for suburban communes (where opposition to linking incomes to output was strongest).

To push more units to link income and output, a People's Daily editorial on April 2, 1980, announced that 80 percent of the teams in the nation had adopted some form of responsibility system, with 20 percent using group contracts, which, the editorial admitted, the People's Daily had criticized one year earlier. Yet, although the paper published a regional report describing the use of specialized contracts in Sichuan Province on the same day, this People's Daily editorial ignored them because in Sichuan they were often signed by individual households. Thus, although the People's Daily could publish regional reports describing household contracts, official policy statements, such as editorials, still drew the limit at group quotas. Throughout this process, responsibility systems which had not yet received official sanction appeared first in the People's Daily as regional reports or letters to the editor. Only after they had passed the political gauntlet were they supported by official editorials. But, with spring planting rapidly approaching and with 20 percent of rural teams still using Dazhai work points, time was of the essence. At a minimum, these teams had to adopt task rates.

Seven days after the April 2 editorial, the *People's Daily* further loosened the boundaries of the responsibility system. Whereas in the fall of 1979 individual contracts were mentioned but not advocated, the *People's Daily* now supported their controlled application under certain conditions.[28] Nonetheless, resistance to linking income to output persisted through part of 1980. On May 15, the *People's Daily* admitted that the responsibility system linking income to output had "constantly incurred censure from all sides." And, although in June, *Economic Research* supported individual contracts, the article still tried to convince units to stop using Dazhai work points.[29]

During the summer of 1980, under increased pressure from many provinces which for two years had been using household contracts for more than just "single households living in remote hilly areas," the Central Committee and the State Agricultural Commission sent out more than a hundred people to collect local data. These research groups found that fluctuations in implementation made farmers uneasy and affected production. So in September 1980, before the fall harvest and winter planting, the Party Secretariat convened a work conference in Beijing with first secretaries of all provinces, cities, and autonomous regions to discuss the responsibility system.[30]

The most important contributions of this meeting were first, its clear recognition that policy implementation would have to be more flexible and consider regional and local conditions—a point critical for successful implementation[31]—and second, that once again the content of the policy had changed in response to local pressures. The conference authorized three responsibility systems: task rates, specialized contracts, and household contracts, including household contracts with fixed levies.[32] The work conference fully integrated household contracts into the responsibility system by authorizing them for all poor areas where farmers had admittedly lost faith in the collective.[33] "Average areas" (*yiban diqu*) with stable collective economies were to avoid household contracts. Where household contracts were already instituted, they were to be permitted to continue, but over time, through the use of various transitionary procedures, the farmers were to be reorganized.

During the winter of 1980-1981, while Central Document (CD) No. 75 was to be passed down for discussion at local levels, Hu Yaobang and Zhao Ziyang traveled across rural China, with Zhao investigating the responsibility system's progress and Hu looking at the issue of "diversifying the rural crop mix" (*duo zhong jing ying*). Leading members of the State Agricultural Commission under Wan Li also carried out investigations.[34] But as the spring harvest of 1981 neared, some local leaders failed to disseminate the policy, others were unsure what form of the policy was appropriate for their locality, and still others began to backtrack on the reforms.[35] However, having completed their research, the reformist group was prepared for another offensive.

Table 2.1

Developments in the Responsibility System, 1980–1981
(percent of rural households)

	January 1980	December 1980	June 1981	October 1981
Task rates	55.7	39.0	27.2	16.5
Specialized contracts	—	4.7	7.8	5.9
Group contracts	24.9	23.6	13.8	10.8
Individual contracts	3.1	8.6	14.4	15.8
Household contracts	1.0	9.4	16.9	7.1
Household contracts with fixed levies	0.02	5.0	11.3	38.0
Totals	84.7	90.3	94.4	94.1

Source: Economic Research (Jingji yanjiu), no. 11 (1982): 6.

A March 2, 1981, *People's Daily* commentary listed several problems: Poor areas had confronted numerous difficulties implementing household contracts; farmers, some of whom left the land fallow, had not fulfilled their contractual obligations; team leaders had abdicated responsibility; and some officials had demanded uniform implementation of household contracts.[36] Yet, while outlining these problems, the *People's Daily* unveiled new trends in the content of the responsibility system.

First, wealthy areas had begun to shift from task rates to specialized contracts, a "developing tendency" that was applauded (see Table 2.1). Second, average areas could now establish individual contracts within large paddy fields, particularly where the work was done manually. Having witnessed successful experiments in Henan, Hebei, and Shandong provinces in early January, Zhao Ziyang supported contracting segments of large paddy fields among individuals, in spite of the complicated irrigation problems.[37] Third, the commentary divided the country into three areas with different levels of economic development— wealthy, average, and poor—and suggested that each area corresponded to the three responsibility systems outlined in CD No. 75.

On the same day the March 2, 1981, commentary was published, the eighty-eighth session of the Secretariat decided, based on Hu Yaobang's winter travels, to further diversify agricultural production. Their deliberations led to CD No. 13 (1981), promulgated on March 30, 1981, which was a significant step toward commercializing Chinese agriculture.

In April and May, the policy's official content continued to evolve. At the end of April, *Ban yue tan* published both CD No. 75 (1980) and CD No. 13 (1981), which demonstrated to all official acceptance of household contracts with fixed levies.[38] Moreover, people now could see that the commentary of March 2 had advanced the content of the policy by supporting individual contracts for paddy cultivation in average areas, something CD No. 75 had not mentioned. Then, on

May 20, 1981, one of the most revealing articles ever published in the *People's Daily* appeared, and when it discussed the responsibility system, the policy's content differed from both CD No. 75 and the March 2 commentary.[39] Rich areas, with strong collective economies and yearly increases in production "in the main, should (*ying gai*) carry out the system of specialized contracts and those carrying out group contracts can, of their own volition, form specialized groups." Task rates, acceptable in March, but which did not link income and output, were no longer mentioned.

In the provinces, changes were occurring quickly. On May 24, 1981, Shanghai's *Liberation Daily* warned all those resisting the responsibility system that their days were numbered and that all units, rich and poor, should link income to output.[40] And, on June 12, 1981, *Hebei Daily* tried to narrow the ideological gap between collectively managed "household contracts" and decollectivized "household contracts with fixed levies" by referring simply to "dual contracts" (*shuang bao dao hu* or simply *shuang bao*). Although both politically and practically these systems differed greatly, this formula of "dual contracts" included the noncollectivist system within the fold of already acceptable responsibility systems.[41]

Development, Disorder, and Retrenchment from July 1981 to March 1982

The Sixth Plenum of June 1981 changed decollectivization's political context. With Hu Yaobang, a member of the reform group, replacing Hua Guofeng as party chairman, opponents of the responsibility system at the middle and local levels could no longer look to the party chairman for support. The Central Committee's decision on Mao, which attributed agricultural problems of the 1960s and 1970s to his errors,[42] indicated to local cadres that a national consensus recognized that Maoist policies in agriculture following the Great Leap Forward (1958) had been wrong. The reforms, therefore, must continue. Following that meeting, Hu Yaobang finally stated that household contracts with fixed levies were part of the responsibility system.[43] Also, in July, Zhao Ziyang visited Lankao County, where farmers were using household contracts with fixed levies.[44]

From July through September 1981, propelled by farmers' spontaneous actions, support for household contracts intensified. Some provinces rejected the relationship between a locality's economic conditions and its responsibility system. *Shaanxi Daily,* July 22, 1981, suggested that average areas could now use household contracts, and five days later admitted that a recent provincial meeting had decided that household contracts for fixed levies could now be expanded to areas not dependent on direct state subsidies. And, on September 1, 1981, the *People's Daily* announced important findings based on another survey by the central party authorities. According to this party report, villagers enthusiastically supported household contracts with fixed levies because this more decentralized system of management stopped cadres from expropriating collective resources for personal benefits and created a stronger incentive for farmers than individual or group contracts, which were based on centralized distribution. The report found "the overall situation is that in this reform, the cadres have been compelled to advance by the masses."[45]

The effects of the Sixth Plenum on decollectivization are shown in Table 2.1. Between December 1980 and June 1981, the use of both types of household contracts increased from 14.4 to 28.2 percent. However, the largest change occurred from June to October 1981, when the number of units using household contracts with fixed levies jumped from 11.3 to 38.0 percent.

The rapid emergence of household contracts with fixed levies, however, created problems during the summer of 1981. Middle-level officials responded in one of two ways: Some county and commune officials, fearful that this policy heralded decollectivization, tried to block its emergence by forbidding propaganda about it and by stopping loans to units implementing it.[46] Other places reacted in the opposite manner. Believing that the policy was unstoppable, these county cadres began to force uniform implementation on local units. In Hebei Province, farmers, forbidden to establish household contracts in the spring, were compelled to do so in the fall.[47] In July, officials in wealthy brigades in Shanxi, Jiangsu, and Fujian provinces admitted that they were under pressure to shift to individual contracts.[48] In many localities the word spread that only by implementing household contracts with fixed levies could leaders show that they had freed themselves from leftist tendencies.[49] In September, the *People's Daily* called for an end to pressure for uniformity.[50]

Team and brigade leaders also responded in two ways. First, to resist changes advocated by both national leaders and villagers, some denied their unit's total dependency on state aid,[51] while others created innovative forms of task rates which did not involve linking income to output.[52] Resistance also was easier when supported by middle-level officials. But persistent national and villager pressures, compounded by evaporating middle-level support, caused many local cadres to simply quit their posts.[53]

Villagers also saw the expansion of household contracts with fixed levies as proof that decollectivization and the reemergence of private agriculture were at hand. Moreover, with local cadres quitting and party branches immobilized, no one disabused villagers of this notion. Consequently, in many areas villagers divided collective property.[54] In addition, fulfillment of the agricultural plan was jeopardized. Acreage allotted for grain decreased; vegetable supplies in state markets shrank as farmers flocked to the free markets; and increased production of cash crops led to waste as marketing organizations refused to purchase above-plan quantities.

These problems precipitated a flurry of national activity and policy readjustments all of which occurred within the context of a conservative shift in national politics. The National Symposium on Agricultural Economic Problems, convened in late August under the auspices of the State Agricultural Commission, suggested that, since the masses were running ahead of the elites and local implementation had exceeded CD No. 75, a new document had to be composed to deal with the changing situation and the diversity of fears at all levels of rural society.[55] In late October 1981, a national rural work conference tried to assuage the aforementioned concerns.[56] First, collective ownership of both land and the basic means of production would persist. On the other hand, since household contracts for fixed levies were now a form of the collective responsibility system, its widescale implementation did not justify dismantling collective property. Also, to ensure plan fulfillment, farmers using household contracts with fixed levies would now sign formal contracts with the collective, committing them to meet the plan's guidelines. The new policy of binding a farmer's production to the state even under household contracts with fixed levies was reinforced by the National Meeting on Problems of Agricultural Responsibility Systems, held in Yunnan Province in December 1981. This meeting also announced that, by the end of October 1981, 45 percent of rural units nationwide were using dual contracts.[57]

During most of the winter of 1981-1982, the reformers' program was in abeyance.[58] Zhejiang Province publicly declined to bring pressure on the recalcitrant 30 percent of its teams that refused to link income to output.[59] Red Flag magazine criticized slogans which implied that people using task rates were ideologically unliberated.[60] Heilongjiang Province rejected household contracts with fixed levies, stating that "draft animals and farm implements cannot be divided among commune members,"[61] and on February 19, 1982, an editorial in Jiangsu Province's Xinhua Daily voiced support for task rates. The provincial press now reported on the deleterious implications of weakening the collective. Fujian's Lunghai County reported that 20 percent of its teams' leaders had withdrawn or held power only in name, while Hunan Province outlined numerous problems resulting from household contracts with fixed levies.[62] Of 260,000 Hunan teams using this system, the leadership had evaporated in 17 percent of them.

That a counter trend had emerged after fall 1981 became even more apparent when, in mid-February, Ban yue tan backtracked from its previous pro-reform position, stating that income could be based on "the quantity or the quality" of the work performed; that is, income need not necessarily be linked to output.[63] Moreover, although many parts of the article were taken verbatim from the minutes of the 1981 Rural Work Conference held in October 1981, the Ban yue tan article was the first public statement emanating from that meeting. However, when its emphasis is compared to that of the minutes as they finally emerged in April 1982, adjustments in the document's contents suggest a viewpoint different from the original minutes. Overall, the Ban yue tan article placed much more importance on "planned production, planned marketing and state monopoly for purchasing and marketing"; played down household production and emphasized the collective management of agriculture; and expressed fears about what decollectivization would mean for water conservancy and capital construction. While these themes may have reflected central concerns about the local problems that had been emerging, they also highlighted issues of concern to more conservative pro-plan and pro-collectivist leaders. Also, although the central work conference had taken place in October 1981, the minutes of the meeting had neither been published when this issue of *Ban yue tan* went to press nor been transmitted to most localities.[64] Therefore, *Ban yue tan*'s spin on the new policies could have had a strong impact on the institutional arrangements that would guide the spring planting. From a conceptual perspective, too, this concomitant change in both policy content and context suggests that the reforms had run into resistance from those who could point to some of the policy's negative effects.

Breakthrough: April 1982 to April 1983

After the retrenchment of the winter of 1981-1982, any new continued rural reform initiatives depended on a more favorable political context. Zhao Ziyang's early March announcement of a major administrative reform of the State Council, and Deng's speech of April 3, 1982, which supported this structural reform, shifted momentum back to the reformers.[65] In addition, on April 3, 1982, a *People's Daily* editorial, while recognizing the rural problems, stated that "compared to the achievements we have made, these problems are secondary, partial and temporary," and that the efforts of the county party committees, not policy changes, would overcome the problems.[66] On April 6, 1982, the *Minutes of the National Rural Work Conference* were published on the front page of the *People's Daily,* and three weeks later an investigatory report by the General Office of the Central Committee finally mentioned "comprehensive contracts" (*da bao gan*) in the *People's Daily*.[67]

Publication of the minutes precipitated a major study campaign, the target of which were county and prefectural leaders who continued to resist the reforms.[68] While the education campaign of the winter of 1981–1982 had focused on local cadres, in May 1982, Bai Dongcai, secretary of the Jiangxi Provincial CCP Committee, emphasized that "in particular, the secretaries and standing committee members of the county CCP committees must unify their thinking."[69] Although the majority of cadres understood the new line in agriculture, "there are some cadres, including some leading cadres at and above the county level, who are muddleheaded."

The pace of reform increased at the end of June. According to the *People's Daily,* the rural situation now was magnificent.[70] This positive view may have resulted from early projections of the 1982 grain harvest, which was almost 10 percent higher than in 1981. Clearly, despite the dislocations that emerged in winter 1981–1982, the responsibility system was having a positive impact on output. Two days later, the *People's Daily* published another speech by Bai Dongcai, in which he argued that dual contracts had helped, not hindered,

Jiangxi Province's rural economy; the breakdown of local leadership that had occurred was due to the lack of ideological work by rural leaders, "the pernicious influence of Lin Biao and the Gang of Four," and middle-level cadres from the province whose political attitudes were behind the times and the changes demanded by the farmers.[71] Therefore, farmers, not cadres, should become "the most active workers of the great reform." In addition, on July 4, 1982, *Sichuan Daily's* commentator reported that a recent provincial CCP committee work conference "took a number of new policy measures for developing the rural economy. Some of these represent a further relaxation of policies, some involve handing over more decision-making powers to the grassroots."[72] The Sichuan report heralded the major policy changes that were soon to come.

From the summer of 1982 on, the content of the rural reforms became more comprehensive. As household contracts with fixed levies became more acceptable and widespread, the reformers began to work toward commercializing Chinese agriculture, with the individual households as the producing, processing, and transporting units. To achieve this goal, the reformers had to divide the collective into independently managed household units, which could either recombine voluntarily into new cooperatives or companies, sometimes competing with both collective and state-run agricultural companies, or persist as individual specialized units. In line with these changes, the reformers began referring to the rural area's "cooperative" rather than "collective" economy. Implementing household contracts with fixed levies and comprehensive contracts had become the linchpin in the reformers' overall scheme. Representatives from more than ten reform-minded provinces met at the July Forum on Agriculture to discuss "further relaxing policy restrictions."[73]

In light of the *Sichuan Daily's* above reference to a "further relaxation of policies," the reformers probably expanded the number of locations that were allowed to utilize this liberal policy at this time. In this way, by November, Wan Li could argue that practice had outstripped the prevailing guidelines. A *Xinhua* report made it clear that a major new reform was in the works. In an interview, a "responsible comrade of the Henan Provincial CCP Committee" said that,

> there has appeared the omen of a new breakthrough and development in the rural areas, and we are needed there *to adroitly guide actions according to circumstances*. It will no longer meet the needs of the situation simply to issue a general call to perfect the responsibility system. We must have a new policy decision and take new action in the face of a host of new things (emphasis added).[74]

Undoubtedly, this Henan official had read a draft policy document, because in November 1982, Wan Li would use the same wording in arguing that owing to local changes, cadres would need to "adroitly guide actions according to circumstances."[75]

In anticipation of the Twelfth Party Congress, support for comprehensive contracts and the major restructuring of Chinese agriculture grew. The August issue of *China Reconstructs* carried an in-depth report from Hunan Province describing a system called "contracting by specialization," which was merely one form of "comprehensive contracts."[76] By August, some "specialized" and "key households" (see appendix to chapter 1) that signed comprehensive contracts could now withdraw from agriculture, leave farming to other specialized farming households, and produce only commodities for enlivening the rural market.[77] On the eve of the Twelfth Party Congress, *People's Daily* announced that, since comprehensive contracts were the "typical form" of the "contract system linked to output," and since even wealthy units must use the contract system linked to output, they, too, might as well establish comprehensive contracts.[78]

Finally, Du Runsheng, director of the newly established "Rural Policy Research Office" (*Nongye zhengce yanjiu shi*) of the Party Secretariat, announced the new policy line on the responsibility system at the Twelfth Party Congress when he said that the decentralized "household contracts with fixed levies" system was no longer simply the major form of the responsibility system; it had now become a "developmental stage" in rural China's historical development.[79]

Over the next few months, the reformers pushed for universal implementation of the dual contract system and linked it to expanded commercialization by presenting individual or cooperatively organized households as the key economic actors of the newly emerging rural economy. Wan Li, in a major speech to the November 1982 Conference of Agricultural Secretaries in Beijing, said that comprehensive contracts and household contracts with fixed levies were "most cherished by the masses." He announced that the Central Committee had officially named the various forms of the responsibility system the "contract system linked to output," and argued that, if villagers in wealthy suburbs demanded the right to use comprehensive contracts, "this demand should no longer be held back."[80] A month later, Premier Zhao Ziyang's speech to the Fifth Session of the Fifth National People's Congress (NPC) supported Wan Li's advocacy of universal use of comprehensive contracts. He said that comprehensive contracts have "now become the principal form of the responsibility system in most rural areas, adopted not only by economically backward brigades and teams that engage in one crop farming, but also popularized in turn among economically advanced brigades and teams that have a highly specialized division of labor."[81] Zhao's public policy posture had changed greatly since early 1981, when he argued that regional variations necessitated flexible implementation of various responsibility systems. One must wonder, therefore, if farmer reactions changed his views or whether his 1981 policy was strategically motivated to undercut opposition and mobilize support for formally introducing household contracts into the rural areas.[82]

During late 1982 and early 1983, while the reformers pushed for universal implementation of comprehensive contracts or household contracts with fixed levies, they also composed No. 1 (1983), which was to lead Chinese agriculture in the direction outlined by Wan and Du. The code word for this overall reform was to "relax policies," and at the end of the December session of the NPC, all responsible officials from all departments, committees, and provinces were told to implement the reforms.[83] Thus, in early 1983 Hu Yaobang gave what *Da gong bao* called "a mobilization order":

> The remarkable success in agricultural reform made the leaders of the CCP who have been determined to carry out reforms understand that the implementation of the system of contracting all-round responsibility (comprehensive contracts), the development of specialized households, the diversified strata of the economy and the use of economic methods in management is the way out for China and is the way for China to launch its social and economic development.[84]

Many provinces convened meetings to implement the new liberal policy. Gansu Province announced that it would "relax its rural policies" and allow villagers to open mines.[85] Guangdong Province recognized that the key to rural prosperity lay in "relaxing and revising policies," and accepting the household contract system as the principal form of the responsibility system.[86] In early 1983, Fujian and Hunan Provinces put out new regulations for enlivening the rural economy.[87]

Widespread mobilization for the commercialization of agriculture greatly expanded the use of the contract system linked to output. Tianjin began to push all its units to accept, at a minimum, individual contracts, if not household contracts.[88] According to a report, 99 percent of Gansu Province's production teams used comprehensive contracts.[89] By the end of January 1983, 10 percent of China's rural families were "specialized households," while over 70 percent of households used comprehensive contracts.[90] Baotou Municipality in Hebei Province reported successful use of household contracts for vegetable production.[91]

Pressure for nationwide implementation of household contracts intensified. *People's Daily* told those who were undermining comprehensive contracts, particularly wealthy localities, that if Yixing County, Jiangsu Province, with its highly diversified economy, and Tao'an County, Jilin Province, where agriculture is highly mechanized, were linking income to output successfully, wealthy areas everywhere should be able to do so.[92] More pockets of resistance caved in. In late February, Chen Zuolin, first party secretary of Zhejiang Province, admitted that the province had seen household contracts as a "question of orientation," and had opposed them, fearing they would undermine the collective economy.[93] But, in August 1982 (after the July forum and before the Twelfth Party Congress), the province promoted household contracts with fixed levies "in the whole province, including some economically developed areas."[94] Two days later *Ming bao* reported that Mao Zhiyong, first party secretary of Hunan Province, purportedly confessed to having opposed linking income to output, fearing it would lead to private farming. He had reported his concerns to then party chairman Hua Guofeng, who said that the system was not applicable to Hunan Province. So Mao stuck with task rates, and, following the publication of CD No. 75, he rejected household contracts at a provincial meeting of county party secretaries.[95] Such confessions increased the danger of further opposition.

A major shift to comprehensive contracts occurred between fall 1982 and spring 1983. According to *Farmers' News* (*Nongmin bao*), the three northeast provinces, which had responded more slowly than much of the rest of the country, reversed their position opposing comprehensive contracts over the winter.[96] The percentage of teams using comprehensive contracts in Liaoning Province increased from 31 percent (October 1982) to 92 percent (March 1983), Jilin Province increased from 29 percent (October 1982) to 94.5 percent (March 1983), and Heilongjiang Province increased from 8.7 percent (May 1982) to 73 percent (February 1983). By March 1983, then, most nonsuburban teams were reporting use of household contracts with fixed levies. Whether these were in fact merely "formalistic" responses to political pressures is impossible to decipher. But, according to official information, from the end of 1982 through July 1983, the number of teams using dual contracts increased by 14 percent to include 93 percent of all teams in China.[97] The goal of wide-scale implementation of the link between income and output and household contracts with fixed levies had been accomplished.

Evaluating Success and the Problem of Unanticipated Consequences

How does one know "successful" implementation when one sees it? Even if initial policy goals are achieved, as has clearly been the case with the responsibility system, how does one deal with possibly deleterious unanticipated consequences? To evaluate this policy's success or failure, therefore, criteria other than the scope of implementation should be considered. Were elite economic goals of increasing agricultural production attained? What were the effects of unintended policy consequences? And, were the reformers able to deal with them? This section briefly considers changes in agricultural output, agricultural productivity, and living standards, as well as the policy's unanticipated consequences and the leaders' responses to them, to determine whether the implementation of household contracts has been a "success."

Following the introduction of the responsibility system, agricultural production increased greatly, particularly after 1981. Table 2.2 presents several indicators showing changes in rural production between 1978 and 1984. Increases in grain output were impressive, particularly since grain acreage decreased. Output of other crops increased even more dramatically. However, if these increases had been the result purely of institutional reforms, they might have been short-lived and had little effect on long-term growth rates. Infusions of technology remain the primary way to increase these long-term growth rates in agricultural produc-

Table 2.2

Indicators of Rural Development, 1978–1984 (in 100,000 tons)

	1978	1979	1980	1981	1982	1983	1984
Grain output	3,047.5	3,321.2	3,205.6	3,250.2	3,534.2	3,872.8	4,070.0
Cotton output	21.7	22.1	27.1	29.7	36.0	46.4	62.5[a]
Oil-bearing crops	52.2	64.4	76.9	102.1	118.2	105.5	118.5
Tea output	2.7	2.8	3.0	3.4	4.0	4.0	4.1
Sugar cane	211.2	215.1	228.1	296.7	368.8	311.4	396.6
Meat production (pork, beef, lamb)	85.6	106.2	120.6	126.1	135.1	140.2	152.5

Sources: 1978–1981: *Ban yue tan*, no. 16 (1982): 27; 1982: *Statistical Yearbook of China, 1982* (Beijing: State Statistical Bureau, 1982); 1983: *Beijing Review*, no. 35 (August 27, 1984); and State Statistical Bureau Communique, April 29, 1984; 1984: *USDA China Outlook and Situation Report* (Washington, D.C.: United States Department of Agriculture, Economic Research Service, 1985).

[a]*Chinese Agricultural Yearbook, 1985* (Beijing: Ministry of Agriculture, 1985).

tion.[98] Indeed, to encourage farmers to invest in land, the period of contracts was lengthened to fifteen to thirty years.

Many costs were suddenly borne by households rather than collectives, creating incentives for individual farmers to increase productivity. Output of grain per *mu* increased by 13 percent from 1981 to 1982, which explains why grain acreage could drop while output rose.[99] From 1978 to 1982, total agricultural production costs, excluding labor, as a percentage of total income dropped 5 percent; for every 100 *yuan* of investment, returns rose from 252 to 288 *yuan*. In addition, after 1978, income was increasing at a faster rate than costs.[100] In short, decollectivization not only contributed to increases in production but improved the economic efficiency of capital.

Finally, the reformers also sought to improve the farmers' living standard. Many rehabilitated cadres, including Deng, had spent the Cultural Revolution in rural areas. Surprised by the villagers' plight, they may have felt obligated to resolve rural poverty. In any case, without an increase in rural living standards, rural productivity and output could not have increased. Table 2.3 shows that, from this perspective the reforms also achieved short-run success. Rural housing construction boomed, and per capita income more than doubled between 1978 and 1983. In that period, the increase in per capita income outpaced growth in income from the collective, which suggests that individuals were more able than collectives to find profitable economic endeavors. If true, that is precisely the kind of change that the responsibility system was intended to achieve. From a short-term economic perspective, the responsibility system appeared to be fulfilling the goals of the reform group. Little wonder, therefore, that implementation was so widespread.

Table 2.3

Villagers' Standard of Living, 1978–1983

	1978	1979	1980	1981	1982	1983
Housing (approximate)[a] (million m^2)	100.0	300.0	500.0	600.0	600.0	700.0
Average per capita net income[b]	133.6	160.2	191.3	223.4	270.1	310.0
Average per capita income from collective[c]	88.5	102.0	108.4	116.2	142.8	169.5

Source: All data are from *Ban yue tan,* no. 16 (1982): 27, unless otherwise marked.
Notes:
[a]Figures from 1982 and 1983 are from State Statistical Bureau Communique, April 29, 1984.
[b]Values for 1982 and 1983 need adjustment to compensate for a change in the price used for valuing distribution in kind by the collective sector. According to Fred M. Surls, *China Outlook and Situation Report* (Washington, D.C.: United States Department of Agriculture, Economic Research Service, 1984), p. 15, the income level for 1982 should be 257.4.
[c]*Chinese Agricultural Yearbook,* 1984.

However, it is impossible to specify clearly what proportion of these economic gains was attributable to higher purchase prices, the opening of free markets, exceedingly good weather overall, and decollectivization. Hartford argued that the yearly increase in villager per capita income from 1979 to 1981 was 76 percent due to increased procurement prices.[101] In different locales, various combinations of factors may have been at work. Nonetheless, there is no question that China's leaders, villagers, and urbanites all believed that the responsibility system had played a major role in agricultural successes in that period. And in politics, perception is nine-tenths of the law.

Major reforms lead to behavioral change. Some changes will be desirable and predicted; others are unwelcome or even unanticipated. If severe or unresolved, unintended consequences can overshadow policy gains and undermine support for the original policy. It would be astonishing if decollectivization, which weakened collective leadership, had not triggered unintended consequences. Some problem areas included population control, capital formation, social unrest, and inequality.[102]

The work of Tyrene White explains the links between the responsibility system and the villagers' desire for more children[103]: (1) allocating land according to family size or number of laborers created strong incentives for more children; (2) weakening collective leadership hurt the state's ability to promote birth control; (3) weakening collective accumulation decreased the collective's ability to ensure old-age security, causing farmers to want more children; and (4) ending collective distribution destroyed the mechanism for sanctioning those who had unauthorized children. These factors increased birthrates in 1982. However, the post-Mao leadership recognized this problem and responded rapidly. Linking the responsibility system and birth policies, they introduced a new form of "dual contracts," combining remuneration for agricultural work with a willingness to abide by birth-control guidelines.

A second long-term problem was the weakening of collective assets and capital formation. While the proportion of total agricultural income accumulated by collective enterprises from 1978 to 1982 stayed stable at 22 percent, income was shifting from teams to households. Production-team income as a proportion of total income dropped from 55.4 to 45.6 percent while the share accruing to household sidelines rose from 22.4 to 32.1 percent.[104] Moreover, the percentage of team income that was reinvested and saved for villager welfare dropped from 14.2 percent in 1978 to 9 percent in 1982.[105] According to the *People's Daily,* many farmers were consuming too much and investing too little,[106] which could have had long-term implications for economic growth, irrigation, rural education, and rural health and welfare.

Many social tensions have increased.[107] Jealousy toward wealthy villagers forced them to perform various services for their neighbors for free and loan money that was not repaid.[108] Thefts increased. Extortion by cadres became so prevalent that the Public Security Bureau had to draft a directive to all its units to protect rural households that were getting rich.[109]

However, although some households became quite prosperous, rural income distribution nationwide became more, not less, equitable.[110] Table 2.4 shows that, whereas in 1978, 82.6 percent of rural households made less than 150 *yuan,* in 1983 only 20.7 percent fell into that category, which represented the official poverty line. Clearly, this policy helped dramatically alleviate rural poverty in much of rural China. Moreover, Table 2.4 also shows that the Gini coefficient, a standard measure of inequality, decreased significantly after 1978. Therefore, the reform group's argument that "everyone is getting rich together" had some validity. Nevertheless, some families were growing quite wealthy while other labor-poor households were running into debt.[111] Furthermore, whereas equality increased in the short run, only time would tell if China would be able to continue following the pattern of equality with growth as occurred in Taiwan and South Korea.[112] Central Document No. 1 (1984), which allowed the hiring of farmer labor and permitted farmers to sublet their contract land to more successful farmers, could lead to greater centralization of land management.[113] Moreover, the wealthy might use their money to increase their political and social standing, which in turn could strengthen and expand overall inequality in the countryside.[114]

Final evaluation of the success of decollectivization must await future developments. The growth rates engendered to date by this policy will be difficult to maintain without a major infusion of capital. Whether private household financing of each farmer's own individual plot will suffice, or whether the state will be

Table 2.4

Distribution of Rural Households by Per Capita Income (percentage)

Income groups (yuan)	1978	1979	1980	1981	1982	1983
Less than 100	33.3	19.3	9.8	4.7	2.7	1.4
100–149	31.7	24.2	24.7	14.9	8.1	6.2
150–199	17.6	29.0	27.1	23.0	16.0	13.1
200–299	15.0	20.4	25.3	34.8	37.0	32.9
300–399	0.0	5.0	8.6	14.4	20.8	22.9
400–499	2.4	1.5	2.9	5.0	8.7	11.6
500+	0.0	0.6	1.6	3.2	6.7	11.9
Gini coefficient	.28	.26	.25	.23	.22	.22
Sample size	34,961	58,153	88,090	101,998	142,286	168,131

Source: Compiled by William L. Parish. First appeared in Mark Selden, "Income Inequality and the State," in William L. Parish, ed., *Chinese Rural Development: The Great Transformation* (Armonk, N.Y.: M.E. Sharpe, 1985), p. 211. Gini coefficients were estimated from the income figures, which are in *Brilliant 35 Years* (Beijing: China Statistical Publishing House, 1984).

forced to pour funds into the rural areas remains unclear. The potentially disruptive effects of several seasons of bad weather, especially given the weakened irrigation infrastructure brought on by decollectivization, must be recognized. Expanding inequalities within China's rural society and the shift from a collective economy offering a protective welfare net to a more unstable economic system replete with household bankruptcies and private financial failures could create a strong base of support for a partial retrenchment of collective and state authority. Still, in the short run, the fulfillment of the reformers' goals of economic growth, increased productivity, and rising rural incomes, while confronting only limited disruptions, argues heavily in favor of viewing this implementation process as highly successful.

Conclusion

Successful implementation of household contracts occurred because the reform group was highly flexible and innovative throughout most of the process. After establishing their preferences, they adjusted the policy's content according to local responses. They had a sense of where they wanted to go, but they also listened to the rural populace. The shift in policy content from the 1977-1978 stress on task rates to the 1983 emphasis on comprehensive contracts was neither prearranged nor randomly achieved. Leaders adjusted the policy's content flexibly, while following their own general policy predilections.

The reform group adjusted the policy's political context to increase their power. At the same time, the economic gains achieved by each incremental shift in policy put opposition leaders off guard. No policy change, in itself, was worth a major fight, but the aggregate of changes produced the decollectivization of Chinese agriculture. The reformers created new political organizations they could control to initiate the policies, and they relied on various ad hoc meetings to advocate the continuation and evolution of the reforms. From 1978 on, they convened major meetings at the end of every year, at which time they put out major policy documents. In the winter of 1978, they rose to prominence at the Third Plenum and set new directions for rural policy. In the fall of 1979, they ratified the New Sixty Points at the Fourth Plenum, and defeated their major opposition the following February. In the fall of 1980, the newly created Secretariat developed CD No. 75, which certified the responsibility system and household contracts. In the spring of 1981, the Secretariat published CD No. 13 on diversification. Four months after Hua Guofeng's ouster as party chairman in July 1981, the reform faction held a rural work conference to maintain momentum during the winter of 1981-1982, although the reforms did slacken during that time. In preparation for the Twelfth Party Congress, they held the July Forum on Agriculture, and following this congress they convened the Conference of Agricultural Secretaries. Then, in early 1983 the reform faction published CD No. 1 (1983), which ultimately defeated the final points of resistance. The consistency of meetings and documents, sustained elite attention, and responsiveness to problems over such a long period constituted a rather remarkable feat and a key ingredient in the successful implementation.

Success also was due to the elite's willingness to allow farmers to experiment locally. According to Cleaves,

> the challenge for reformers lies in utilizing the discipline inherent in a closed system to loosen the structure and thus to permit the system to adapt and learn, rather than remain persistently sealed from the social forces in its midst. When this task is accomplished, the resources available for policy implementation are recombined and increased.[115]

Through careful manipulation of their political power, the reformers loosened the structure of the system. Then, by appealing to the villager's pecuniary interests, they set loose these previously sealed "social forces," which helped propel the reforms. As Mao himself had learned, changes in rural policy were doomed without mass support.

The major problem that plagued this policy's implementation process and that affected the implementation of many other rural policies was the disastrous tendency toward uniformity and the refusal to allow variations in policy implementation based on local characteristics. Although the reformers stressed the importance of local conditions throughout 1981 and most of 1982, in July 1982, they began to demand universal implementation of comprehensive contracts, even in wealthy areas that did not support the policy. In the past, radical elites who desired to impose their utopian view uniformly on society were often the culprits. Middle-level cadres, more concerned with protecting their political careers than developing the economy, always pushed local leaders to implement unsuitable policies that emanated from Beijing. This study shows that pragmatic elites also fell prey to this error, as if uniform implementation validated the correctness of their political line as well.

Most important, however, the reform group delicately matched the content of the policy to their ability to affect its political context. They continually monitored the rural areas and, when unforeseen local responses changed that context, the reformers quickly adjusted the content. When confronted by fearful cadres, they offered soothing words to calm them, even as they laid the groundwork for future changes and pressed the cadres to accept new forms of the responsibility system. As soon as the political context was again conducive to the reformer's goals, they changed the content and forcefully pressed on. Meetings and documents signaled bureaucrats throughout China that the reforms would continue. Each political success created a new political context, allowing the reformers, through salami-type tactics, to change the content of the policy and move the rural areas toward widespread use of household contracts and the decollectivization of Chinese agriculture.

Notes

1. For analyses of policy in the United States and Third World, see, respectively, Jeffrey L. Pressman and Aaron Wildavsky, *Implementation: How Great Expectations in Washington Are Dashed in Oakland* (Berkeley and Los Angeles: University of California Press, 1973); and Merilee S. Grindle, ed., *Politics and Policy Implementation in the Third World* (Princeton: Princeton University Press, 1980).

2. By July 1983, 93 percent of all production teams in China had divided the land among households for farming. *Farmers' News (Nongmin bao)*, July 21, 1983, p. 1. For the guidelines of collective agriculture established in 1962, see "Regulations on Work in the Rural People's Communes (revised draft)" (Sixty Articles), *Issues and Studies*, vol. 15 (October and December 1979), pp. 93–111, and 106–115.

3. For example, much of the former Soviet Union has experienced enormous difficulty dismantling collective agriculture.

4. Provincial reporting and reactions spiraled back to Beijing, affecting policy formation and implementation. In this way, outcomes, initially dependent on the policy, rebounded back to the center, generating new policy directions. See H. Hugo Heclo, "Review Article: Policy Analysis," *British Journal of Political Science* 2, part 1 (January 1972): 92. For a summary on evaluating policy "success" or "failure," see David M. Lampton, "The Implementation Problem in Post-Mao China," in David M. Lampton, ed., *Policy Implementation in Post-Mao China* (Berkeley: University of California Press, 1987), pp. 3–24.

5. Grindle, *Politics and Policy*, pp. 5–6.

6. For a discussion of the political battles in that period see Christopher Clark,

"Changing the Context for Policy Implementation: Organizational and Personnel Reform in Post-Mao China," in Lampton, ed., *Policy Implementation in Post-Mao China,* pp. 25–50.

7. For the content of "household contracts with fixed levies" and "comprehensive contracts," see the appendix to chapter 1, pp. 55–56.

8. *People's Daily,* August 29, 1977, page 3, and October 22, 1977, p. 3.

9. An Gang, Song Cheng, and Huang Yuejin, "There Is Hope for the Vigorous Development of Agriculture in China," *People's Daily,* July 9, 1981, in *Foreign Broadcast Information Service* (hereafter cited as *FBIS*), no. 141 (July 23, 1981): K 11-18.

10. *People's Daily,* February 3, p. 1, and March 23, 1978, p. 1.

11. Wan Li, "Energetically Carry Out the Party's Rural Economic Policy," *Red Flag* (*Hongqi*), no. 3 (1978): 2-7.

12. Clark, "Changing the Context," p. 30.

13. *FBIS,* no. 209 (October 27, 1978).

14. A direct link between income and output would improve agricultural yields by giving farmers incentives to be concerned with the entire production cycle rather than only a segment of the cycle. Thanks to Tom Bernstein, who clarified this point.

15. *Hebei Daily,* October 11, 1978, p. 1, compiled in *China's People's University Materials Room, Materials Republished from the Press, Agricultural Economics* (*Zhongguo renmin daxue shubao ziliao, baokan ziliao, nongye jingji*) (hereafter cited as *People's University*), no. 10 (1978): 235.

16. *Henan Daily,* November 2, 1978, p. 1, in *People's University,* no. 12 (1978): 121-122.

17. In 1982, Wan Li admitted that he had avoided using such terms as long as possible. See *People's Daily,* December 23, 1982, in *FBIS,* no. 002 (January 4, 1983): K 6.

18. See Tang Tsou, Marc Blecher, and Mitch Meisner, "Policy Change at the National Summit and Institutional Transformation at the Local Level: The Case of Tachai and Hsiyang County in the Post-Mao Era," *Select Papers from the Center for Far Eastern Studies,* no. 4 (Chicago: University of Chicago, 1979–1980): 242–392.

19. If a policy has a nonsensitive political content, it is more likely to be implemented successfully. See Grindle, *Politics and Policy,* p. 28.

20. See point 3 of "Decision on Some Questions Concerning the Acceleration of Agricultural Development," in *Issues and Studies,* 15, no. 7 (1979): 102-19, and no. 8 (1979): 91-99. *People's Daily,* December 2, 1978, p. 3, subscribed to a "three fixes" quota system which excluded output quotas.

21. *Issues and Studies* 15, no. 7 (1979): 111.

22. For reports on the pilot projects, see *People's Daily,* September 16, 1982, in *FBIS* (September 21, 1982): K 15-16. For a report on Anhei Province, see *Xinhua Monthly* (*Xinhua yuebao*), no. 11 (1982): 91.

23. *People's Daily,* May 20, 1981, p. 1, reported Deng arguing that "it is necessary to enable every family to try its way. . . . It may even be necessary to allow farming groups or even individual farmers to enter into contracts for a fixed output" (translated by the author).

24. *People's Daily,* October 6, 1979, p. 1.

25. For changes in Guangdong Province, see *People's Daily,* May 20, 1981, pp. 1, 4 and in Anhui Province, see *Problems in Agricultural Economics* (*Nongye jingji wenti*), no. 5 (1981).

26. *People's Daily,* April 2, 1980, p. 1. An informed Nanjing source told me of Zhao's "discovery" of this system. It is worth noting that the *People's Daily* article which first discussed this system originated from Chengdu, Sichuan Province, only one month after Zhao became a member of the Politburo's Standing Committee.

27. For a discussion of resistance to these reforms in wealthy suburban areas, see chapter 3.

28. *People's Daily*, April 9, 1980, p. 2.

29. Ye Xin, "An Exploratory Discussion of the Reform of the People's Commune's Quota Payment System," *Economic Research* (*Jingji yanjiu*) (June 1980), pp. 45–49. Some parts of rural China, including Jiangsu Province, were still using Dazhai work points until the fall of 1980.

30. Changing the locus of decision making from the Politburo to the Secretariat removed Hua Guofeng, who opposed linking income and output, from the decision making process. See *Ming bao*, in *FBIS*, no. 039 (February 25, 1983): W 1-2. For an in-depth discussion of the decision-making process for Central Document No. 75 (1980) and CD No. 13 (1981), as well as expressed provincial support for and opposition to "household quotas," see *People's Daily*, May 20, 1981, p. 1.

31. Peter S. Cleaves, "Implementation Amidst Scarcity and Apathy: Political Power and Policy Design," in Grindle, *Politics and Policy*, pp. 284-285.

32. Both CD No. 75 (1980) and CD No. 13 (1981) were published in *Ban yue tan*, no. 8 (April 25, 1981), pp. 4 and 11–13, respectively.

33. *Ban yue tan*, no. 8 (April 25, 1981): 8. See also Yu Guoyao's article in *Hongqi*, no. 20 (1980): 12-15, who explained why household quotas with fixed levies had to be introduced in poor areas.

34. *People's Daily*, May 20, 1981, p. 1.

35. See letter to the editor in *People's Daily*, March 7, 1983, p. 3.

36. See "Summarize Experience, Improve and Stabilize the Agricultural Responsibility System," *People's Daily*, March 2, 1981, p. 1.

37. *People's Daily*, May 20, 1981, p. 1.

38. *Ban yue tan*, no. 8 (April 25, 1981), p. 8. On March 7, 1981, the *People's Daily* first referred to this system when it ran a letter from Sichuan Province showing that household contracts with fixed levies had been in effect there for over a year. At the same time, Sichuan's Provincial Party Committee published a circular advocating household contracts with fixed levies. See *Sichuan Daily*, July 13, 1981, p. 2, in *FBIS*, no. 154 (August 11, 1981): Q 3.

39. Entitled "Time to Consider 800 Million Peasants," this article explained much about the decisions behind these two documents.

40. "Even Shanghai County Can Link Income to Output," *Liberation Daily* (*Jiefang ribao*), May 24, 1981, p. 1. Since Shanghai's leadership had opposed *household quotas* at the September 1980 meeting, this article showed that, by May 1981, they had changed their views.

41. *Hebei Daily*, June 12, 1981, in *FBIS*, no. 131 (July 9, 1981): R 1-7.

42. See "On Certain Questions in the History of Our Party Since the Founding of the People's Republic of China," *Beijing Review*, no. 27 (July 6, 1981), pp. 10–39.

43. See An Gang, Song Cheng, and Huang Yuejin, "There Is Hope for the Vigorous Development of Agriculture in China," *People's Daily*, July 9, 1981, in *FBIS*, no. 141 (July 23, 1981): K 11-18.

44. See *Zhejiang Daily*, July 26, 1981, in FBIS, no. 143 (July 27, 1981): W 6, and *People's Daily*, September 1, 1981, p. 4.

45. This joint report by the CC-CCP Administrative Office (*Ban gong ting*) and the investigation group of the CC-CCP Party School was based on rural investigations from March 20 to May 30, 1981. See *People's Daily*, September 1, 1981, in *FBIS* (September 9, 1981): K 7-15.

46. See *World Economic Herald* (*Shijie jingji daobao*), November 2, 1981, pp. 1–2, in *Da gong bao*, November 8, 1981, and *Sichuan ribao*, November 7, 1981, p. 2, in *FBIS*, no. 224 (November 20, 1981), pp. Q 1–3.

47. *People's Daily*, September 22, 1981. The Chinese refer to this demand for policy uniformity as "cutting all with one knife" (*yi dao qie*).

48. David Zweig, "Chinese Agriculture: Pragmatism Gone Too Far?" *Asian Wall Street Journal,* August 12, 1981, p. 4. See also *FBIS,* no. 185 (September 24, 1981), pp. D 5–6, and chapter 1 of this book.

49. *Shanxi ribao,* September 22, 1981. Those who still suffered from "leftist" tendencies were at risk politically in an environment that was clearly shifting to the right.

50. *People's Daily,* September 22, 1981, p. 1.

51. *Shanxi ribao,* July 22, 1981, in *FBIS,* no. 161 (August 20, 1981): R 1-6.

52. Interview by the author in suburban Nanjing, Spring 1981.

53. See *Hebei ribao,* August 23, 1981, which referred to these two responses as first "locking horns" and then taking a "laissez-faire" attitude. See *FBIS,* no. 171 (September 3, 1981): K 7-9.

54. See *People's Daily,* August 15, 1981, in *FBIS,* no. 162 (August 21, 1981): K 21-22; *Shanxi ribao,* October 3, 1981, in *FBIS* (October 22, 1981): T 2-3; *People's Daily,* editorial, October 4, 1981, in *FBIS* (November 12, 1981); and *FBIS* (December 31, 1981): O 3.

55. See *Nongye jingji wenti,* no. 10 (October 28, 1981): 3-6, in *Joint Publications Research Service* (hereafter cited as *JPRS),* no. 79741 (December 24, 1981).

56. A commentary in *People's Daily* (October 30, 1981), entitled "Uphold Collective Ownership of Land, Uphold the Direction of Collectivization," referred to "the recently called national agricultural work conference." *See FBIS* (November 6, 1981): K 1-2.

57. *FBIS,* no. 245 (December 22, 1981): K 8. This figure matches the one in Table 2.1.

58. Politically, Deng's influence was briefly eclipsed by Chen Yun, Li Xiannian, and Ye Jianying, all of whom were more supportive of central planning or administrative control of the economy. Chen Yun was particularly assertive during this period, trying to insure stable grain production.

59. *FBIS* (November 24, 1981): 03–5, and *FBIS* (December 3, 1981): 02–3.

60. *Hongqi,* no. 1 (1982): 49.

61. *FBIS* (February 1, 1982): S 1-2.

62. See *Fujian ribao,* April 12, 1982, and *People's Daily,* February 6, 1982, in *FBIS* (February 18, 1982): K 12-16, respectively.

63. See "Several Questions Concerning Our Present Work in Agricultural Economics," *Ban yue tan,* no. 3 (February 10, 1982), pp. 22–25.

64. In Hebei Province, meetings for transmitting the minutes were not held until February, and other places did not distribute the minutes until March. See *FBIS* (February 24, 1982): R 3-4 and *FBIS,* no. 062 (April 8, 1982): K 6-8, respectively.

65. For Zhao's speech, see *New China News Agency,* March 8, 1982, in *FBIS,* no. 46 (March 9, 1982): K 1-7. Thanks to Mike Oksenberg for pointing out this speech. According to Deng Liqun's speech of November 1, 1982, Deng Xiaoping supported the policy to "restructure the administration and economic setup." See *FBIS* (November 8, 1982): K 10.

66. *People's Daily,* April 3, 1982, in *FBIS,* no. 073 (April 15, 1982): K 1-3.

67. *People's Daily,* April 27, 1982, p. 1.

68. *People's Daily,* April 3, 1982, p. 1. The Central Committee also published a booklet called "Several Issues on Further Strengthening and Improving the Responsibility System in Agricultural Production," to explain the major reforms inherent in the minutes. FBIS, no. 092 (May 12, 1982): O 1-2.

69. *FBIS,* no. 092 (May 12, 1982): O 1-2.

70. *People's Daily,* June 27, 1982, in *FBIS,* no. 129 (July 6, 1982): K 8-11.

71. *FBIS,* no. 129 (July 6, 1982): K 1-4.

72. *FBIS,* no. 132 (July 9, 1982): Q 2-3.

73. Wan Li referred to this forum in November. See *People's Daily,* December 23, 1983, pp. 1, 2, 4.

74. See *Xinhua,* July 25, 1982, in *FBIS,* no. 144 (July 27, 1982): K 4-5.

75. *People's Daily,* December 23, 1983, pp. 1, 2, 4.

76. *China Reconstructs* 31 (August 1982): 52.

77. Xinhua Commentator, August 12, 1982, in *FBIS,* no. 157 (August 13, 1982): K 11-12.

78. *People's Daily,* August 29, 1982, in *FBIS,* no. 171 (September 2, 1982): K 24-26.

79. *Xinhua yuebao,* no. 9 (1982): 139.

80. *People's Daily,* December 23, 1982, in *FBIS,* no. 002 (January 4, 1983): K 2-20.

81. *FBIS,* no. 240 (December 14, 1982): K 31.

82. Wan Li, in part, admitted that farmers in more advanced areas had pushed the reforms into this new stage. In his November speech, he admitted that, since a number of places had gone beyond the current state regulations, including some "key" and "specialized households," the CCP Secretariat decided that it was better to relax the restrictions and "adroitly guide action according to circumstances," rather than simply forbid these areas to advance the reforms. *FBIS,* no. 002 (January 4, 1983): K 18.

83. *Da gong bao,* February 6, 1983, p. 1, in *FBIS,* no. 028 (February 9, 1983): W 1-2.

84. Ibid.

85. *FBIS,* no. 247 (December 23, 1982): T 1-S.

86. *FBIS,* no. 249 (December 28, 1982): P 4.

87. *FBIS,* no. 009 (January 13, 1983): K 17, and *People's Daily* (editorial), January 22, 1983, pp. 1, 4, respectively.

88. *FBIS,* no. 247 (December 23, 1982): R 4-6.

89. Ibid.

90. *FBIS,* no. 009 (January 13, 1983): K 17, and *People's Daily* (editorial), January 22, 1983, pp. 1, 4, respectively.

91. *People's Daily,* January 13, 1983, pp 1, 2.

92. *People's Daily,* January 23, 1983, p. 2.

93. *People's Daily,* February 21, 1983, in *FBIS,* no. 038 (February 24, 1983): O 7.

94. This change of policy and posture may have resulted from the removal of Tie Ying who had just been replaced as first party secretary of Zhejiang. Thanks to David Bachman, who pointed out this fact.

95. *Ming bao,* February 23, 1983, p. 5, in *FBIS,* no. 039 (February 25, 1983): W 1-2.

96. *Nongmin bao,* March 22, 1983, p. 1.

97. *Nongmin bao,* July 21, 1983, pp. 1, 3.

98. See Steven Butler, "The Rural Responsibility System: A Fresh Answer to China's Agricultural Problems?" in David Zweig and Steven Butler, eds., *China's Agri-cultural Reform: Background and Prospects* (New York: Asia Society, 1985), and Nicholas R. Lardy, *Agriculture in China's Economic Development* (Cambridge: Cambridge University Press, 1984).

99. *Nongmin bao,* July 21, 1983, p. 1.

100. The rate of increase in total expenditure as compared with the rate of increase of total income dropped 3.9 percent between 1978 and 1982. See *Nongmin bao,* August 4, 1983.

101. Kathleen J. Hartford, "Once More with Feeling" (unpublished manuscript, 1984).

102. For a list of problems, see Chen Chung-min and Owen Hagovsky, "Agricultural Responsibility System: An Irresponsible Retreat or a Responsible Readjustment?" Presented at the workshop, "Studies in Policy Implementation in the Post-Mao Era," Social Science Research Council–American Council of Learned Societies Joint Committee, Co-

lumbus, Ohio, June 20-24, 1983. One important problem that is not addressed is water management.

103. See Tyrene White, "Implementing the 'One-Child-per-Couple' Population Program in Rural China: National Goals and Local Politics," in Lampton, ed., *Policy Implementation in Post-Mao China,* pp. 284–317.

104. *Nongmin bao,* August 4, 1983.

105. Ibid.

106. *People's Daily,* September 7, 1983, p. 1.

107. See chapter 4 of this book.

108. *Nongmin bao,* March 6, 1983, p. 1.

109. For a report on the extortions, see *People's Daily,* March 10, 1983, p. 1; for the Public Security Bureau's directive, see *Nongmin bao,* March 6, 1983, p. 1.

110. One survey found that, from 1978 to 1982, the income gap between rich and poor in suburban Shanghai narrowed. See *China Daily,* October 11, 1983, p. 4.

111. See "Village Volunteer Youth Groups," *China Reconstructs* 32 (November 1983): 4-6.

112. Li Chengrui of the State Statistical Bureau stated that the 1984 Gini coefficient of rural inequality was slightly higher than the 1978 coefficient, which suggests that inequality had begun to expand. See Li Chengrui, "Economic Reform Brings Better Life," *Beijing Review,* no. 29 (July 22, 1985): 22.

113. See *FBIS* (June 13, 1984): E 2. Over the past 15 years, land concentration has not been very extensive as people cannot make a lot of money given the relatively low prices available for crops.

114. Educational differences help explain income inequality today. According to *Nongmin bao,* July 21, 1983, 36.9 percent of specialized households, 40.3 percent of rich households, and 18.2 percent of poor households had a lower-middle school education. (Nationwide, 13 percent of farmers had lower-middle school education.) Clearly, the better educated one is, the more likely one is to make it into the ranks of China's new wealthy villagers.

115. Cleaves, "Implementation Amidst Scarcity," in Grindle, ed., *Politics and Policy,* p. 301.

3

Explaining Diversity in Rural China

Embedded Interests and Decollectivization in Jiangsu Province, 1978–1983

Rarely have analysts been able to view unbridled popular interest at play in the PRC. When Mao demolished the Chinese Communist Party (CCP) and the forces of order in the Cultural Revolution, long festering divisions among students and among workers burst into view. However, most reflections of popular views in China, particularly before the advent of surveys in the mid-and late-1980s, were reconstructed by government "spin doctors" whose role was to filter citizen beliefs through a thick veneer of state interests before presenting them in official reports. Awareness of these distortions often leads us to wonder what people actually thought.

Looking at rural China in 1983, one would have assumed that all farmers, regardless of the socioeconomic, ecological, or political context in which they lived, strongly supported individual farming and the deconstruction of the collective system of agriculture. No doubt, many farmers were strong advocates of the dismantling of the communes; and some analysts argue that it was the farmers themselves who led the movement to end collective agriculture in China (see the introduction). Nevertheless, by 1983, all of rural society had completed the shift to individual agriculture. Despite provincial resistance and demands for some policy alterations, the state, through its power to impose policy conformity, had reconstructed rural institutions and norms into one pattern. Household farming good! Collective farming bad! Uniformity good! Diversity bad!

However, the process of socioeconomic change is a window through which we can view the interests embedded in a country's society, polity, and economy. At these moments of significant historical shifts in China, the blinds that often block our view are lifted, allowing us more fully to understand the social forces that influence China. Our problem is that frequently we lack the spotlight to illuminate those interests that, in the early stages of change, motivate individual and collective action. One thinks, for example, of the Hundred Flowers campaign and the cacophony of interests that emerged at that time or the deafening silence that followed its eclipse.[1] Had the results of decollectivization varied significantly across regions, we could have dissected those final local institutions to understand how socioeconomic, political, and ecological variations among regions shaped or explained the outcome. But the relative uniformity of decollectivization complicates that post hoc process of explanation enormously—we cannot explain the impact of different forces if there is no variation in the outcome. In fact, the final, uniform pattern of decollectivization strengthens arguments that the Chinese central government's or poor farmers' interests totally dominated that process and that regional variations and the interests resulting from those differences played no meaningful role in the policy-making process.

This chapter challenges those assumptions. Through firsthand observations and field research on the ongoing, step-by-step process of decollectivization, and by comparing the responses of three different localities before a generally uniform outcome was attained, we can demonstrate with certainty that a locality's social, political, economic, and ecological context structures individual perceptions of state policy, and in the absence of state pressures, would determine the final policy outcome. We can also demonstrate which local variations had the greatest influence on local interests and attitudes towards decollectivization. Moreover, while it may be assumed that regional variations resulted in large part from the differing views of provincial elites towards the reform process, the diversity documented in this study occurred among villages in different counties or districts, but all within the same municipality. In the end, one can only imagine the true complexity of rural China and the enormous diversity that underlies the relatively uniform facade that China's leaders and many analysts try to impose on the countryside.

Therefore, three interrelated points form the central issues here. First is the question of the relationship among freedom of choice, bureaucratic coercion, and economic rationality. Did the local units studied here adopt these techniques for increasing labor accountability on their own initiative or under bureaucratic pressure? If the impetus for change came from the bottom up, farmers and local leaders[2] must have recognized the economic rationality of the policy before the central leaders attained consensus and officially sanctioned it. Moreover, local leadership was probably important in guiding farmers to adopt these changes. If implementation was due to pressure from above, middle-level bureaucrats enforced compliance either because local officials underestimated the policy's benefits or because they saw it as a threat to their own interests, or they imposed conformity to prove their political fealty, irrespective of the policy's utility to the specific locality.[3] If the latter interpretation is true, China again failed to learn from past errors.[4]

The second issue, the nature of the Chinese farmer, also relates to the proper locus of decision making for this policy. Farmers respond to the world based on their own economic interests.[5] Local leaders, by consulting with farmers, should have been best situated to determine which policies would maximize economic production, which was the goal of China's central leadership. Similarly, if local interests had been allowed to influence outcomes, different natural conditions and levels of economic development should have led localities to respond in dissimilar ways to opportunities to alter the collective system.

Finally, the leaders of the CCP have never really succeeded in resolving the conflict among rural households, the collective, and the needs of the state, and this period was no different. Rather than strike a balance among the three, the leadership chose to remove one actor, the collective, from the equation. But, as the state permitted individual interest to play a greater role in the rural economy, how did farmers respond to the increased freedom? Did they support the collective or did private interest propel them to dismantle the collective? Although by 1983 the result of the reforms had become obvious, this brief glimpse of rural China in transition helps us understand how farmers and cadres would have responded to these incentives had they been allowed to determine the outcomes that best suited their local interests.

The Local Setting

From January through July 1981, I carried out field research in three different areas of Jiangsu Province. I talked with local leaders and farmers about the methods they were adopting for increasing labor accountability and their attitudes toward them. Although all three sites are in the greater Nanjing Municipality, they differ enough in leadership, wealth, terrain, and cropping patterns so that comparing their different responses to various incentive systems provides valuable clues as to the appeal and liabilities of these systems throughout China. Table 3.1 sets out the major differences among the three units.

The decisions in these units concerning these incentive systems were based on political, psychological, environmental, economic, and technical factors. Politically, the attitudes of bureaucratic superiors and the authority local leaders had within their own unit shaped the adoption of new incentive systems. By rearranging labor organization and remuneration in the countryside, these accountability systems involved questions that had long generated political conflict between farmers and cadres. For local leaders, these risky political changes were less dangerous when their bureaucratic superiors supported the policy shifts, while the danger quotient increased if local leaders ignored the views of middle-level

Table 3.1

Major Characteristics of Three Research Sites in Jiangsu Province, 1980

Brigade	Distance from Nanjing (kms)	No. of Teams	No. of Villages	Major Crops	Per Capita Income (*RMB*)	Population	Farmland (hectares)	Land/ Labor Ratio	Terrain	Level of Mechanization (no. of tractors)
Mushuyuan	2	7	4	Vegetables	320	1,594	35.5	.06	Flat	17
Qingxiu	30	26	14	Rice, wheat	230	3,866	424.2	.37	Mixed	27
September First	50	8	8	Rice, wheat, cotton	120	1,824	114.3	.21	Hilly	9

Source: Information in this table was obtained by the author through interviews in China during the spring and summer of 1981.

officials. Finally, within each team or brigade, strong leaders imposed their own will, while weak brigade leaders allowed for more variety in implementation among the teams.

Psychologically, some farmers, fearing future flip-flops in agricultural policy, hesitated to invest energy in land that could suddenly revert to the collective. And local cadres, remembering the 1960s and 1970s when political rather than economic mistakes threatened their careers, decided that being "left" was safer than being "right" (*ning zuo wu you*). From a Maoist perspective, the stress on material incentives was clearly *rightist;* therefore, local cadres had to wonder if today's implementation could become tomorrow's rightist error. Given these farmers' and cadres' fears, some localities did not accept the new policy until authoritative statements emanated from the Central Committee in Beijing.

Environment, economics, and technology also influenced village decisions. Suburban units are usually rich and possess strong brigade economies. With these economic resources, which include capital, equipment, and access to employment in commune- and brigade-run enterprises, brigade leaders influenced team decisions in ways that their counterparts in poorer areas could not. Because suburban units also have less land per capita, incentive systems that sped up work were generally superfluous, but in hilly, more isolated regions, some farmers welcomed the new independence that came with "household production contracts" (*baochan daohu*).

Cropping patterns directly affected the choice of incentive systems. Vegetable production, with its numerous varieties, involves complicated accounting and organizational problems, creating disincentives for the introduction of individual quotas. Wet rice cultivation, particularly in hilly areas, requires complicated irrigation schedules and careful coordination among households. Under these conditions, rationality favored continued collective incentives. However, for cotton, for which output depends on handpicking, and for other dry-field crops that do not have irrigation problems, household or individual quotas could succeed; the only exception occurred during droughts. Thus, household contracts appeared first in areas more dependent on dry-field crops.

Still, local leaders' choices about incentive systems depended not only on local conditions, but on the special character of the leadership and economy of Jiangsu Province as a whole. Jiangsu Province probably sells more grain to the state than any other province in China.[6] Maintaining this high output needs continuous water projects. Jiangsu's rapidly developing brigade- and commune-run enterprises supported agriculture through the reinvestment of their industrial profits. Therefore, high levels of capital formation, necessary to establish collectively owned industries and finance water and field improvement projects, have played a crucial role in the enrichment of Jiangsu Province.

But many policies after the Third Plenum of December 1978 directly threatened the provincial leadership. Xu Jiatun, provincial party secretary until 1983, had built his reputation on Jiangsu's high grain output, both as the provincial officer responsible for agriculture in the early 1970s and as provincial party secretary. But restrictions on rural capital construction limited Xu's power to improve Jiangsu's irrigation system.[7] Distributing more money to the farmers decreased the funds available for expanding collectively owned enterprises and capital construction projects.[8] And the emphasis on economic crops threatened Xu, who had been praised by Hua Guofeng and Li Xiannian for enthusiastically "taking grain as the key link."[9] Both of them, and particularly Hua, reportedly had helped to elevate Xu to the post of first party secretary after Peng Zhong had moved to Shanghai.

Using individual and household quotas or contracts exacerbated these problems by altering the relationship among farmers, local leaders, and state officials. Mobilizing farmers for capital construction projects through contractual agreements would leave local units free to refuse to participate if projects were not to their benefit. Second, household or individual contracts would weaken the collective's ability to accumulate capital. Finally, surplus grain would fall under the control of teams and households threatening the province's continued high levels of grain sales.

Not surprisingly, Jiangsu Province lagged behind much of the country in establishing more individualized accountability systems. Only after Zhao Ziyang or Hu Yaobang criticized him and told him to repent for his "leftist errors" did Xu Jiatun return to Jiangsu Province and convene a provincial meeting to discuss the new policies. He is reported to have made a public "self-criticism" there. From then until shortly before the Sixth Plenum in June 1981, when he publicly lauded the successful implementation of household production quotas in northern Jiangsu, Xu Jiatun's name rarely appeared in the provincial press. Within this political context, lower level cadres, aware of the provincial opposition, probably felt little compulsion to change their incentive systems, particularly with regard to adopting more individualized ones.

Mushuyuan: A Rich Vegetable Brigade

Mushuyuan Brigade sits right outside the western gate of Nanjing. Comprised of four villages, it was Zijingshan Commune's model brigade and the wealthiest brigade in the commune. For seven years it grew only vegetables and no grain. Every year the brigade lost rich cropland to an ever-expanding city, and the brigade party secretary believed that in approximately twenty years the brigade would disappear. I did my research there in January and February of 1981, and returned occasionally until July of the same year.

This brigade played a greater role in the daily activities of its teams and team members than most brigades in China. Although a 1978 experiment in brigade accounting was undone a year later, in 1981, all machinery was still owned by the brigade. Over a third of the labor force worked in commune- and brigade-run enterprises. And for several years, income from these industries had surpassed the total agricultural income of the teams, comprising 62.7 percent of the brigade's total gross income in 1980. The brigade and commune had also underwritten a new sprinkler system, plastic tents, and other investments for agriculture, as well as a new old-age pension system.[10] Such extensive financial involvement probably created strong support for the brigade among its inhabitants.

This vegetable brigade was slow to change its incentive system. The teams adopted "task rates" in 1978 but only for a few activities; as of 1980, time rates were still used for most jobs. In 1980, the commune accountant advocated scoring work points after each day's labor ("flexible time rates" [*sigong huoping*]) to establish a closer link between quality of work and payment received. Team leaders, however, fearful that disagreements would arise daily, preferred to rank farmers once a month, if not once a year.

In 1980, in fact, one team still allowed farmers to rank themselves in open meetings (the Dazhai system of "self-assessment and public discussion") because he feared they would get angry if he set their work point values too low. When I asked him why he still used a system that the national government had rejected, he responded that changes were too troublesome. With much work and few laborers, time constraints made it simpler to let the farmers decide themselves. In fact, because each field laborer in this team *did* work far more land than farmers in any other team, the team leader probably was pressed for time.[11] But, in 1981, the brigade pressured him to adopt time rates, for which the team leader set the work point values, which finally expunged the last remnants of the leftist Dazhai system in this brigade.

In January 1981, a brigade official told me that all teams were going to shift to task rates. In one team I observed a freewheeling management committee meeting at which members discussed their personal preferences between time and task rates. Although four months earlier Central Document No. 75 had rejected time rates, men at this meeting argued vociferously for them. The women, on the other hand, strongly supported task rates. With time rates, the number of days worked, multiplied by relatively fixed work point values, determined the number of points earned each year. But, because work point values for women invariably were fixed below those for men, women preferred task rates, for which the task's value was fixed. Although women might work more slowly, they would have the opportunity to earn as much as men. Task rates, therefore, would restrict sexual discrimination,[12] unless women were consistently given less valuable jobs. Although team management committee members freely expressed their views, they could not affect the final decision. Their team leader was extremely strong willed and firmly held the reins of political control. During the Cultural Revolution he had led one faction that had usurped commune administration for a time. The day after the committee meeting, he told me that he had decided unilaterally to use task rates, not out of fairness to women but because people would work faster. Nonetheless, all other teams still paid people on a time rate basis.

While its incentive system for organizing and paying general field labor failed to keep pace with national policy, this brigade was far more flexible about the incentive system it used to raise vegetable seedlings that were subsequently transplanted into the fields. In 1978, it placed quotas on the agricultural inputs for the seedlings, and in 1979, soon after the Third Plenum sanctioned it, the brigade gave a bonus for meeting the quotas. The bonus, given to the one or two technical specialists each team had for raising vegetable sprouts, was based on the quality and quantity of sprouts raised. The brigade also had a technical team that produced sprouts not only for its own fields, but for other teams as well. The agricultural prosperity of the brigade depended heavily on all these technical specialists, which accounted for the brigade's readiness to give bonuses. As one brigade official remarked, "Things that have been good for the countryside, we begin to do early on."

The brigade wanted to make workers in all its enterprises more accountable for their work, but it had troubles in the brigade-run piggery. The female laborers there told me that they already worked hard enough. In addition, they feared accepting personal financial liability for each piglet that died. In their experience, one piglet died in almost every litter. Due to this opposition, the brigade, as of July 1981, had still not established a personal incentive system in the piggery.

Even as team leaders began contemplating a shift to task rates, brigade leaders began devising a new scheme. They had only alluded to it in January, but by March their proposal had taken shape. Two or three work groups within each team would work separately, and the total number of work points and the amount of money that the group could use for planting, raising, and harvesting specific crops would be fixed. Because any financial savings would revert to them, the groups would work harder and more frugally and would complete the tasks sooner. But, if the work groups failed to meet the input quotas, they would be fined. However, the brigade still would not give them a production quota. This method, called "long-term task rates" (*da duan bao gong*), first appeared in public in the *Nanjing Daily* in the late spring or early summer of 1981, when pressure on all units to link income to output was mounting. By adopting long-term task rates, local leaders could argue that they were improving labor accountability without instituting output quotas.

By July 1981, however, brigade officials said that, due to the strong propaganda campaign in the press and other undefined pressures that advocated linking income to output, the brigade would "link output to the individual" (*lian chan dao lao*) for all crops. Even though an accounting nightmare could arise, particularly because teams in the brigade no longer had accountants, the necessity of this move had become clear to the brigade after a May 20 article in the *People's Daily*.[13] One brigade official had already gone to Hangzhou and Shanghai to see how other prosperous brigades linked individual income and output. Commune officials concurred that pressure was intensifying and that people were a little afraid.

If you start any type of system of responsibility and then it doesn't work, well, okay. But if the weather is bad one year, they may shift to "household quotas." We don't like that here, so we are a little afraid of it.[14]

Due to high per capita income and a stable brigade economy, team and brigade leaders were comfortable using time rates. Nonetheless, they changed this local policy because of pressure from above. After Central Document No. 75 had been circulated in the winter of 1980-1981, leaders began the transition to task rates. And, although they were frightened of doing so, by July 1981, the brigade was preparing to cross the threshold and join other units across the country that were linking individual income to the quantity of crops produced.

Qingxiu: A Rich Grain Brigade

Qingxiu Brigade is situated in the southwest corner of Jiangning Commune, Jiangning County, thirty miles south of Nanjing. On the east it borders the Jiangning River, which flows directly to the larger Yangze River. Due to massive water conservation projects in the 1960s, most teams have had an abundant water supply. Grain production has been high, surpassing 15,000 kgs per hectare. According to the brigade secretary, every year it sold more grain per capita to the state than any other brigade in the province. Therefore, it benefited greatly from the 50 percent price increase in 1979 for above-quota grain sold to the state. In 1973, when he heard about its extensive land leveling projects, Xu Jiatun made the brigade a provincial model. Leadership had been relatively stable. After many years, the old brigade secretary became an official in a neighboring commune, and by 1981, the new secretary had managed the brigade firmly since 1975. I lived in this locality for fifteen days in June 1981.

As with the vegetable brigade, the role of this brigade in the economy of the teams was very large. Since 1978, the gross income of the brigade's five enterprises had equaled or surpassed the total agricultural income from the twenty-six teams. Including laborers in commune-run enterprises, over which the brigade had veto power, over a third of all laborers worked in collective industries. In 1981, factory workers in the brigade were still paid work points and their salaries were remitted to their respective teams for distribution among all members. These funds were crucial for maintaining the brigade's impressive per capita income of 230 *yuan,* the highest in the commune.[15]

All teams employed "task rates" *(bao gong)* for harvesting wheat and rice, and only during the 1968 Three Loyalties Campaign did they cease using them. At that time, teams also introduced the Dazhai system of "self-assessment and public discussion." Although people worked harder in the first year, these initial successes resulted from the "milieu of activism" generated by the political campaign, rather than from the particular incentive system.[16] According to one brigade official, teams returned to time and task rates in 1971 because

If you don't give people work points for a long time they don't work. In the end there was no benefit [from Dazhai work points], so we stopped in 1971. To start the policy the upper levels called a meeting. This was the commune. They had learned about it from the outside. When we stopped, we did it on our own. The whole brigade stopped. Production wasn't good, and the masses said they were working more but not getting more. They said that "Dazhai" work points had become *dagai* [approximate] work points.

In 1981, many production teams extended task rates to the work group within the team. Each group received work points, based on the area of land they worked that day, which were then redistributed to the individuals in the group based on time rates. A few units adjusted this procedure by daily evaluating each individual's work so that the quality of work directly affected income. The team leaders employed this method only for rapeseed because, if it is not well planted, it will die. Thus, the first link between income and output occurred for rapeseed cultivation. In fall 1980 the leader of the wealthiest team "linked output to the group" (*lian chan dao zu*) for two groups, with a 30 percent bonus/10 percent fine system. For two years, many seedlings had died, but with this method the 1981 harvest improved significantly. In 1982, he planned to give two groups output quotas for wet wheat and rice fields as well. Unlike many teams in the brigade which are in the hills, this team had flat land. Irrigating each group's wet fields would not cause problems.

Although his team was the richest in the brigade, the team leader, rather than conservatively avoid risk, responded as a "rational peasant,"[17] using his team's financial surplus to try out new ways to get even richer. For many years, this team had been the test point for all new seeds in the brigade. Although this, too, involved risks, the team benefited first when the strains were successful. The team leader's experiment with "group quotas" had already triggered a "demonstration effect." A neighboring team leader, related through marriage to this risk taker, knew of his successful experiment in rapeseed and told me that he would give "output contracts to each household" (*baochan daohu*) for rapeseed in fall 1981.

Nonetheless, most team leaders opposed the policy and argued that their team members were unhappy with the prospect of using it. The possibility of a fine frightened the peasants most. They felt that on their own they would be unable to meet quotas based on the high output per hectare achieved by the collective. The leader of another prosperous team expressed it this way:

> They're not willing. Now they have machines, so the work is lighter. . . . They don't mind more private plots, but if they "fix production" (*bao chan*) then they have a target they must meet. I don't want to do it either. I called a team meeting and told the farmers that anyone who wanted to work on their own could do so. . . . But no one wanted to do it. Now the output per hectare is high, and they would have to meet the output that the team gets.

The brigade's attitude toward this policy was unclear. One official told me that brigade leaders supported the policy, but the way it was introduced into the brigade left some doubts as to their true feelings. In March 1981, the county announced that poorer hilly areas could institute household production quotas.[18] However, according to some informants, as they returned from this meeting brigade officials confronted farmers on the street, asking them if they wanted to work the land on their own, and using the highly explosive term, *dan gan*.[19] One person said, "they blew a wind" (*gua yige feng*), implying that brigade officials triggered a spontaneous popular reaction. In most cases, it was fear. When the team leaders were called together and invited to try out the policy, there were no takers. Next, when the poorest team in the hills was offered the chance to experiment with individual quotas for wet rice, it resisted. Brigade officials told me that only 10 percent of the people supported household farming.[20] Of the remaining 90 percent, 60 percent opposed it passively and 30 percent opposed it totally. "They curse it," they said. "These people either had many family members working in collective enterprises or were weak laborers."

Although Western analysts assume that all farmers prefer private farming, I found serious hostility toward any prospects of this transition. I first talked with a farmer in a team in which, due to the increase in the number of farmers working in brigade factories, per capita income had not dropped from 1979 to 1980. His family had three field laborers and two factory workers, but he claimed to have an average income for the team. I asked him the one request he would have for an investigation group from the Party Central Committee. His preferred financial situation notwithstanding, the frankness of his answer was rather surprising.

> Before we were so poor and now the economic work is done well. The new policy is a backward retreat. If you divide the land you will have "polarization" (*liang ji fen hua*). We will have the return of the landlords and capitalists. Collective socialism is good. Chairman Mao is good. We do not want to move off Chairman Mao's road. The collective is done well. If you divide the land to the household, how will we use the machinery? If you divide the land to the household then the team leader will have no power and the place will be chaotic. Even the households with five laborers do not want to divide the land.

His attitude was corroborated by a villager in another team. Due to the brigade's liberal policy of the past two years on opening barren land as private plots, he farmed as much land in 1981 as he had before land reform. Because his relatively stable income from the collective was supplemented by his private plot, he opposed dividing the collective fields. Of interest, he also extolled "Chairman Mao's socialist line." A farmer in yet a third team, who also had greatly expanded his private plot, preferred collective farming because it was easier simply to work where and when they told him to.[21]

One team leader attributed the farmers' enthusiasm for the collective to the brigade enterprises.

The farmers here work hard. They do their work quickly. If I give them one day to do the work, they do it in half a day. So, if the people want to go work in their private plots, they can. But most prefer to work on the collective fields. This year our income from sidelines increased by 7,000 *yuan,* mostly due to the fact that we sent more people to the brigade enterprises. Last year our team had twenty-one people in the factories and now we have sixteen more. The collective income will increase and the farmers know this. They can calculate. They know the collective income will increase.

The issue of mechanization, which surfaces in two of the above quotations, also explains the farmers' antipathy toward the new policies. In 1981, after this brigade became a test point for mechanized farming, the County Agricultural Mechanization Bureau donated ten twelve-horsepower tractors. The brigade had already purchased fifteen tractors, so all twenty-six teams now had at least one twelve-horsepower tractor. In this brigade, which was the only place I visited where plowing was done primarily by tractor, tilling land by hand was hardly an enticing prospect.

Commune officials agreed with the farmers and the brigade officials.

At present, output in our commune is very high for the county. Our technical level is also high. Our rice output is especially high. So, on this basis, we recently began to say that if the masses want production quotas to the household or the labor power it could affect per capita output. But the masses in the whole commune are not willing to have production quotas to the household or the laborer for wet fields. They do not have this desire. They still want to do it on the same basis and in that way increase production and mechanization.

Nonetheless, the commune permitted one brigade which grew cotton and wheat in dry fields to establish household quotas. The brigade had never changed these fields into paddy, and with the restrictions on large-scale field construction, output could be increased only by adopting the new incentive systems.[22]

As with most of Jiangsu Province, Qingxiu Brigade was not at the forefront of organizational change. Hesitancy by provincial officials was reinforced by resistance to household quotas by commune and probably brigade leaders as well. The high level of technology, the high grain output (which farmers felt they could not match privately), and collective enterprises that supported per capita income in the teams made the farmers fear changes in the well-established collective system. In addition, larger private plots and increased sideline incomes made the incentives in the household quota system less enticing. Nonetheless, the most prosperous team was willing to risk experimenting with new incentive systems. These changes occurred first for rapeseed, a dry-field crop involving careful planting but not complicated irrigation procedures.

September First: An Average, Hilly Brigade

The September First Brigade lies in Tangquan Commune, Jiangpu County, on the north side of the Yangze River. Although located in Nanjing Municipality, it borders the Qu River, with Qu County in Anhui Province on the other side. Its per capita income of 120 *yuan* was 50 percent higher than the national average in 1980, but the September First Brigade was the poorest brigade in the commune. Disparities within the brigade were also significant; two of its eight teams were short of arable land and received a state grain supplement. Farmers in these teams grew grain in their private plots to avoid purchasing it at state shops. Although the irrigation system was adequate, half the land in some teams could grow only dry-field crops.

Leadership in the brigade had not been outstanding. Brigade officials had lacked the prestige and authority of the leaders in the two brigades discussed above. While I was there for a month from April to May 1981, one vice brigade secretary, who was illiterate, retired. His replacement, a young ex-army officer who had led one team for three years, was selected to add vitality to the leadership ranks.

Economically, the brigade's impact on the production teams was far less significant than in the two brigades discussed previously. The only brigade-run enterprise, a pig-bristle factory, was donated by the commune in 1975 because this brigade alone, of thirteen in the commune, had no factory. The teams had purchased almost all their own machinery; the county had supplied two tractors to the poorest teams. And, in 1976-1977, when the factory paid the farmers work points, it had remitted less than half as much to the respective teams as in Qingxiu, the model grain brigade. In 1981, due to low monthly wages, few farmers sought employment in the factory, preferring to work in the fields or outside the collective. Only 13 percent of the brigade's total labor force, mostly young women, the handicapped, and the weaker males, worked in the factory. This economic ineffectiveness led one team leader to refer to the brigade as "an empty shell."

Throughout much of the surrounding countryside, the farmers responded quickly to the opportunities to farm on an individual or household quota basis. In spring 1978, as agricultural policy was just beginning to change but still more than half a year before the Third Plenum, thirty-nine of the ninety-three teams in the commune established household production quotas for cotton. Although the county tried to prevent this, commune officials decided not to tell the brigade leaders of the criticism they had received for permitting these changes. "If I had said anything to the brigades, they would have stopped. So, I simply kept quiet," commented one official. And, in 1979, when the county remained silent, the scope of household quotas increased.

In early 1980, antagonism toward household quotas intensified in Jiangsu Province. City and county governments intervened, demanding that local units stop using individual incentive systems for crop production that linked income to output. Only "specialized fixed tasks" (*zhuanye chengbao*) were acceptable. This time commune officials passed on the instructions, albeit they still suggested that units already having production quotas for groups at the sub-team level continue to use them. Household quotas, however, had to be discontinued. However, by fall 1980, almost all the commune's teams were using household quotas for cotton and rapeseed, both dry-field crops. And, after the *People's Daily* editorial of March 2, 1981, which for the first time supported individual production quotas for wet fields in average income areas,[23] six of the commune's poorest teams decided to experiment with this policy. Forty-seven teams agreed to shift to group quotas for wet fields, while the remaining forty stuck with task rates. As policy options expanded, people and leaders in this locality willingly partook of the new innovations.

Farmers in Jiangsu Province began to use household quotas in 1978, because of this area's proximity to Anhui Province, which was one of the first provinces after Mao's death and the fall of the "Gang of Four" in 1976 to experiment with these new incentive systems. News from Anhui travels quickly due to livestock marketing across the provincial border and extensive personal ties.

The farmers and leaders in the September First Brigade, however, did not respond as quickly. In 1978, they still planted as a team using task rates, and in 1979, only four of eight teams had household quotas for cotton. Under pressure in 1980, the brigade retreated; three teams followed the city's guidelines, using special contracts for raising cotton, but the rest cultivated the cotton fields collectively.[24] According to commune officials, this brigade, compared with others in the commune, panicked in 1980 and overreacted to the outside pressures. Only in 1981, after the political environment sanctioned it, did the brigade uniformly adopt household quotas for rapeseed and cotton.

Even weak leadership, which made the brigade vulnerable to external political pressures, is inadequate to explain its slow response. Because this brigade had the lowest per capita income in the commune, farmers here should have favored these incentive systems in 1978, particularly since agricultural output and per capita income had dropped in 1977. They knew of the successes across the provincial border. Moreover, unlike the two other brigades where the wealth of the collective caused farmers to resist the new accountability systems, the effect of this hilly brigade's economy was less significant. Changes in the collective system should not have frightened the farmers. Nonetheless, technical problems and mistrust of the party's future policies were at work in this brigade. In addition, some farmers were more interested in increasing sideline income than collective agricultural output.

For twenty-five years, agricultural policy in this area had been volatile. During the Great Leap Forward, the commune collectivized and sold to the state private land that the farmers had planted with trees just a few years earlier. During the 1968 Three Loyalties Campaign farmers lost their private plots for three years. In 1975 and 1976, responding to political pressures from a leftist county party secretary, local officials uprooted crops in some private plots. And in 1980, commune leaders again tried to eradicate private tree-seedling cultivation.[25] The swiftness with which the incentive systems were introduced in this locality probably made the farmers cautious. According to the leader of one team,

> The farmers still do not trust things. At the meetings they ask me how long the policies will last. One year? Two years? Five years? It's important for household quotas because if farmers trust you and the policy, they'll exert more energy and will plant deeper. In this way, in dry seasons the roots will be deep and they'll get more water. Also, the wind won't blow them down. In the wet season, if the roots are deeper they won't get waterlogged.

The technical problem of irrigating uneven wet fields also played a role. In a December 1980 meeting, the county announced Central Document No. 75. After brigade officials passed down this report to their teams, one team prepared to introduce group quotas for wet rice cultivation. However, after determining the precise payment system to employ, the team hesitated. Its paddy fields, created by leveling hilly land, were uneven in height, and with only one portable pump capable of raising water six feet, some fields got water later than others. Conflicts that arose during the planning sessions convinced the team leader that the problems exceeded the potential benefits. Therefore, the team planted the rice as a village with task rates. Another team also considered using group quotas for their wet fields in 1981, but because it had the poorest water supply in the brigade, a shortage of water would have caused the groups to fight there as well.[26]

Another technical problem was the inexperience of some young farmers. If rice seedlings are raised in densely packed clusters, great care is necessary when digging them up, separating them, and replanting them in neat rows within the paddy fields. Because they lacked these skills, young people would not have gotten a good harvest and might have faced a fine. For this reason, the brigade opposed household quotas for wet fields.

Other examples of hesitancy and risk avoidance occurred in the brigade. In 1979, the wealthiest team rejected household quotas and used only group quotas for cotton because, with task rates its 1978 cotton production had surpassed all teams in the brigade. At the other extreme, the poorest team in the brigade had grown accustomed to being poor and receiving state assistance. After losing ten hectares of land during the Great Leap Forward to the building of the commune reservoir, it could not grow enough grain to feed its villagers. Since 1963, it had relied on state grain subsidies. In line with 1981 policy, whereby farmers in teams relying on the *three supports*[27] were permitted to farm without any quotas under "household contracts with full responsibility" (*da baogan*), the commune offered this opportunity to this poor team.[28] But, in spring 1981, after discussions with the farmers, the team leader decided not to do it. His explanation?

> Most people oppose the policy because there would be no collective economy. People fear "total responsibility" (*da baogan*). They like the collective

Table 3.2

Land/Labor Ratios, September First Brigade, 1979

Team Number	1	2	3	4	5	6	7	8
Land/labor ratio (hectares)	.25	.23	.31	.24	.25	.11	.12	.20
Adopted household quotas for cotton	No	No	Yes	Yes	Yes	Yes	No	No

Source: Information in this table was obtained by the author through interviews with members of the September First Brigade during April 1981.

method [household quotas] because they get fertilizer, insecticide, and thirty-five points for managing the fields, all from the team. If they get sick and can't plant, the team plants for them. Also, they will still get their grain ration. They will lose their work points but they can borrow money to buy their share of "collective grain" (*gong liang*), and pay back the money when they can.

With total responsibility they would probably produce enough grain to feed themselves, but it would obviate state support. The insecurity of freedom can be a frightening experience, especially when one is accustomed to being coddled by the state. As a result, the team rejected all policies linking income to output until 1981, and then accepted them only for cotton and rapeseed.

Private sidelines might have affected the adoption of household quotas, because after 1977 the number of families raising tree seedlings increased greatly. Farmers drawing out their personal capital to invest in tree-seedling cultivation might hesitate to accept household quotas due to the potential fines. But in spring 1979, when four teams decided to plant cotton on a household quota basis, the number of households raising tree seedlings in these teams also increased, often significantly. Perhaps the situation was reversed: farmers planning to invest in tree seedlings hoped for a bonus to help pay off their new investments. In addition, due to low collective agricultural output, farmers here may not have feared the fine.

Land/labor ratios could play a role in the decision on incentive systems, but the fit is not good (Table 3.2). Undoubtedly, team 3 needed a remuneration system that quickened the pace of work, but in 1980 it reverted to collective labor and not group quotas. Also, based on these ratios, why did team 6 adopt household quotas and team 7 did not?

The question of leadership explains some of these anomalies. The strongest leaders were in teams 2, 4, 5, and 6. Lineage conflicts made team 8 impossible to run, while in team 7, the old leader stayed in office only because no one else was willing to manage this poor village. Similarly, leadership had been weak in team 1. Many people told me that the team leader, often criticized as a "rightist," feared the political bureaucracy. He was precisely the type of leader least likely to experiment with a new incentive system. Last, team 3 did not adopt any quota system in 1980 due to a leadership change. Therefore, only teams with strong leaders were willing or able to adopt household quotas.

Also, the two teams (7 and 8) most dependent on sideline occupations (compared with crop production) for their collective income were the slowest to adopt new accountability system (Table 3.3). Teams 7 and 8 both had links with outside units, such as construction and forestry companies, and sent excess laborers to work there. The change since the 1978 Third Plenum that interested them most was undoubtedly the new liberal policy on sidelines. Only after Central Document No. 75 made the incentive systems official policy did these two teams finally adopt household quotas for rapeseed and cotton.

Compared with the other two brigades studied, the variations among teams in this hilly brigade and the yearly shifts within teams are striking. The brigade leadership reacted swiftly to external intervention and, in the absence of those pressures, each unit's or leader's characteristics determined the response to the incentive system. And, because of large interteam variations, each team's policy was rather different.

Certain trends, however, continued. Major innovations occurred first with dry-field crops. Technical complications, inherent in irrigating paddy fields in hilly areas, again caused hesitation in establishing household or group quotas. And once more, farmers were nervous about the new changes. Of interest, however, the feebleness of the collective did not increase popular support for its further weakening. For farmers in the September First Brigade, the subsistence guaranteed by the state and the collective provided a welcome base from which they could increase their household sideline income.

Conclusion

Although in many localities the new incentives were quite popular, not all farmers warmly welcomed these adjustments to the collective system. Opposition lay in wealthier, more developed units, where farmers knew that their household's prosperity was intertwined with a strong collective. Even as national leaders downplayed mechanization, farmers in areas where machine use was practical still believed that this was one way they could escape the drudgery of agricultural labor. Ironically, these were the units that in the 1960s and 1970s learned well from Dazhai: They had built extensive irrigation systems, had leveled fields, and had sacrificed immediate aggrandizement to speed up capital formation and build strong collectives. In 1981, farmers in these areas were hostile to policies that threatened those hard-earned gains.

Cropping patterns and terrain consistently affected policy implementation. In both grain-producing brigades, the first breakthrough in household quotas occurred in dry fields, and even after leaders overcame political fears, conflicts over irrigating paddy fields still caused teams to hesitate. Also, because vegetable-

Table 3.3

Ratio of Collective Profits Derived from Sidelines, September First Brigade, 1973–1980

	1973	1974	1975	1976	1977	1978	1979	1980	Average
Team 7	.62	.53	.67	.89	.54	.61	.62	.60	.61
Team 8	.40	.43	.58	.50	.62	.83	.62	.75	.59
Average of other six teams	.36	.33	.35	.23	.35	.37	.37	.29	.33

Source: Information in this table was obtained by the author through interviews with members of the September First Brigade during April 1981.

producing units cultivate a wide variety of crops, leaders there eschewed individual quotas as long as possible. Psychological factors, too, were important, but farmers and local leaders in the hilly brigade mistrusted the permanency of the changes and feared future policy shifts much more; policy there had been more unstable and unpredictable.[29]

Twice the bureaucracy intervened in the local decisions. Before the publication of Central Document No. 75 in September 1980, provincial, municipal, and county officials sought to prevent experimentation with incentive systems linking income to output, even if they could help agricultural production. Units with weak leaders succumbed swiftly to these bureaucratic interventions. But for leaders of wealthy units who themselves opposed the changes, the middle-level hostility to the policy increased their resolve to persist in their own opposition.

After September 1980, however, central policy shifted. As direction from Beijing intensified and became more specific, some units that preferred to move slowly found themselves under pressure to introduce new incentive systems quickly. Seeing that the tide had changed, middle-level bureaucrats swung full circle and began demanding policy conformity, oblivious again to the issue of local independence and economic rationality.

Finally, major problems resulted from the concomitant implementation of broad policy changes that crisscrossed a large spectrum of issue areas. The unintended consequences of one policy undermined the goals of another. This fact may explain why policy shifts in China, which often have been all-encompassing, have quickly run into unexpected complications. The leaders in Beijing may have correctly assumed that farmers would respond to these new incentives. However, liberalization in other spheres, such as the expansion of private plots, resurrection of rural trade fairs, and increased freedom to pursue household and collective sidelines, in the short run may have made this new policy less attractive. The incentives from the former sectors involved fewer risks and greater opportunities for increasing household incomes than the inducements built into these accountability systems, particularly those that involved the meeting of a production quota. Therefore, more rapid and voluntary implementation of household, group, and individual quotas should have occurred in areas with few avenues for increasing private or collective sidelines. However, when farmers were able to get rich by methods other than laboring in collective fields, it should not have been surprising to find that they did not warmly welcome these new incentive systems.

Notes

1. One marvelous portrait of the silence in the countryside engendered by political campaigns is Liu Binyan, "Sound Is Better than Silence," in Perry Link, ed., *People or Monsters?* (Bloomington: Indiana University Press, 1983), pp. 98–137.
2. The term "local leaders" refers to team and brigade officials who differ from mid-

dle-level cadres at the commune, county, district, and provincial levels, because they are not state-salaried officials. Their incomes depend directly on the production levels in the village or villages they manage.

3. Jonathan Unger, "The Decollectivization of the Chinese Countryside: A Survey of Twenty-Eight Villages," *Pacific Affairs,* no. 58 (Winter 1985–1986).

4. This phenomenon, called "one knife to cut all" (*yi dao qie*), was regularly criticized after the Third Plenum of December 1978. During the Movement to Learn from Dazhai in Agriculture many localities, with natural conditions differing greatly from Dazhai's, still had to do things the way Dazhai did.

5. See Victor Nee, "Peasant Household Individualism," and Jonathan Unger, "Remuneration, Ideology, and Personal Interests in a Chinese Village, 1960–1980," in William L. Parish, ed., *Chinese Rural Development: The Great Transformation* (Armonk, N.Y.: M.E. Sharpe, 1985).

6. According to an assumed model of the interregional movement of grain, Jiangsu Province has the largest surplus, with Heilongjiang Province next. See Japan Economic and Trade Research Organization (JETRO), *China Newsletter* 34 (September–October 1981): 16.

7. During a visit to the Ministry of Water Conservation in Beijing in early 1981, I was told that half the staff was busy deciding which projects to cancel. Jiangsu Province took a public position against cutbacks on water conservation projects in an article in Red Flag (*Hongqi*) magazine, the Communist Party's leading journal. In that article, the authors attributed Jiangsu's prosperity to continued improvements in the irrigation system and stressed that, unlike other provinces, Jiangsu's large projects had been well managed and not wasteful. See "An Investigation in Jiangsu," *Hongqi,* April 1980.

8. The movement to "lighten the peasants' burden," part of the "Xiangxiang experience" propagated by a central document in summer 1978, signaled this change. See *People's Daily,* July 5, 1978, p. 1.

9. Much of this information on Xu Jiatun was obtained from personal conversations with well-connected Chinese in Nanjing.

10. Begun in 1981, this system allowed women to retire at age fifty-five and men at age sixty, giving them .80 *yuan* per month for each year worked. Thus, a villager who worked for twenty years received sixteen *yuan* per month.

11. For 1980, the average land/labor ratio for the brigade was .06 hectares per person, and the standard deviation of all the teams was .017. Therefore, the land/labor ratio for this team of .09, the highest in the brigade and almost two standard deviations from the brigade mean, indicates that the difference between this team and the others was considerable.

12. A commune official told me that, although this was official commune policy, as of January 1981, only 20 percent of the teams were giving women equal pay for equal work, implying that the vast majority of teams in the commune still used time rates.

13. See "Time To Consider 800 Million Farmers," *People's Daily,* May 20, 1981, p. 1.

14. Interview with commune official, Nanjing, July 1981.

15. From 1979 to 1980, average agricultural income of all teams dropped 33 percent, but per capita income decreased by only 4.8 percent. This occurred because, in the same period, the average increase in team industrial income, which was derived almost totally from these remitted salaries, was 37.5 percent. To demonstrate the importance of these factory jobs for the high standard of living in Qingxiu Brigade, I regressed the percentage change in industrial income, the percentage change in agricultural income, and the percentage change in population, all for 1979-1980, on the percentage change in per capita income from 1979 to 1980. I did this for all twenty-six production teams in the brigade. These three independent variables explain a great deal of the variation in the change in per

capita income (R^2 = .594). While the influence of agriculture on per capita income remains most important, with a standardized least squares coefficient of .725, industrial income also had a great effect on per capita income in each team. Its standardized least squares coefficient was .560. Without these factory jobs, all of the farmers would have been significantly poorer. While results were significant at the .01 level for both these variables, the result was not significant for population change.

16. See Jonathan Unger, "Collective Incentives in the Chinese Countryside: Lessons from Chen Village," *World Development* 6 (1978): 583-601.

17. Samuel L. Popkin, *The Rational Peasant* (Berkeley: University of California Press, 1979).

18. This position meshes more with the political line advocated in the March 2, 1981, editorial in the *People's Daily* than with Central Document No. 75 of fall 1980, because the poor, hilly areas in Jiangning County were still twice as prosperous as the national average. They did not fit the criterion of "poor" units as outlined in Central Document No. 75.

19. In the Chinese communist lexicon, *dan gan* refers to the private farming that was criticized in the 1960s by Mao.

20. When I accused them of triggering opposition by offering "individual" rather than "group" quotas, which given the financial level of the team seemed inappropriate, they explained that this team had a history of factionalism. The work groups would have divided on factional lines, creating endless and bitter conflicts over water and machinery.

21. The party secretary of a brigade at my third research site liked the new incentive systems because they helped overcome precisely this attitude. I translated a little ditty from the 1960s that for me reflects this problem: "When the bell rings, begin your task./ Questions on the job? The team leader you can ask./ After work, go home/ and just relax."

22. They had planned to transform the sandy soil into paddy to increase the commune's total grain production. However, in April 1979, when the Third Plenum documents were presented for discussion, the county stressed that "natural conditions must be respected" (*yin di zhi yi*). The commune canceled its plans for changing the fields. Then, in fall 1980, after the drafting of Central Document No. 75, the commune let the brigade establish household quotas.

23. See "Summarize Experiences, Improve and Stabilize the Agricultural System of Responsibility," *People's Daily,* March 2, 1981, p. 1.

24. Limiting contracts to sidelines did not really end the use of household contracts for cotton. In 1980, under specialized contracts, individuals accepted responsibility for meeting quotas and received bonuses for surpassing those quotas. In form they stopped household quotas, but in reality, by using specialized contracts, individuals within households still contracted to produce cotton under an agreement that linked their remuneration to output. Policy evasion at the local level in China is often based on the difference between formalistically implementing a policy and really doing it. See David Zweig, *Agrarian Radicalism in China, 1968-1981* (Cambridge: Harvard University Press, 1989), pp. 91–97.

25. See chapter 4 of this book.

26. Liuhe County in Nanjing Municipality, the northern region which is quite poor, used group and household quotas for wet fields in spring 1981. In April and May, however, after the area suffered a drought, *Nanjing Daily* reported that farmers, work groups, and collectives all battled over water.

27. The "three supports" refers to stale grain for eating, state loans for production, and state aid for living expenses.

28. Even though there were no quotas, farmers were still accountable for meeting the State agricultural tax and for making small payments to the collective welfare fund. In

most cases, however, the state tax was already waived in these poorer localities. For an analysis of these contracts, see Frederick W. Crook, "The 'Baogan Daohu' Incentive System: Translation and Analysis of a Model Contract," *China Quarterly,* no. 102 (1985): 291–303.

29. One farmer, who with his brother and brother-in-law made over 5,000 *yuan* raising tree seedlings in 1980, admitted that he would not be surprised if he were again criticized. He had simply decided to make as much money as he could as quickly as possible. For this reason, he had stopped working on the collective. When Zhang Jingfu, first party secretary of Anhui Province, discovered during a rural investigation that Anhui farmers still feared future changes, he announced that the Central Party Committee had no thoughts of making farmers change. "The length of time we had set will not change. Before we had set a three-year limit. But, if the farmers do not want to change, we will not ask them to change. Only if the farmers ask for change can it then be changed." See *People's Daily,* June 9, 1981, p. 4. By 1984, Central Document No. 1 on agriculture announced that contracted land would not change for fifteen years. See *People's Daily,* June 10, 1984, p. 1.

Part II

Conflicts, Norms, and the Search for New Institutions

4

Prosperity and Conflict in Post-Mao Rural China

In 1980, the *People's Daily* reported that 200 million Chinese farmers were living below the poverty line, while in 1982 Vice Premier Wan Li admitted that "for many years in the past, more than 150 million farmers had not solved the problem of not having enough to eat."[1] To enrich the rural economy, Party leaders established new normative guidelines that legitimized the private pursuit of household prosperity. The new policy, highlighted by the phrase, "permit some farmers to get rich first" (*rang yixie nongmin xian fuqilai*), allowed households that were more industrious and innovative and, of course, had better personal and economic ties to use their skills, personal relationships, excess labor power, and comparative advantages to accrue wealth quickly.

The search for rural prosperity has not come without costs. Increased competition over the inputs and outputs of rural production has generated conflicts and "antisocial" behavior in rural China. During the 1960s and 1970s, the collective and the state controlled the inputs—labor, machinery, fertilizer, water—and possessed a monopoly on the outputs—crops and the goods of brigade and commune factories. The collective had no local competition, while the state used taxes and prices to expropriate its share of the goods produced. The local state also suppressed most spontaneous interpersonal conflict, relying on state-led violence to maintain its control. Today, as rural China undergoes a major shift from plan to market, the state and collective have tried to ensure that the newly created wealth falls into their coffers. But the legitimization of the household's expanded economic role and its usurpation of economic activities previously monopolized by the collective have generated new conflicts between households and among households, the collective, and the state.

National Policy and the Search for Household Prosperity

Chinese elites have expressed three divergent tendencies toward the role of household sidelines in China's rural development: radical, bureaucratic, and marketeer perspectives.[2] During the late 1960s and most of the 1970s, radical elites opposed all private economic activity on ideological grounds, fearful that it would lead to the *revanche* of capitalism. For them, household sidelines were the "tail of capitalism," which undermined the transition to higher stages of social- ism, and communism by reinforcing the farmers' "petty bourgeois" mentality and providing a breeding ground for a new class of rural exploiters.[3]

The bureaucratic elite's primary goal of plan fulfillment and extraction of society's resources by the state depends heavily on the administrative allocation of resources. They see local state and collective economic organizations as their most reliable allies in the search for economic stability, prosperity, and control.[4] Although they see the private sector as a "necessary adjunct to the planned economy," bureaucratic elites quickly demand restrictions on private economic activity when it undermines the plan, threatens the role of local state agencies, or creates rural instability.

Finally, the market line supports the commercialization of Chinese agriculture and the household's primary role as commodity producer in rural areas. Marke- teers advocate a "quasi-rich peasant rural economy" that relies on the wealthy to pull the poor out of the quagmire of poverty.[5] Since 1978, they have promul- gated a series of central party documents on agriculture,[6] the latest of which, Central Documents No. 1 of 1983 and 1984, represented a wholesale commit- ment to developing commercialized farming with individual households serving as the growing, processing, transporting and marketing units.[7] These reforms often place households in direct conflict with state and collective agencies, as well as local party officials, and attack the interests of the bureaucratic line, at both the national and local levels.

Strategies of Conflict over Household Prosperity

The responses of local cadres and rural households to the new economic oppor- tunities vary. While some farmers and cadres resist these reforms, others move quickly to get rich through their own labor, by managing the labor of others, or by expropriating wealth from wealthy households. These three responses to the opportunity for household prosperity may be categorized as (1) protectionist, (2) entrepreneurial, and (3) exploitative strategies.

Protectionist cadres and villagers have tried to prevent private household economic development in their localities. Some are motivated by ideological predilections, fearing capitalist restoration and increased "class polarization" in the rural areas.[8] Leftist ideology remains quite potent among some rural cadres.[9] Land-reform cadres, now working at the county level, as well as "Cultural Revo- lution" cadres, are likely to fear the return of "class polarization."[10] Some farmers may be concerned that they will not get their share of the limited pie;[11] if new opportunities allow some people to prosper, others, in this case the farmers themselves, may lose. Labor-weak households or lazy villagers who eschew sideline labor may favor restrictions to ensure that others cannot get rich.[12] Farmers in places where few economic opportunities exist, and those who rely on the collective's welfare net or support the collective for economic reasons, may favor restricting the growth of the household sector.[13] This local tendency reflects the egalitarian nature of the Chinese farmer and the moral economy interpretation of villager behavior.[14]

Some cadres implement protectionist strategies less from ideological predilections and more for economic or political reasons, such as fears of "rightist" labels. After years of policy fluctuations, rural cadres are already anticipating a "leftist" policy shift.[15] As soon as the Central Committee publishes one directive attacking economic crimes, cadres overreact, suppressing all entrepreneurial activity.[16] No doubt, some oppose these reforms because they weaken the power of the production team leader.[17] Finally, some cadres fear the economic competition of private entrepreneurs.[18]

The entrepreneurial strategy for increasing household income involves actively pursuing the private road to prosperity.[19] These entrepreneurs have become "specialized households," signing contracts to meet their village's agricultural, industrial, commercial or sideline quotas. Their total income often depends on fulfilling these contracts, and if they have invested their own funds, rather than simply privatizing the collective's property, they have taken major risks to advance the welfare of their families.[20] This local entrepreneurial strategy reflects the marketeer tendency at the national level.

A second entrepreneurial strategy involves cadres using their economic and political authority to expand collective wealth. Strong collectivist norms, reinforced by the local governments' important welfare functions, facilitate efforts by local officials, particularly in localities with a modicum of collective property, to assert the collective's right to expand its property base. As we saw in chapter 1, members of strong collectives, who benefited from the redistributive capabilities of local governments, resisted decollectivization, fearing the loss of public goods. In addition, as we will see below, even where collectives were not strong, cadres could invoke the collective's authority to expand its share of a burgeoning economy. Yet, even as cadres use collective resources to increase the delivery of public goods, they also use their control over the distribution of resources and labor to improve their own standard of living. In fact, their ability to use collective resources to expand their personal wealth and power gives them a strong incentive to adopt a more collectivist entrepreneurial strategy. Nevertheless, because the focus in this chapter is more on the commercialization of agriculture, rather than on the expansion of rural industry, we focus more on the many cadres who set out on their own and tried to translate their political authority into individual economic advantage.[21]

According to one study that was widely reported inside and outside China, 43 percent of specialized households in one county were currently brigade and team cadres or ex-cadres, who, according to the report, responded quickly because of managerial skills.[22] Probably interpersonal ties established while they were in power were more important, because these connections gave them preferred access to resources and marketing outlets. The second group, comprising 42 percent of specialized households, was made up of urban-educated rural youths and demobilized soldiers who had developed special skills in the army. All had lower–middle school education or better. Another 9 percent were skilled craftsmen, while another 5 percent had good managerial skills, although, because they were targets of the radical repression of the private economy in the 1960s and 1970s, they had not used them. Finally, less than 1 percent had "historical problems"; they may have been peddlers, "rich peasants," landlords, petty capitalists, or old nationalist officials.

Of note, with 43 percent of these specialized households current or former cadres, and another 42 percent potential future cadres, 85 percent of the new wealthy villagers in this county were candidates to become rural cadres under the Maoist collective system; now they had become entrepreneurs. Power and education have remained highly correlated with wealth under the new rural order. Second, only 6 percent of specialized households suffered repression during the radical era, suggesting that the other 94 percent had avoided private economic endeavors at that time. Third, that Wan Li chose as an example a county where many cadres or prospective cadres had become wealthy entrepreneurs suggests that the Beijing leadership still needed to persuade local officials to end their resistance, stop seeing commercialization as a zero-sum game, and get on board the prosperity train themselves.

The third, or exploitative, strategy has occurred when some villagers and cadres, recognizing that they cannot stop the reforms, siphon off resources produced by entrepreneurs.[23] Today, dwindling collective accumulation funds, which erode cadre income supplements, cause officials to blackmail or extort money from the newly prosperous villagers.[24] Some state or commune officials have imposed unauthorized taxes to get their share of the entrepreneurs' new products.[25] These activities prompted the Public Security Bureau to put out a directive attacking extortion of wealthy villagers by local officials and their rural neighbors.[26]

Some villagers, jealous of their neighbors' prosperity, shame or frighten the wealthy neighbors into parting with some of their income. According to Xu Jiatun, former first party secretary of Jiangsu Province:

> There is a jealous tendency prevalent now in society. Some people are jealous when they see others become rich; those who have become rich also fear being envied by other people.[27]

Jealous villagers spread rumors that those who become conspicuously wealthy will be accused of economic crimes.[28] Entrepreneurs parry this jealousy by washing others' clothes for free in their new washing machines, holding banquets as a means of sharing their wealth, similar to Native American potlatch celebrations, building cultural centers or schools, and in some cases giving loans to neighbors which they know will never be repaid.[29] The *People's Daily* "Commentator," June 9, 1984, compared this situation to the time when rural armies also advocated "robbing from the rich to help the poor."

The Case Study: Politics of Rural Prosperity in Red Flag Commune

Protectionist, entrepreneurial, and exploitative strategies that were at work in the late 1970s undermined the pursuit of household prosperity and generated conflicts in localities where the commercialization of agriculture policy was first promoted.[30] The events traced in this case study are both a preview and microcosm of the dilemma China faces as it increases the household's role in the search for rural development and prosperity.

Policy Fluctuations: The Historical Setting

All the oscillations in policy that have been the hallmark of China's agricultural decision making affected Red Flag Commune.[31] Located about 60 kilometers from a major Jiangsu Province city, the commune's per capita income was above average; but it was not a prosperous commune. In the early 1960s, famine struck this commune in the wake of the Great Leap Forward, but very few people died. However, the river which separates this commune from Anhui Province reportedly was filled with the famished who collapsed at the river's edge. When villagers in Anhui divided the land and resorted to household production quotas in 1960 to remedy this disaster, one brigade in Red Flag Commune followed their example and was one of the few units in Jiangsu Province to experiment with group production quotas. During the Cultural Revolution, Red Guards invaded Red Flag Commune and severely criticized the brigade official who had sanctioned this institutional reform.

In the late 1960s and throughout most of the 1970s, villagers in Red Flag Commune faced tight controls on their private pursuit of prosperity. In 1968, the commune's leadership vigorously restricted private plots and household sidelines. Under its auspices, all villagers marched to the commune headquarters carrying placards representing the private plots they were "donating" to the collective.[32] Following Lin Biao's 1971 demise, restrictions were relaxed somewhat, but in 1975 and 1976, due to leftist pressures from county party officials, commune leaders prevented the raising of cash crops, such as ginger, tomatoes, and tree seedlings. A poem, current in this commune at that time, expressed the official distaste for seeking prosperity from sideline production.

If you grow ginger, onions and cabbage,
Hundreds of *yuan* you can make,
But the spirit and interest to learn from Dazhai,
That you will surely forsake.[33]

In summer 1976, in the wake of Deng Xiaoping's second fall from power, county leaders increased their efforts to prove their "political redness." They called on local leaders to measure the size of private plots, and if the plots were larger than the county's guidelines, the cadres were empowered to pull out the crops. Although most brigade officials tried to drag their feet on this policy, Prosperity Brigade officials carried it out, even though farmers reportedly tore the clothes of the brigade officials who did it. Trees outside the boundaries of the private plots were collectivized. The commune and brigade maintained these strict controls on the private sector through 1977.

Due to its proximity to Anhui Province, which, under the leadership of then provincial Party secretary, Wan Li, became a model for agricultural reforms, in 1978 Red Flag Commune began to adopt more liberal economic policies. In the same year, a third of this commune's teams established "household production quotas" (*bao chan dao hu*) for cotton. In 1979, more teams adopted these new incentive systems. Commune officials, who during the radical years of the 1960s and 1970s had restricted the private sector, began to emphasize the positive aspects of individual and material incentives. These reforms led many villagers and cadres to reassert long suppressed entrepreneurial interests. However, this outburst of enthusiasm for the pursuit of prosperity brought private and collective interests into direct conflict by attacking the commune's monopoly on the production of tree seedlings.

Economic Development and the Conflict over Tree Seedlings

The history of raising trees commercially in Red Flag Commune can be traced to 1958, when the commune began its tree farm in the surrounding hills. Throughout most of the 20 years until 1978, the commune dominated this line of economic activity. But big trees were not profitable, so after the slight political thaw of 1971, the commune began to raise and market tree seedlings. The ensuing larger profits were reinvested in new projects, and the commune's economy expanded. During 1974-1977, when economic endeavors undertaken by even lower-level collectives, not to mention individuals, were heavily restricted, the commune's activities were also tightly controlled. Its sales representatives could not roam around China, forcing the commune to rely on formal bureaucratic ties to sell its seedlings. The state Flower and Tree Company and the Parks and Forest Management Group in the large urban center 60 kilometers away handled all sales. Yet these formal relationships and political pressures helped the com-

Figure 4.1 **Tree Seedling Cultivation in Prosperity Brigade**

(By Income and Number of Households)

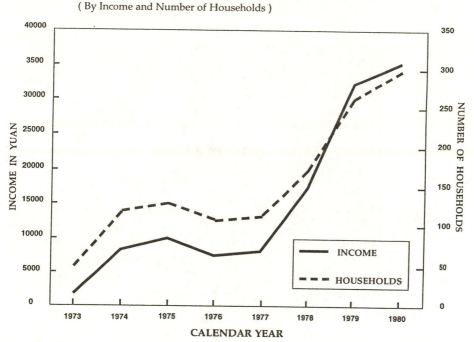

mune maintain a monopoly throughout most of the 1970s. Although some teams and individuals began to raise seedlings in 1973, controls imposed in 1975 and maintained through 1977 limited private activity (Figure 4.1). In 1975, the commune increased its profits by expropriating land with impunity from a team in Prosperity Brigade, which bordered the commune's tree farm. Only in 1977-1978 did private tree seedling cultivation begin to expand, and by 1979-1980, it was playing a major role in the local economy.

Throughout most of rural China, agricultural production in 1979 reached record levels. Red Flag Commune also prospered that year. But, in 1980, when national and local agricultural output decreased, per capita income in Red Flag Commune still increased by 13 *RMB*, due primarily to the cultivation and sale of tree seedlings. Seedlings bought for .03 *RMB* in 1979 were sold for .30 *RMB* in 1980. As demand grew in 1980, costs rose to from .30 to .50 *RMB* per seedling, but resale values after a year's cultivation also rose, to from 1 to 3 *RMB*, depending on size and quality.

This new economic opportunity was suddenly having a major impact on incomes and equality within the locality. In 1980, total collective and individual income in this commune from raising tree seedlings was approximately 600,000 *RMB*, an average of 33 *RMB* for each of the 18,000 citizens whose total average per capita income was 130 *RMB*. The commune tree farm, employing 38 villagers,

Figure 4.2 **Sources of Household Sideline Income, Prosperity Brigade, 1973–1980**

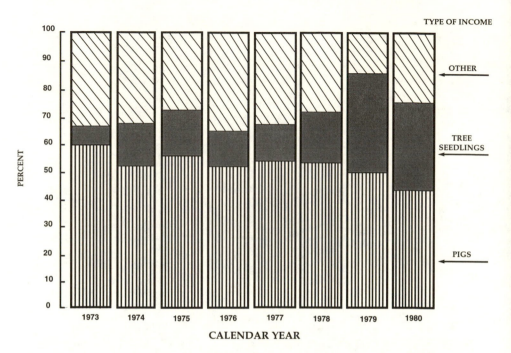

made over 80,000 *RMB* in profit. One brigade made 30,000 *RMB*, which constituted 50 percent of its total agricultural income. The sale of tree seedlings increased the income of some teams by as much as 30 percent, and some individuals also made enormous sums of money. The manager of the commune's agricultural machinery factory made over 6,000 *RMB* in 1980.

Villagers, however, still relied on their collectives to sell the tree seedlings for them. Seedlings were marketed to twelve provinces, as far away as Gansu Province, and mostly to institutions and factories for the "greening of China," not for reforestation. The commune's guest house was often full, as sales representatives came from various localities to buy tree seedlings. By 1980, five of eleven brigades had "sales representatives" (*cai gou yuan*) traveling across China. In many ways and in a short time, tree seedling cultivation was enriching this commune's inhabitants and its collective institutions.

As Figure 4.1 demonstrates, the number of households in Prosperity Brigade raising tree seedlings and their income from tree seedlings increased dramatically after 1977. In addition, according to Figure 4.2, the role of tree seedlings in sideline incomes increased as well.

What was the impact of this new wealth on equality? Figure 4.1 suggests a relatively equitable distribution of income because the slopes of the two lines are

Figure 4.3 **Variation among Teams in Prosperity Brigade: Average Per Capita Income from Tree Seedlings**

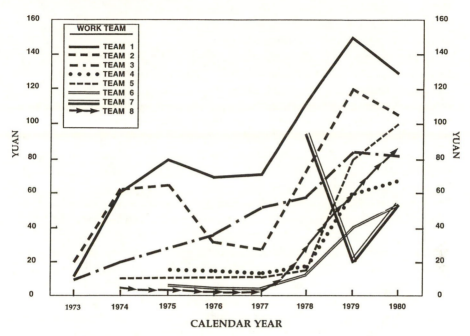

similar; the number of households and total income increased at similar rates. Nonetheless, the 1978-1979 increase in income was much greater than the increase in the number of households raising tree seedlings, suggesting that, in 1978-1979 some households made much more money than others. Although I have no household-level data, team-level data shown in Figure 4.3 suggests that the increased income within Prosperity Brigade was not evenly distributed. Some teams were much more active and their per capita income from tree seedlings was greater. Moreover, teams 6 and 7 were already the poorest teams in the brigade, while team 2 was the wealthiest. Therefore, tree seedling cultivation may have reinforced, rather than ameliorated, inequality among teams within Prosperity Brigade.

Conflicts Erupt: 1979 to 1980

Changes of such diametric proportion are unlikely to occur without new social conflicts. After the commune's tree farm made a large profit, and income in Prosperity Brigade from tree seedlings in fall 1978 doubled, interest in cultivating tree seedlings increased across all levels of the collective and among individual households. In autumn 1979, there were large profits at all levels: household income in Prosperity Brigade from tree seedlings again doubled, and the number of households raising tree seedlings also jumped as before. According to one brigade official, "Everyone's doorway was blocked because everyone was doing it. You couldn't walk around here without tripping."

However, demand suddenly surpassed supply, triggering conflict among the households, the collective's leaders, and the state.

During the winter of 1979-1980, entrepreneurial farmers and cadres from Red Flag Commune turned to the urban sector to resolve the shortage. Some people clipped the ends of fir trees in the city's most prestigious park. According to a brigade cadre in a suburban commune, residents of Red Flag Commune stole tree seedlings from his yard and from the homes of other suburbanites. Finally, they resorted to the "back door," bribing officials in the city's tree farm to sell the remaining supply. City officials with jurisdictional supervision over the commune called in Red Flag Commune's leaders and chastised them, particularly because of cadre participation in these activities.

Commune officials, angry that they had been criticized, overreacted and responded in a protectionist manner, reminiscent of the radical years. In March 1980, they convened a three-day "study meeting" (xuexi ban) to prepare other commune, brigade, and team officials for restrictions on tree seedlings. As in the mid-1970s, they tried to generate a radical environment to frighten team and brigade cadres into implementing unpopular policies which attacked private interests.[34] The "study meeting," in which commune officials criticized individual cadres, villagers, and teams by name, rekindled memories of days when "rightist caps" had been distributed freely to those who emphasized individual over state and collective interests. The use of the term "study meeting" had menacing implications for cadres and villagers.

According to a commune official, at the meeting they had advocated punishing perpetrators of four types of misdeeds: (1) people who had harmed the beauty of the city's parks; (2) people who had stolen seedlings; (3) people who had speculated (i.e., bought at one price and resold at a higher price); and (4) people who had bought seedlings with collective money and then sold them to team members for their private use. The collective was to expropriate the seedlings of the perpetrators of these offenses and fine all speculators. This official claimed to have admonished villagers against moving plants until they were developed enough to survive replanting. Further, until plants were moved to the collective's tree farm, the original owners were to be paid for tending them. Villagers who were raising seedlings but who had not committed any of the four offenses were not to be punished in any way.

Other officials had strikingly different recollections of that meeting. One claimed that the attack was far more indiscriminate, while another suggested that the commune's response had been "ultraleft," because officials had tried to end the private raising of tree seedlings altogether. These individuals remembered that people who stole seedlings were to lose them immediately and were not to be paid for taking care of them under collective auspices. More important, the right of private cultivation was withdrawn for all people who had bought seedlings in 1979-1980. The commune offered only two choices: immediately turn the seedlings over to the team or immediately transfer ownership to the team but manage them privately in return for work points. In either case, innocent villagers were to lose title to their own private property.

Responses varied across brigades. Although villagers with many seedlings were angry, some cadres, frightened by the commune's threats, clamped down on all private cultivation. One brigade leader immediately uprooted the seedlings in half the cultivated area of his brigade. Others registered seedlings and transferred ownership, but the farmers, resenting the expropriation of their private property, let the newly collectivized seedlings die.

Some brigade leaders, however, reacted more cautiously, unwilling to ignite villager ire or contravene national political trends. Many cadres and villagers knew that restricting private activity in 1980 was against the spirit of the post–Third Plenum rural policies; the commune had no legal authority to collectivize the seedlings of those who had not committed a crime. In addition, since teams lacked funds to buy the seedlings, most brigade leaders procrastinated. One evasive strategy was to record the number of tree seedlings each brigade member owned but neither transfer the title nor move the seedlings to collective plots. By implementing the form of the policy, but not its essence cadres could make it appear that they had implemented the policy, when in reality they had not. In registering the number of seedlings, but avoiding the final step of expropriation, cadres were positioned to complete the implementation process if upper level pressure were to persist.[35] Brigade officials who had themselves invested in private cultivation of tree seedlings were more attentive to villager complaints. In one instance, villagers supposedly offered a brigade leader one *RMB* per person if he did not collectivize the seedlings. In 1980, this entrepreneurial brigade official, who placed himself on the "right" end of the political spectrum, had made six hundred *RMB* from tree seedlings, as much as anyone else in his brigade, giving him a strong incentive to resist the collectivization of private property.

Finally, some brigades remained untouched by these events, neither benefiting from the new wealth nor confronting new conflicts. Strict, collective-oriented brigade leaders, such as one who labeled himself a leftist, had prohibited any private economic activity even after 1977. Probably out of fear of retribution, no villager in his brigade had either raised tree seedlings or stolen any from other villages. This brigade leader, who served as a member of the commune management committee from 1981 to 1984, had imposed a strong collective orientation on his brigade's villagers.[36]

In the end, the stalling strategy paid off. By fall 1980, the furor in the commune subsided and villagers quietly sold their seedlings. According to one official, about 80 percent of the seedlings remained unaffected by these restrictions. Yet many people suffered financially due to a protectionist response by commune leaders.

The Commune's Strategies for Expanded Prosperity

Once commune officials realized that they could no longer suppress private cultivation, they adopted two strategies to increase their share of the new income. They tried to expropriate part of the villagers' profits by levying their own surtax, and they tried to increase the commune's income from tree seedlings by illegally enlarging the commune's tree farm.

By the autumn of 1980, at the time of the Central Party Secretariat's Central Document No. 75 on the responsibility system, which significantly intensified the pace of decollectivization,[37] the spring 1980 restrictions in this commune had passed and private cultivation blossomed. But since Jiangsu's provincial government still voiced a preference for collective over private agriculture, commune leaders devised a new scheme to increase their coffers. Henceforth, all sales—collective and individual—were to be handled by three commune management committees, which alone could distribute the sales receipts required by the bank to pay teams and individuals.[38] Not only did the commune prevent direct interaction between buyer and seller, which could facilitate the development of relationships (*guanxi*) among teams and outside units, but the commune imposed a surcharge of 10 percent on all sales.

The villagers, resenting the commune's new intrusion, sent heated letters to the city government, which dispatched an investigation team. Its report determined that the new "tax" was indeed exorbitant, but the commune was allowed to levy a 3 percent surcharge on every sale. City officials probably favored strengthening commune control over private entrepreneurship and marketing, as well as increasing the commune's financial base. Such actions by local state officials mirrored the bureaucratic tendency at the national level.

Commune officials had often expanded the size of their landholdings at the expense of Prosperity Brigade. In 1980, one commune official tried to steal more land from Prosperity Brigade.[39] While overseeing the strengthening of the walls of the commune's reservoir, he ordered the laborers to close off and plow one *mou* of adjoining land and prepare it for tree seedling cultivation. The leader of the team which owned the land was outraged. This team had been losing land to commune projects since 1958. With only 79 *mou* for 200 people, its land/labor ratio was dangerously low. Only in the past two years, through hard work and careful planning under the leadership of a newly demobilized officer, had the team attained grain self-sufficiency, improving the villagers' self-respect and their official's political prestige. This team leader, who came from a leading family in the village and who became a brigade cadre in summer 1981, protested to the commune leader but to no avail. Prosperity Brigade's party secretary was also vexed; due to its proximity to commune projects, his teams were always losing land to the commune. In 1975, one team had lost land to the commune tree farm. Therefore, the party secretary confronted the commune official directly, and a heated argument ensued. For several months afterward, these officials avoided all contact, but in the spring of 1981, the production team plowed this patch of land and planted rice. The commune leader had backed down, although he never apologized for his heavy-handed actions.

Inter- and Intravillage Conflicts

Not only did the introduction of tree seedlings in Red Flag Commune trigger conflicts between households and the state, or among different levels of the collective, but as theft increased, interpersonal relations suffered as well. Following a rash of late night robberies, some villagers bought fierce guard dogs and built strong walls around their plots to keep out intruders. Small shacks guarded the entrances to most tree seedling compounds, where one family member always passed the night. The social climate had indeed intensified.

The criticism of individual villagers at the commune-run study meeting also triggered conflict. One villager in Prosperity Brigade, who with his brother and brother-in-law had made over 5,000 *RMB* in 1980, had been named during the meeting. Not only had he withdrawn from collective labor to work full time on his tree seedlings, which in 1980 was not yet legal,[40] but he had used personal connections to buy seedlings for his team when none was available on the open market. In return, his family received some of the team's seedlings for personal use. According to the commune's criteria, this villager should have lost his seedlings; jealous neighbors, therefore, took the opportunity to beat him and loot his yard with impunity.

This same villager's pursuit of personal wealth also precipitated the division of one team into two and created serious unrest among his team's remaining members. Since 1962, he had raised tree seedlings. In the early days he had helped the brigade, but in the late 1970s, he worked only as an unofficial adviser to his team's tree seedling farm for two *RMB* a day, which at that time was a rather large sum. And, although he used his long-standing personal ties to get seedlings for his team when other teams searched in vain for supplies, the team leader, his nephew, had awarded him and his brothers 650 of the team's 2,500 kilograms of seedlings. In addition, his nephew sold him collective grain at the lower collective price without his making the necessary contributions to the team's accumulation fund. Finally, when the villager enlarged his private plot beyond official guidelines, the team leader not only failed to object, but instead helped him by closing off the land from the collective fields.

Most team members resented these machinations, but the man's family was part of a three-lineage faction or "trait group" that dominated the village.[41] Therefore, in 1980, the original production team split, with households favoring the collective forming one team, while those preferring private endeavors stuck with the three families, hoping to benefit from their extensive outside connections. After the division, however, this villager's purchasing of inexpensive collective grain without contributing money to the team created another fissure in the now smaller team. In spring 1981, the conflict peaked. The accountant refused to keep the books, and other villagers went on strike, refusing to follow the team leader and work in the fields. Only direct intervention by brigade officials resolved this dispute. They ruled that this villager had two choices: contribute 120 *RMB* yearly to the team's accumulation fund and continue to buy collective grain, or buy grain on the free market at twice the collective price.

Economic Development, Social Conflict, and the Future of Rural China

The foregoing case study was an in-depth look at how emerging marketization of the rural economy in the context of significant changes in economic institutions can lead to social and political conflicts at all levels of rural society. The diversification of agriculture and the growth of a cash crop economy, after many years of suppression and stagnation in this sector, led to new opportunities for generating income that had not existed since the early 1950s. Not surprisingly, rural entrepreneurs rushed to reap the large profits that awaited those who could fill the market void. At the same time, the legitimization of private interests and the resurgence of traditional ties meant that individual families or groups of families became major players pursuing this new wealth.

However, the norms governing who could get rich and who had the right to benefit from collective land were undergoing serious transformations. While radical reformers in the party center supported privatization as the shortcut to rapid economic growth, conservative leaders stressed the collective economy. This normative ambiguity over the rights to the new wealth, unclear property rights, particularly with regard to land, and cadres' continuing administrative authority to intervene in the local economy gave cadres incentives to grab as much of the new wealth as possible. However, increased acceptance of private strategies emboldened farmers as well to try to strike it rich. These conflicting trajectories insured that villagers and cadres were on the fast track to a major political collision.[42]

The pattern of conflict mirrored both traditional and Maoist society. Lineage or trait groups reemerged, as ascriptive ties took on greater significance in the search for private prosperity. It is not surprising that these traditional organizations led to a serious restructuring of collective organizations—the demise of the production team—left over from the Maoist era. Boundaries created during the readjustments of the 1960s broke down as social conflicts over the product of society created a new fusion of informal and formal organizations. From this perspective, we can see that the nature of conflict in reformist rural China changed as well. During land reform, social conflict was directed by the Communist Party against landlords and their agents. In the radical years of 1968-1978, rural conflict was also state directed. People's Liberation Army Mao-Thought Propaganda Teams attacked local cadres, and during the "One Hit

Three Antis" Campaign some were killed. Collective cadres in turn threatened violence against class enemies who were attacked to frighten villagers into accepting the predominance of state and collective interests that were not consonant with household economic interests. Under these protectionist pressures, state and collective cadres, in particular commune cadres, not only maintained control, but expropriated private and production team resources, expanding their own political and economic bases. Once referred to by former party chairman, Hua Guofeng, as "the three-level ownership system, where two levels have nothing" (*san ji suo you, liang ji mei you*), rural China under Mao created an environment conducive to the alienation of household and team property by brigade or commune officials.

The arrest of the radical "Gang of Four" undermined the national radical line and seriously weakened the local protectionist strategy. Deng Xiaoping publicly enunciated that prefabricated "class conflict" and "class struggle campaigns" would no longer be tools with which local officials could limit privatization and maintain their dominance over the local political economy. However, the case presented here has shown that, during the early years of transition to a new political economy, when the breakdown of market order and illegal activity by entrepreneurial villagers allowed for the resurgence of the bureaucratic tendency at the national level, local protectionists were quick to use these opportunities to close down both legal and illegal private activity. Ironically, this local reaction to national bureaucratic pressures—the restriction or closure of legitimate private activity—led to the local implementation of solutions preferred by the deposed radical elites. Looking only at local outcomes might convince outside analysts that proponents of a radical line still influenced Chinese decisions, when, in fact, they had been cleared from the national political scene. This anomaly may explain why, almost a decade after the national radicals were purged, local cadres and farmers remain deeply concerned that the radical line may reemerge.

Nonetheless, the market-oriented strategy dominates today. The widescale implementation of household farming greatly weakened the team leader, whereas dividing the economic and political functions of the commune and liberalizing local commercial activity somewhat eroded the power of the exploitative cadres. Moreover, as collective officials lose their ability to suppress local conflicts in the name of economic stability, they confront more open opposition to their exploitative strategies from villager and cadre entrepreneurs. As a result, it is not surprising that, as competition over resources intensifies, conflicts among entrepreneurs at different levels of the collective, among villagers, the collective, and the state, and among villagers themselves have increased.

Once the lid of radical repression is removed, all kinds of conflicts burst to the surface. Yet, when private economic activity remains restricted, the rural economy does not grow very rapidly, and a great deal of entrepreneurial talent is wasted. In part, the choice appears to be either more rapid economic development, higher household incomes, greater inequality, and more social conflicts that may need to be legally mediated, or more restrictive policies that suppress social conflict and ensure plan fulfillment but suffocate personal initiative. It is little wonder that the establishment of a stable and liberal rural economy has long eluded the leaders of modern China.

Notes

1. *People's Daily,* April 9, 1980, p. 1, established a poverty line of fifty *RMB* per year per person. For Wan Li's speech, see *People's Daily,* December 23, 1982, p. 1.

2. The three-line model comes from Dorothy J. Solinger, *Chinese Business Under Socialism* (Berkeley: University of California Press, 1984). Solinger drew her "tendency analysis" from Franklyn Griffiths, "A Tendency Analysis of Soviet Policy-Making," in H. Gordon Skilling and Franklyn Griffiths, eds., *Interest Groups in Soviet Politics* (Princeton: Princeton University Press, 1973), pp. 335-378.

3. David Zweig, *Agrarian Radicalism in China, 1968-1981* (Cambridge: Harvard University Press, 1989). See also Yu Lin County Theoretical Study Group, *The Socialist Collective Ownership System* (*Shehuizhuyi jiti suoyouzhi*) (Guangxi renmin chubanshe, 1976).

4. According to Solinger, bureaucratic elites stress "economic stability relatively more than they do economic growth, and find any competition with state sector-led exchange to be a serious threat." See Dorothy J. Solinger, "Commerce: The Petty Private Sector and the Three Lines in the Early 1980s," in Dorothy J. Solinger, ed., *Three Visions of Chinese Socialism* (Boulder, Colo.: Westview Press, 1984), p. 74.

5. Similarly, in 1925 Bukharin called for liberalizing restrictions on the prosperous upper-stratum and middle-income farmers who, through commodity production, could pull up the incomes of lower strata farmers. See Stephen F. Cohen, *Bukharin and the Bolshevik Revolution* (Oxford: Oxford University Press, 1980), p. 176.

6. Central Document No. 75 of September 1980, which established "specialized households" as an official form of the responsibility system, allowed some farmers to pursue full-time nonagricultural sideline activities. Central Document No. 13 of March 1981 legitimized household sideline production by permitting "private people"*(zi liu ren)* to withdraw totally from collective labor and work full time on private plots. For both central documents, see *Ban yue tan,* no. 24 (April 25, 1981), pp. 11–15. See also Jurgen Domes, "New Policies in the Communes: Notes on Rural Societal Structures in China, 1976-1981," *Journal of Asian Studies* 41 (February 1982): 253-267; and chapter 2 of this book.

7. See *People's Daily,* April 10, 1983, p. 1, and *China Quarterly,* no. 101 (1985), pp. 104-142, for a translation of Central Document No. 1 of 1984 and several analyses of its implications by various China scholars.

8. See chapter 1 of this book, pp. 47–50.

9. According to Mao Zhiyong, first party secretary of Hunan Province, local cadres remain influenced by "ultraleftist" propaganda put out by that province's party committee in the late 1970s. *Foreign Broadcast Information Service* (*China Daily Report*), no. 211 (November 1, 1982): P 4-5. Hereafter, all references to *FBIS* are to the *China Daily Report.*

10. The uproar created by one incident in Feixing County, Hebei Province, shows that some cadres still maintained these beliefs in 1982. On December 16, 1982, a cadre in the county agricultural bureau, who joined the Party in 1965 at age 42, criticized the reforms at a party meeting. Press articles claimed that his mistaken position was the result of his "erroneous view" of the Cultural Revolution. *Farmers' News* (*Nongmin bao*), May 29, 1983, pp. 1, 3.

11. George Foster, "Peasant Society and the Image of the Limited Good," in Jack M. Potter, Mary N. Diaz, and George M. Foster, eds., *Peasant Society: A Reader* (Boston: Little, Brown & Co., 1967), pp. 300–323.

12. An older villager spoke bitterly about the opportunities for private prosperity opening up in her locality. She wanted to retire, but some of her neighbors were working hard and making "too much" money.

13. When, during the Cultural Revolution, villagers employed in collective factories were paid in work points rather than salaries, factories often remitted their workers' incomes to their respective production team. Since this money increased the total income that the production team could distribute to its members, even those who worked in the fields benefited from the collective factory.

14. James Scott, *The Moral Economy of the Peasant* (New Haven: Yale University Press, 1976).

15. *FBIS*, no. 214 (November 4, 1982): K 1; *People's Daily,* November 2, 1982, p. 1; and *FBIS*, no. 39 (February 27, 1984): R 2-4, cited in Thomas P. Bernstein, "Reforming China's Agriculture," prepared for the conference "To Reform the Chinese Political Order," June 18–23, 1984, Harwichport, Mass., sponsored by the Joint Committee on Chinese Studies of the American Council of Learned Societies and Social Science Research Council, p. 33.

16. *FBIS*, no. 066 (April 6, 1982): K 6-7; and *FBIS*, no. 95 (May 17, 1982): K 9-10. A spring 1982 directive on preventing economic crimes led local officials to attack villagers who had bought machinery privately or who got rich through sidelines. Only work on the land was deemed acceptable. *FBIS*, no. 95 (May 17, 1982): K 9-10. In another case, local officials held a mass rally to criticize a villager for "seeking private interests," forcing the county party committee to criticize local officials for undermining national policy. *People's Daily,* May 20, 1982, p. 1.

17. Richard Latham, "The Implications of Rural Reforms for Grass-Roots Cadres," in Elizabeth J. Perry and Christine Wong, eds., *The Political Economy of Reform in Post-Mao China* (Cambridge: Harvard East Asian Monograph Series, 1985), pp. 157-174.

18. One commune party secretary, angry about a farmer-managed soy sauce factory that competed with the commune's vinegar factory, persuaded the county industrial bureau to revoke the farmer's license. *FBIS*, no. 30 (February 13, 1984): K 11, cited in Bernstein, "Reforming China's Agriculture," p. 69.

19. These villagers fit Popkin's model of the peasantry, that is, as rational calculators who see economic opportunity in changing times. See Samuel Popkin, *The Rational Peasant* (Berkeley: University of California Press, 1979).

20. Some brigade officials have divided collective property, such as factories and trucks, and used this equipment to set themselves up as specialized households. See Anita Chan, Jonathan Unger, and Richard Madsen, *Chen Village: The Recent History of a Peasant Community in Mao's China* (Berkeley: University of California Press, 1984), p. 276.

21. For a discussion of the debates as to whether cadres can use their political authority to benefit more from market opportunities, see the introduction to this book.

22. The study, which looked at all 20,989 specialized households in Shanxi's Ying County, was publicized by Vice Premier Wan Li, one of the strongest supporters of the marketeer line in China. *People's Daily,* January 18, 1984, pp. 1, 2. *One Hundred Examples of Rural Specialized Households Getting Rich Through Labor* (Beijing: People's Publishing House, 1983), however, which presents a study in which a smaller percentage of specialized households had been cadres, suggests that the Shanxi study was probably not representative of national conditions. Thanks to John Burns who brought this study to my attention.

23. Commune- and county-level expropriation of production team resources, what Chinese call "equalization and transfer" (*ping diao*), was a major problem during the Great Leap Forward and the 1960s and 1970s. See Tom Bernstein, "Stalinism, Chinese Peasants, and Famine: Grain Procurements during the Great Leap Forward," *Theory and Society* 13 (May 1984): 339-378, and Zweig, *Agrarian Radicalism,* chapter 7.

24. In one case, the original leader of a commune revolutionary committee, the militia head, an old team leader, the father of the head of the Women's League, and a relative of the brigade secretary all became one villager's partners. They appeared for work only on the day the villager sold his fish, whereupon they took their share of his profits. *Nongmin bao,* March 6, 1983, p. 1.

25. *Nongmin bao,* July 10, 1983, p. 1. Some taxes supplement an underdeveloped rural tax base that relies primarily on taxing grain and draws little benefit from the expanding sideline sector. As William Parish points out, this threatens (1) to create gross inequalities as grain-producing families shoulder the major tax burden; and/or (2) to leave local governments unable to meet welfare, educational and infrastructural expenses. Personal communication with the author, May 12, 1984.

26. *Nongmin bao,* March 6, 1983, p. 1. Other articles warned wealthy farmers to put their money in banks and not to leave it at home.

27. *Economic Daily (Jingji ribao),* March 9, 1983, p. 1, in *FBIS,* no. 052 (March 9, 1983): K 15-16.

28. *FBIS* (June 17, 1982): O 2.

29. *Nongmin bao,* March 6, 1983, p. 1.

30. In 1981, through Nanjing University and the assistance of provincial officials, I carried out research in three brigades in three different communes in Jiangsu Province. The information in this case study was compiled through interviews with commune- and lower-level officials in one locality where I lived for 27 days. The data for the tables were compiled for me by local accountants. To protect my informants, I refrain from naming any organization or individual involved in the following events, and have given the commune and brigade a false name.

31. The brigade where I carried out most of my research, which I call "Prosperity Brigade," was near the commune town but was one of the poorest brigades in the commune. Average per capita income was 80 *RMB* per year, just above the national average. Because the terrain was hilly, the brigade had leveled land and carried out water conservation work to increase agricultural output.

32. According to my interviews in China, during 1968-1978 private plots were collectivized in many counties in southwestern Jiangsu, as well as in many other parts of China. Zweig, *Agrarian Radicalism,* chapter 6.

33. In Chinese, the poem is *Shengjiang, yangcong, dabaicai, yi nian gao guo ji bai kuai, na you xingqu xue Dazhai?* Translation by the author.

34. See Jon Unger, "Collective Incentives in the Chinese Countryside: Lessons from Chen Village," *World Development* 6 (1978): 583-601. He refers to a "milieu of activism" from which I draw my concept of a "radical environment."

35. For a more extensive discussion of the role of form versus essence in policy evasion, see Zweig, *Agrarian Radicalism,* pp. 91–97.

36. In 1984 when local officials were rectified, the brigade leader was demoted for his unswerving leftism.

37. See chapter 2 of this book.

38. At that time, all sales in China of over 30 *RMB* had to be carried out through banks.

39. During 1968-1978, commune officials all over China often expropriated resources from teams and brigades during field and water conservation campaigns. See Zweig, *Agrarian Radicalism,* chapter 7.

40. Central Document no. 13 (April 1981), on agricultural diversification, allowed "private individuals" (*zi liu ren*) to withdraw from collective labor.

41. Some anthropologists refer to factions based on locality or lineage as "trait groups," differentiating them from factions based on dyadic ties. See Arthur J. Lerman, *Taiwan Politics: The Provincial Assemblyman's World* (Washington: University Press of America, 1978), pp. 102-103.

42. See Elizabeth J. Perry, "Rural Collective Violence: The Fruits of Recent Reforms," in Perry and Wong, eds., *The Political Economy of Reform,* pp. 175-192.

5

Struggling over Land in China

Statist Hegemonies and
Villager Resistance, 1966–1986

When one thinks of monolithic states, few countries leap to mind faster than Maoist China. After 1949, the Chinese Communist Party (CCP) and its state machine reached out to control more and more aspects of China's economy, polity, and society. At no time in the past 350 years has the state exercised as much power over the lives of its citizens.[1] Fortified by a loyal army of communist cadres, who, imbued with Marxist-Leninist ideology, attacked society through incessant mass campaigns, the state appeared to have penetrated all aspects of Chinese society and to have maximized its control over it. In the rural areas, the state forced villagers into collectives and imposed a bureaucratic hierarchy on the countryside to control the means of production—land, labor, and capital—as well as the production and distribution of almost all rural produce. While terms such as "totalitarianism," "Oriental despotism," or the "Asiatic mode of production" have flaws as analytic categories, they do impart the flavor of the statist world of the Chinese farmer under communist rule.

Yet throughout the history of the People's Republic, villagers successfully employed a variety of "weapons of the weak" to protect their interests against this ofttimes oppressive state.[2] Ironically, much of their success has been due to the same factors that increased state control. While ideology served as a powerful weapon for mobilizing local cadre support for tightened state controls, ideological battles among competing factions in Beijing engendered frequent policy shifts that weakened the state's authority and created local political and policy vacuums through which villagers advanced their own interests. Yet, fearful that the state would label overt political action as ideologically unsound, farmers usually adopted less obvious forms of resistance.

Villager resistance is intimately entwined with their relationships with local officials. In most instances, rural inhabitants have relied on Janus-faced local cadres who determined the extent and success of those efforts. When cadre and villager interests coincided, collusion was likely. When cadre and villager interests collided, or state pressures intensified due to a mass campaign, many cadres ignored the farmers and responded to their own or the state's demands. In addition, while the state bureaucracy, running from the county to the village, controlled rural wealth and siphoned resources from the countryside, weaknesses in its monitoring mechanisms allowed for much formalistic or partial compliance.[3] Finally, although campaigns pressured cadres and villagers to comply with state, rather than local, interests, their limited duration afforded some leeway for local resistance. Thus, the same tools the state used to expand its control—ideology, personnel, bureaucratic structure, and campaigns—created "cracks in the monolith" and facilitated villager resistance to this quite powerful state.

Dramatic post-Mao changes, however, have altered the nature of villager resistance. First, the state is no longer the main target of resistance; local cadres and new entrepreneurs are. Under the *enrichez vous* brand of socialism introduced by Deng Xiaoping, the state ended political campaigns and withdrew some of its tentacles from society. The weakening of the collective system and the growth of markets has meant that local officials can no longer rely totally on the rural bureaucratic structure to channel resources into their hands. Under the current mixed economy, they must aggressively pursue their own personal interests.[4] At the same time, a new class of rural entrepreneurs has begun to increase their share of rural wealth.[5] Still, decollectivization, the end of campaigns, and the demise of Maoist ideology have significantly freed the villagers as well, making them more assertive in defense of their interests. Fear of cadre recriminations still suggests judicious use of these weapons of the weak, but confrontations among cadres, entrepreneurs, and villagers are more widespread as they now conflict directly for control of the means of production and prosperity.

Clearly, politically powerful cadres and wealthy villagers with economic contacts are dominating Deng's new order.[6] Nevertheless, common farmers have shown an ability to resist these new assaults by resorting to several strategies. First, to undermine the development of private wealth, villagers have resurrected Maoism's stress on an equitable distribution of income and have used slander and threats of social sanctions against those who would get rich. Second, villagers have been fighting cadre corruption and other efforts to cheat them with the assistance of county cadres and county courts. These efforts have often involved anonymous letters to higher-level officials or newspapers. And third, when other localities or officials have tried to dictate how farmers should behave, villagers have turned to their local officials to protect their individual and collective interests. These cadres have often resorted to foot-dragging or false compliance.

Thus, even as they defend their own rights, villagers remain highly dependent on officials at various levels.

To explain villager resistance against cadres and the state during two eras—under Mao and under Deng—this chapter examines local conflicts in three Nanjing communes[7] concerning five aspects of land policy: private plots; villager homes; crop types in collective fields; expropriation of team land by brigades, communes, and counties;[8] and the constant battle over whether land should be farmed collectively or privately.[9] These local events are analyzed within the context of national trends. While more systematic nationwide data on local resistance might help convince readers of the generalizability of the local case studies, it must be recalled that access to rural China remains limited. Moreover, reports of these events are rare precisely because villagers who employ "everyday forms of resistance" seek to avoid detection. This desire for anonymity is inherent in Scott's very definition of the concept we are analyzing.[10] Finally, the Chinese have not wanted to admit that widescale resistance to national policies exists.

Villager Resistance in China: A Framework for Analysis

Before looking at villager resistance, the framework in which these local battles occur must be understood. As outlined above, villager efforts at resistance have been influenced by four major factors—ideology, personnel, rural structure, and campaigns—each of which has both constrained and facilitated villager efforts to protect their own interests.

Maoist ideology or "hegemony" glorified collective rather than individual values and invalidated any political interests outside those defined by the state.[11] Moreover, a constant emphasis on class struggle increased the probability that villager efforts to defend their economic and political interests would be labeled counter-revolutionary. Yet, shifting coalitions or factional alignments created fluctuations in values emanating from Beijing.[12] These elite perspectives mixed with two dominant local values, a desire for prosperity and a fear of expanding inequality, generating jealousy and egalitarianism.[13] Thus, when Maoist egalitarianism ruled in Beijing, egalitarianism was the dominant local value; villagers who pursued private wealth suffered opprobrium.[14] However, under Deng's reforms, which legitimized individual prosperity, villagers have been able to expand and protect their own interests. Nevertheless, egalitarianism and jealousy aimed at new rich villagers have still strongly limited the pursuit of private wealth.

The state's hegemonic values, and the policies emanating from them, were introduced into rural China through a series of rural campaigns that forced villagers to demonstrate political support for CCP policies and preempted their efforts to raise political issues. Inflammatory rhetoric about anti-Party "class enemies" and symbolic beatings of remnants of the old classes—common occurrences during such campaigns—sent a clear message to villagers not to fight back. Their resistance became indirect and depended on presenting economically based challenges to politically motivated policies that limited their control over resources.[15] Political campaigns also taught rural cadres to be circumspect in opposing state interests, which complicated their efforts to help the villagers.[16] However, the use of campaigns, with pressures for immediate compliance but weak monitoring mechanisms, meant that cadres who dragged their feet until the campaign ended could avoid implementation.

The local bureaucracy sharply curtailed resistance by placing farmers in a tightly controlled environment and taking all decisions out of their hands. Each rural resident lived in a production team, the basic unit of labor and account,[17] comprised of about twenty to thirty households, and each team had a team leader, usually chosen by brigade officials, and a team management committee of three to five members.[18] The farming tasks villagers performed were determined by these officials, and work outside the production team was sharply curtailed.[19] Each brigade had approximately seven teams (a thousand people), a management committee, and a party branch. This party branch, the lowest formal level of CCP penetration into the countryside, had a brigade party secretary, the most powerful local official, who was always from a village in the brigade. In fact, farmers could work outside the village only with the written permission of the brigade secretary. While these committees usually had three to five members, the number of brigade and commune cadres increased dramatically during the 1970s, expanding bureaucratic control. Above the brigade stood the People's Commune (approximately seven to ten thousand people), with a party and management committee which could comprise two dozen or more cadres. Their leader, the commune party secretary, was a state cadre brought in from the outside by the county—the lowest level of the state bureaucracy directly above the commune—to support state interests.

This political structure, which combined economic and political organizations in one bureaucracy, maximized the power of the cadres who, after land reform (1947–1952), replaced the old landlord class as the ruling strata in rural China. Cadres monitored local activities and used their party authority to dominate village politics. They also were the major agents of state interests in the countryside. However, as members of the local community, team and brigade officials had to consider the interests of their fellow villagers. Squeezed from above and below, the local cadres' behavior varied according to the pressures they confronted.[20] Particularly when elite pressures abated or villager economic losses were great, villagers used personal relationships to compel cadres to negotiate with them, to approve their resistance tacitly by turning a blind eye to it, or to help them protect their interests.

Finally, the vastness of the Chinese bureaucracy and the distances county and commune officials covered to check on policy conformity helped cadres and villagers mask their opposition and feign compliance. These spatial factors also permitted cadres in the post-Mao era to ignore calls for more liberal land policies or to use this openness to their own advantage.

In short, villager resistance in China has been no easy task. Prisoners of a bureaucratic structure that controlled its actions, buffeted by ideological and coercive campaigns decrying efforts at self-protection, and dominated by rural officials who often pursued their own interests at the farmers' expense, China's rural inhabitants, not surprisingly, were rather passive through the mid-1980s. One need only recall that, although twenty-five million rural residents starved to death in 1960–1962, due in part to government overrequisitions, there have been no reports of major rural collective action during that time.[21] Yet, within this constrained environment, villagers employed various "weapons of the weak" to fight back. Moreover, as the shackles of the Maoist order were removed, they were more assertive in protecting their expanded interests from ever more rapacious rural officials.

Pre-1966 Struggles over Land

Property rights over land have been a major source of tension and a target of villager action since the early 1950s. While land reform divided the land among farmers and gave them contracts for it, the state reasserted control over that land and its product through collectivization. But, even after land ownership was transferred nationwide to the cooperatives in 1956, the state still controlled land use, leading one scholar to describe ownership rights as a "hybrid form of corporate and public land ownership."[22] Further complications in delineating de facto land ownership arose in the 1960s and the 1970s from the villagers' lingering memory of which land had been theirs. Therefore, when the opportunity arose, they reasserted their property rights to the collectivized land.[23]

State management of land, however, turned into state ownership of land under the impetus of the radical ideology of the Great Leap Forward and the state's ability to manipulate ownership rights within the rural bureaucracy. During the Great Leap Forward, when ownership of the means of production shifted up to the commune level, national-level state officials used their control over commune leaders to expropriate a great deal of collective land. They morally justified this "land grab" by announcing the imminent advent of communism, under which land ownership would be transferred from small collectives to "ownership by all the people." Because of intense ideological pressure, rural resistance was futile; in fact, many villagers may have accepted this chiliastic vision,[24] especially since in several localities food was given for free in fall 1958. With free food, who needed land? In any case, the locus of decision making on this issue was well out of the villagers' reach.

Local events around Nanjing reflected these national trends. In Red Flag Commune, west of Nanjing, the state transferred hilly land belonging to several teams over to the state tree farm.[25] But, after the dizziness of the Great Leap

Forward dissipated, and land ownership reverted from the larger People's Communes to the much smaller production team, this land remained the state's. Although no one has researched this issue, China's historical lack of property rights, the dramatic growth of state agricultural farms in 1957–1962, and the continuing state expropriation of land since collectivization suggest that similar land thefts by the state occurred throughout China.[26] Communes, too, stole land during the Great Leap Forward. In 1957–1958, while building a reservoir, leaders in Red Flag Commune took half of one team's land. Thereafter, until the early 1980s, this village's disastrous land/labor ratio forced it to rely on state aid for food grain and made its per capita income one of the lowest in the commune.

Although villagers in this locality were unable to prevent this land transfer, they reacted to the expropriations in several ways. Villagers living around this commune's reservoir unsuccessfully petitioned commune leaders to give them commercial fishing rights in the reservoir, while farmers in villages near the hills who lost land to the state tree farm, frequently cut down state-owned trees.[27] This poaching mirrors what Scott calls "state-created crime."[28] These villages that had too little land suffered from overemployment; therefore, to prevent further theft, the state tree farm employed their surplus laborers. Although villagers could not regain the rights to their land, stealing trees forced the state farm to repay them indirectly for the land it had stolen from them. This *de facto* property redistribution, which avoided the legal issue of ownership, is one clear example of a weapon of the weak.

Struggles over Land under the Collective System, 1966–1978

The disastrous Great Leap Forward set the stage for future battles over land. In response to the famine of the early 1960s, rural inhabitants in parts of China shifted to private farming,[29] and particularly in provinces such as Anhui, they introduced a form of household responsibility system. Moreover, through a series of party documents, the CCP relegitimized the private sector and transferred decision-making authority to the lower levels of the rural bureaucracy. Each team in China was allowed to divide 5 to 7 percent of its cultivated land into private plots, and farmers were allowed to open wasteland for private cultivation, so long as the total acreage of private plots did not exceed 15 percent of collective land.[30] In 1962, party documents admonished cadres not to compel villagers to move their homes without villager agreement, while the state insisted that the basic cooperative—the production team—be allowed to make its own decisions as to what crops it would grow without interference from commune and county officials. Finally, in the same 1962 document, the state criticized commune and county officials for expropriating team land, as well as labor and capital, during the Great Leap Forward.

These liberalizing trends expanded during the initial political vacuum brought on by the Cultural Revolution, which allowed villagers in many parts of China to further expand their private plots. In Nanjing, during the early stages of the Cultural Revolution, cadres were busy fending off political attacks or had abrogated their leadership roles. Therefore, in 1967–1968, people in suburban Everbright Commune opened up many small strips of marginal lands while villagers in Eternal Happiness Commune, 30 kilometers south of the city, cultivated as much as a fourth of a hectare.

In 1968, however, the state struck back, using ideology and terror to increase control over the private sector. At this time, a radical Maoist elite, bent on saving China from the villager's "petty bourgeois mentality," organized a series of political campaigns designed to bring the rural areas under their control. Indoctrination in the Maoist cult ensued under the guidance of People's Liberation Army "Mao Thought Propaganda Teams" that during the Three Loyalties Campaign descended on the rural areas. By beating so-called "class enemies," or what the Chinese call "killing the chickens to teach the monkey," cadres used the threat of coercion to prevent public resistance. After all, who wanted to be accused of being anti-Mao? Thus, when radical leaders called for a major contraction, if not outright elimination, of private plots in 1968–1969, labeling them the "tail of capitalism," local cadres in many parts of China responded.[31] In counties east of Nanjing, private plots were farmed collectively, while in Red Flag Commune outside Nanjing, villagers marched to party headquarters with a placard signifying the private plots they were "donating" to the collective.[32]

However, even in the face of this intense pressure, villager protests and cadre self-interest in maintaining their own access to private plots led local cadres to adjust these policies. In the near and distant suburbs of Nanjing, some officials decided only to halve the private plots rather than collectivize them. Similar collusion occurred in other parts of China. According to a Hong Kong informant, when villagers in a south China village complained directly to local cadres that without private plots they would be unable to grow tobacco, brigade officials allowed them to clear hilly land, but only for tobacco, and only if they promised not to tell outside officials. Because many cadres in this locality smoked, they also wanted land for tobacco. During this radical period, villagers were forced to rely on the good will of their local officials. One commune official claimed that he helped the villagers keep some of their private plots by "opening one eye and closing the other."

To expand the size of their private plots, some villagers built brick walls around their yards and cultivated the land within the yard, but walls could not always keep the long arm of the state at bay. In 1975–1976, the radical faction in Beijing tried to control this land as well. The resulting national mobilization led a county party secretary in Nanjing Municipality to call on local officials to restrict these yard plots, but farmer resistance complicated these efforts. When some local cadres in Red Flag Commune tore up tomato patches, villagers fought back, ripping these cadres' shirts. According to one team leader, he had refused to tear up the plots precisely because he feared getting beaten. While such confrontations were not common during the Cultural Revolution, the beatings were probably because the cadres were destroying crops that were already in the ground.[33]

Some farmers also used the Cultural Revolution's chaos to divide land surreptitiously among households for independent farming. While such actions did not occur in Nanjing, an informant from Fujian Province reported that, in 1967, his village divided the land among its residents with each household's income dependent on the output of its own plots. Reportedly, county officials colluded in this strategy by warning villagers of impending visits by higher level officials; at these times, farmers worked the fields in large groups, creating the appearance of collective agriculture. A novel about the Hunan countryside during the Cultural Revolution told of a similar strategy that backfired. After the land was divided and the rapid rise in output made the village famous, outside officials came to make it a provincial model of collective agriculture. Once the truth was uncovered, however, officials from the commune level down were purged for their pro-capitalist behavior.[34]

While farmers actively resisted state efforts to restrict their access to private land, they were much less successful in controlling the crops grown in the collective fields. After 1965, and especially after the 1969 Sino-Soviet border conflict, pressure to grow grain reached almost ludicrous proportions.[35] According to a Hong Kong informant, villagers in one locality in Guangdong Province were forced to level bamboo trees, terrace the hillsides, build irrigation canals, and lay pipe to a distant reservoir to make the hills appropriate for growing grain. Communes in parts of Nanjing were compelled to plant two crops of summer rice and one crop of winter wheat. Although local team cadres argued that three crops produced less grain, and at a higher price, than two crops, fixed quotas made overt resistance impossible. However, some localities found ways to resist these pressures. Teams in Sputnik Brigade, Eternal Happiness Commune, did not report new land brought under collective cultivation in the late 1960s, so they increased total grain output without completely shifting to three crops. Keeping 20 percent of their land off the official records helped them meet state quotas and apparently increase per hectare output without directly confronting the state.

State efforts to control the allocation of land for housing formed another area of contention for which villagers relied on weapons of the weak to resist the government. In Sputnik Brigade, when the state tried to introduce collectivist residential planning, farmers and cadres resisted the trend.[36] As a provincial model, Sputnik Brigade always had to respond to national trends. However, since relocating their homes in the hills and making them into row houses would have left no land for growing trees or pilling straw, villagers protested. Consequently, the brigade never forced anyone to move, and only stipulated that new homes had to meet brigade guidelines. Still, some farmers who moved into the hills ignored the state's plan and built bigger homes. According to a brigade official, the rich families "moved early [and] got the good locations."

In other places cadres ignored villager complaints. In a village in Red Flag Commune, a team leader forced everyone to move and, although many could not afford the expense of moving, he gave financial assistance only to families within his personal network. Several years later, when five or six children of the villagers whose families had moved without assistance returned from school, they got revenge by forcing the team leader from his post.

Finally, in the name of strengthening the collective and the state, commune and county cadres nationwide transferred a great deal of property, including land, from the teams and placed it under their own control. They built collective factories and new office buildings with which they dominated the local political economy. Various commune organizations, such as supply and marketing cooperatives, grain stations, animal husbandry stations, schools, and hospitals, took land from the villagers and their production teams.[37]

In rural Nanjing farmers tried to prevent these land expropriations. In 1976, when Prosperity Commune needed team land to build a reservoir, several families refused to move their homes. The commune secretary invoked slogans from the ongoing campaign and blocked their front doors with piles of dirt, forcing the families into sheds, where they lived for three years until the county built new homes. When national party leaders called for a massive mobilization for irrigation projects, this commune leader brooked no opposition.

During these years, Friendship Brigade, Everbright Commune, in suburban Nanjing, lost land to the city for factories and new housing units. However, while villagers and local cadres could not resist most land transfers during the radical era, new policies begun in 1974 gave local leaders more bargaining power. For each fixed amount of expropriated land, the new plant had to pay a small sum of money and hire one villager permanently, giving him an urban-residence permit and supplying him with subsidized grain. Friendship Brigade's party secretary was an excellent bargainer who persuaded a watch factory that took the brigade's land to help them build a watch parts factory. While he could not stop the land grab, he did improve the livelihood of his villager constituents. This trend persisted. By 1986 that brigade had almost no land, but 85 percent of its villagers were collective factory workers.

Similarly, anticipated retribution over land expropriations helped villagers in Sichuan Province increase the price they received for their land. One Hong Kong informant, who had managed a construction site in Sichuan Province, admitted overpaying the villagers for the land taken by his project; if he had not increased the low state price for land, he argued, villagers would have stolen his equipment nightly. And, since he and his company were from outside this area, he knew local officials would ignore their complaints about villager theft. This manager, therefore, overpaid to protect state property, responding to a weapon of the weak.

Although in 1962 state policy had returned control over the land to villagers and their production teams, from 1966 to 1978 the central government tried to reassert its control over the villagers' private land and decision-making authority on collective land. Ideological campaigns and threats of coercion dramatically increased the risk of resistance. Because many rural officials responded to these endeavors, the state was quite successful. However, particularly when state policies hurt local cadre interests, as well as those of the villagers, cadre-farmer collusion was more likely, allowing rural inhabitants to wield their weapons of the weak to get better deals for their lost land. But, if cadre-villager interests conflicted or external pressures were too great, cadres often chose the safer route of self-protection and forced state policies on the farmers. Without cadre support, villagers often quietly acquiesced. Clearly, villager dissatisfaction with these and other radical policies was known to some national and provincial leaders who visited the countryside. However, it was not until these people, the "reform faction," came to power and changed national ideology and policy that the villagers could gain more effective control of the land.

Post-1978 Struggles over Land in Rural China

In 1978, a new leadership group came to power determined to reinvigorate China's moribund rural economy. They introduced a series of reforms aimed at increasing the farmers' individual incentives and decreasing state and collective cadres' abilities to interfere in local decisions. They liberalized and restructured the rural economy and created economic opportunities previously unavailable under the collectives.[38] These reforms significantly changed the nature of the struggle over resources and the weapons employed in that struggle. A concomitant shift in the distribution of power from cadres to villagers also altered the nature of rural resistance and villager-cadre relations, as cadres showed less concern for state interests and more openly pursued their own.

The demise of "agrarian radicalism" and its stress on strengthening the collective through class struggle and mass mobilization meant that cadres were no longer as free to use coercion against farmer resistance or to invoke collectivist values as a cover for their own property expropriations. Moreover, decollectivization represented an historic watershed in productive relations, as well as a shift in the ethos of the state's hegemonic values.[39] The cadres' mechanisms for controlling the farmers and the economic product were greatly weakened. Team funds reverted to the households, leaving little for cadres to expropriate directly. By developing sideline enterprises, some villagers prospered and began to compete for control with local cadres. Reform leaders in Beijing even called for a split between the economic and political functions of local organizations, directly threatening the basis of cadre domination—the fusion of political and economic power; to signify this shift, communes were renamed "townships" and brigades were called "villages." In the face of all these threats to their long-term supremacy over the rural political economy, cadre relations with villagers became more conflicting, making cadres less reliable as allies in the villagers' struggle with the state. Instead, cadres resorted to old and new stratagems:

their authority as members of the CCP, their influence through personal net-works, and their access to and control over the bureaucratic allocation of the resources necessary for economic development. In addition, cadres tried more aggressively to expand their own economic power base and limit the burgeoning threat from emerging entrepreneurs.[40] These actions often brought them into direct conflict with the villagers. As one of the primary sources of wealth, land became a focus of conflict.

Still, while the rural reforms have made cadres more rapacious, they have also increased the villagers' willingness and ability to protect their land. First, the growth of inequality has made the gap between rich and poor, between winners and losers, more noticeable. Since the benefits gained from exploiting them have become greater and more obvious, villagers are more aware when they are being exploited. Second, the weakening of collective controls and the end of ideologi-cal campaigns have increased the villagers' freedom of expression. They use letters to newspapers, anonymous petitions to officials, and even the ballot box to express their dissatisfaction. And, while cadre recriminations can be costly, economic sanctions are far less constraining than political labeling, which had been used effectively in the previous era. Third, a new legal code, replete with contract law, has created a new sphere for villager resistance. Although cadres may manipulate the law more effectively than illiterate farmers, the replacement of arbitrary cadre decisions by impartial rulings can only benefit the villagers.[41] Finally, even as the new hegemony has fostered the search for private wealth, farmers have maintained an egalitarian ethos and used the local prohibition against immoral behavior to undermine those who would grow wealthy or, at a minimum, to force *nouveaux riches* to share their money with the community.

All these national changes have had ramifications for rural resistance in Nan-jing and elsewhere. The expansion of the private plots offered some villagers a chance to increase their incomes dramatically; at the same time, cadres and villagers who opposed this increase generated some defensive actions. For exam-ple, Sputnick Brigade, south of Nanjing, sold more grain to the state than any brigade in Jiangsu Province. To maintain this lead, rural consumption of food and cooking oil had suffered since the mid-1960s. After Mao's death in 1976, commune and brigade officials decided that, rather than decrease grain acreage, which would undermine their "model" status, they would resolve the villagers' food shortage by letting them open barren land. In 1978–1979, national policy publicly supported this expansion of barren land, and by 1981 some villagers in this brigade privately farmed as much land as they had after land reform. In one team, farmers spent more time during the busy summer season planting potatoes in their own fields than working on collective land. But the demise of radical ideology prevented the team leader from using coercion or threats to get villagers into the fields. Instead, this cadre was forced to increase the financial rewards for those who participated in collective work, allowing villagers to extract more funds from the collective. He also relaxed labor obligations, giving farmers more time off from collective labor to work their own fields.[42]

Expanding private land holdings had increased the villagers' leverage over the collective, but, in 1981, powerful team leaders in several villages in Sputnik Brigade insisted that all opened land be farmed collectively. According to one woman, her team leader expressed concern that conflicts among villagers would erupt if some families opened more land than others. More likely, this cadre simply wanted to keep all land under collective, that is, his own, control. Although, as in other villages, many farmers favored privately opening land and told the leader so, "when we raise this to the team leader he says that we can go and live there, if we think that it is so much better. . . . People here do complain about the fact that we cannot have more private land, but he refuses to accept it." Since he had a reputation for beating villagers who disagreed with him, farmers did not press the issue.

In part, the team leader was correct, in that a moral battle ensued within the brigade over the wealth this new land was creating. One old woman in another village chastised people who opened new land for being different: "These people have different thoughts. They don't think about resting or playing." Her sharpest criticism, evoking Maoist morality, was that "they sell on the private market," which indirectly suggested that these people preferred the "capitalist" or individual, rather than the "socialist" or collective, path to development. However, industrious villagers fought back against this effort to denigrate their efforts; they blamed poverty on laziness and saw nothing virtuous in it. According to a farmer who had opened land, "the strong people don't say anything [about opening land]. It is those who are lazy who complain."[43]

Even in 1985–1986, social pressure based on egalitarian morality still prevented an entrepreneur in Red Flag Township from getting rich. Although he was extremely skilled at raising fruit trees, this villager refused to subcontract more land for a big orchard because managing it would have entailed hiring labor. And, while hiring labor was legal, he had been beaten in the past for his "capitalist tendencies," and, therefore, feared the villagers' wrath should Maoist policies return. As of 1986, he had still not expanded his land beyond the half hectare he and his immediate family could work.[44]

In addition, the issue of hiring labor to work one's land has been contentious in this locality. One inhabitant of Red Flag Township who had been hired to tend another's tree seedlings received a handsome yearly salary. However, when his employer made ten times as much from the sale of the trees, he took him to court. County court officials tried to dissuade him, since he had signed a contract; moreover, under the reforms this profit was legal. Yet, this villager wanted to make his own point—that this vast income discrepancy was immoral—and demanded that the courts legitimize his viewpoint. While court officials thought him foolish for pushing his case this far and, therefore, refused to grant him a legal hearing, his actions gained countywide attention for him and his cause.

Moral issues forced other entrepreneurs in Red Flag Township to handle their newfound wealth cautiously which led to a ritual of redistribution. While many *nouveaux riches* built new homes, most also bought insurance against moral and political recriminations by giving some of their profits to their relatives, friends, and villages as loans that were unlikely to be repaid. One cadre who had earned 20,000 *yuan* from raising trees admitted loaning over 10,000 *yuan* even though it was rather clear that people would not pay him back.

Because new opportunities for profitmaking from commercial crops increased the value of land, some cadres increased their efforts to expropriate it, and villagers once again had to fight to protect their interests. In some cases, local cadres helped them fend off threats from higher-level officials. For example, in Red Flag Commune in 1979–1980, farmers who raised young trees doubled their funds in one year, triggering a local tree-growing mania. Consequently, when a tree-seedling shortage developed, some villagers clipped the ends off trees in Nanjing parks, plundered seedlings from the yards of suburban villagers, and bought seedlings through the "back door" from state companies. Criticized by the city government for permitting this outburst of pilfering, commune officials convened an inflammatory meeting, reminiscent of the Cultural Revolution decade, and pressured officials to tear tree seedlings from villagers' private plots. Villagers approached local officials for help. According to one brigade official, villagers had entreated him to resist the policy. Given his own sizable investment in trees; his personal political predilections, which favored the private sector; and his awareness that the current national policy opposed such expropriations, he dragged his feet until the affair passed and never pulled up the seedlings. Shared interests and a new hegemony prompted local cadres to protect villager private land.

When commune cadres tried to increase their share of the tree-seedling business, villagers also resisted them vigorously. After the commune imposed a 10 percent tax on all tree sales, villagers wrote protest letters to the city party committee.[45] A city investigation team reduced the tax to 3 percent. A commune official, who was supervising repairs to the reservoir's dikes, cordoned off some land belonging to the team that had lost half its land to the reservoir in 1958, declaring it commune property. The team's leader argued heatedly and was supported by the brigade party secretary, who for a full six months thereafter publicly ignored this commune official. While public and private criticism did not lead to a formal recantation, local pressure prevented this commune official from planting any trees, and the land eventually reverted to the team.

In other cases, intravillage conflicts pitted farmers against their local officials, as in the case in which villagers were forced to fend off a land grab by a local cadre and his allies. In this village, a team leader, part of a subteam alliance of three families, cordoned off a small parcel of collective land and allocated it to his cousin. After commune officials criticized the cousin by name at the commune-wide meeting, villagers reportedly beat him and plundered seedlings from his yard. Other villagers refused to obey the team leader. This opposition forced the brigade leader to intervene and replace the team leader.

This way farmers used local government efforts to restrict private activity and stop individuals from expropriating collective land.

When localities contracted collective property, factories, fishponds, and orchards, to individuals, this transfer of management rights over the means of production from collective to individual control led to many rural protests.[46] The quota payments that the contracting parties were to pay to the collective accumulation funds often underestimated the extent to which a motivated individual could outproduce a collectively managed business. Huge individual profits made from land into which they had sunk "economic rents" incensed most farmers. Some complained that since collective fields had been divided evenly, the orchards should be as well. Cadres used villager anger to demand that entrepreneurs renegotiate the contracts at a higher quota. If the entrepreneurs refused, their orchards could be pilfered and they themselves beaten. However, when cadres contracted the collectively owned orchards, timid villagers sometimes took them to court, accusing them of using their power to get rich, even though in many cases only cadres dared take the economic risk of signing a contract. In the late 1980s, more and more of these cases were being decided by the courts, which sought both to uphold the law, a reflection of the reigning hegemonic values, and to respond to the underlying morality of Chinese rural society, which was pressuring them to protect collective property.

Housing, and the land needed for building new homes, became a major source of villager-cadre conflict in the 1980s. As rural incomes grew for the first time in two decades, villagers poured their funds into new housing. However, with decollectivization blurring the line between collective and private land,[47] cadres sought to get rich by selling off collective land.[48] Private sales of collective land led the CCP's Central Discipline Inspection Committee in early 1981 to issue a circular criticizing cadres, "mainly at the commune and county levels," who abuse their power.[49] In the southern Zhejiang district of Wenzhou, famous for its independent politics and entrepreneurial behavior, rural officials sold 1 percent of all arable land in the county for housing in 1979 alone.[50] Since land in 1979 was still under collective control, only cadres could sell it.

While occupying collective land for house building was not a problem around Nanjing in 1981, by 1985 it had become the major issue in Red Flag Township.[51] Because Red Flag Commune's former party secretary had always lived in the commune town, he had prevented other cadres from moving into town. However, when the new township party secretary left his village several kilometers down the road and moved onto land owned by a village bordering the township center, he lost the moral authority to stop other cadres from following suit. Between 1984 and 1986, over 175 cadres and their relatives had moved into villages around the town, but building homes on collective land undermined each villager's income, because the collective had to redistribute and decrease the amount of land each household farmed to ensure a continuing even distribution. For example, when the township party secretary and another cadre moved into one village, each household's holdings shrunk by 20 percent.

Rural resistance to these expropriations varied. One team leader was so angry at the continuing loss of village land to outsiders that he refused to sign any more forms; brigade support strengthened his resolve. Since township leaders preferred to persuade team officials to sign these land transfers voluntarily, foot dragging was showing results in 1986. A township cadre who wanted to move into this leader's team had been waiting for several months. His bricks were sitting there, but the signed form was not. On the other hand, residents of the village into which the township party secretary moved were so enraged that they sent photographs of the two homes to the county government.[52] They may have responded more forcefully because their loss had already occurred. Unfortunately, county cadres phoned township leaders and asked them to investigate the problem, which meant, of course, that nothing happened. Unfortunately, city officials who also knew of the problem took no action.[53]

While land issues were critical during the Maoist era, few farmers dared confront state cadres who stole their land or rural officials who collectivized it. In Deng's China, however, while myriad opportunities for prospering from the land have intensified the conflicts over it, political and legal reforms have brought more of those struggles into the open. The press regularly reports such stories, encouraging villagers to resist or take cadres or other villagers who act unethically to court. Clearly, the role of the state and its institutions has changed. Although decollectivization forced rural cadres aggressively to seek a large share of the new rural wealth, villagers, often with state assistance, have been encouraged to fight back against cadres and wealthy villagers who try to expropriate their rightful share of rural land.

Conclusion

The Chinese case offers an opportunity to witness villager resistance under two different situations. The first involves the villagers' response to a powerful state that ruled firmly for most of two decades. Through ideological and political campaigns, and the establishment of a collective bureaucracy, the CCP penetrated Chinese society and controlled most aspects of the villagers' political, economic, and social life. The state even tried to determine what farmers could plant in their private plots or their yards. The collective structure also created a new strata of rural bureaucrats, particularly at the commune level, who often surreptitiously used their power to extract wealth from the villagers to establish its own control. Farmers, however, could at times turn to local—team and brigade—cadres, who, when they shared common interests, helped villagers resist state and collective encroachment.

During the post-1978 era, the state progressively withdrew its controls and, through decollectivization, the attempted separation of economic and political organizations, and the introduction of a new legal system, increased the villagers' freedom of action. The state's withdrawal, however, and the shift in hegemonic values from Maoist moral egalitarianism to a more profit-oriented viewpoint have intensified the conflict between cadres and farmers and between richer and poorer villagers. In both cases, the former have become the major target of more vigorous resistance.

While the mode of resistance varied across time periods, and also depended on which land issue was at hand, constraints imposed by the collective system from 1958 through 1978 made approaching cadres in informal settings, and asking them to intervene, the villagers' major weapon. Some cadres devised solutions amenable to both themselves and the villagers and, through foot dragging, false compliance, and other strategies, deflected the demands of the state. At other times, they simply limited the harshness of state policy. Yet, when political events weakened state controls, villagers could unilaterally advance their own interests, either by expanding private holdings or shifting to individual farming. They needed only the acquiescence of local cadres who, in any case, often abdicated decision-making authority during times of political unrest.

The critical role of cadres also meant that villager resistance was most constrained when cadres acted in accordance with state policies. This coordination was often the result of intense mobilization, when cadres could invoke the heavily ideological, hegemonic values of the regime—which from 1958 to 1978 involved building the state and the collective through "class struggle"—and use harsh techniques to suppress resistance. The coordination of state goals and cadre behavior placed villager efforts to protect their rights from state or collective assaults beyond the pale of acceptable actions. The specter of so-called "class enemies" often melted villager resistance. However, even when radical influence persisted at the national level, cadre actions, such as pulling up crops in private plots, that violated local morality could be met with violent local resistance.

After 1978, however, when cadres pursued their own interests or prevented the implementation of new state policies benefiting villager interests, thereby making themselves the target of resistance, farmers responded in various ways. They circumvented the cadres and wrote letters to newspapers and state officials, an action most likely to succeed when cadre behavior conflicted with the formal values or laws of the extant regime. Thus, in 1978–1979, many letters to the editor in the national press criticized local opposition to the "responsibility system." More assertive or better-educated villagers turned to the developing legal system to seek redress from corrupt cadres or unjust decisions. However, despite efforts by the state to strengthen those aspects of the local environment that permit farmers to protect their own interests, the history of the People's Republic of China suggests that, even under Deng's regime, cadres will come out on top.

Finally, the Chinese case offers an interesting perspective on the issue of hegemonic control and values, for the battle over land is tied to both policy and morality. Under the CCP, the hegemonic value system changed frequently, which allowed competing rural value systems concerning the use of land and private property to emerge in the same locality. When state leaders invoked a Maoist morality, emphasizing collectivism and egalitarianism, state and collective cadres carried out their respective land grabs and easily established effective control over land. In the post-Mao, post-radical era, however, the hegemonic values of the state changed, while those of some farmers and many cadres did not. Maoist values persisted locally, albeit perhaps as part of a defense strategy against new entrepreneurs and the weakening of collective controls. In the face of, or behind the backs of, industrious neighbors, villagers resorted to rumormongering and criticizing the hiring of labor to hold entrepreneurs back from getting rich; when possible, they pressured them to distribute some of their profits, or sometimes they simply beat them. This local morality, which reflected the passing hegemonic Maoist values, assisted the weaker villagers to battle the new entrepreneurial class. It also helped collective cadres, the reigning, rural ruling class, to undermine the rise of this competing class of rural entrepreneurs, whose activities more closely reflected the new elite hegemony.

Notes

1. For a discussion of some of these issues, see Vivienne Shue, *The Reach of the State* (Stanford: Stanford University Press, 1988); and William L. Parish and Martin K. Whyte, *Village and Family in Contemporary China* (Chicago: University of Chicago Press, 1978).

2. See James Scott, *Weapons of the Weak* (New Haven: Yale University Press, 1985). This chapter focuses on everyday forms of villager resistance, to which the work of Scott has sensitized us, rather than historic shifts in productive relations, such as decollectivization. By focusing on these small-scale strategies of resistance, I am not arguing that villagers were powerless to influence policy outcomes; clearly, they played a major role in decollectivization. However, as I have shown in chapter 2, central reformers were also critical to successful decollectivization. Moreover, large-scale social change, such as decollectivization, which depended to a significant extent on local initiative, has rarely occurred under communist rule, while much of the villagers' political struggle with cadres and the state revolved around successfully employing these weapons of the weak. Ignoring that struggle understates the strong, ongoing battle among villagers, cadres, and the state that was an important hallmark of rural China after 1949.

3. For a discussion of villager-cadre relations and formalistic cadre compliance with state policies during the Cultural Revolution decade (1966–1976), see David Zweig, *Agrarian Radicalism in China, 1968–1981* (Cambridge: Harvard University Press, 1989).

4. See Jean C. Oi, "Commercializing China's Rural Cadres," *Problems of Communism* 25 (September 1986): 1–15.

5. See chapter 4 and the discussion in the introduction to this book.

6. See Gordon White, "The Impact of Economic Reforms in the Chinese Countryside: Towards the Politics of Socialist Capitalism?" *Modern China* 13 (October 1987): 411–440.

7. In 1981, I spent three months living and researching in three communes in rural Nanjing; in summer 1986, I returned for further field research. I have also drawn on press reports from 1968 to 1986 and interviews in Hong Kong in fall 1980 to supplement the

argument and demonstrate that events described here are not unique to this area alone, while recognizing that regional variations are important in China.

8. Loss of arable land can be attributed to specific causes: the expansion of pasture land, forestry, rural industry, national construction, and rural housing. See George P. Brown, "Arable Land Loss in Rural China: Policy and Implementation in Jiangsu Province," *Asian Survey* 35 (October 1995): 922–940. Note that four of the five reasons primarily involve local state activity, rather than the actions of individual villagers. For a more general discussion, see Leo A. Orleans, "Loss and Misuse of China's Cultivated Land," in Joint Economic Committee, U.S. Congress, *China's Economic Dilemmas in the 1990s: The Problems of Reforms, Modernization and Interdependence* (Armonk, N.Y.: M.E. Sharpe, 1993), pp. 403–417.

9. In 1955–1956, 2 to 5 percent of the collective's land was divided among villagers on a per capita basis as private plots. Villagers paid no tax on produce raised in these plots. See Kenneth R. Walker, *Planning in Chinese Agriculture: Socialization and the Private Sector, 1956–1962* (Chicago: Aldine Publishing Co., 1967), pp. 10–12. Their homes, however, were privately owned, although the land on which they sat belonged to the collective. Nevertheless, while land was to be owned by the basic collective, the production team, cadres at higher levels of the rural bureaucratic structure often tried to take over that land for their own use.

10. See James C. Scott, "Everyday Forms of Resistance," in Forrest D. Colburn, ed., *Everyday Forms of Peasant Resistance* (Armonk, N.Y.: M.E. Sharpe, 1989), pp. 3–33.

11. For a discussion of hegemonic values, see the concluding chapter of Scott's *Weapons of the Weak*.

12. At the elite level, the values of various leaders include efficient economic development, political stability, equality, and high moral behavior. For the first three values, see Dorothy Solinger, *Chinese Business Under Socialism* (Berkeley: University of California Press, 1984).

13. For a discussion of the villagers' desire for wealth and fear of inequality, see Zweig, *Agrarian Radicalism,* chapter 4. Villagers also expect local officials to behave morally towards others and distribute fair justice. See Richard Madsen, *Morality and Power in a Chinese Village* (Berkeley: University of California Press, 1984).

14. For a story of how a bean curd saleswoman who prospered in the early 1960s became the target of a political attack in 1964, see Gu Hua, *A Small Town Called Hibiscus* (Beijing: Panda Books, 1980).

15. This is the argument of John P. Burns, *Political Participation in Rural China* (Berkeley: University of California Press, 1988).

16. The key campaigns affecting local cadre behavior were the 1959 Anti-Rightist Campaign, the Four Cleans Campaign of 1964–1965, and the Cultural Revolution. See, respectively, Liu Binyan, "Sound is Better than Silence," in Perry Link, ed., *People or Monsters?* (Bloomington: Indiana University Press, 1983), pp. 98–137; Richard Baum, *Prelude to Revolution: Mao, the Party and the Peasant Question, 1962–1966* (New York: Columbia University Press, 1975); and Anita Chan, Richard Madsen, and Jonathan Unger, *Chen Village: The Recent History of a Peasant Community in Mao's China* (Berkeley: University of California Press, 1984).

17. Collectivization made land which had been owned privately into the corporate property of all team members. Thereafter, each villager received "work points" for each day's labor based on task rates (each task had a particular value) or time rates (the value of a labor day depended on a villager's personal work-point value determined by the team leader and based on his or her skills or strength). At year's end, after the team deducted funds for taxes and reinvestment, it divided its net income by the number of work points it had distributed to determine the value of each work point. The total number of points a

villager earned times the team's work-point value determined individual income. See Fredrick W. Crook, "The Commune System in the People's Republic of China, 1963–1974," in Joint Economic Committee, U.S. Congress, *China: A Reassessment of the Economy* (Washington: Government Printing Office, 1975), pp. 366–410.

18. In northern China, each village was a team; in southern China, where the villages are larger, each village was often divided into several production teams.

19. For the structural constraints imposed on rural residents, see Jean C. Oi, "Communism and Clientelism," *World Politics* 37 (January 1985): 238–266, and Sulamith Heins Potter, "The Position of Peasants in Modern China's Social Order," *Modern China* 9 (1983): 465–499.

20. See Thomas P. Bernstein, "Problems of Village Leadership after Land Reform," *China Quarterly*, no. 36 (1968): 1–22.

21. See Thomas P. Bernstein, "Stalinism, Chinese Villagers and Famine: Grain Procurements During the Great Leap Forward," *Theory and Society* (May 1984): 1–39; and Anonymous (introduction by Thomas P. Bernstein), "Starving to Death in China," *New York Review of Books* 30 (June 16, 1983): 36–38.

22. Fleming Christiansen, "Private Land in China? Some Aspects of the Development of Socialist Land Ownership in Post-Mao China," *The Journal of Communist Studies*, no. 3 (1987): 57.

23. According to a May 1975 interview conducted by Fred Crook with a mainland refugee in Hong Kong, some villagers in Shanxi Province collectively cultivated land outside their commune's borders, because the land had been cultivated by their ancestors. See The China Group, *Reports on Rural People's Communes*, unpublished data set, compiled by Fred Crook.

24. See Franz Schurmann, *Ideology and Organization in Communist China* (Berkeley: University of California Press, 1968), p. 49; and David and Isabel Crook, *The First Years of Yangyi Commune* (London: Routledge and Keegan Paul, 1959).

25. Although the names of the three communes, Red Flag, Everbright, and Eternal Happiness, and the brigades within them, are fictitious, they will be used consistently to protect my informants.

26. While 440,000 villagers plowed 1 million hectares of land in 804 state farms in 1957, by 1962 the number of state farms had jumped to 2,123, with 2,168,400 villagers farming 2.74 million hectares of land. (Few major changes occurred in the next twenty years.) This growth in acreage was not due solely to the clearing of land. In 1957, at the peak of a nationwide irrigation campaign, state farms cleared only .20 million hectares for their own use; in 1962, they cleared only .1 million hectares. Thus, the dramatic increase between 1957 and 1962 of 1.75 million hectares in the amount of land under state farm control probably came during the 1958 Great Leap Forward and at the expense of villagers and the people's communes. See *Chinese Agricultural Yearbook (Zhongguo nongye nianjian)* (Beijing: Nongye chubanshe, 1980), p. 5, which unfortunately gives data only in five-year intervals.

27. According to one team leader, villagers felt more secure stealing from the state's, rather than the commune's, tree farm, because the commune would protect them if they got caught stealing from the state, but no one would protect them if they stole from the commune.

28. Scott, "Everyday Forms of Resistance."

29. See Fredrick W. Crook, "Chinese Communist Agricultural Incentive Systems and the Labor Productive Contracts to Households: 1956–1965," *Asian Survey* 13 (May 1973): 470–481.

30. For this and the following points, see "Regulations on the Work in the Rural People's Communes (revised draft)," *Issues and Studies* 15 (December 1979): 106–115.

31. See Han Ke-chuan, "Recent Development in Rural Communes on the Chinese Mainland," *Issues and Studies* 5 (May 1969): 4–11.

32. Collective farming of private plots occurred in parts of Hebei Province in 1964, no doubt in response to the 1964 Learn from Dazhai Movement (personal communication from Mark Selden, 1996).

33. A *People's Daily* report (January 18, 1979), p. 2, also told how villagers in Jiangxi Province beat their cadres in April 1976, when they tried to uproot sugarcane from the villagers' plots.

34. See Gu Hua, *Pagoda Ridge and Other Stories* (Beijing: Panda Books, 1985). Although this is a novel, written to criticize the Cultural Revolution in the countryside, it reflects the tenor of the period. For similar events in Wenzhou District, Zhejiang Province, see *People's Daily*, January 1, 1978, p. 2.

35. See Nicholas P. Lardy, *Agriculture in China's Modern Economic Development* (Cambridge: University Press, 1983).

36. Residential planning moved villager homes into neat rows on nearby hills to increase the acreage of valley land and the state's control over the villagers' private domain. Such homes often had no yards in front or back for private economic activity. The national model for collectivized agriculture, the Dazhai Brigade, employed this measure to increase the collective's authority.

37. A district in Inner Mongolia returned over 600 hectares of collective land that it had taken during the previous decade. See *People's Daily*, July 9, 1979, p. 3. In Yunnan Province, factories and mines in a commune in Kunming's suburbs had taken over 450 hectares of land from the villagers. See *People's Daily*, August 15, 1978, p. 3. For similar reports see *People's Daily*, July 28, 1978, p. 2, August 19, 1978, p. 2, and November 6, 1978, p. 3.

38. The acreage for cash crops, fish ponds, and orchards increased at the expense of grain acreage. The percentage of collective land allocated to private plots rose from 5 to 15 percent by 1980. From 1978 to 1983, decollectivization gave households more control over the land. The resultant leap in villager per capita income, a fourfold increase between 1978 and 1986, precipitated a housing boom of worldwide historic proportions. For an excellent study of the early rural reforms, see William L. Parish, ed., *China's Rural Development: The Great Transformation* (Armonk, N.Y.: M. E. Sharpe, 1985).

39. For a discussion of the importance of historical shifts in productive relations on the employment of everyday forms of resistance, see Scott, *Weapons of the Weak*, p. 49.

40. Collectivization created new bureaucratic organizations at the brigade and commune levels but did not necessarily give those organizations the capital or property to pay for the tasks or services expected of them. In 1977, former party chairman Hua Guofeng in 1977 referred to the rural structure as "three levels of ownership, with two levels that have no property" (*San ji suo you, liang ji mei you*). Cadres wanted to rectify that situation.

41. See chapter 6 of this book.

42. This reappropriation of time from the collective to private activities has been a significant means of resistance to state socialism. See Scott, "Everyday Forms of Resistance."

43. For a similar circumstance, in which the wealthy asserted that poverty was the result of villagers lacking industriousness, see Scott, *Weapons of the Weak*, p. 146.

44. Similar problems have been reported in China since 1983. See the speech by Xu Jiatun, then first party secretary of Jiangsu Province, in *Economic Daily* (*Jingji ribao*), March 9, 1983, p. 1. See also chapter 4 of this book.

45. Writing letters to party and government officials, as well as to newspapers, is common in China. See Hugh Thomas, ed., *Comrade Editor: Letters to the People's Daily*

(Hong Kong: Joint Publishing Co., 1980); and Paul Godwin and Leonard Chu, "Parties in Conflict: Letters to the Editor of the People's Daily," vol. 31, *Journal of Communication* (Autumn 1981): 74–91.

46. For a more lengthy discussion of this and similar legal cases, see chapter 6 of this book.

47. Christiansen, "Private Land in China?" *Farmer's Daily*, June 28, 1985, p. 1, recognized that the responsibility system made land ownership unclear in some places.

48. See chapter 6 of this book, as well as *Nanjing Daily*, April 21, 1981, p. 1, and *Foreign Broadcast Information Service* (September 21, 1981): O 1.

49. *Foreign Broadcast Information Service* (October 6, 1981): K 6.

50. See *People's Daily*, March 17, 1981, p. 4.

51. For some national reports in 1985, see *Farmer's Daily*, August 30, 1985, p. 1, and October 26, 1985, p. 1.

52. According to *Farmer's Daily*, October 26, 1985, p. 1, villagers in another location wrote letters to the National People's Congress to protest against cadres buying and selling houses and collective land.

53. While villagers under the collective system relied almost entirely on interactions with their brigade secretary or team leader, farmers under the reforms now interact with many more local officials and are less dependent on their team or brigade leader. This has resulted in a more pluralistic patronage system. See Jonathan Unger, "The Decollectivization of the Chinese Countryside: A Survey of Twenty-Eight Villages," *Pacific Affairs*, no. 54 (1985–1986): 585–606.

6

Law, Contracts, and Economic Modernization

New Institutions for Conflict Resolution under the Rural Reforms

Introduction

The reintroduction of household farming in the People's Republic of China (PRC) and the transition to a more commercialized rural economy have loosened the bonds of the command economy that had previously subordinated the rural people's communes and their members to the dictates of the state plan. As a result, as early as 1981, procurement agencies in some locations were deluged with more produce and livestock than they could manage, while in other locations procurement of vital products, including grain, fell woefully short of state plans. To resolve these dilemmas, establish a more flexible link between plan and market, and implement the new developmental strategy based on the commercialization of Chinese agriculture,[1] the PRC in 1982 began to introduce a system of rural contracts that controlled commercial relations among rural producers, the state, and collective agencies that were responsible for agricultural inputs and outputs. In April 1985, the government further refined this system by abolishing the system of unified purchased sales (mandatory sales quotas) estab-

---

This chapter was originally co-written, but I have edited it extensively for this volume. My co-authors on the original article were Kathleen Hartford (Professor of Political Science, University of Massachusetts at Boston), James Feinerman (Professor of Law, Georgetown University Law Center), and Deng Jianxu (Professor of Law, Faculty of Law, Shenzhen University, Shenzhen, Guangdong Province, People's Republic of China).

lished in 1953,[2] replacing it with a system based on "voluntary" contracts between the producer and the state. Henceforth, the Chinese Communist Party (CCP) and the state have expected contractual obligations to govern commercial relations between rural producers and state purchasers and even to regulate private commercial transactions in the vastly expanded free-market sector.

The success of the rural economic reforms depends on whether contractual relations can facilitate rural China's transition from a command economy to one based on an amalgam of indicative-planning and market mechanisms. It is no easy task to introduce a commercial system more reliant on the rule of law, based on legal, rather than particularistic, procedures and norms, into a rural economy that has been dominated by the arbitrary actions of local officials.[3] To determine which factors impede or promote the implantation of these new notions of rights[4] and legality, this chapter analyzes the development of China's new rural legal system and the adjudication under it of several specific rural contract cases previously unpublished outside China. Based on these cases, and the legal and political circumstances discussed below, the particular conditions under which people resort to the legal system to consolidate the gains of rural economic reform and the factors that determine the successful resolution of rural contractual disputes are assessed. Finally, the role of the courts and legal processes in establishing an environment conducive for implementing China's chosen strategy of economic development is discussed. China's success in introducing an effective legal system will have an enormous impact on rural reform and rural development.

Economic Development, Legal Philosophy, and Rural Contracts

Evolution of Commercial Relations

Before the reforms of 1978, producers, that is, production teams and brigades, enjoyed little bargaining power vis-à-vis the purchaser, that is, the state.[5] Producers were subordinates in primarily "vertical," hierarchical relationships; "horizontal" or competitive relationships with other producers or providers of services were rare (except for black-market transactions). In the early 1980s, production teams and brigades were permitted to give individuals the responsibility for operating small-scale enterprises, agricultural machinery, technical services, and irrigation works of the commune, brigade, or team, as well as responsibility for managing all agricultural land. Individual contractors were given considerable flexibility in selling their services or agricultural goods to other farmers or to units managed by the collective or the state. By 1984, party policy permitted private individuals to provide goods and services in the rural areas. The change inevitably brought these individuals into direct competition with the collective or state organizations.[6]

The party and the state changed economic policy as well as the structure of commercial relations. As the volume of rural commercial production increased, farming households could increasingly choose where to dispose of their surplus goods and even how much of a surplus to produce. Between 1978 and 1982, farm and sideline products sales increased by 99 percent, and the average commodity rate (output sold as a proportion of total output) had risen from 41 to 59 percent.[7] During the same period, the number of rural markets increased nearly 25 percent, and the volume of trade in the rural market increased by 130 percent.[8]

The state now had to compete with other buyers, including other state units, for the increased output. As a result, the command economy required new mechanisms to govern the hierarchy of producers still subservient to the state plan. New mechanisms were also required for managing horizontal exchanges of goods and services, both within units, which had previously managed these transfers administratively, and among units which had rarely engaged in transactions.[9] By introducing the "contract system" (*chengbao hetong zhi*), the state hoped to replace the political-command system with formal legal notions of economic rights and obligations that would transform these new complex relations into a streamlined and efficient rural economy.

Law and Economic Modernization

Many states recognize that a modern legal system is a precondition for economic development.[10] In the China of the 1980s, this proposition correlated well with a long-existing instrumental attitude towards law.[11] Important features of such a modern system include centralism, professionalism, and uniform and universal application of rules. Legislated norms of general applicability replace customary rules, and a bureaucracy administers the legal system, employing trained specialists.[12] The central government administers a hierarchy of courts, from courts of first instance at the local level to higher courts of appeal and review that ensure regional conformity to national standards.

Modernizing the legal system also requires altering community attitudes towards law, which the populace must internalize.[13] The state must protect economic transactions, eliminate family and local influence in determining economic rights and responsibilities, and rely on published norms interpreted by trained legal personnel in a fair and impartial manner. By overcoming such societal forces as regionalism, particularism, and nepotism, legal development, in the official view, will enhance economic growth.

However, attempts to establish Western legal systems in Third World countries have demonstrated that non-Western societies must also accommodate existing basic legal traditions in the course of introducing modern institutions.[14] As a result of its own ambivalence towards the rule of law, which could limit the party's ability to control outcomes and intervene at times of crisis or social conflict,[15] China seems to be using a Western form of political and legal institution, that is, contract, in a socialist economic system, with considerable modification to accommodate Chinese tradition and socioeconomic realities. By replacing state directives with market-related mechanisms such as contracts, Chinese leaders hope to ensure compliance with state policy, delimit the permissible range of behavior (both within and outside the state plan), and protect private economic activity from bureaucratic interference. However, promulgation of laws cannot by itself establish the rule of law in China; the state must use its power to make the rule of law one of the people's mores. Many Chinese still prefer to rely on informal arrangements in governmental, business, and personal dealings. The formalism required of a modern legal system remains anathema to many illiterate or semiliterate farmers and particularly to government officials who prefer to rule with a vague paternalism, unfettered by legal restrictions or guidelines.[16]

Laws which create a "rights consciousness" challenge fundamental notions of the individual's subservience to state authority. The specter of a litigious citizenry, armed with knowledge of its legal rights and willing to confront those who govern them, might be profoundly threatening to local Chinese leaders. Moreover, both Confucian norms and Chinese communist forms of dispute resolution emphasize conflict avoidance through mediation and consensual settlement. These norms would be challenged by a Western system of adversarial proceedings which vindicates certain individual and collective rights to the detriment of others. In theory, as some modernizing societies develop their legal systems, mediational dispute resolution evolves into more formal types of adjudication by third parties. In other modernizing societies, the social pressures and interrelationships which bind informal institutions are early casualties of changing mores, leaving state coercive power as the only force potent enough to command adherence and to inculcate a modern attitude towards law.[17]

Finally, legal codes entail precise standards and an element of permanence which limits the flexibility the CCP needs to respond to rapid political and economic changes. The government is also reluctant to promulgate detailed regulations which would publicly commit it to certain policies. But vague standards and general statutes are less beneficial than specific regulations to the economic development that remains critical to the success of the economic reforms. In the long run, the PRC might choose to amplify existing law through greater detail and more deftly tailored regulations. At present, short-term flexibility and the advantages of vagueness have outweighed long-term considerations.

Contracts under the PRC Legal System

Since the early 1950s, the state has used contracts to control economic exchange by units subordinate to it. But state interests always had precedence over any contractual agreements, leaving the state free to ignore or abrogate contracts according to its needs.[18] However, after the Third Plenum of the Eleventh Party

Congress, in December 1978, state leaders stressed that contracts can introduce flexibility into China's planned economy while preserving state control. The Economic Contract Law, which became effective in 1982,[19] and several sets of related regulations, including arbitration rules and the Agricultural Sideline Production Contract Regulations,[20] have encouraged formation of contractual relations. These laws and regulations apply only to economic relations between collectives and between collectives and individuals. Article 54 of the Agricultural Sideline Regulations provides that, although the Economic Contract Law does not govern contracts between individuals, contracts between individuals should nonetheless be signed "with reference to it." The new civil code should provide some guidance concerning the law that governs contracts.[21]

To increase the central plan's predictability, most socialist systems used contracts to allocate responsibility for production among economic units, to make economic units accountable for fulfilling their quotas, and to coordinate the distribution of scarce inputs ranging from bank credit to raw materials. They also used contracts to extend government control to economic activity outside the state's purview. Yet, while the relative emphasis on the state plan or contractual responsibility has fluctuated, contracts have remained subordinate to the plan.

The PRC uses contractual responsibility for agricultural output to increase production. The remarkable results it has achieved have focused party and state attention on the mechanism, but their commitment is to the result, not to the means. Contracts remain important only as long as they are effective. The PRC also uses the institution of contract to control the newly decentralized economy. The CCP and the state hoped that this new system would provide, in a way that *dirigiste* central planning has never achieved, the means to calibrate output and requirements and improve coordination of the various sectors of the Chinese economy. Furthermore, they hoped that economic sectors outside the plan would be able to determine with some certainty the degree of their involvement with the planned sector and then act accordingly. Finally, the attention being given to the contracts themselves and to recent leading cases in the PRC provides a useful guide to dispute resolution—for adjudicators, disputants, and potential disputants.

Recent regulations governing contracts differ from earlier Chinese practice in three ways. First, the state has established a corps of notaries public whose chief purpose is to review and validate the terms of the contracts. Legally, notarization is *prima facie* evidence that the contract is valid and lawful.[22] In practice, notarization is essential for any claimant seeking to establish the binding force of a contract.[23] Second, state and local units now encourage contractual parties to engage legal advisers who can ensure that contracts comply with relevant laws, protect clients' interests, and apprise their clients of their legal rights in cases of breach. Thus 56 legal offices set up in Beijing in 1985 handled more than 4,000 lawsuits in six months and reduced the number of disputes by examining and notarizing contracts for local enterprises and households.[24] In the provinces, however, legal representation occurs less frequently.[25] Third, the law and regulations provide reliable and public guidance concerning the formal process for resolving disputes.[26]

The new laws and regulations formalize the contract responsibility scheme and fix it in the framework of the state economy. They also legitimate the contract approach and establish norms for its enforcement. While the CCP and state always stress the primacy of the plan, promulgating these codes legitimizes contractual economic relationships so that state officials may not arbitrarily challenge agreements that conform to these laws and regulations. Therefore, agreements sanctioned by these rules should be enforceable through either formal or informal dispute resolution mechanisms. And, while those who stand their ground might be reviled for their stubbornness, the state promotes the current system as a form of protection for their contractual rights.

Implementing Rural Contracts

Two sets of guidelines based on the Economic Contract Law and current party policy govern rural contracts. The first set, the Agricultural Sideline Production Contract Regulations, covers purchasing contracts, to which organizations rather than individuals are usually parties.[27] The second set includes all local policies or regulations for production responsibility systems and commercial relations which remain unstandardized due to divergent ecological, social, and economic conditions in rural China. (Nonetheless, the local regulations should be consistent with policies of the Central Committee.)[28]

To systematize contracts, the Agricultural Sideline Production Contract Regulations require that each contract specify the following: the exact product, quantity, and units of measure; the "variety, grade, and quality of products"; packaging materials and methods; price; date and location of delivery; procedures for settling accounts; and methods of quality control.[29] The regulations also stipulate the responsibilities of "high-level leading organs" if their actions render one of the contracting parties unable to perform its obligations under the contracts. However, the softness of the regulations is evident; they permit alteration or cancellation of the contract if the state plan is changed, and the "responsible organ involved" may absolve a contracting party of its obligations in whole or in part if *force majeure* (an "irresistible force") prevents fulfillment of the contract.

Although individuals, collectives, and the state may all be party to contracts, the most common combinations are individual-collective agricultural or sideline production contracts and collective-state purchasing contracts. Individual-state purchasing contracts began to proliferate in the early 1980s, especially for cash crops, livestock, and sideline products, but the Chinese press has emphasized contracts between collectives and individual farmers, which to date have formed the vast majority of rural contracts. These contracts are unlikely to generate major difficulties. In fact, court officials in Jiangpu County, Jiangsu Province, said that contract disputes between villagers and their production team are usually resolved by the actors themselves or through the intervention of higher-level local leaders. The ease with which these disputes are resolved probably derives both from the standardization of the ordinary responsibility contract,[30] and from the fact that farmers and cadres resort to traditional patterns of discussion and accommodation.[31] County governments print standard forms and distribute them to all households that sign contracts with their teams for responsibility plots. The team distributes the land according to each household's population, labor power, or both. It then assigns obligations to deliver produce, cash, or both, according to the amount and quality of land each household manages.[32] The change in the procurement system in 1985 presumably allows a more voluntary formation of the contract;[33] however, in many locations old procedures, whereby localities are given delivery quotas and cadres must apportion the needed production and sales among villages and the farmers, remain in effect.[34] Voluntarism was more the exception than the norm.

Specialized contracts, however, are rarely standardized. For example, vegetable contracts in Shanghai County often specify only how much the cultivator should deliver in a given year, without specifying the times of delivery or the varieties of vegetables.[35] The contracts often fix the price without regard to variety or quality.[36] In Fujian Province, vegetable growers sign contracts with their team for land suitable for vegetable cultivation, but often at delivery assessments higher than those charged for grain land.[37] After 1985, more and more collective enterprises, such as factories of various sizes, small-scale repair shops, fish ponds, orchards, brick kilns, construction work, agricultural services, and transportation equipment, were contracted out to individuals, who retain most of the profits.[38] Other households, having turned very small-scale cottage industries into major income-earning pursuits, also sign contracts, either voluntarily or under some duress, with state or collective agencies to sell their product or to buy inputs.[39]

Other types of agreements have been proliferating. Individual-individual contracts (oral or written; between specialized or individual households; for transport, purchase, and sale of services) are becoming more important as the size of the rural private sector expands.[40] In Jiangpu County, specialized households now sign contracts for purchases of inputs and sales of products, as well as for the use of collective property, rather than rely on verbal agreements. But, as the web of contractual relationships becomes far more complicated, problems within one contractual relationship create difficulties for others. Nonetheless, contracts between collectives for the purchase of resources, labor, and technical services will probably proliferate.[41]

Such major readjustments of economic relations among producers and purchasers and between units with disparate interests have generated many problems. Introducing the rule of law into transactions previously subject to state fiat and the personal interventions by state and collective authorities has been difficult.

Moreover, the higher stakes of rural economic activities under the reforms inevitably increase the potential for local conflicts, and the number of contract disputes has risen significantly. In Jiangpu County, there were only eight such cases in 1983, but this figure increased to twenty-four in 1984 and sixty-one in 1985. By May 1986, there were already thirty-four cases, and court officials suggested that the number would increase dramatically by the end of the year.[42] Finally, rural economic specialization and the contract responsibility system have altered local power relationships in the Chinese countryside. For example, a number of rural entrepreneurs have sought protection from the exactions of local officials imposed on those who have profited from the economic reform, or from attempts to alter or evade contractual responsibilities. In all reported cases, the people's courts upheld the contracts and imposed lawful (but perhaps inconsistent) sanctions on the breaching parties or interfering officials. Such decisions affect the socialist political relationship between those in power and local villagers and, consequently could affect general attitudes towards authority on the part of average Chinese citizens.[43]

Philosophy of Enforcement, Court Procedures, and Enforcement of Rural Contracts

Overview of the Court System

The PRC's judicial system comprises the public security organs, the procuratorates, and the courts.[44] In criminal cases, the public security administration investigates crimes and detains suspects, the procurators approve arrests and initiate prosecutions, and the courts adjudicate the cases. In civil cases, the people's courts have greater discretion in investigating and adjudicating cases; however, in that the people's procuratorates retain some rights to supervise court actions, a complete, formal separation of functions does not exist. Moreover, the CCP often monitors the justice system through a parallel network of party committees, whereby party functionaries limit judicial independence.

A hierarchy of judicial organs established by law operates in most of China. It comprises the people's courts at four levels (basic, intermediate, high, and supreme) and a number of special courts with narrow jurisdiction in particular areas. Unless specific legal provisions require that a higher court assume jurisdiction, most civil and criminal cases originate in the basic-level people's courts established in county seats, towns, autonomous counties, and urban districts of larger cities. These courts of general jurisdiction have been divided for administrative purposes into chambers which hear criminal, civil, or economic cases.

The Chinese legal process also relies on informal methods of dispute resolution outside the judicial framework. Mediation committees, established in every urban and rural locality, have customarily been forums in which preliminary efforts are made to mediate civil disputes, encouraging disputants to settle their differences in a nonconfrontational manner. The trial Code of Civil Procedure reiterates this commitment to mediation; it stipulates that courts should attempt to mediate the dispute before going to trial, and disputants who resist going before a mediation committee can still expect a protracted period of mediation in the court.[45] And, while the trial Code of Civil Procedure stipulates that participation in mediation is voluntary, in that a party has the legal right to take the case to court, the voluntariness of this decision may be rather illusory. Between 1983 and 1986, mediation had already resolved 73 percent (93 of 127) of all cases in Jiangpu County, Jiangsu Province; in only four cases did the court issue a decision, and thirty were still pending.[46]

Overview of Contract Dispute Resolution

While a number of rural contract disputes involve individual farmers bringing suit against a collective for breach of contract, rural cadres have not used the dispute-resolution mechanism against individual villagers. Whether this indicates that villagers rarely breach contracts, that collectives rely on their reserve funds to cover losses, or that cadres use their political power to enforce contract resolutions is unknown.

In the contract cases analyzed below, in which simple agreements between farmers and the production team involve little money, disputes are heard in the economic chamber of the basic-level people's court. No fixed monetary amount determines which disputes go to which level of court, but intermediate-level courts usually hear disputes involving larger amounts.[47] Jurisdictional boundaries also determine where a case is heard. Intermediate-level courts usually hear contract disputes between parties in different counties, but sometimes the basic-level court in the county where the work was to be completed hears the case.[48] Intermediate-level courts also take potentially precedent-setting cases and sometimes cases with which the county courts have little experience. For example, at the beginning of the agricultural reforms, municipal courts heard responsibility-contract cases to demonstrate how such cases should be handled.

Regardless of which level has jurisdiction, its economic chamber follows the same basic steps in a contract dispute. The petitioner writes a complaint and mails or delivers it to the court. The complaint should state the names of the complainant and the respondent, their respective units, the content of the contract between them, and the nature of their dispute. The court may reject the case if the contract did not follow the provisions and regulations of the Economic Contract Law, or if the terms of the contract are unclear.[49] The court may decide not to reject the case, however, because it wishes to prevent a lingering dispute.[50] The economic chamber may also move a case to the criminal chamber if the contract promoted illegal activities.

Since the typical county court has as few as five or six judges, the economic chamber attempts to persuade the disputants to settle out of court or accept solutions determined at higher levels of the rural bureaucracy—a strong practical option that supplements the norms and laws emphasizing mediation. Both parties' fear of losing at trial often helps the court to achieve a negotiated settlement. Should the parties persist, however, and the court accepts the complaint, the court must first register the complaint, making it a case (*anjian*). It then sends the respondent a copy of the complaint, to which she or he must respond. In some cases, the respondent simply accepts the accusation specified in the complaint. On receipt of the response, the court appoints a collegial bench of three to supervise the case.[51] Two members of this panel, or one member accompanied by a clerk, then visit the location of the dispute and investigate the case. Two people attend to prevent corruption or bias.

The team considers four categories of evidence: (1) written documents, such as the contract itself, the complaint, the responses; (2) oral testimony of complainant(s) and respondent(s); (3) testimony of witnesses (usually interviews without cadres present to prevent intimidation and encourage frank testimony); and (4) results of inspection of the site where the contract was to be performed. Customary practices are also a source of law in Chinese cases, but their evidentiary weight is greater in the urban industrial sector of the economy than in rural agricultural areas. The court might also examine past practices of the parties to an agreement—a kind of informal customary law.

In simple cases, the investigation team may use the field trip to encourage the parties to reach an agreement. Should the parties agree, they must specify their agreement to abide by the contract in writing. The entire collegial bench must approve the agreement, not only those conducting the investigation; the parties must sign it, and the court must affix its seal.[52] If the parties will not agree, the investigation team reports to the other members of the collegial bench, and the three members of the court of first instance discuss the case. A clerk records notes of their discussion. In reaching a decision, the votes of all members have equal weight, and split decisions are possible. If the decision is clear, the panel may try to persuade the parties to come to an out-of-court settlement. The mediation solution that the bench proposes represents the majority opinion of the panel members. If the parties accept the settlement, they sign the letter of agreement. However, if either party insists on litigating the dispute, the court must provide a hearing.

The three judges then form the bench for the courtroom trial.[53] According to the trial Code of Civil Procedure, each party presents its version of the dispute in oral argument, and the court investigates further with questions. The parties may then debate their positions, after which each may make a final statement. The court then attempts a final mediation, and, if it fails, must render a decision. The judgment must state the facts as determined by the bench and its reasons for the judgment, as well as the bench's determination of the expenses that each party must bear and the deadline for filing an appeal of the decision. Once that deadline passes, the judgment can be executed.

Contract Dispute Cases

The six cases that follow have been disseminated by Chinese legal officials among legal specialists to provide insight and advice as to the proper procedures for settling contract disputes.[54] These cases demonstrate the importance that Chinese officials ascribe to avoiding breaches of contract and their tendency to favor mediation over court decisions. At the same time, they demonstrate the difficulties involved in introducing a legal code and contractual agreements into a society in which economic law previously had a minimal role. In the light of these difficulties, it is not surprising that judicial actions often blend formal legal codes and informal societal ones.

Case 1: The Apple Orchard Case

In August, 1981, when [XX] Township's team no. 1 contracted its apple orchard to a commune member, the terms provided that the contract would not change for three years; in addition, besides bearing all expenses, the contractor would pay the team 500 *yuan* (approximately US$135) a year at the end of September.[55] The contractual fee was not to be reduced for any drought, waterlogging, wind, rain, or hail. Anyone contravening the contract was to pay a double fine. As the highest bidder, Wang XX, a team member, won the contract. After signing the contract, [Wang] and his two brothers wholeheartedly threw themselves into it; they engaged a technician and expended a great deal of labor to increase the orchard's productivity. In 1982 and 1983, Wang paid the full contractual fee on time and obtained double that in profit. As a result, some people became envious. In the first month of 1984, during a meeting of team members, the team leader, on the pretext that the contract had been drawn up imperfectly, and without consulting Wang, unilaterally announced that Wang should prepay the 1984 contract fee; otherwise, the contract would be annulled. Because Wang would not agree, they [the team members] annulled the contract. Consequently, the team hastily conducted new bidding, requiring that each year [the contractor] must pay the team 1,500 *yuan,* and signed a new contract with four households. Remaining dissatisfied, Wang raised objections. He was accused of "being deliberately provocative" and was jointly attacked by the contracting households, forcing the contractor [Wang], on June 24, 1984, to lodge a complaint with our court.

In our hearing on this case, neither plaintiff nor defendant took exception to the stated facts. Through organizing [sic] the litigants earnestly to study Central Document No. 1 and the Economic Contract Law, we raised the litigants' sense of legality and level of policy [sic]. We solemnly criticized the team leader's erroneous activity, drawing a clear distinction between right and wrong, and under the principle of contract and in line with the spirit of benefiting production, the two parties voluntarily arrived at an agreement, namely: that the original contract should be upheld, and the newly signed contract was without effect.

After the case was concluded, the team leader said, "Before we generally didn't study, didn't read the newspapers, didn't understand the Party's policy, and even less understood the law, and did some things contravening the law. We feel extraordinarily ashamed. From now on, we certainly must conscientiously study Document No. 1 and state law, actively support the contracting households in developing commodity production, and protect their contractual rights." [Wang] feelingly said, "with the Party's Document Number One and state law, the more we do the more zeal we have."

Through the handling of this case, we learn: (1) Economic adjudication work must unswervingly follow the Party's direction and policies, securely establish the idea that economic adjudication serves the four modernizations, promotes the reforms of managerial structures, and develops production; (2) We must maintain consistency with the Central Committee and correctly and in timely fashion handle contract disputes among contracting households, specialized households, economic associations, and juridical persons; support the legal rights and interests of the "two households, one body";[56] and promote the development of the rural economy; (3) The reason why some rural communes and brigades are abrogating contracts, aside from prejudice, is that commune and brigade cadres' sense of legality is weak. They are accustomed to handling matters through administrative commands and treat signed contracts as merely another purely administrative method to be handled arbitrarily. Not only are the legal rights and interests of contracting households infringed on and their production enthusiasm seriously dampened; but the thorough implementation of party [policy] is also adversely affected. Given the present situation, preserving the legality of rural contracts and conscientiously safeguarding the legal rights and interests of contracting households has become a major task of the People's Court.

Case 2: The Tangerine Orchard Case

On July 17, 1983, the [XX] County People's Economic Adjudication Chamber at the place in question publicly heard a case involving a dispute in which the contracting households, Guo XX and Ni XX, sued their production team for tearing up their tangerines contract.[57] Through the hearing, we maintained the solemnity of the Economic Contract Law and the legitimate rights and interests of specialized households, and obtained good results in developing the various rural specialized households, [and] key-point households, [in] promotion of rural commodity production, and [in] enlivening the rural economy.

"Envy" Destroys the Agreement and the Aggrieved Party Brings Suit

[BB] Brigade team No. 3 of [AA] Commune, [XX] County, had a tangerine orchard (among which were 192 tangerine trees bearing fruit and 492 seedlings).

In the past several years production management was poor, and in the best years they could harvest only about 200 kilograms of tangerines. So, after team cadres and members had many times discussed and studied the problem, they decided, in March 1982, to contract out the orchard to team members. Without gaining the members' consent, the team head [Guo XX] and the tangerine technician [Ni XX] jointly contracted for the orchard. The two parties signed a three-year contract, and had it stamped by the vice chairman of the brigade management committee. After the contract was signed, the two parties had no disagreement. Because they worked as one and conscientiously managed the orchard, that year the gross output jumped to over 5,500 kilograms. The net income of each of the contracting households was over 800 *yuan*. With bumper harvests of tangerines, the contracting households' income increased. A minority of team members grew envious, so they looked for a pretext to fabricate facts and create contradictions. Arguing that the contracting households had used the power of office to force a contract, they unilaterally repealed the contract. In April of last year, they divided all the tangerine trees equally among all households. The contracting households maintained that it was a legal contract and demanded that the original contract be maintained. Because of this, the two parties raised a dispute. In the commune and brigade, mediation was conducted repeatedly without success, and the contracting households were forced to bring the suit to the court's economic chamber.

"Registering the Case and Investigation:
Distinguishing Clearly Between Right and Wrong"

Handling rural, specialized-household, contract-dispute cases poses a new problem for economic adjudication work. Before registering the case, we had some misgivings: first, rural contract disputes involve a broad range of issues, the policy ramifications are great, and we feared that we lacked experience, and if we handled it badly it would be hard to wind up the case. Second, the circumstances of this type of case were complicated; since each side was sticking to its own position, mediation could not succeed. Also, any judgment would be hard to implement. Third, after the rural responsibility system was implemented, the number of specialized households was increasing, so we feared that in future many cases such as this one would be brought to our court. But, the personnel of the economic adjudication chamber were few, and if we received many cases, the burden would be onerous.

With these problems in mind, we talked to the commune party committee and the district and county leaders, conscientiously listening to their opinions. Leading cadres in the district and county argued that some of the masses, who misunderstood the question of specialized households prospering under the new circumstances, grow envious and provoke disputes, thereby harming the consolidation and development of specialized households. Therefore, the court decided to handle several of these model cases and use the law to uphold the legitimate rights and interests of specialized households and support their efforts to get rich. We also repeatedly organized the comrades of the entire chamber conscientiously to study the Central Committee's policies concerning enlivening the rural economy, as well as articles in periodicals and newspapers concerning the protection of specialized households. Thus, we recognized that specialized and key-point households emerging in the countryside under the contract responsibility system are a new phenomenon which leads to the development of rural commodity production and the enlivening of the rural economy. We must cherish them and actively support them; the people's court then should handle the case and use legal methods to support their rights and interests, so as to facilitate their healthy development. This case should definitely be accepted.

After accepting the case, the personnel handling it conscientiously checked over the complainants' report of their suit and listened in detail to their statements. The agent for the team raised four arguments: (1) the contracting households had used the powers of office to force through a contract; (2) the contracting households had picked and sold unripened fruit without the team's authorization or unified weighing, so team members had not shared in any bonuses; (3) the contracting households hadn't done their winter mulching and fertilizing, or whitened the bark to prevent freezing, so some tangerine trees [had] died; and (4) if large fields could be contracted to all households, then tangerine production could also be contracted to households. We conducted [an] investigation on all these points.

Concerning charges about the use of Guo and Ni's powers of office, the brigade management committee's vice chairman and registered contractor [Deng XX] and the commune's vice secretary handling diversification[58] [Zhang XX] testified that to do the contracting of the tangerine orchard well, the team had convened three consecutive member assemblies and had given the members a sample tangerine contract to discuss and revise. Afterward, each household had signed and affixed its seal. To manage this orchard well, and given that no one else wanted to take on the contract, Guo and Ni finally formed this partnership. Fundamentally, there was no problem in their using the powers of office to ram through a contract.

As for the unauthorized sale of unripened fruit, the fact is that in August 1982, when the tangerines had to be sprayed with insecticide and fertilized, the contracting households were financially strained. To protect tangerine production, they sold 100 kilograms of unripened fruit at the state-negotiated price, which earned them 46 *yuan* for the tangerines. Not only did this not contravene the contract, but it could not have harmed tangerine output. Regarding the alleged fruit picking without unified weighing, because the number of tangerines to be sold to the team had already been fixed in the contract, and any increase or decrease of output was entirely the responsibility of the contracting households, they did not have to let the team weigh them. Finally, regarding the quantity of tangerines to be distributed to team members, the contracting households gave a detailed list of the original distribution, enumerated household by household, which accorded with that amount stipulated in the contract, so the team members had received their proper share.

As for the failure to winter mulch and fertilize, we invited the tangerine technician and the district, commune, and brigade management committees and the two parties to come to the orchard to inspect whether this work of mulching, fertilizing, and painting [the bark] had been done. Actually, it had not been done. The reason was because, after the team abrogated the contract, the contracting households' thought vacillated; they lost interest in the orchard and therefore didn't sufficiently mulch or fertilize the mature trees, and applied 50 kilograms less chemical fertilizer and 3,500 kilograms less household manure. The team had not mulched or fertilized the immature trees according to the contract stipulations, which definitely harmed the raising of the tangerine trees.

As for dividing the output among the households, we specifically asked county committee leaders for instructions. The county vice head, who was also in charge of diversification, told us that given the diversification under the rural production responsibility systems, the contracts already signed should be supported by law, and we must give expression to the solemnity of law. Contracting out the tangerine orchard to specialized households accords with state policy, and we must certainly protect the contractors' rights and interests. The facts indicate that the production team was wrong to tear up the contract and redivide the trees equally among member households. They must bear the chief responsibility for the dispute. The contracting households' failure to discharge all their contractual responsibilities before expiration of the contract was also incorrect, and they should bear responsibility for the dispute.

Mediation Is Unsuccessful; Judgment According to Law

After the facts were clearly ascertained and the responsibilities clarified, in line with the principle of "emphasizing mediation" we went twice to the team to organize [sic] the cadres and masses to study the Party's rural policies and Economic Contract Law, so as to raise the masses' sense [sic] of policy and law. We conducted active mediation work. During the investigation, we first tried to change both parties' viewpoints and discretely consulted with them. We also did painstaking work with the agents designated by the two parties. But, because the demands raised by the team's agent were excessive, the contracting households would not accept them, and we could not get a mediated agreement. Later, we again brought the two parties face to face for discussion, but that mediation also failed. This situation meant that the ill effects of this case in the county's rural areas would be relatively great. So on July 17, 1983, to educate the masses and propagandize the law, we conducted a public hearing on the spot. In the court session we stated the facts clearly, explained the reasoning, and studied the relevant policies and laws. The two sides conducted a thorough debate. We further clarified right and wrong and distinguished responsibility. Afterward, the court again tried mediation, but the two parties still could not agree. Based on the Civil Procedure Law, article no. 111,[59] we rendered the following judgment: (1) the contract signed between Guo and Ni and the production team was still in effect and should be upheld; (2) the reduced application of fertilizer and mulch by Guo and Ni should be remedied by their buying good fertilizer to apply; (3) the team should again apply fertilizer to the immature trees which had been insufficiently fertilized; (4) the costs of this case, 25 *yuan,* should be shouldered at 15 *yuan* by the team and 10 *yuan* by the contracting households.

After the case was concluded, we conducted a return visit. The commune party secretary said that all the commune cadres had been in the audience when the case was heard, and unanimously considered that the court had handled it in a timely, suitable, and fair fashion. In the entire commune there were fifteen commune and brigade farms and forty-five team farms. Of those originally conducting responsibility contracting, seven farms had intended to abrogate the contracts. After this case was settled, they recognized that the specialized households receive legal protection, and now all have been stabilized, promoting development of the commune's specialized households. In 1983, the output of tangerines in the commune reached 436 tons; 414 tons were delivered to the state, a relatively great increase over 1982. Guo and Ni, seeing that the people's court was upholding righteousness and supporting and protecting specialized households' legal rights and interests, were reassured, and their confidence in specialized contracts was even greater. They claimed that henceforth they would manage the tangerine trees well, repay the previous losses, and make more contributions to the state.

Case 3: The Grain Station Case

In August 1983, drought threatened the late rice crop of a team in [XX] county; they needed water from the irrigation station, but could not get it until they paid electrical expenses and bought the necessary tools.[60] But the team's accumulation fund was empty. The grain station still owed the team over 1,000 *yuan* for tea oil, but a dispute over this had been dragging on for three years. The team head decided that the matter should be taken to court.

The team head and several team members went to the court's economic chamber and reported the circumstances as follows: In winter 1981, the team sold 200 kilograms of tea oil [at the fixed price] and 450 kilograms at the above-quota [surplus] negotiated price to balance its funds. The sales receipts were lost because they were not well taken care of. So the team suffered a loss from the grain station. They went repeatedly to the grain station seeking payment but without success.

The court's chief judge and two comrades of the economic chamber, after hearing the team head's complaint, considered the problem serious and decided to solve it immediately. They worked hard to investigate and solve the case within two to three days. The court vice head and one other comrade hurried to the brigade and found that the team had indeed made the sale as claimed. The second day, the person handling the case went to the grain station, looked up the receipts for the 1981 grain and oil purchases, and found that the amount of money for which [sic] the team had lost its sales receipts was still at the grain station. The third day, [the investigators] called the two parties together to make adjustments. The head of the grain station immediately agreed to pay the team the amount owed. The team went home with 1,110 *yuan,* and got its water and tools.

Case 4: The Mushroom Factory Case

In July 1980, [XX] County commune and brigade enterprises bureau [hereafter CBE] staked a mushroom spores factory formed by five persons.[61] At the time they rented three rooms of a house and successfully experimented with growing *pinggu,* woodears, and monkeyhead mushrooms. Some pinggu were as heavy as 6.5 kilograms. During this period, the average monthly wage for the five was nearly sixty *yuan.* So, in January 1981, the county CBE bureau decided to establish the factory formally and expand it from the original five to eleven persons.

Various units with poor production conditions, such as the county chemical factory, the cement factory, as well as [YY] Brigade, and two individual households asked to buy the factory's spores and also requested technical guidance. Around the same time, in March 1982, the county agricultural repairs factory signed a contract with the spores factory for raising pinggu. The agricultural repairs factory was to supply the land, manpower, and funds for raw materials, estimated at more than 1,900 *yuan.* The spores factory was responsible for supplying the spores and the technology for mushroom cultivation. The contract specified that 5,000 kilograms of cottonseed husks would produce 3,000 kilograms of mushrooms. If under 3,000 kilograms [were produced], the spores factory was to repay the agricultural repairs factory's losses. Profits were to be divided between the two on a four-to-one basis. But after the spores were planted, not a single kilogram was harvested within the stipulated period, and a dispute between the two parties arose.

The agricultural repairs factory took the complaint to court, saying that the spores provided by the spores factory were defective and could not grow mushrooms. The spores factory claimed that the problem stemmed from air pollution caused by the materials the agricultural repairs factory had burned to raise the indoor temperature. In fact, the spores factory was not too clear on why no mushrooms had sprouted. The two other factories were unsuccessful as well in growing mushrooms and also accused the spores factory of cheating. Investigation yielded different stories from different people within the spores factory, causing its credibility to suffer. Not only did no one contract again with the factory, but there was no one left raising anything in the spores factory. After selling the products, 70 percent of the workers' wages still could not be paid, leaving [the factory] no option but to shut down.

The county court's economic chamber, based on the plaintiff's complaint and the defendant's response, figured that the key to resolving the dispute was to determine whether or not the spores were viable, and, if they were, why they hadn't sprouted. This was a technical issue new to the adjudicating personnel. They needed to ask a scientific research unit to study it. So they took spore samples to the Provincial Biological Research Institute and to the Municipal Vegetable Research Institute. Results showed that the spores were good. There were two reasons why the mushrooms hadn't grown: (1) things had not been properly managed, and the humidity was too low; (2) the temperature was not kept constant. In May, the [outdoor] temperature had gotten very high and humidity had dropped fast. Also, they said the spores could still produce mushrooms under the proper conditions.

Upon their return, the investigators called the two parties together for mediation. The spores factory realized their technical guidance had been at fault; the agricultural repairs factory recognized that their original way of proceeding was also wrong. Both gave up their original stances. The spores factory voluntarily assumed the 1900 *yuan* loss suffered by the Agricultural Repairs Factory. The two set up an agreement, and the dispute was entirely resolved.

But the county court reckoned that the problem was not entirely solved since the spores factory had ceased production and the workers had scattered. The economic court personnel were not satisfied. Responsibility for the four modernizations means that, for each problem that arises during the handling of the cases, the court must propose legal opinions, help improve economic management, and raise economic results. Especially in the case of a factory that has closed, the court has the responsibility to help them restore production so as to guarantee stability of the workers' livelihoods. Therefore, they proposed a method for raising the level of technical management so that mushroom cultivation could resume. Motivated by the court's sense of responsibility, the spores factory accepted their opinion and followed the advice on cultivation and management proposed by the scientific unit. Altogether they harvested 2,000 kilograms of mushrooms, received nearly 3,000 *yuan,* and in one season repaid the losses and had some extra left over.

As more and more places bought mushrooms from this factory, demand exceeded supply. In the beginning of 1984, we interviewed the manager of the spores factory and discovered that the factory had expanded to eleven rooms, had bought a truck, and supported its own technical expert. In the past year, production had exceeded 10,000 bottles [of spores]. In January and February of this year, they already had signed contracts with outside units for 15,000 bottles.

XX, XX, and XX were preparing to sign contracts, and the factory estimated that this year they might attain 30,000 bottles. The number of workers had also increased to fifteen, with day and night shifts.

Case 5: The Brick Kiln Case

On March 18, 1984, our court publicly tried a contract dispute case in [XX] Township Hall.[62] The accused, [XX] township's village committee and team no. 1, were punished by law. This educated nearly 1,000 people.

In October 1982, [XX] Commune's [YY] Brigade members Luo XX and five others, inspired by the Party's policy of allowing people to prosper, signed a contract for a brick kiln with the brigade and team no. 1. The contract stipulated: "The brigade and production team no. 1 (hereinafter Party A) contracts the brigade kiln out to Luo XX and five others (hereinafter Party B) for a period of three years, at a contractual charge of 11,000 yuan to be paid in installments. Party A guarantees the kiln's land for production, electricity, water supply, and roads. Party B is responsible for additional purchases of kiln production equipment. After the end of the contract period, any equipment is to be given to Party A without compensation." In order to make the contract legal, both parties signed and affixed seals, and then took the contract to the county notary's office to have it notarized. After the contract took effect, Party B strictly abided by the contract, and spent 25,000 *yuan* on kiln investments, repaired the kiln and roads, paid for additional equipment, and quickly plunged into production.

After one year, they could see results. At this point, certain responsible persons of the brigade committee and team no. 1 got envious, considered that they had sustained a loss, and made harsh demands on the contractors, such as that each year the contract fee should be raised by 10,000 *yuan,* and so on. After these demands had been rejected, the brigade's responsible person(s) sent someone to shut off the kiln's electrical supply; [and] divided up the land used by the kiln [as a source of clay] among commune members as responsibility fields, forcing the kiln to stop production and creating serious losses. In this dispute, the [XX] township government mediated many times without success. Thus, on February 13, 1984, the contractors of the kiln filed suit in our court, demanding that we defend their legal interests.

After our court accepted this case, we immediately sent someone to investigate and after ascertaining the facts called the two sides together for mediation. The plaintiff agreed to make suitable concessions under the court's mediations. But the defendant "stepped back an inch and advanced a foot" and was unreasonably fierce. When our court sent someone to investigate, [the defendant] organized the masses to surround him and hurl abuses. To consolidate socialist economic order, guarantee thorough implementation of the Party's various rural economic policies, defend the contractors' legal interests, uphold the sanctity of the law and the solemnity of contract, and punish and educate the transgressors, the Economic Chamber's Trial Committee decided that the economic tribunal, according to law, should form a collegiate panel and conduct a public hearing of the case.

Following its inquiry, the panel decided that the content of the "brick kiln contract" signed by the two parties was legal, the responsibilities were clearly divided, the procedures were faultless, and it was legally binding. There was much evidence that the defendant, [YY] Brigade Committee and team no. 1, had clearly contravened the contract. Based on articles 6, 32, and 35 of the PRC [Economic] Contract Law, they made the following decision: (1) to uphold the original contract; (2) the defendants were to reimburse the plaintiff 500 *yuan* as penalty for breach of contract, and 1,000 *yuan* in compensatory damages, while the person directly responsible, Zeng ZZ [head of team no. 1], was to reimburse the kiln 100 *yuan*; (3) the land that had been distributed was to be returned for the kiln's use; (4) court costs of 550 *yuan* were to be paid by the defendants. After the judgment was passed, the plaintiff Luo XX, the defendant [Zeng ZZ], and the responsible person of [YY] Brigade, expressed obedience to the decision, but the defendant Zeng ZZ, acting for team no. 1, did not accept the decision.[63]

After the hearing ended, the masses who had been in the audience discussed it bit by bit, [generally approving that those who violate contracts should be punished and that everyone is equal before the law]. Some masses said, "The village cadres talk but it doesn't mean anything, and they tear contracts to shreds. They bully everybody and specialized households; they should be fined a bit more." The representative(s) of the specialized households participating in the audience said: "In the past, we feared that the policies would change. This year's CC Document No. 1 has reassured us. Today the people's court has also backed up our households."[64]

Case 6: The Apple Sales Cases

Example A. "Resolutely Uphold the Rights and Interests of the Parties Concerned"

In January 1984, an apple-raising specialized household [Fang XX] brought a complaint. In November 1983, two transport households, Zhang and Peng, having been sent by the municipal mayor to the market town to procure apples, negotiated with Fang.[65] With Fang as guarantor,[66] they went to the apple-raising households in his brigade and agreed to pay for the apples three days after taking them to the city. Based on this oral agreement, Fang collected altogether 24,775 kilograms (or 9,910 *yuan*) of apples from some apple specialized households. In December, Zhang and Peng took these apples to town to sell them. But a month later, no word had arrived from them. By spring festival, the fruit growers needed this cash for handling their new year's purchases. So the dispute fell on the guarantor Fang. Some wanted to take things from his house in payment of the debt. Fang went repeatedly to the Public Security Bureau, the Industry and Commerce Bureau, and other officials without success. Just when he was about to disregard the consequences and risk a fight with Zhang and Peng, someone suggested "going to people's court."

Because this had been a verbal contract and Fang could not produce written proof, some of our comrades said our court could not handle such cases. After he left, we had a heated discussion over whether we should take on a case based on an individual household's verbal complaint. All felt that since the Party's economic policy supporting increased interactions between individual and specialized households would indirectly give rise to conflicts, we had to settle this case.

So the court carried out an intensive investigation and very quickly ascertained the facts. Originally, when Zhang and Peng brought the apples back to town, their poor quality caused delays in selling them; so they rotted, causing losses. Since the apples were not of good quality, the plaintiff bore part of the responsibility; at the same time the mediated agreement stated that the defendants would pay 8,650 *yuan*, making Fang very grateful.

*Example B: "The Parties Concerned Should Be Treated
Without Discrimination Regardless of Whether They
Are from Another Province or Another County"*

Among the sixteen cases we handled, 15 percent involved litigants from other areas. The defendants in this type of case think that, because they are on their home turf and dealing with familiar people, legal proceedings with outsiders, even those who are in the right, will still be settled to their own advantage. Therefore, they often end up in our courts entangling our administrative staff. How can we overcome this "localist" attitude and correctly uphold the rights and interest of outsiders according to state law? To handle this kind of case well, we must deal impartially, regardless of whether people are from another county or another province and strictly handle the case according to law. For example, the head of the court judged a case involving an individual and a specialized household, Xiao XX and Du XX, both from [AB] Commune of Henan Province's [YY] County. They accused the DD Railroad's RR Section Youth Store [in a dispute] over a purchase and sale contract.

On September 27, 1981, Xiao and Du had signed a purchase-and-sale contract with the Youth Store for 25,580 kilograms or 16,005.23 *yuan* of apples. According to the contract, Xiao and Du had brought the apples to FF Station in [DD] City, Henan Province, to give them to the Youth Store. After the Youth Store had taken the apples back to [DD] City, they discovered that the apples were of poor quality and they refused to pay for the goods. Because of this, Xiao and Du came to [DD] City to bring suit, although they feared that in eight of ten cases they'd lose by bringing the cases here. The Youth Store's legal representative had secretly told the head of the court that he expected that the court would not find in favor of an outsider. Not only did the head of the court reject this attitude, he conducted a detailed explanation and sternly pointed out that "we state work personnel cannot adopt localist attitudes." After that, the head of the court conducted a conscientious investigation. After clarifying the facts of the case, he placed principal responsibility on the Youth Store. He discussed this with the leaders of the Youth Store nine times and smoothly arrived at an agreement. Regarding the actual losses of 10,591.3 *yuan,* the Youth Store was responsible for 70 percent; because of the defective quality of the apples Xiao and Du had delivered, they voluntarily took responsibility for 30 percent. After signing the adjustment agreement, Xiao and Du were ebullient in praising the court's impartiality.

Example C: "Conform Only to Whether a Case is Standard; Don't Distinguish Between Large- and Small-Scale Cases; Handle Them All Equally"

For example, Zhejiang Province's LL County, [GG] Commune's food processing factory in [LL] County, Zhejiang Province, accused an individual industrial household in [DD] City in a purchase-and-sale dispute. However, although the amount at issue was only 75.48 *yuan,* and we were concurrently in the midst of a very serious criminal case, leaving only one person in the court to deal with other cases, we thought that the rights and interests of the parties in question merited protection. So we decided to handle all cases, however small. After investigation and discussion, the court decided that repayment was necessary. However, the defendant's financial problems meant that he couldn't pay, so the person handling the case got the plaintiff to agree to extend the repayment period. When that expired, the defendant brought the money to the court, and the person handling the case personally sent it to the plaintiff, who sent us a letter of thanks.

Evaluating the Cases

This section draws general conclusions from the six cases and the circumstances surrounding them. They are cases that the state chose to publish, and one cannot be certain that unpublished decisions resemble these. Nevertheless, the cases illustrate that the courts' paramount consideration is avoiding breach of contract; otherwise, this new institution was unlikely to thrive within China's traditionally nonlegalistic culture. A breach by one party does not relieve the other party of its contractual obligations, and the courts admonish parties who claim they cannot meet their obligations to exert every effort to fulfill the terms. Otherwise, the state plan and production will suffer. Modifications of original obligations are also discouraged to prevent repercussions for third parties.

The courts also strive to preserve contractual relations as well as contracts, aware that the disputants are often from the same locality and are likely to be living in close proximity for most of their remaining lives. Therefore, long before disputes reach the court, the courts try to persuade litigants to participate in nonconfrontational mediation, organized informally by influential local officials or consisting of informal sessions of the people's mediation committees. They doggedly seek to preserve the relationship of the parties and ensure at least general fulfillment of the contract. Even after the petitioner insists that the court register the case, civil procedure requires that mediation efforts continue while the case is under court investigation. Until the very moment that a judgment is announced, the legal system encourages out-of-court settlements. In this way, the courts try to reconcile the contract responsibility system's goals with Chinese reality. The state, by demonstrating that it will strictly enforce contracts, clearly strives to impress on producers their responsibility to fulfill the original terms. However, the novelty of the system has required flexibility, as producers and cadres discover the uses and limitations of the new institutions. Furthermore, strict enforcement of the original terms would contravene the long tradition in Chinese rural communities of seeking to maintain harmonious relations and impede popular acceptance of the contract mechanism. The courts, therefore, constantly try to balance legalism and prevailing social norms, a critical aspect of helping new legal institutions sink roots in traditional cultures.

The courts also seek equitable remedies. If both sides have attempted to fulfill the contract, the courts apportion responsibility accordingly. However, arbitrary action by one party in disregard of the contract tends to elicit unilateral judgments. Even without arbitrary action, court judgments more often place responsibility for losses on one side, whereas mediated settlements usually apportion damages.

The new laws and regulations establish minimum requirements for contracts and for the existence of contractual relations. Contracts must be voluntary, written, and certified. Only such contracts form the normal basis for contractual relations, although in certain instances, consistent with local practices, courts have even honored oral agreements. If the terms of the contract are unclear or the contract lacks proper verification, courts usually disallow its validity.

The introduction of notaries public into the legal system over the past few years has also changed the way in which contracts are signed and disputes are resolved. Notaries public have legal training; notary offices throughout China's large cities, provincial towns, and county seats, are supervised by the Ministry of Justice. In addition to their initial review and certification of contracts, state officials give notaries some power to settle disputes; the office which notarized the contract can interpret ambiguous provisions, act as the final arbiter of a contract's substance, and order reluctant parties to perform their obligations. In Jiangpu County, the head of the notary office was also director of the Ministry of Civil Affairs' mediation office, and had responsibility for the work of the local mediation committees.[67]

The cases above share certain fundamental characteristics. Each case presented substantial evidence that contractual relations existed, usually with special focus on a written contract. The basic-level court accepted each case only after early attempts at out-of-court mediation had failed. The courts undertook extensive pre-trial mediation to encourage the parties to settle and to educate parties who were clearly in the wrong about their erroneous behavior.

However, there are important differences among the cases. While in most cases both parties shared the blame for disrupting contractual relations, in a significant minority of cases, local officials demonstrated a callous disregard for the terms of the contracts, and one party alone was judged to be at fault. Even in these cases, the court took considerable pains to urge a settlement, and if the party at fault refused to change, the language of the report and the final judgment was quite harsh. While the courts are using these cases as models to promote the state's new economic policies, the courts are also demonstrating a willingness to abide by new norms.

Ironically, the very successes of the contract responsibility system in increasing agricultural and industrial output may have complicated the establishment of a stable contracting system. Many parties apparently abrogate contracts due to jealousy (what the Chinese often call "red eye disease") or outrage concerning the rich economic returns that accrued to the target of the complaint. Even if they were to be committed to the ideal of economic reform, some parties might have second thoughts when the other party reaps large profits. In cases in which specialized households' net return far surpassed that produced under collective management, cadres often tried to increase fees paid by the contracting party, arguing that collective inputs had been undervalued at the time the contract was negotiated. These claims have sometimes been true as local cadres' inexperience and the lack of effective incentives generated enormous lost opportunity costs for collectively owned assets. However, once those collective assets were essentially privatized through the contract responsibility system, which allows individuals to recoup those sunken economic rents, farmers became angry at the sight of collective prosperity enriching a few hard-working households. Nevertheless, in these cases, once the contract was signed, even if the transferred resources were undervalued, the sanctity of the contract was upheld. Despite these local difficulties, the central government has made known its priorities, and these cases at the grassroots level underscore them. Abuses of contract or attempts to disavow legally binding agreements must be publicly condemned, and meaningful penalties must be imposed for violations of the Economic Contract Law and regulations. Parties must respect the institution of contract.

The cases decided under the new Economic Contract Law display the thrust of the new economic policies toward formalizing and legalizing economic relationships. Reliance on sometimes standardized, sometimes specific, and carefully documented delineation of responsibilities; the use of notaries public to scrutinize contracts; and legal checks on the discretion of local administrators and

party cadres all depart from previous PRC practices. The judiciary, by overseeing the enforcement of these new requirements, is assuming a new political role.
The new freedoms provided to the contracting households and the constraints
placed on cadres are altering the political landscape. But before local cadres
undertake a more limited supervisory role and allow villagers to enter freely into
contractual relationships, the state and the courts must help them unlearn habits
inculcated during decades of Maoism. Under the new reforms, government fiat
no longer determines the relationship of agents in the economy; subtle coercion
has given way to greater freedom to make contracts, choose economic partners,
and determine the level of output or services that will be offered. In resolving
contract disputes, the courts have taken on the mandate of educating cadres in
their new tasks.

Strengthening the rule of law has enhanced the role of formal, especially
judicial, methods of dispute resolution. Mediation committees remain the first
recourse for formal resolution of contract disputes, but the number of cases
resolved by the courts is increasing.[68] Perhaps responding to the courts' new role
and norms, many disputants want a definitive allocation of fault and costs. The
state has yet to fix the scope and substance of the judiciary's duties, but litigation
should assume a greater role in rural China than has existed since 1949. As more
villagers successfully challenge local leadership through litigation, the contract
system itself may affect the nature of power in rural China, shifting some authority to the courts as well as strengthening the farmers' relationship vis-à-vis local
cadres.

The cases cited above, which limit local cadres' previously wide, discretion-
ary power, also promote greater administrative efficiency. In the past, local
cadres benefited greatly from the ambiguities of the old method of economic
management. Under marketization, they have incentives to specialize and to
participate in the processes they used to supervise; the emergence of contracts
also means they can attend less to the minutiae of economic life. However, if
they try to protect their interests by contravening the new economic norms and
challenging the legal interests of newly prosperous farmers, the courts' responses
may be almost as painful as the criticisms local cadres endured during the campaigns of the Maoist era.

The new rural entrepreneurs, however, should be heartened by the state's
commitment to resolving contracts through legal procedures. As the cases
demonstrate, the state wants to discourage those actions that threaten contract
fulfillment and encourage and protect those that instill respect for contracts. This
should bring a new measure of stability to the rural economy.

Yet, while the role of economic laws in managing the PRC's economy has
never been greater, their fundamental subservience to party policy remains unal-
tered. Policy has dictated that market mechanisms, which require contractual
relationships, be employed to invigorate the economic system. To that effect, as
the cases demonstrate, local courts will disallow egregious violations of contract

discipline, all the while seeking to mediate the disputes. However, should the new policies not manage rural social and economic relationships, the local party structure may limit its efforts to create a hospitable environment in rural China in which to inculcate the new legal norms.

Conclusion

The new rural contracts have far-reaching implications for China's future. This is particularly true as the contracts establish the rule of law, revamp rural politics, and link complex economic relations in a mixed plan-and-market economy.

In establishing the rule of law, China's leaders must institute formal legal structures and processes and instill respect for formal legal principles and procedures. China's new institutions of the "rule of law" and "contract" do not include (at present) contracts between individuals. Such contracts do not enjoy formal legal protection (although, as the Apple Sales Case indicates, local officials may choose to protect such agreements as if they were binding contracts). Moreover, farmers' concepts of justice and "collective rights" often challenge respect for formal contracts. While numerous breaches and cases originate in cadres' miscomprehension or contempt for contractual agreements that limit their power, a more intractable conflict exists between community claims to "economic rents" on previously collective property, developed over decades of collective labor and investment, and the individual's contractual rights to the profits of production. While the terms of the contract might include a tax on those economic rents, changing market conditions and previously inefficient collective management make such calculations almost impossible.

In the future, more astute bargaining by both sides might reconcile individuals and collectives, as the risks to the producer and the potential profits become clearer to all when contract negotiations begin. Experience, however, will not be enough. The requirements of the state plan and the inequality of bargaining positions dictate the limits of China's present legal norms. Even with the recent reforms in the state procurement system, contractual agreements may well be involuntary for ordinary farmers; otherwise, localities will be unable to fulfill sales targets set by the state. In contract negotiations generally, most farmers remain in very unequal bargaining positions vis-à-vis the collective—which still owns the land, the water and the electricity, and other means of production—and the state or cooperative purchasing agencies—which control access to scarce inputs such as fertilizer, seeds, breeding stock, and technical services. Specialized households can be especially vulnerable because they need more technical inputs and credit, while their commercial output may require bulk sales that only state or cooperative agencies can manage.

Despite these limitations, at least one new principle of rights and obligations has been introduced: signed and notarized contracts place clear legal limits on the demands that state, collective, or cooperative bodies (or their agents) may impose on farmer-producers. This principle has never characterized relations between villagers and officials in the Chinese countryside since collectivization was completed in the late 1950s. As a consequence, new institutional relations and norms may be emerging in the countryside that significantly alter farmer-cadre and farmer-state relations. However, even this principle suffers from countervailing influences. Mediation remains a powerful principle, one that places individuals, who believe that their contractual rights have been violated, under considerable social and legal pressure to yield their legal rights somewhat in informal compromise solutions. The pressures on farmers confronting state cadres to accept a mediated solution must be enormous. Even when the dispute moves into formal court proceedings, contractual rights and obligations are often not the major issue. The six opinions demonstrate that the emphasis on contractual rights derives from an insistence on observing the CCP's current policy, not from an inalienable right to due process under law. "Party policy" rather than "legality" remains the ultimate determinant of contractual obligations. The courts' primary responsibility is to promote the four modernizations, as the Mushroom Factory Case demonstrates. Of course, if the CCP continues its policy on contracts, contractual rights and obligations may become legitimate in their own right.

Second, the new, rural contract norms have changed rural politics. A major transformation of rural political processes has been under way since 1978, but the new formal legal structures in rural China have established an alternative power structure to the local rural bureaucracy. If the courts uphold individual claims against cadres or collectives, farmers, particularly specialized households, may prefer to use the courts rather than traditional mediation to resolve disputes.

Farmers' perceptions of the courts' receptiveness may depend heavily on the nature of county and provincial political forces. The courts' willingness to settle cases strictly according to legal principles does vary from locality to locality. The six cases demonstrate that, in some instances, the courts need the cooperation and support of other party or state bodies at the same and higher levels. Without that assistance, they are unable to overcome staunch resistance by local party officials. As a result, farmers in some locations, particularly specialized households, might prefer to rely on the courts and the new legal code, while ordinary farmers and collective cadres might prefer contracts with the collective that follow community norms. Great regional differences and the variable power of local party officials may mean that the attempt to establish legal institutions will not create a homogeneous polity in which all villagers can effectively pursue their interests.

Nevertheless, local cadres, particularly those at the administrative village level (the former brigade) and above, remain quite powerful. Because the collective controls many goods and opportunities, individuals might hesitate to assert their contractual rights; legal victories could become pyrrhic ones, when resentful cadres and neighbors block further opportunities for economic gain. Relationships with other collective and state cadres developed during the years of collective administration give local cadres influence in their own areas far beyond the formal powers of their office. Recognizing this situation, the prudent farmer may eschew opportunities for legal redress and instead rely on personal relationships. Moreover, cadres guide the farmers to their decisions regarding how much to contract, and oversee implementation of programs; whether farmers should even be directly involved in the contract-negotiating process remains an issue.

Finally, the new rural contract norms will link rural economic relations to more complex economic operations. Rural economic development requires more flexible, specialized, and commercialized rural economic relationships; such relationships, in turn, require legal contracts. Only through the introduction of legal contractual relations can an indicative state plan be implemented in an economic environment that provides producers a necessary degree of predictability and insurance from risk. As farmers become more convinced that the Party, the state, and other farmers will observe contractual rights and obligations, they will make more long-term investments.

Contracts assumed an important role in the economic development of Western market economies, and one might interpret the introduction of rural contractual relations as proof of China's transition to capitalism. However, China apparently has instituted contractual relations to restructure its economy. In China's mixed plan-and-market economy, contracts provide the new glue that holds together the claims of the state, collective property holders, and individual producers. Rhetoric aside, China appears to be creating its own variant of a socialist rural economy. The successful institutionalization of contractual relations will provide another bellwether by which to gauge the twists and turns, advances and setbacks, in the ongoing reform process.

Notes

1. See David Zweig, "From 'Agrarian Radicalism' to 'Cooperative Commercialization': Competing Visions of China's Rural Development," in Steven Butler and David Zweig, *China's Agricultural Reform: Background and Prospects* (New York: China Council of the Asia Society Occasional Paper No. 1, 1985). See also William L. Parish, ed., *Chinese Rural Development: The Great Transformation* (Armonk, N.Y.: M.E. Sharpe, 1985).

2. Jean C. Oi, "Peasant Grain Marketing and State Procurement: China's Grain Contracting System," *The China Quarterly*, no. 106 (1986): 272–290.

3. "Arbitrary" action on the part of Chinese officials is difficult to describe in a systematic fashion, although, as Justice Stewart said of obscenity, one knows it when one sees it. A new recognition is emerging: that legal norms and basic conceptions of rights must govern even China's rulers. See "Strengthen the People's Concept of Rights," *Renmin ribao,* August 26, 1985, p. 5, in *Foreign Broadcast Information Service*, Daily Report—China (hereafter cited as *FBIS*) (September 5, 1985): K 13–15.

4. These "rights" must be understood in the context of Chinese tradition, which sharply diverges from Western liberal tradition. For a detailed history and description of Chinese concepts, see Andrew J. Nathan, *Chinese Democracy* (New York: Alfred A. Knopf, 1985), pp. 107–132.

5. For a discussion of the powers and resources available to the production teams, production brigades, and communes, see Fredrick Crook, "The Commune System in the People's Republic of China, 1963–1974," Joint Economic Committee, United States Congress, *China: A Reassessment of the Economy* (Washington: U.S. Government Printing Office, 1975).

6. See "Circular on Rural Work During 1984," articles 4 and 5, *People's Daily*, June 12, 1984, which accorded farmers the right to compete with state agencies. See also chapter 8 of this book.

7. Ding, "Reform of the System of Grain Commodity Buying and Selling," *Economic Research (Jingji yanjiu)*, August 20, 1984, p. 26, in Joint Publication Research Service (hereafter cited as *JPRS*), *China, Report on Agriculture* (October 16, 1984): 42.

8. *Statistical Yearbook of China, 1985 (Zhongguo tongji nianjian)* (Beijing: Chinese Statistical Publishing House, 1985), p. 477; and *Chinese Statistical Yearbook, 1983 (Zhongguo tongji nianjian)* (Beijing: Chinese Statistical Publishing House, 1983), p. 386.

9. See William L. Parish and Martin K. Whyte, *Village and Family in Contemporary China* (Chicago: University of Chicago Press, 1978). Before 1979, the command economy generally governed vertical relationships, and informal communication facilitated horizontal relationships (if they existed at all). The new legal conceptions was applied equally to both types of relationships and reduced the sharp distinctions made between them in an earlier period.

10. See Max Rheinstein, ed., *Max Weber on Law in Economy and Society* (Cambridge: Harvard University Press, 1954), pp. 39–40.

11. Jerome A. Cohen and W. Gage McAfee, "China Builds Legal Framework for Modernization," *National Law Journal* 1 (36) (May 21, 1979): 30, 32.

12. See Lawrence M. Friedman, "Legal Culture and Social Development," and Marc Galanter, "The Modernization of Law," in Lawrence M. Friedman and Stewart Macaulay, eds., *Law and the Behavioral Sciences* (Indianapolis: Bobbs-Merrill, 1969), pp. 1007 and 989, respectively.

13. Friedman, "Legal Culture and Social Development," pp. 1004–1008, 1012–1013; and Galanter, "The Modernization of Law," pp. 993–998.

14. See Friedman, "Legal Culture and Social Development," pp. 1011-1013; Galanter, "The Modernization of Law," pp. 992-998; and Merryman, "Comparative Law and Social Change: On the Origins, Style, Decline and Revival of the Law and Development Movement," *American Journal of Comparative Law*, 25 (1977): 483.

15. Acceptance of a role for law in China has never implied the prominence it enjoys in liberal democracies, and communist parties have often disregarded law when party dominance has been threatened. China's recent commitment to the rule of law must, therefore, be seen as an instrumental and expedient use of law. For example, see Shao Chuan Leng and Hungdah Chiu, *Criminal Justice in Post-Mao China: Analysis and Documents* (Albany: State University of New York Press, 1985), pp. 51-55.

16. See chapter 4 of this book, as well as Jean C. Oi, "Commercializing China's Rural Cadres," *Problems of Communism* (September–October 1986); and "Breach of Contract Hurts Peasants," *China Daily*, April 6, 1983, p. 4.

17. See Galanter, "The Modernization of Law." However, some analyses of the post-Mao reforms suggest that informal institutions have remained quite strong.

18. For an example, see Richard M. Pfeffer, *Understanding Business Contracts in China, 1949–1963* (Cambridge: Harvard East Asian Monographs, 1973), pp. 48-64; see also Jerome A. Cohen, "Kiangnan Shipyards Case Interview," in James Feinerman, ed., *Materials for Chinese Law Seminar*, Georgetown University Law Center, 1987, pp. 299, 312-314 (unpublished collection).

19. "Economic Contract Law," in *China Law Reporter*, no. 2 (1982): 61–80.

20. "Agricultural Sideline Production Contract Regulations" (date unknown), *Farmers' News* (*Zhongguo nongmin bao*), February 7, 1984, p. 2, in *JPRS—China Report, Agriculture* (September 10, 1984): 61.

21. See "General Principles of Civil Law of the People's Republic of China," (*"Zhonghua renmin gongheguo minfa tongze"*), articles 111-116 (1986) ("Civil Liability for Breach of Contract"), adopted by the Fourth Session of the Sixth National People's Congress, April 12, 1986 (hereafter cited as General Principles of Civil Law), *American Journal of Comparative Law* 34 (1986): 736-737.

22. Code of Civil Procedure of the People's Republic of China (trial implementation) (*Zhonghua renmin gongheguo minshi susongfu* [Shixing]), article 59 (March 8, 1982) (hereafter cited as Code of Civil Procedure [trial implementation] in *JPRS China Report: Political, Social, and Military Affairs* (March 22, 1982): 32–67; see also Tung-Pi Chen, "The Chinese Notary: An Overlooked Cornerstone of the Legal System of the People's Republic of China," *International Law and Comparative Law Quarterly* 35 (1986): 80–81.

23. "Notary Public Gives Legal Guarantee to Zhejiang Peasants," *China Daily,* March 31, 1983, p. 3; and "Seriously and Conscientiously Do a Good Job in Notarization and Authentication Work," *Renmin ribao* (commentator's article), July 10, 1986, p. 4, in *FBIS* (July 15, 1986): K 30. According to officials in Jiangpu County, Jiangsu Province, notarization was not necessary if both sides agreed to the contract and if the contract did not break the law. David Zweig, interview, Jiangpu County Court Building, Nanjing Municipality, Jiangsu Province, June 11, 1986 (hereafter cited as Interview of June 11, 1986).

24. "Legal Firms Spur Rural Economy," *Beijing Review,* November 4, 1985, pp. 9–10.

25. In a court case in Jiangpu County, Jiangsu Province, on July 3, 1986, involving a contract dispute between a township agricultural company and a specialized household, only the latter defendant had a lawyer, who had to come all the way from Nanjing proper, because there were no lawyers in Jiangpu County.

26. "A Fundamental Measure to Deepen the Citizens' Concept of the Legal System," *Renmin ribao* (commentator's article), November 23, 1985, p. 1, in *FBIS*, December 2, 1985, p. K 19.

27. See "Agricultural Sideline Production Contract Regulations," article 2, p. 61.

28. "Circular on Rural Work During 1984," articles 1, 2, p. 132.

29. "Agricultural Sideline Production Contract Regulations," article 8, p. 62.

30. Deng Jianxu made these findings in his field research.

31. Crook, "The Commune System," pp. 292–295.

32. David Zweig, interview with the manager, Tangguan Township Grain Station, Jiangpu County, July 2, 1986 (hereafter cited as "Interview with Grain Station Manager").

33. Oi, "Peasant Grain Marketing and State Procurement," pp. 284-287.

34. The Heilongjiang provincial government guidelines for implementing "contract procurement" stipulate that the grain procurement targets of each county must be implemented level after level down to the village. While farmers may initially report their own sale amounts for procurement, the village head, through consultation and on the basis of the various households' planting situation, will "assign a target amount of procurement for everybody." *Heilongjiang Daily* (*Heilongjiang ribao*), March 24, 1985, p. 1, in *JPRS—China Reports, Agriculture* (June 11, 1985): 77, 80. Similarly, farmers in Tangquan Township report to grain station officials how much they plan to sell. The officials enter the total for each village on a form and forward it to the township grain station, which confirms whether the total matches the quota given to the township by the county. If the total is short, the township apportions the shortage among all villages, the leaders of

which then persuade the farmers to increase their quota. Zweig, Interview with Grain Station Manager.

35. "Self-Employed Specialized Households Are a New Type of Individual Economy—Third Discussion on Diversified Development of the Rural Economy," *Renmin ribao* (commentator's article), June 21, 1984, p. 1, in *FBIS* (June 26, 1984): K 14.

36. These findings are based on investigations by Deng Jianxu.

37. Kathleen Hartford, interview with confidential source, Hong Kong, June 1983.

38. See He Kang, "Agriculture: The Chinese Way," *Beijing Review,* May 12, 1986, p. 23.

39. The Chinese farmer does not have the "freedom of contract" to refuse to deliver quota amounts to agricultural purchasing units; similarly, specialized households may find that, if they fail to sell their output to certain state purchasing departments, they will be excluded from normal, commercial distribution channels. See "A Call for Fair Treatment for Township and Town Enterprises," *Farmer's Daily* (*Nongmin ribao*) (commentator's article), December 1, 1986, p. 1 in *FBIS* (December 12, 1986): K 7.

40. See "Two Important Links in Improving the System of Contracted Responsibilities with Payment Linked to Output," *China's Farmers' News* (*Zhongguo nongmin bao*) (editorial), January 19, 1984, in *FBIS* (January 31, 1984): K 11–12.

41. Ibid., K 11.

42. Interview of June 11, 1986.

43. "Specialized Rural Families Get Legal Protection," *FBIS* (April 19, 1984): K 27.

44. See "Law for the Organization of the People's Court of the People's Republic of China" (*"Zhonghua renmin gongheguo renmin fayuan zuzhi fa"*) (1979) (hereafter cited as Law for the Organization of the People's Court), in *FBIS* (July 29, 1979): 20; Shaochuan Leng, "The Chinese Judicial System: A New Direction," in Sidney L. Greenblatt, Richard W. Wilson, and Amy Auerbacher Wilson, eds., *Organizational Behavior in Chinese Society* (New York: Praeger, 1981), p. 112; and Stanley Lubman, "Emerging Functions of Formal Legal Institutions in China's Modernization," *China Law Reports 2* (1983): 205–221.

45. Code of Civil Procedure (trial implementation), articles 6, 97, translated in *JPRS—China Reports, Political Social and Military Affairs* (March 22, 1982): 32–67.

46. Interview of June 11, 1986.

47. The relationship between the size of the financial dispute and the court taking jurisdiction varies from place to place. In wealthier areas, the amount must be higher before the intermediate court takes the case. In general, intermediate-level courts lack the time to deal with the vast number of disagreements that develop between teams and farmers. In addition, villagers find it more convenient to go to court in the county seat than in distant cities. David Zweig, interview with Deng Jianxu in Cambridge, Mass. (December 24, 1984); Kathleen Hartford, interview with Deng Jianxu in Cambridge, Mass. (January 14, 1985).

48. Interview of June 11, 1986.

49. Code of Civil Procedure (trial implementation), articles 82, 83, 85, in *JPRS—China Report, Political, Social and Military Affairs* (March 22, 1982): 32–67.

50. "Specialized Rural Families Get Legal Protection," *FBIS* (April 19, 1984): K 27.

51. The *collegial bench* consists of judges and people's assessors, who are citizens selected either through election or invitation. See Leng and Chiu, *Criminal Justice in Post-Mao China,* p. 67.

52. Code of Civil Procedure (trial implementation), article 101.

53. In the case observed by Zweig, one judge and two citizens sat on the bench.

54. These six cases became available to the authors under conditions requiring that their source remain confidential. Close examination of the documents established their

authenticity as actual case records of decisions in district court cases from several areas of China. The records were translated by Kathleen Hartford. With the exception of a few leading cases published in *Supreme People's Court Gazette* (*Zuigao renmin fayuan gongbao*) and teaching texts which have made their way to the West, no other case reports provide such unique information about the nature of legal decisions in the PRC and the range of issues subject to court adjudication.

55. Judgment of February 25, 1984, *Shenpanting* [XX xian] *renmin fayuan* [XX County] People's Court, Adjudication Chamber], PRC, Case No. 3 ("Implement Document Number One: Maintain the Legal Rights and Interests of Contracting Households").

56. *Two households* refers to specialized and key-point households.

57. Judgment of March 1984, *Jingjiting* [XX xian] *renmin fayuan* [XX County] People's Court, Economic Chamber, PRC ("Handling a Contractual Dispute: Rescuing a Tangerine Orchard").

58. "Diversification" refers to expanding the varieties of crops and developing the output of livestock breeding, forestry, and fisheries, among others.

59. The court refers to the Code of Civil Procedure (trial implementation), article 111, translated in *JPRS—China Reports: Political, Social, and Military Affairs* (March 22, 1982): 32–67.

60. Judgment of April 5, 1984, *Jingjiting* [XX xian] *renmin fayuan*, PRC ("Over One Hundred *Mu* of Paddy Land Are Saved"). One acre comprises six *mu*.

61. No information about this case is available. Its title in translation is "Investigating XX County People's Court Economic Adjudication of a Mushroom Contract Dispute."

62. Judgment of March 1984, [XX xian] *renmin fayuan* [County] People's Court, PRC ("Punish Actions in Violation of Contract: Uphold Strict Obedience to Law").

63. The material on the final resolution of the case is not available to the authors.

64. According to a Zhengzhou, Henan Provincial Radio report, higher-level officials intervened after the plaintiff wrote a letter to "Comrade Liu Jie, first secretary of the provincial CPC [Communist Party of China] Committee. Comrade Liu Jie immediately instructed the . . . [municipal party] Committee to promptly investigate and handle the matter. Backed by the leaders of the provincial, city and county CPC committees the . . . [XX] County People's Court publicly tried the case." *FBIS* (March 23, 1984): p. 1.

65. Judgment of April 1984, *Jingjiting* [XX] *renmin fayuan* [Economic People's Court], PRC ("Actively Assist Individual and Specialized Households' Economic Dispute Cases; Protect Their Legal Rights According to Law").

66. The exact nature and responsibilities of the Chinese "guarantor" are unclear, and it is also uncertain whether the Economic Contract Law defines legal responsibilities of a guarantor. The Economic Contract Law, article 15 (1981), states that one who provides a "guarantee that one of the parties concerned will fulfill the contract" is "responsible for making up for the losses incurred."

67. Interview of June 11, 1986.

68. Zhou Zheng, "China's System of Community Mediation," *Beijing Review*, November 23, 1981, p. 25; see also Wilkinson, "China Plans to Expand Trials," *Los Angeles Times*, January 20, 1981, p. 5.

Part III

Markets, Hierarchy, and the Restructuring of Urban-Rural Relations

7

From Village to City
Reforming Urban-Rural Relations

Introduction

Notwithstanding Mao Zedong's rural roots and the rural origins of the Chinese Revolution, Mao's China did little to narrow the urban-rural gap. By placing tight constraints on the countryside, the state controlled most interactions—commercial, financial, technological, and personal—between villagers and workers and between the urban and rural sectors. Although the two sectors were not hermetically sealed off from each other, this "new Great Wall" between town and country exacerbated urban-rural inequalities and contributed to the low, rural living standards that prevailed at the end of the Maoist era. China's current reforms, particularly those begun after 1983, and the national introduction of the household responsibility system, have facilitated increased interactions between the urban and rural sectors. The reform of urban-rural relations has not only called into question the Maoist model of development, but it also offered potentially important lessons on economic development and agricultural reform for other Third World and communist societies. Nonetheless, the path of the ongoing reform remains fraught with numerous problems as various sectors and a lingering antirural bias resist continued liberalization of urban-rural relations.

The Maoist Model and Urban-Rural Relations

Although Mao often spoke of the need to overcome the urban-rural gap, the Chinese Communist Party's policy did not seek to reintegrate the urban and rural sectors. Beginning in 1953, and continuing well into the 1970s, the Party used the massive state and party bureaucracy and the imposition of collective controls on China's villagers to regulate all commercial interactions and labor migration between town and country. China maintained two ownership, management, and remunerative systems with state ownership in the cities and collective ownership in the countryside. While the state-owned sector received massive state subsidies, the post-1956 rural sector was forced primarily to fend for itself. Even the rural factories, which offered farmers an escape from the drudgery of agricultural labor and a chance to learn modern skills, were developed for the purpose of making the rural areas less dependent on urban centers.

State-imposed price controls and a policy favoring industrial goods kept the prices of rural produce artificially low, forcing farmers to subsidize urban living standards.[1] In addition, demands for excessive grain production to feed the cities undermined the production of commercial crops and regional comparative advantage, impoverishing many parts of rural China, while the household registration system prohibited villagers from moving to urban centers where they could seek a better life.[2]

Since the mid-1950s, the state has strengthened its monopoly over the marketing and transportation of rural produce. Supply and marketing cooperatives, which had played a significant role in the 1950s, were transformed during the Cultural Revolution from collectively oriented organizations into state-managed and state-centered ones. Private sidelines and service sector activities in the countryside were labeled "petty bourgeois capitalism" and strictly controlled. The collective directly delivered the product of the farmers' labor to the state, which controlled its distribution. According to Du Runsheng, China's leading analyst of the rural reforms, this system

> cut agricultural producers off from their market. This threw the rural economy into a state of isolation over a long period. . . . Commodities were not tested by market authorities, and in the absence of competition and elimination of shoddy goods, the quality of products could not improve; production costs could not be reduced; and technical progress was slow.[3]

Because prices were fixed, and the supply of staple and nonstable foods for urban citizens was planned,

> consumer's demands could not be reflected through market price changes, and the peasants could not gear their production to needs. . . . Furthermore, because there was a lack of competition, a bureaucratic business style was engendered among state-owned commercial departments, giving rise to a complicated multilevel management system, which resulted in a long period of circulation, huge waste, and high costs.[4]

Under the collective system, the free-rider principle was constantly at work. The collective system contained a great deal of disguised overemployment, especially during the Cultural Revolution when farmers' remuneration was based primarily on a general evaluation of their work and their political attitudes, rather than on just the quality or quantity of their work.

One reason the Maoist regime accepted rural overemployment was its desire to limit urban expansion. Not only were villagers prohibited from seeking employment outside the collective, but from the mid-1960s into the mid-1970s, over seventeen million urban residents were forcibly moved to the countryside. However, with so many youths gone from the cities, government organs and factories had to recruit staff and workers from the rural areas. Between 1966 and 1976, over fourteen million workers were recruited from the countryside,[5] but after 1978, most rusticated urban youths returned to the cities in the form of "compensatory migration," creating a serious employment problem.[6] Not only was "China's rate of urban population growth and urbanization ... comparable to those found in other populous developing countries,"[7] but the Maoist strategy prohibited the institution of policies which really resolved the problem of excess urban youth.

The income gap also increased. The growth of small urban collective factories increased the proportion of members of the average household that earned salaries, increasing urban household incomes and the urban-rural gap in relative incomes.[8] In addition, the urban state-ownership system paid workers fixed salaries, while villagers relied on the collective's profits. Tight restrictions on rural, private economic activity ensured that the overwhelming majority of farmers received less money than urbanites. Finally, diminishing returns on labor and capital, due to the overemphasis on grain production imposed on villagers during the 1960s and 1970s, further suppressed rural incomes in wealthy areas.[9]

As a result, rural collective per capita income rose only 10 *yuan* from 1965 to 1976 (in 1987 one *yuan* was approximately 27 cents), and the income gap grew from 2 : 1 to at least 3 : 1 and possibly 6 : 1 from the late 1950s to the late 1970s.[10] Villagers' average annual rate of increase in consumption levels also lagged behind until the post-1978 reforms; between 1971 and 1975, rural consumption levels rose by only 1.3 percent compared with 4.2 percent for nonagricultural inhabitants, while between 1979 and 1984, rural consumption levels increased 9.2 percent annually compared with 4.1 percent for nonagricultural inhabitants (Table 7.1.)[11]

Due to Mao's belief that labor only in the goods-producing sector, but *not* in service or transportation sectors, could create value, and because of the state's monopoly on tertiary industry, the service sector remained a gaping hole in China's post-1958 economy. Having clothes washed and goods repaired, buying a quick meal at irregular hours, and finding a nanny were difficult. Before 1966, Beijing had 60,000 restaurants, but by 1974, there were less than 6,000, all state-run; in Kui City, Xinjiang Province, there were 200,000 residents, but no laundry.[12] Even critical services such as transportation were deficient in the rural areas under the Maoist regime.

Table 7.1

Average Annual Rate of Increase of Consumption Levels, 1953–1984

Period	National average	Rural inhabitants	Nonrural inhabitants
1953–1978	2.2	1.8	3.0
1966–1970	2.1	2.5	2.1
1971–1975	2.1	1.3	4.2
1976–1980	4.8	4.1	4.9
1979–1984	7.8	9.2	4.1

Source: China: A Statistical Survey in 1985 (Beijing: New World Press, 1985), p. 95.

Finally, the impoverished nature of the rural economy severely restricted the flow of technology from the city to the countryside throughout the 1960s and 1970s. According to one Chinese economist, the average capital assets of production teams in 1977 in China was under 10,000 *yuan*; the same held true for the average brigade. Because neither teams nor brigades had enough money to buy a no. 55 tractor, which costs approximately 14,000 *yuan,* tractor sales occurred through administrative allocation, not market forces.[13] The results were low quality and a shortage of spare parts; when problems developed, machines sat idle and decayed.

Maoist policies improved rural health care, literacy, and irrigation, but in terms of the urban-rural gap, the policies of his era were clearly detrimental. According to Whyte, "In a number of important respects, the Maoist reforms in the pre-1976 period had consequences contrary to their stated purposes and actually contributed to a substantial widening of the gap between town and countryside in China."[14]

China's New Development Model

Although Western analysts of Chinese society disagree concerning the extent of urban-rural integration in the premodern era,[15] most agree with Skinner and Rozman that vibrant economic exchange between urban and rural sectors, channeled through a hierarchy of small market towns and middle-sized cities, was critical for economic and technical development in China.[16]

The current developmental strategy has arisen piecemeal since 1978. Household farming has been reinstated, giving farmers greater decision-making power over the mix of crops to produce and the technology with which to produce them. Particularly since 1983, farmers are allowed to move more freely within the countryside and between the countryside and the cities. The centralization of land in the hands of specialized households is expected to reestablish private economies of scale and increase the commodity rate of agricultural production.

Rather than allow villagers to freely migrate into the cities, however, China has reintroduced the idea of developing small rural towns (townships) as the centers for rural commerce, trade, and industry. They are to be linked with expanding middle-sized cities, which in turn are to serve as the link between rural and urban production. At the same time, rural demands for consumer and producer goods are expected to promote further urban industrial expansion. Thus, the new strategy's position on urban-rural interactions fits some of the contours of the premodern period.

Surplus rural labor and the capital that flowed into the countryside as a result of the 1979–1980 increase in the price of agricultural products are expected to reinvigorate the moribund service sector in these lower-level urban centers and supply the necessary labor force for the ever-expanding township industries. These rural factories have been directed to turn agricultural products into export-able commodities to defer the cost of importing foreign technology.[17] Neverthe-less, to ensure the fulfillment of the state plan, the state maintains ultimate control over the direction of economic development.

These changes have occurred more rapidly in rural areas which are contigu-ous to cities, and in coastal areas which are well situated to benefit from China's "open door" on foreign trade and foreign investment.[18] Wealthier provinces or parts of those provinces, such as southern Jiangsu, coastal Fujian, Shandong, and Zhejiang provinces; the Pearl River Delta; and the Liaotong Peninsula, have also taken advantage of these new economic opportunities. On an individual level, villagers with skills and capital have also benefited more from these reforms than rural inhabitants with few skills or economic opportunities.

Changes in Urban-Rural Relations

The Marketplace

The reformers have urged villagers to expand commercial farming, which should increase the villagers' interest in the urban economy and markets.[19] Supply and marketing cooperatives are slowly reverting to their original form, in which they were owned and managed by villagers directly, purchased the goods farmers produced, and helped farmers market them. To resolve the problem in the rural-urban marketing process of "too many links," by which "people at each level try to make a profit out of the goods," supply and marketing cooperatives, as well as collective businesses and individual traders, are expected to bring agricultural produce directly to wholesale distributors who have expanded warehouse storage space. Cities are also expected to "provide the space and conditions to make it convenient" for rural people to sell directly to city people.[20]

Lifting many price controls and establishing more direct links between rural producers and urban consumers have allowed farmers to respond to market opportu-nities and price incentives. Urban needs, more than state directives, are beginning to determine urban residents' food supplies. Villagers are flooding China's cities with various types of agricultural produce. To compete, state-run markets in Beijing have

Table 7.2

Villagers' Sales of Farm and Sideline Produce to Nonagricultural Residents, 1977–1983

Year	Value of sales (in billion *RMB*)
1976	2.20
1977	2.18
1978	3.11
1979	4.75
1980	6.90
1981	8.94
1982	11.08
1983	13.30

Source: Statistical Yearbook of China, 1984 (Beijing: State Statistical Bureau, 1984), p. 364.

had to diversify the sources of their produce and seek high-quality produce from Shandong and Hubei provinces; as a result, vegetable suppliers in Beijing were much more plentiful in July 1985.[21] In Nanjing, I observed how state salespeople were forced to go outside the state agricultural market building and sell their produce in the streets on the free market; otherwise, they made few sales.

The avenues through which marketing occurs have also expanded. In May 1985, Beijing rescinded its prohibition on villagers entering the city to market vegetables.[22] A Kunming vegetable company owned and operated by a township government did over 20,000 *yuan* of business each month.[23] As early as 1983, in remote areas such as Guizhou Province, some villagers began to purchase sideline produce, transport it to the county seat, and bring the products farmers wanted back to the mountainous villagers.[24] In spring 1985, private traders in Changchun marketed grain and spices in the free market. By 1986, private sales of fish in Nanjing Municipality's free markets had reached such proportions that the state-run fish companies had been all but destroyed.[25] In all, villagers' sales to nonagricultural residents increased dramatically from 2.2 billion *yuan* in 1976 to 6.9 billion *yuan* in 1980 and 13.3 billion *yuan* in 1983 (Table 7.2).[26] Similarly, the volume of sales in urban free markets increased from zero in 1978 to 2.4 billion *yuan* in 1980 and 8.0 billion *yuan* in 1984, and the number of urban market fairs increased from zero in 1978 to 6,144 in 1984. Also, as a percentage of the total volume of trade, the amount sold in urban areas increased from zero percent in 1978 to 10 percent in 1980 and 17 percent by 1984 (see Table 7.3 on page 192).[27]

Rural Factories

Rural factories have begun processing rural produce for consumption by urban residents and the urban industrial sector so that "rural production is aimed at the

urban centers, and suburban towns produce goods according to the needs of urban consumption."[28] Processing rural produce where it is grown employs surplus rural labor, keeps that labor in the rural areas, and reduces waste. This change in rural production is strikingly evident. Mushuyuan village in suburban Nanjing closed its watch factory and began processing locally produced vegetables. By 1986, the village owned a soda pop and ice cream factory, a bakery, a candy factory, a workshop that processed peanuts, and was soon to open a textile factory. Due to these developments, the percentage of villagers employed in industry rose from 43.5 percent in 1981 to 54.5 percent in 1983 and 74.2 percent by May 1986.[29] Baoziyan Village, outside Changchun, Jilin Province, established what the Chinese call a "dragon" (yi tiao long), which is an integrated enterprise whereby villagers raise cattle privately and sell milk to the village milk powder factory, whose produce is marketed by the township government. Also, 80 percent of the bricks made in Baoziyan's brick factories are used for urban construction.[30] Finally, a new national model, the White Lotus Washing Machine Factory in Beijing, produces over 85 percent of its parts in suburban collective enterprises, which reflects the growing linkages between urban and rural industries.[31]

Labor Migration and Urbanization

The household responsibility system has already freed up over 30 percent of the rural labor force, and the proportion of rural laborers leaving agriculture is increasing. Although Chinese projections may be unrealistic, Du Runsheng's view that over 70 percent of China's villagers will leave agriculture by the year 2000 is considered conservative by some Chinese analysts.[32]

Where is this excess labor to go? During 1978–1980, many rusticated urban youth, as well as villagers, entered the cities. With the number of newly employed migrants reaching a high of 1.3 million by 1980,[33] the state began a campaign in 1981–1982 to force rural laborers back to the countryside.[34] From mid-1981 to year's end, Anhui Province sent 102,400 villagers back to the countryside and in March 1982 persisted in this policy.[35]

Nevertheless, restrictions on rural-urban migration, one of the few permanent themes in China's otherwise quixotic developmental strategy, are weakening.[36] In April 1983, and again in early 1984, the state council promulgated new regulations allowing rural laborers to "leave the land but not the countryside" (li tu bu li xiang). Under these rules, farmers could move to nearby rural market towns to engage in nonfarming jobs, but only if they "supplied their own grain" (zidai kouliang), which they could bring from their family farms.[37] In October 1984, villagers who set up or managed businesses in China's 60,000 townships became eligible for urban residence permits.[38] As a result, 1.2 million farmers entered cities and towns in 1984, almost doubling the number in 1982 or 1983 (Table 7.4).[39]

Villagers are encouraged to settle in cities with less than 200,000 inhabitants

Table 7.3

Data on Urban and Rural Markets and Trade, 1978–1984

	1978	1979	1980	1981	1982	1983	1984
No. of market fairs	33,302	38,993	40,809	43,013	44,775	48,003	56,500
Urban	—	2,226	2,919	3,298	3,591	4,488	6,144
Rural	33,302	36,767	37,890	39,715	41,184	43,515	50,356
Volume of trade (100 million *RMB*)	125.0	183.0	235.0	287.0	333.1	385.8	470.6
Urban	—	12.0	24.0	34.0	45.2	55.9	80.3
Rural	125.0	171.0	211.0	253.0	287.9	329.9	390.3
Total urban (%)	0.0	0.06	0.10	0.12	0.14	0.17	0.17

Source: China: A Statistical Survey in 1985 (Beijing: New World Press, 1985), p. 84.

Table 7.4

Number of Persons Entering Employment in Cities and Towns, 1978–1984 (in 1,000s)

	1978	1979	1980	1981	1982	1983	1984
Total	5,444	9,026	9,000	8,200	6,650	6,283	7,215
From rural areas	1,484	708	1,274	920	660	682	1,230
Total rural (%)	0.27	0.08	0.14	0.11	0.10	0.11	0.17

Source: China: A Statistical Survey in 1985 (Beijing: New World Press, 1985), p. 28.

but are accepted in middle-sized cities of 200,000 to 500,000.[40] Middle-sized cities can give farmers "living permits" (*zu zhu zheng*) to stay and work in the cities without making them eligible for some benefits that accrue to those holding "urban residence permits" (*chengshi hukou*), the most important being the right to buy state-subsidized "commercial grain" (*shangpin liang*). Although they, like other villagers, must supply their own grain, in some circumstances these rural residents bring their families into town and enroll their children in urban schools. This third kind of residence permit, somewhere between the rural *hukou*, which prohibits urban habitation, and the more highly prized urban *hukou*, will create first- and second-class urban citizens with the lower class determined by their more recent rural roots.

According to some observers, the living permits policy is a compromise between officials who feel that villagers must expand the urban service sector and those who oppose further burdens on municipal budgets. In summer 1985, the floating population of Beijing and Tianjin surpassed one million.[41] Final policy direction remains unclear. In some locations, the level of urban centers in which villagers may reside is expanding. In May 1985, Anhui Province announced that villagers could move into Hefei, the provincial capital, if they brought their own grain. Beijing now permits farmers who market particular products to reside in the city, including residents of Yixing County, Jiangsu Province, who are allowed to move into Beijing to market their famous pottery.

Rural contract labor is also flowing into the cities. As of February 1985, Tianjin had over 1.67 million villagers working there,[42] many in construction teams whose speed, quality, and lower labor costs have created stiff competition for state-run urban construction companies. In 1984 alone, 160,000 villagers built a quarter (in square meters) of the new buildings in Beijing.[43] The most sought after construction team in Nanjing comes from one rural township (formerly commune) in Qidong County in northern Jiangsu Province.[44] However, the green light for farmers to move into middle-sized cities was under reevaluation as of fall 1985,[45] so the permanent mixing of the urban and rural population may be reserved for China's small towns rather than large- or middle-sized cities.

Developing Rural Small Towns

In late 1980, then Communist Party General Secretary Hu Yaobang argued that developing a "socialist commodity economy" depended on resurrecting small market towns.[46] These "rural small towns" (*xiao chengzhen*) would be expected to provide villagers with cultural, political, marketing, transportation, and service opportunities previously unavailable outside large cities, and to serve as commercial, cultural, informational, and technological bridges between the urban and rural sectors.[47] In addition, small-scale industries, such as food processing plants, brick kilns, and clothing mills, would introduce new technologies into the rural areas and process rural produce for urban consumption. In 1984, township enterprises in Wujiang County, Suzhou Municipality, Jiangsu Province, earned over US$50 million in foreign exchange by turning agricultural produce into exportable commodities.[48] Rural towns will also become marketing centers for household sidelines. By the year 2000, these small towns are expected to accommodate 40 percent of China's total population as more and more farmers leave agricultural production.[49]

From 1982 to 1984, the number of these rural towns increased from 2,800 to 7,280, and their population grew from 66 to 139 million. Although this "bottom heavy" urban population distribution[50] was due partly to redefinition of the criteria for urban areas, major growth has occurred in these rural towns mostly as a result of the boom in township industries.

These towns may play a major role in raising rural productivity and incomes. As they draw in more and more of the surplus agricultural labor to work in their service sectors and township enterprises (currently over 70 million former farmers work in these enterprises), the agricultural productivity of the farmers remaining behind must increase to supply these new urban residents with enough food. Also, growing demands for agricultural produce by consumers and rural enterprises in these towns will offer the shrinking rural labor force new opportunities for further expanding rural production and potentially increasing their agricultural incomes.

More urban planners are being trained to help develop these rural towns.[51] In Wujiang County, Jiangsu Province, homes for migrants are being constructed in specific areas where roads and marketing facilities have already been built.[52] In a major departure from previous policy, villagers in Hu County, Shanxi Province, can build their own homes on "peasant enterprise streets" in four small towns, or they can rent the houses to others.[53] Establishing farmer streets in rural towns has become an important indicator that the township government is responding to the model proposed by Fei Xiaotong and the national government, and also demonstrates that a township is in tune with this important aspect of the new development strategy. However, developments vary nationwide. In a township in Jiangpu County, outside Nanjing, only one village family had moved onto the farmer street by summer 1986.[54]

Developing the Service Sector

In cities and towns throughout China, villagers are helping revitalize the service sector. Since rural, not urban, residents prospered under the household responsibility system, and since entrepreneurs must put up 50 percent of the capital before they can get a bank loan,[55] villagers are financially better situated than urbanites to invest in the service sector. From 1982 to 1984, Guangzhou's (Canton) farmers capitalized on the tourist trade to build hotels, restaurants, shopping malls, car parks, piers, and even skyscrapers.[56] A farmer-run company in Tianjin spent three million *yuan* building a six-story restaurant, while in September

Table 7.5

Number of Persons in Service Trade Nationwide, 1978-1983 (in 1,000s)

	1978	1979	1980	1981	1982	1983
Urban	460	716	890	1,095	1,266	1,430
Rural	100	168	236	388	558	844
Total	560	884	1,026	1,483	1,824	2,274
Total rural (%)	17.8	19.0	20.1	22.8	30.1	38.9

Source: *Statistical Yearbook of China, 1984* (Beijing: State Statistical Bureau, 1984), p. 377.

1985, rural inhabitants opened an eighty-seven-bed hotel in Tibet, replete with shops, restaurants, and color televisions in each room.[57]

Although urban residents view working in restaurants and hotels or doing various repairs as low status jobs,[58] most farmers view any urban job as a step up. According to a 1984 survey in *Society* (*Shehui*), housemaids, barbers, and service personnel were among the lowest 20 percent in terms of occupational prestige in Beijing, while cooks, sales clerks, and sewing workers were in the lowest 40 percent.[59] Urban residents with state jobs and state salaries have hesitated to trade security for higher paying, but more risky, jobs in the service sector.[60] As a result, rural surplus labor freed up by the household responsibility system is moving rapidly into the service sector. Over 10,000 young women from rural Anhui Province were working in Beijing as nannies in 1985; they also formed the core of nannies in Nanjing. Total service jobs have increased from 0.56 million in 1978 to 2.27 million in 1983, with the rural share increasing from 17.8 to 39 percent (Table 7.5).[61]

Nevertheless, relying on the expansion of the tertiary sector as the sole means to resolve the surplus rural labor pool cannot totally replace investment in training, institutions, and facilities that is necessary to ensure that this historic rural-urban population flow occurs smoothly and successfully.[62]

Technology Flows to the Countryside

During the initial stages of the post-1978 reforms, rural demand for small tractors declined considerably, from a 1979 peak of 3.77 million horsepower of walking tractors to a 1982 nadir of 2.80 million horsepower. (Chinese sales statistics are measured in terms of total horsepower.) However, as farmers increased their control over their economic decisions, the demand for tractors increased as well, pushing sales back up to 4.1 million horsepower in 1983.[63] The 1985 World Bank report on China recognized this "continued strong demand for small-scale pedestrian tractors."[64] Most of these tractors are bought by "transport specialized households" to fill a gap in rural transportation. Similarly, as farmers' freedom of choice increases, they are refusing to buy poor equipment and machinery for which there are no spare parts.[65]

Technicians and specialists have begun to transfer technology to the countryside. Urban specialists and technical institutions are forming consulting groups which work with rural units to improve output, and their income may be linked to the profits and losses they generate.[66] Some urban technicians work part-time in suburban villages, while some urban managers work full-time or part-time in rural factories. However, very few give up their urban residency and its "iron rice bowl" to take up "clay rice bowls" in the countryside.[67] To facilitate the influx of technicians into the countryside, Anhui Province established a "talent exchange service center."[68] Some specialists are organizing technical schools in the countryside, while some rural technicians are attending urban technical institutes.[69] Nonetheless, of 328,000 agricultural technicians in China, fewer than 40,000 are working at the county level or below, where they are in regular contact with farmers. Combined with the 200,000 rural technicians undergoing on-the-job training, there are only 3.1 agronomists per 10,000 rural inhabitants.[70]

Finally, sophisticated rural small-scale industries, as in the Pearl River Delta or Suzhou and Wuxi municipalities in Jiangsu Province, improve the level of rural technology. According to Yu Guangzhou, Chinese Premier Zhao Ziyang called on his county to follow a developmental strategy of "turning agriculture into industry in order to promote foreign trade" (*mao gong nong de fazhan*). According to some foreign visitors, factories in the Pearl River Delta in 1985 earned 25 percent of their income from making integrated circuits for export. These localities are also helping to link the rural economy with the world market.[71] Nevertheless, rural demand continues to outstrip the urban-rural technology flow.

The Urban-Rural Gap

After 1978, changes in the income gap appeared to favor China's farmers. By comparing data from 1979 to 1983, the World Bank argued that the reforms have "significantly narrowed urban-rural income differentials,"[72] and the Chinese, using their own data, have shown that, between 1979 and 1984, the average annual growth rate in family income was faster in the rural than in the urban sector (15.0 percent vs. 8.2 percent, respectively). Although over the same period villagers' expenses (13.2 percent vs. 7.0 percent) and consumption levels increased more rapidly compared with those of urban residents (Table 7.1), due in large part to the building of new homes (something urban residents in that period could not do), their average annual growth rates in bank deposits have also outstripped those of urban residents by 41 percent to 31 percent. In fact, as a proportion of total national bank deposits, rural savings have increased consistently since 1976, going from 26 percent of the total in 1978 to 36 percent in 1984 (Table 7.6).

Table 7.6

Year-End Savings Deposits, 1957–1984 (in 100 million *RMB*)

Year	Total	Urban Residents	Rural Residents	Rural/Total (%)
1957	35.2	27.9	7.3	20.7
1965	65.2	52.3	12.9	19.7
1978	210.6	154.9	55.7	26.4
1979	281.0	202.6	78.4	27.9
1980	399.5	282.5	117.0	29.2
1981	523.7	354.1	169.6	32.4
1982	675.4	447.3	228.1	33.8
1983	892.5	572.6	319.9	35.8
1984	1,214.7	776.6	438.1	36.0

Source: China: A Statistical Survey in 1985 (Beijing: New World Press, 1985), p. 105.

Although by the mid-1980s, the income gap between urban and rural residents appeared to have returned to 2 : 1, the rate of change in urban incomes is increasing (see chapter 13 in this book). According to official reports, from 1983 to 1984, it rose by 12.5 percent after an adjustment for price increases, while change in rural incomes was steady at 14.7 percent.[73] Moreover, the new urban reforms begun in October 1984 could permit urban residents to make much more money than at any time since 1949. The creation of extra budgetary funds by many enterprises and administrative units, as well as the current decentralization efforts, has left some managers with more money to distribute as they please.[74] Moonlighting, which increases urban incomes, is unlikely to appear in official statistics; therefore, while the official income gap may be narrowing, the current reforms may help urban incomes increase more rapidly. Thus, despite many positive changes, recent trends do suggest that the terms of trade could again swiftly turn against China's rural residents.

Continued Urban Bias

Given the new problems that drastic socioeconomic changes can generate, it is remarkable that the process to date appears to be avoiding major dislocations. Nevertheless, competition with urban residents and an "urban bias" in local and national policies persists.

Young villagers who desire the good urban life are the most likely to migrate, meaning that agriculture in China, as in the Soviet Union, Japan, and many Third World countries, will become the domain of old men and women; while the latter perform fieldwork, the former manage by reviving old "networks."[75] However, migrating rural youths must compete with the young generation of town residents and unemployed youths in the bigger cities. With six million people entering the urban work force yearly, urban areas need to develop the service sector to resolve their own unemployment problem.[76] Also, according to informed sources, up to 15 million urban workers in state-run enterprises could become redundant in the next few years. Should such demands for urban industrial efficiency increase urban unemployment, unemployed workers could vent their anger on rural migrants working in the urban service sector. Already, numerous *Farmers' News* articles tell how urbanites, jealous of current rural prosperity, extort money from unsuspecting farmers and beat them up.[77]

Similarly, urban state-run enterprises use their ties with state administrators to drive rural competitors (such as villager-run film companies, marketing firms, and even food stalls) out of business.[78] In Heilongjiang Province, farmers' private buses were smashed and drivers beaten, while in Hubei Province, farmers who competed with a township enterprise that unloaded boats were beaten and their equipment destroyed.[79] State-run stores also resist selling rural commodities, even if they are of better quality.[80]

Finally, by imposing "hard budget constraints" on rural enterprises and "soft budget constraints" on state-run factories,[81] the state has been far more willing to let rural collective enterprises go bankrupt, arguing, "This phenomenon is not frightening. Those who are better can win, and those who are worse can lose. This is law that promotes progress and development."[82] This type of mentality clearly reflects the biased approach of state administrators who use their control over resources to prevent state-run firms from closing, making urban workers' jobs more secure than those of the vast majority of rural factory workers.

Lessons for Third World Development

China's rural policies and attempted integration of the urban and rural economies call for a reevaluation of current Third World development strategies. For ideological and political reasons, the urban bias in Third World development has helped the cities dominate the countryside (although some dispute this thesis).[83]

According to Bates, conscious state policy, particularly agricultural pricing policies, impoverished much of Africa's rural economy.[84] In most of these societies, elite power rests on support from the urban sector, and increased food prices generate urban unrest which threatens state power. In China, however, the increase in agricultural prices in 1979 and 1980 contributed greatly to a subsequent burst in agricultural output, and other Third World villagers may also respond positively to better prices. Increasing agricultural procurement prices did burden China's state budget, prompting belt-tightening in 1981–1982, but that indirect rural investment bore fruit. A stronger, richer rural sector, demanding urban consumer and producer goods, is fueling urban industrial growth. Yet, in many Third World countries where prices favor the cities, rural poverty inhibits economic development across all spheres of the national economy.

Moreover, China's overall development strategy, with its emphasis on narrowing urban-rural differences and bringing down the barriers between urban and rural China, has been singularly successful. Rural industry has improved rural living standards; urban technology has moved into the countryside; and villagers and urbanites are meeting in the marketplace, with the former supplying vastly increased qualities of foods and the latter supplying cash for rural entrepreneurs and farmers. One result has been the largest housing boom in world history. Despite all the hoopla for many years about how Mao's collective system improved the lives of rural inhabitants, reformist policies since 1978 have really transformed rural-urban ties and with them the face of rural China.

No doubt China's uniqueness—the size of its domestic economy, the existence of numerous exportable commodities, its ability to avoid the current Third World "debt crunch," and state-directed industrialization emphasizing labor-intensive production of basic commodities rather than capital-intensive production of luxury goods—may limit the applicability of China's developmental experience for the Third World or other communist societies. Nonetheless, a more liberal rural economy, comprised of villagers who are free of excessive burdens imposed by landlords or the state and buoyed by fair prices and acceptable terms of trade, may create resources for light industry and generate sufficient demand to propel urban economic expansion. The engine of economic development lies in the countryside and its link to the cities, not in the cities alone.

Notes

1. Nicholas P. Lardy, *Agriculture in China's Modern Economic Development* (Cambridge: Cambridge University Press, 1983), p. 127.

2. Martin K. Whyte and William L. Parish, *Urban Life in Contemporary China* (Chicago: University of Chicago Press, 1984), pp. 18–19.

3. Du Runsheng, "Second Stage Rural Structural Reform," *Beijing Review,* no. 25 (1985): 15–17.

4. Ibid.

5. Feng Lanrui, "On Factors Affecting China's Labor Employment," *People's Daily* (*Renmin ribao*), November 16, 1981, p. 126.

6. Judith Banister, *Urban-Rural Population Projections for China* (Washington: U.S. Bureau of the Census, Center for International Research, CIR Staff Paper #15, March 1986).

7. Kam-wing Chan, "Urbanization Issues in China's Development," in Miriam Chen and Lawrence N. Shyu, eds., *China Insight: Select Papers from Canadian Asian Studies Association Annual Conference Proceedings* (Ottawa: Carleton University, 1985), p. 201.

8. Martin K. Whyte, "Social Trends in China: The Triumph of Inequality?" in A. Doak Barnett and Ralph Clough, eds., *Modernizing China: Post-Mao Reform and Development* (Boulder, Colo.: Westview Press, 1985), pp. 103–123.

9. Thomas P. Wiens, "Poverty and Progress in the Huang and Huai River Basins," in William L. Parish, ed., *Chinese Rural Development: The Great Transformation* (Armonk, N.Y.: M.E. Sharpe, 1985), pp. 57–94.

10. For these two estimates, see William L. Parish, "Egalitarianism in Chinese Society,"

Problems of Communism, no. 1 (1981): 37–53; and Thomas Rawski, "The Simple Arith-metic of Chinese Income Distribution," *Economic Research (Keizai kenkyu)* 33, no. 1 (1982): 12–26.

11. State Statistical Bureau, *China: A Statistical Survey in 1985* (Beijing: New World Press, 1985), p. 95.

12. *Farmers' News* (hereafter *Nongmin bao*), February 22, 1985, p. 2.

13. Yang Shun, "Energetically Summarize Historical Experience, Change the Back-ward Face of Agriculture," *Problems in Agricultural Economics (Nongye jingji wenti),* no. 1 (1980): 15.

14. Martin K. Whyte, "Town and Country in Contemporary China," *Comparative Urban Research* 10, no. 1 (1983): 9–20.

15. Susan Mann, "Urbanization and Historical Change in China," *Modern China* 10, no. 1 (1984): 79–113.

16. See William G. Skinner, "Introduction: Urban Development in Imperial China," in William G. Skinner, ed., *The City in Late Imperial China* (Stanford: Stanford University Press, 1977), pp. 3–32; and Gilbert Rozman, *Urban Networks in Ching China and Tokugawa Japan* (Princeton, N.J.: Princeton University Press, 1973).

17. See chapter 11 in this book.

18. See chapter 12 in this book.

19. Bernard Gallin, "Rural to Urban Migration in Taiwan: Its Impact on Chinese Family and Kinship," in David C. Buxbaum, ed., *Chinese Family Law and Social Change in Histori-cal and Comparative Perspective* (Seattle: University of Washington Press, 1978), p. 264.

20. See *Foreign Broadcast Information Service* (hereafter cited as *FBIS*) (February 14, 1984): T 1–4, which also argues that there were more than ten procedural links in transporting industrial, agricultural, and sideline products. It was hoped that the number of steps could be cut down to three or four.

21. *China Daily,* July 11, 1985, p. 4.

22. *Nongmin bao,* May 31, 1985, p. 1.

23. *Nongmin bao,* February 14, 1985, p. 2.

24. *Nongmin bao,* April 3, 1983, p. 2.

25. Interview with Nanjing Municipality Agricultural Work Office, June 1986.

26. *Statistical Yearbook of China, 1984* (Beijing: State Statistical Bureau Publishing House, 1984), p. 364.

27. *China: A Statistical Survey in 1985,* p. 84.

28. *Nongmin bao,* January 11, 1985, p. 1.

29. Interview with Mushuyuan village party officials, suburban Nanjing, June 5, 1986.

30. The author visited this village in April 1985.

31. Wan Li, "Speech on Rural Work," *FBIS* (March 4, 1985): K 1–10.

32. Interview at the Chinese Academy of Social Sciences, Agricultural Economics Research Institute, Beijing, April 1985.

33. *China: A Statistical Survey in 1985,* p. 28.

34. *FBIS* (December 8, 1981): Q 1–2; *FBIS* (December 11, 1981): T 1–3; and Joint Publication Research Service, *Chinese Agriculture Report* (December 9, 1981): 23–24.

35. *FBIS* (February 2, 1982): O 1; *FBIS* (March 22, 1982): O 1, respectively.

36. Dorothy Solinger, "Temporary Residence Certificate Regulations in Wuhan, May 1983," *The China Quarterly,* no. 101 (1985): 98–103.

37. Y. Hu, *"Huji dengji fagui de gaige yu jingji fazhan de xuyao,"* Social Science *(Shehui kexue),* no. 6 (1985).

38. *Beijing Review,* no. 46 (1984): 8.

39. *China: A Statistical Survey in 1985,* p. 28; and Banister, *Urban-Rural Population Projections,* Table 3.

40. Interviews with the China Urban Rehabilitation Mission, Toronto, April and September 1985. There are eighty-one cities with 200,000 to 500,000 people.

41. *Globe and Mail* (Toronto), July 5, 1985.

42. *Nongmin bao,* February 26, 1985, p. 3.

43. *Nongmin bao,* September 30, 1984, p. 2.

44. Interview with Qidong County construction team officials, Nanjing, May 1986.

45. Interview with the China Urban Rehabilitation Mission. For ten years, however, people have been able to settle in medium-sized cities, but were kept out of the very large ones.

46. Jiangsu Province Study Group on Small Towns, ed., *Small Towns, A Big Issue* (*Xiao chengzhen, da wenti*) (Nanjing: Jiangsu renmin chubanshe, 1984), p. 7.

47. Ibid, p. 9. See also chapter 8 of this book.

48. Interview with Yu Guangzhou, magistrate of Wujiang County, Toronto, September 21, 1985.

49. Fei Xiaotong, "The Social Significance in China of the Development of Small Towns," *Liaowang,* no. 32 (1984): 8–10.

50. Banister, *Urban-Rural Population Projections,* p. 5.

51. *Nongmin bao,* January 14, 1985, p. 2.

52. Interview with Yu Guangzhou.

53. *Nongmin bao,* January 5, 1985, p. 3.

54. The author visited this township in summer 1986.

55. Interview with Yu Guangzhou.

56. *Nongmin bao,* January 19, 1985, p. 1.

57. See *Nongmin bao,* February 26, 1985, p. 1; and *Nongmin bao,* September 16, 1985, p. 1, respectively.

58. Interview at the Agricultural Economics Institute, Chinese Academy of Social Sciences, April 22, 1985.

59. Z. Xuan, J. Zhang, and W. Xie, "Study Research on Occupational Status," *Society* (*Shehui*), no. 15 (November 4, 1984): 20–22.

60. On a May 1986 trip to Beijing, I found that barbers, who can double their income working privately, are beginning to prefer private employment.

61. State Statistical Bureau, *State Statistical Yearbook of China, 1984,* p. 377.

62. Jeffrey Taylor, *Employment Outlook for China to the Year 2000* (Washington: Center for International Research, U.S. Bureau of the Census, 1986).

63. State Statistical Bureau, *State Statistical Yearbook of China, 1984,* p. 374.

64. The World Bank, *China Agriculture to the Year 2000* (Washington: The World Bank, 1985).

65. *Nongmin bao,* January 18, 1985, p. 2.

66. *Nongmin bao,* February 11, 1985, p. 1.

67. *Iron rice bowls* refer to the security of state employment, while *clay rice bowls,* which are more fragile, reflect the insecurity of incomes based on rural production. See *Nongmin bao,* May 7, 1985, p. 1.

68. *Nongmin bao,* September 18, 1984, p. 1.

69. *Nongmin bao,* November 6, 1984, p. 1; and *Outlook* (*Liaowang*), May 9, 1985, respectively.

70. *Nongmin bao,* May 9, 1985, p. 1. The World Bank, which estimated four agronomists per 10,000 rural inhabitants, was critical of this aspect of the current investment policy in agriculture, emphasizing that China had to spend much more money if it was to build "an effective national research capability." See World Bank, *China Agriculture in the Year 2000,* pp. 17 and 52.

71. Zhao Ziyang, "Why Relax Agricultural Price Controls," *Beijing Review,* no. 7–8 (1985): 16–18.

72. The World Bank, *China Agriculture to the Year 2000,* p. 25.

73. *China Reconstructs,* vol. 34 (July 1985).

74. A small city urban planner, moonlighting in the evenings, made over 10,000 *yuan* in 1985, while a Beijing factory sales representative was averaging 1,000 *yuan* per month bonus in early 1985. Interviews in China, April–May, 1985. On "extra budgetary funds," see Barry Naughton, "The Decline of Central Control over Investment in Post-Mao China," in David M. Lampton, ed., *Policy Implementation in Post-Mao China* (Berkeley: University of California Press, 1987), pp. 51–80; and Vivienne Shue, "Beyond the Budget: Finance Organization and Reform in a Chinese Country," *Modern China* 10, no. 2 (1984): 147–186.

75. Helen Siu, "Politics of Migration in a Market Town," in Ezra Vogel and Deborah Davis, eds., *Chinese Society on the Eve of Tiananmen* (Cambridge: Harvard Contemporary China Series, 1990), pp. 61–84.

76. Feng Lanrui, "On Factors Affecting China's Labor Employment," *People's Daily,* November 6, 1981, p. 5, in *FBIS* (November 20, 1981): K 5.

77. See *Nongmin bao,* June 29, 1985, p. 3; July 24, 1985, p. 3; October 12, 1985, p. 3; and August 17, 1985, p. 3.

78. See *Nongmin bao,* December 16, 1984, p. 2; August 12, 1984, p. 1; and May 14, 1985, p. 1.

79. See *Nongmin bao,* May 13, 1985, p. 1; and August 19, 1985, p. 2, respectively.

80. *China Daily,* April 30, 1985, p. 1.

81. Janos Kornai, *Economics of Shortage* (Amsterdam: North Holland, 1980).

82. *Nongmin bao,* January 12, 1985, p. 1.

83. Michael Lipton, *Why Poor People Stay Poor: Urban Bias in World Development* (Cambridge: Harvard University Press, 1976).

84. Robert Bates, *Markets and States in Tropical Africa* (Berkeley: University of California Press, 1981).

8

Dilemmas of Partial Reform

State and Collective Firms versus the Rural Private Sector

Introduction

To speed up the commercialization of China's rural economy, China's leaders decided to foster the growth of the rural private sector. The limited growth of the rural economy under the Maoist system of bureaucratic control and the improving rural standard of living following the liberalization and expansion of the private sector demonstrate the usefulness of this policy. Nevertheless, while studies addressing the reemergence of the private sector in China have taken as their starting point the myriad problems confronted by private entrepreneurs,[1] this chapter considers the dilemmas confronted by some of their competitors—the supply and marketing cooperatives (SMC), service companies, and other state-run service industries that to date have administered important functions in the rural economy.

This is no plainted plea for the superiority of socialism; these companies were formed by expropriating the private property of often far more efficient entrepreneurs. However, approaching this reform from their perspective highlights the regulatory constraints that restrict the behavior of some rural collective and state firms even as the Maoist, rural political economy is being deregulated and liberalized. These businesses are confronting reverse discrimination, a form of state-imposed, negative affirmative action, while other businesses are receiving special dispensations or assistance. In essence, they are functioning under different economic institutions.[2] This approach also helps pinpoint one source of the lingering hostility to the rural reforms, that is, the economic interests of managers and employees in local state firms, and suggests that the level of opposition to reform might drop if reforms were to be advanced further, rather than reversed; for these regulated units, simply stopping in midstream may be the worst option.

Characteristics of Partial Reform

Under the Maoist, rural political economy resources flowed primarily through a vertical, bureaucratically dominated system that controlled the goods produced in the countryside and transferred them according to the dictates of a command economy. State and collective rural cadres from the county level down managed the labor, capital, and land of the collectivized farmers, and withdrew resources from them to expand their own sinecures.[3]

After the nationwide introduction of the household responsibility system, China's reform leaders called for the second stage of the rural reforms. A market mechanism and increased privatization of the nonagricultural sector have increased the amount of goods flowing horizontally among individuals and units beyond the purview of the bureaucracy's vertical controls.[4] In addition, to increase the free flow of commodities and services, the second stage of the rural reforms has introduced policies that weaken the state and collective sector's monopoly over rural marketing and services. In response, a resilient private sector now cuts into their markets and challenges them for business. And yet, as these commercial and service companies confront this new competition, they find themselves constrained by the dilemmas of partial reform.

Whereas one may think of a centrally planned economy as a highly regulated one, with guidelines emanating from the national government that constrain most commercial interactions, "partial reform" involves only limited deregulation and a limited introduction of market forces. First, the market remains constrained by continued intervention by state bureaucrats who seek to guide its development in ways that help them fulfill their political obligations to their bureaucratic superiors. Second, these officials may limit market access to protect firms that generate taxes that are important revenue sources for the local government. Under these conditions, only certain firms are free to operate according to market rules, while the decisions of others are still determined by the bureaucracy; this limits their ability to compete in the market. And, although these regulated units might have a comparative advantage in the marketplace, under partial reform both central and local governments invoke certain regulations or guidelines that severely shackle their economic activities and strip them of their competitive edge.

To return to the vertical/horizontal perspective, under partial reform some actors who were part of the vertical bureaucratic system are forced to continue to work under that system, and remain guided by its collective norms, while others are now free to work under a horizontal market-oriented system, with fewer constraints. And yet, the commercialization of the rural economy, the expansion of the commercial sector, the increase in the role of the service sector, the private transportation of goods, the introduction of a dual price system—with goods sold outside the plan inviting the higher prices—and a variety of other semi-market changes are resulting in new opportunities that are expanding daily. These sectors are ones in which money can be made. However, state and collective firms remain under the control of local governments that admonish them not to seek quick profits but direct them to demonstrate a socialist ethos when they serve the people, while private businesses remain freer to serve the people for a quick profit. Ironically, whereas under the Maoist system, units controlling the vertical hierarchy used their power to dominate individual farmers and expand their resource base, under partial reform some of them, particularly commercial and service sector firms, are currently being more constrained than private entrepreneurs, who are better positioned to take advantage of the new market opportunities now available under the reforms.

Finally, the continued existence of agricultural planning at both the national and local levels forces state and local bureaucrats, who continue to receive planned quotas from above or who must meet societal needs, to respond in a manner which creates inequality unique to partial reform. Driven by these responsibilities, they may impose production obligations on a particular set of units, such as those closer to a city or situated in valleys rather than hills, leaving another set of units free to pursue market-oriented interests. For example, suburban units may be forced to grow vegetables or rice while more distant, hilly units can grow medicinal herbs or more valuable fruits. Moreover, the former units must sell their goods to the state at planned or negotiated prices, but the latter units produce goods that can be sold at higher market prices. In this way, too, partial reform binds one set of units while giving those in different locations or with different endowments the freedom to make more money by participating in the newly expanding market sector.

Changes in the Rural Commercial System

The ongoing rural reforms, begun in 1983 but expanded in 1985, have increased the number of private businesses as well as their freedom to compete with collective and state companies. At the same time, these latter companies remain regulated in their market activity, even as they are pressured to reform their internal operations and adjust their relationship to the external economic environment.

Growth and Problems of Private Businesses

Since 1978, the state has opted for managing, rather than policing, the private sector,[5] and has facilitated its development. As a result, from 1978 to mid-1986, the number of private businesses in towns, cities, and rural areas, as well as the volume of their sales, has increased dramatically (Table 8.1). Data from Nanjing

Table 8.1

Development of Small Business in China, 1981–1986 (in 1,000s)

	1981	1982	1983	1984	1985	1986[a]
Number of businesses						
Nationwide	1,829	2,636	5,901	9,304	11,710	11,340
In cities and towns	868	1,132	1,706	2,222	2,798	2,734
In rural areas	961	1,504	4,195	7,082	8,915	8,610
Compared with the preceding year (percentage change)	+44.1	+44.1	+124	+57.4	+25.9	—
Number of persons						
Nationwide	2,337	3,198	7,464	13,031	17,661	17,190
In cities and towns	1,056	1,358	2,086	2,911	3,839	3,790
In rural areas	1,281	1,840	5,378	10,120	13,822	13,400
Compared with the preceding year (percentage change)	—	+40.6	+133	+74.3	+35.5	—

Source: "Basic Data on Individually Owned Small Businesses Since the Third Plenum of the Party's 11th Central Committee" (*"Dangde shiyi jie san zhong quan hui yilai geti gongshang hu jiben qingkuang"*), *Industry and Business Administration (Gongshang xingzheng guanli)*, no. 24 (1986): 13.

Note:

[a]Figures for this year are through June 1986.

Table 8.2

Development of Private Business in Nanjing, 1978–1985 (in 1,000s)

	1978	1980	1982	1983	1984	1985
Number of households	1,738	5,535	10,443	21,577	34,137	49,977
Number employed	1,758	5,770	10,788	24,191	42,465	61,634

Source: Nanjing Industrial and Commercial Management Bureau, June 3, 1986.

Table 8.3

Individual Business Employment Structure, Jiangpu County, 1978–1986

	1978	1980	1982	1983	1984	1986[a]
Industry	22	27	71	106	286	341
Commerce	33	195	613	778	1,190	1,281
Food	41	57	108	137	384	369
Service	12	20	35	44	152	123
Repairs	17	53	91	104	249	252
Transport	—	0	2	2	275	1,008
Construction	—	2	3	7	10	12
Other	3	3	4	5	5	20
Total households	128	357	927	1,183	2,551	3,406
Total employed	128	553	1,368	1,690	3,344	4,362

Source: Industrial and Commercial Bureau, Jiangpu County, June 10, 1986.
Note:
[a]Data as of May 1986.

Municipality and Jiangpu County, near Nanjing, show a similar pattern of growth in the number of private businesses between 1978 and 1985 (see Table 8.2).

In Jiangpu County, many of these private businesses have focused on the food, service, and commercial (store ownership) sectors (Table 8.3), and compete directly with the SMCs and the state-run service companies. In this county in 1986, 1.4 million *RMB* of a total business volume of 3.0 million *RMB* carried out by private businesses were earned in commercial exchange. In addition, of 234 private businesses located in Tangquan Township, Jiangpu County, in 1984, 115 were small shops and 31 were food businesses. In fact, according to local officials in Tangquan, the commercial sector developed too rapidly and quickly became saturated.

State policy has fostered this growth. Under State Council guidelines, private businesses, especially "those who indeed have difficulty in running a handicraft, repair service, other service trade or catering service," were promised special treatment "in the form of loans, *favorable prices or tax reduction or exemption or necessary technical assistance from the state*" (emphasis added).[6] When private businesses came under attack from local bureaucrats, Nanjing's city government promulgated an eight-point document in January 1985 on "protecting the legal rights of the private businesses" (*baohu getihu de jingji hefa quanyi*). Yet, many of these small businesses do not really need major tax breaks. In theory taxes are assessed at 3 to 5 percent of sales plus a graduated tax ranging from 7 percent for a gross income of less than a thousand *RMB* per month to 60 percent on a gross income of 30,000 *RMB* per month and above.[7] According to owners of a private restaurant in Nanjing, they must pay 55 percent if they make more than six thousand *RMB* per year.

However, many private businesses do not keep good books if they keep them at all. According to one 1,000–household survey in Changchun in Jilin Province, 61 percent of businesses kept no books, 24 percent had records only of current accounts, and a mere 15 percent had a full set of books.[8] As a result, officials are often forced to estimate the income of private businesses. Yet, local officials in Nanjing recognized that they really did not know how much entrepreneurs made.[9] And, if they remain as "specialized households," and not private businesses, they need pay no taxes at all.

To get more farmers into county-towns to compete with extant collective businesses, the state moderated its formerly rigid ban on rural-to-urban migration and introduced a new "long-term residence permit" (*chang zhu hukou*), which allows them to live in towns, so long as they supply their own rice. In addition, since a main problem for private businesses is a lack of suitable space for selling their wares, some counties, such as Jiangpu in Jiangsu Province and Shulu in Hebei Province are constructing "private business centers" (*geti dalou*) for them.[10] Similarly, the Tangquan Township government, a county model for promoting private businesses, charged farmers 900 *RMB* and built them brightly painted stands along the main road. Not only could they better observe the private business activity, but they could improve the aesthetics of privatization. In other ways, too, township officials demonstrated strong support for these businesses.[11]

In Jiangpu County, the "Individual Business Division" (*getihu gu*) of the "Commercial and Industrial Bureau" (*gong shang ju*) was also extremely supportive of private businesses. These bureaucrats took their responsibility to help these private businesses seriously, and supported them in almost all conflicts with state or collective units. Although they establish guidelines and requirements that must be passed, such as tests for drivers and construction contractors and health certificates for restaurateurs, they also give private businessmen classes to help them pass these tests; in most cases, the teachers are state cadres.

Still, private businesses have confronted serious problems since 1978.[12] Supply and marketing cooperatives and other state or collective enterprises have expended great efforts to undermine the growth of private businesses. They have approached Commercial and Industrial Bureau officials to get them to revoke the licenses that had been given to the private businesses.[13] Overall, the kinds of bureaucratic restrictions and hostile reactions small businesses have met are legion.[14] Getting supplies is also a major problem, although deregulating the markets for timber, grain, and other products in 1985 alleviated some of these difficulties. For example, many restaurants need coal for cooking, but firms established after July 1, 1985 cannot buy coal from the state and thus pay higher coal costs.[15]

Government constraints on marketing and wholesaling leave private firms dependent on their competitors, the SMCs. According to some sources, private firms cannot go into the wholesale business very easily, reportedly because the government still sees the state and collective as the major marketeers.[16] As a result, private businesses in more distant rural areas must buy from their competition, the SMCs, which do not supply them with top quality goods.[17] Even increases in the production and supply of agricultural and industrial goods have not totally undermined the power of the SMCs; they remain a critical channel through which farmers market some of their surplus and, given their control over resources, the SMCs can wield even more influence if supplies of commodities on the market shrink.

According to the directors of one suburban Nanjing SMC, the private businesses with whom they compete are less under the control of the SMCs than those businesses in more distant locations. In near suburbs, such as this one, individual businesses buy about 65 percent of their goods from the SMC, but they compete on over 95 percent of the goods the township sells. However, "in the more distant countryside, . . . they must rely more on selling their goods to the [SMC]. This fact gives the [SMC] in those areas more power."[18]

The Changing Environment for State/Collective Units

Significant changes have occurred in the SMC's property rights arrangements and subsequently in their financial incentives, opportunities and behavior. Since 1949, SMCs have shifted back and forth between cooperative ownership (1949–1958, 1962–1970, 1975–1978) and state (1958–1962, 1970–1975, 1978–1982) ownership.[19] In February 1982, the SMC's administrative organization was incorporated into the Commerce Ministry to show that the SMC system was not a separate, administrative bureaucracy but was, in fact, now a competitive commercial network.[20] In response, in 1983, Jiangsu Province changed all SMCs from "all people's ownership" (state) to collective ownership. The state no longer covers their losses, particularly after Central Document No. 1 of 1985 announced that all SMCs "should have completely independent accounting systems, be responsible for their own profits and losses, and operate on their own under democratic operation by the masses."[21] In addition, all new employees with urban residence permits would be collective, not state, workers, and SMCs could now hire rural "contract workers" (*hetong gong*).

To replace the loss of state funding, SMCs can now raise funds directly from farmers, and the results have been significant.[22] In return, the cooperatives now return dividends to villagers at year's end. In addition, after 1984, over 77 percent of the SMCs in Jiangsu Province had divided their various divisions, such as food companies and individual stores, into 9,490 financially independent units.[23] However, following the cancellation of compulsory sales of agricultural products in 1985, SMCs were expected to help farmers market their produce all over the country, expand the information network for marketing and technical innovation, make loans to rural entrepreneurs, and, in particular, promote the commercialization of agriculture.[24] Many companies are clearly reluctant to perform these kinds of services, particularly since these rural entrepreneurs are competing directly with them.

Therefore, when I went to China to do research in summer 1986, I expected to find the villain among these semi-state, semi-collective enterprises. But interviews in rural Nanjing showed that at this critical stage in the rural reforms, government bureaus at both the city and county levels still control major parts of the rural economy. To maintain social and economic order, they are demanding that state-run commercial and service companies follow the plan and "serve the people." At the same time, the bureaus are responding to central government signals to loosen the constraints on the private sector, as well as on other parts of the collective sector, creating serious disadvantages for units still working under local bureaucratic control. In the end, I found a partially planned, partially market-oriented economy, for which officials still regulated a great deal of local economic activity and, therefore, predetermined which sectors had the competitive edge and comparative advantage under the emerging rural market economy.

Dilemmas for State/Collective Firms Under the Reforms

According to *Beijing Review,* the SMCs are the main target of the second stage of rural reforms,[25] while Central Document No. 1 (1985), which deregulated the exchange of most rural commodities, called on state companies to "enliven their operation because they will be subject to market regulation." At the same time, the state has called on the companies to help farmers prosper, even though villagers' private businesses may compete with shops or processing factories now run by SMCs and other state-run businesses, such as food wholesaling and transport.[26]

Thus, SMCs; service companies, which run hotels, restaurants, bathhouses, barbershops and photo shops in county towns; and other similar firms, such as "small collectives" (*xiao jiti* or *hezuo qiye*) in township towns,[27] face major problems resulting from the state's financial and tax policies, local labor regulations, heavy retirement demands, and local political interference.

Problems of Finance and Taxes

According to Chinese sources, SMCs in many ways are much worse off than state firms, even though they are free to go out and raise money.[28] First, the Finance Ministry regulates their expenditures while taxing some of the bonuses for their employees. Second, profits on agricultural products are small, but SMCs get no credit assistance to cover the seasonal outlay of funds, as do state grain companies. Third, the rate of taxation for SMCs rose from 39 to 50 percent, the same as for state companies, but unlike state wholesalers, who do not pay taxes, SMC wholesalers pay a 10 percent tax. Finally, according to Meng, even though their financial resources are strained, SMCs remain the best source of funds for local governments and financial institutions that increase the contributions demanded of them.

These kinds of financial issues were raised by officials at the lower levels. When a county SMC manager compared his problems with those of the collective enterprises, he complained that, if an SMC opens a new store, it gets only one year tax free, the same as a state company, whereas if a collective opens a store or factory, it gets three tax-free years. In addition, bonuses given out by SMCs are more tightly regulated.[29] If the bonuses they give are more than two and a half times their monthly salary, they must pay taxes on that money.[30]

Finally, due to bureaucratic complications, all transactions of the SMC must go through the bank; therefore, it takes them several more days to complete transactions than are required for a private business, which often has no bank accounts. According to another source, as of 1984–1985, "cooperatives" (*hezuo zongdian*) in local towns could draw out 30 *RMB* of their funds from the bank without permission, while managers of smaller "branch shops" (*menshi bu*) could draw out only 10 *RMB*.[31] In addition, state service companies work under regulations that stipulate how many people are needed to run a restaurant—a chef, a server, someone to take in the money, and someone to buy the food. This imposed division of labor increases their labor costs compared with private restaurants which do not confront such regulations.

Problems of Labor Allocation

Due to recent policy changes, SMCs can now legally hire contract laborers; however, most of the workers in Jiangpu County and Nanjing SMCs (in Nanjing's immediate suburbs) who were hired under previous policies are still collective or state workers. As of 1986, only 20 percent of workers in Jiangpu County's SMCs and only 3 percent (ten of three hundred) in Zijingshan Township's SMC were contract laborers. The greatest impediment comes from the Labor Department (*renshi bumen*); as an official in Jiangpu County complained, the reality of trying to hire contract workers is much more complicated than the "spirit of the documents."

While private businesses are free to hire and fire contract workers, Tangquan Township's SMC cannot. The problem originates in the large number of unemployed youths in rural towns who have urban residence permits but refuse to work in unstable township factories. The Labor Bureau, which must find these urban residents jobs, has turned to the SMCs for help, demanding that they hire the children of SMC workers first. But if the SMC is to improve its level of service and finances, it needs to be able to fire slovenly workers;[32] however, the children of SMC workers, as urban residents, must be hired as semipermanent collective workers, who, for anything short of committing a major crime, cannot be fired. From 1983 to 1985, SMCs in Jiangpu County needed only the permission of the county government to hire rural workers, but by late 1985, the Labor Bureau had reasserted its control and told the SMC that, if it hired villagers, the Labor Bureau would not help SMC employees' children find jobs in the state sector. Similarly, in Zijingshan Township outside Nanjing, the SMC has failed to introduce a responsibility system for each worker, because the workers are resisting it.

The county service company works under similar constraints. Before 1982, if it could not make enough money to pay its workers, it could bargain with the state which would cut its income tax. But now, because each store is an independent enterprise, confronting a "hard budget constraint," if it performs poorly, its workers' salaries are cut. However, even as they are pushed into the market, SMCs do not control their own hiring and firing. Since 1980, Jiangpu's Labor Bureau has given them twenty new workers, and whenever one retires, the state sends a replacement, whether they want one or not.

Retirement Problems

A major problem for all these firms is their obligation to supply retirement benefits to their former workers, even though for most of the past twenty years their profits went to the state's coffers and not into the SMC system. But now, as older workers retire, the SMC system is expected to cover the workers' retirement benefits from its management costs. In some places, one current employee may support .5 to 2 retired workers, undermining current workers' benefits and labor enthusiasm.[33]

In Jiangpu's service company, retirement benefits have been a major problem. Persons who retired after twenty years have been receiving 75 percent of their salaries, while those who worked fifteen to twenty years have been getting 70 percent of their salaries; all of them have received free medical treatment. These funds reportedly came from this company.

In Tangquan Township, the small collective, where sixty retired workers are supported by seventy current employees, pays 3,000 *RMB* per month in salaries and medicine for retired workers. Because it, too, is an independent accounting unit, poor business means lower salaries. A 1986 local recession meant that eighty-two workers in 1985, who generated a profit of 35,000 *RMB,* became only sixty-eight current employees in 1986 accounting for profits of only 15,000 *RMB.* Six workers retired, but others quit because of unstable salaries. Officials believe that private businesses took away 40 percent of their profits. Still, they had to continue to support their retired workers. Finally, when a state- or collective-run shop goes broke, it must take care of its workers,[34] whereas rural entrepreneurs who go bankrupt can go back to the fields.

Political Problems

Supply and marketing cooperatives confront a great deal of local bureaucratic interference, even as they try to balance their books. Although they are the same as other "large collectives" (*da jiti*), they are supposed to "serve the people" rather than be "too busy managing their own businesses, making money, issuing rewards or even competing for profits. . . . struggling to handle that which yields big profits while leaving those making little profits alone, thus lacking sufficient consideration for their social effects."[35] So that villagers will not scream about difficulties marketing their produce, the county government forces the SMC to buy products they do not want. Still, if the SMC loses money on these deals, the state does not supplement its funds. Similarly, a SMC plan to combine several unprofitable stores in neighboring townships was turned down by the government because it could inconvenience the villagers. Thus, although these firms are expected to "stand on their own financially" (*zifu yingkui*), they are not totally free to pursue those goals.

In addition, some county officials may favor private businesses. Private businesses serve some needs of the general population better than the state and collective companies; local governments may also feel political pressure to conform to public policy and demonstrate that the private sector is growing under their stewardship.[36] As a result, in Jiangpu County there was a close relationship between the "Private Business Association" (*getihu xiehui*) and the Industrial and Commercial Bureau (ICB); in fact, they are run out of the same building, and the deputy head of the ICB, himself a former director or the ICB, heads the association. As a result, managers of collective businesses complained that the state checks the quality of produce in their shops more carefully and more often than that of the private shops. In fact, one township official in the SMC system argued that each time the ICB, the "Tax Office" (*shuiwu ju*), the "Price Investigation Office" (*wujia jiancha suo*) or the Health Bureau came to investigate, they checked only those shops run by the SMC. According to this official, "we have raised this many times, and only now is there beginning to be a change." In fact, while I was in the township, the restaurant run by the SMC was closed temporarily for health violations.

Many of these local problems result from a lack of political support at higher levels of the political system. Nationally, the SMC organization is an "empty shell,"[37] and as part of the Ministry of Commerce, its fate under the reforms depends on that ministry's political clout. Supply and marketing cooperatives are particularly vulnerable on issues of price reduction, which often harm their income, especially in localities where there is a high degree of specialization.[38] In addition, although they are part of the Ministry of Commerce system, and therefore must buy their products from Commerce Bureau wholesalers in the county, they compete in the county seat with stores owned and operated by the county's Commerce Bureau, which passes on the best products to its own stores.

Nevertheless, officials in the Nanjing city government's Rural Work Department believe that the township SMC has much more freedom today than under the "radical line," when the commune party committee's "horizontal control" (*kuai kuai lingdao*) gave commune leaders great influence over the grain station, the SMC, and the bank, among others. Now a major part of the reform is to get the township government to reduce its efforts to control local SMC stores. According to Rural Work Department officials, many township SMCs do not listen to the township government, preferring instead to respond to the "vertical authority" (*tiao tiao lingdao*) of their county bosses "because if they go bankrupt, the upper levels are responsible."[39] Still, if the ICB and the Individual Business Association are this closely tied nationwide, those who compete with private businesses are likely to face continued discrimination by ICB officials.

Commercialization of the Rural Economy

Finally, the continued existence of production quotas and local governmental responsibility for ensuring urban food supplies, both reflections of partial reform, demonstrates how the concomitant existence of plan and market generates new inequalities of opportunity. Units that do not fall under the constraints of the plan and are free to pursue other economic opportunities have profited greatly from commercialization; those restrained by the plan have done less well.

For example, although the state formally ended the compulsory grain sales,[40] each county, township, and village still receives a production quota. However, because land can now be used for commercial endeavors, decisions on its use are much more important than before 1978, when marketing opportunities were minimal. Thus, villages that avoid grain quotas and shift to commercial crops are in a better position to profit from new opportunities, creating inequalities among villages or brigades in the same township. In fact, the price differential between grain and some commercial crops has made it worthwhile for some villages to shift their production into cash crops and fulfill their grain quota through purchases on the free market.

In Tangquan Township, hilly brigades which quickly began raising tree seedlings got very wealthy in 1983–1985. This occurred in part because the township lowered its grain quota. However, crops grown in paddy areas are more tightly regulated; only recently have they shifted some of their poorest land out of grain, expanding their melon production and turning some of the land into fish ponds. As a result, the living standard of teams in paddy areas is visibly lower than that of the hilly teams.

Consequently, Tangquan Township's overall prosperity has resulted in part from a low grain quota which other, less privileged townships supplement. Nanjing officials recognized this dilemma: "No doubt, we need to adjust the grain quota from the county level and below to allow those areas that specialize to pursue those interests, while at the same time ensure the grain output. But if the other area helps you out by helping to fulfill your quota, then you need to pay them back."[41] At this point in the reforms, Tangquan Township's limited quota has helped them grow rich at the expense of other localities who are fulfilling their own quota. The fairest solution would be either to force everyone to grow grain or simply let the market come into full play.

The production of food, such as vegetables and milk, was also still regulated in parts of rural China in 1986. In fact, the policy of the "cities leading the counties" (shi lingdao xian), was instituted to help city governments control the crops grown for urban consumption. To ensure sufficient supply, 80 percent of the crops grown in Zijingshan Township, in suburban Nanjing, were set by the city and 20 percent were planted at the township's own discretion; if the township ignored the plan and failed to meet its vegetable quota, the state would cut its grain ration, forcing the township to buy more expensive free-market grain.[42] The city also relied on its party authority to ensure cooperation with its directives.

In fact, in all conversations, party officials in Zijingshan Township constantly stressed the township's role in feeding the city; city officials had made their point emphatically to the township's leaders. But privately, other township officials expressed disappointment and frustration that some of their leaders had been too concerned with fulfilling the state plan. As a result, some plans these other officials devised to take advantage of the commercialization of the rural economy had been turned down.

As a result of these and other constraints, Zijingshan Township had not industrialized as rapidly as some neighboring townships located farther from the city, because it had to use its funds and land to ensure a rich supply of good quality vegetables. In addition, because this township must sell all its milk to the state, it cannot establish a factory for processing its own milk. Were they not part of this plan, they might find it profitable to process and sell their own milk in the city. However, the city, which runs its own milk factory, refused the township's request to build a factory, thereby maintaining its monopoly.

Finally, a freer fish market that permits rural entrepreneurs to sell directly to factory mess halls has led to hard times for state-run fish companies in Nanjing. Their share of the market has shrunk considerably. In 1985, almost 1 million

Table 8.4

Private Agricultural Sales as a Percentage of State Agricultural Sales, Nanjing, 1983 and 1985

Products	1983[a]	Percent of State Sales	1985[a]	Percent of State Sales
Grain	8,735	2.1	3,610	0.8[b]
Pork	419	0.8	2,234	4.9
Beef	152	11.5	293	24.2
Eggs	3,151	34.7	4,430	67.8
Fowl	3,380	41.6	5,040	133.1
Fish	2,847	156.8	5,800	756.0
Vegetables	36,712	16.4	68,890	42.7

Source: Industrial and Commercial Management Bureau, Nanjing, June 3, 1986.

Notes:

[a]Figures are in 1,000 *RMB.*

[b]In 1985, as compared to 1983, people were eating less grain in Nanjing and more meat, fish, and vegetables.

kilograms of fish in Nanjing were sold by rural entrepreneurs.[43] Moreover, state company sales of 20 million kilograms in 1983 dropped to 9.5 million kilograms in 1984. As of 1985, when the state stopped giving state-run fish companies a subsidy, they had problems feeding their workers. These problems arose "because the state controls on them were quite tight, with restrictions that others did not have." Although this problem needs more meticulous analysis, similar problems have developed for numerous other food companies in Nanjing (Table 8.4), suggesting that the existence of state controls on some but not all economic sectors has created a common dilemma at this stage of the reforms.

Reflections on a Visit Two Years Later

This chapter is based on data collected in summer 1986 and was written in summer 1987. In 1988, I returned briefly to Jiangpu County and had the opportunity to talk with some of the same actors. Rather than entirely rewrite this chapter, an unnecessary task given that the transitional nature of the phenomena is acknowledged, I decided simply to add some comments describing the changes I observed.

First, continued reforms have relieved some hostility generated by constraints imposed by local governments. For example, according to the new director of the SMC in Jiangpu, its economic situation improved dramatically after 1986 due to an expansion of its wholesale efforts. Whereas in 1986 its SMC sales and purchases occurred only within the county, it is now able to buy better quality products outside the county and market them in other counties as well. One of the SMC stores in a township bordering Anhui Province serves as a wholesale outlet for sales in Anhui. As a result, sales in 1986 of over 90 million *RMB* have increased by 55 percent (not controlling for inflation); by June 1988, the sales were already over 70 million *RMB*.

Labor and retirement problems have receded as well. According to the new director, pressures from the Labor Bureau to hire children of SMC workers have passed and reflected a particular period when jobs in the county were few and unemployment high. Perhaps, too, rural industries have expanded and become slightly more stable. As for pension problems, efforts are being carried out nationwide to resolve this welfare dilemma. In Jiangpu County, the SMC now draws 24 percent of total salaries of all employees from its yearly profits, and gives it to a state labor insurance company. The insurance company handles all retirement payments. Although one wonders what happens to companies that cannot afford these payments, under this new system retired workers are more secure since their retirement payments do not come directly from their old firms.

Finally, the recent expansion of the SMC in Jiangpu County may merely reflect the slow nature of the commercial reform that has taken place in this county. After 1986, several older officials were replaced by more active, younger county officials who sought to increase the pace of development. One need only compare the SMC in Jiangpu County with the more prosperous and powerful SMC organizations in southern Jiangsu Province, which rapidly expanded their commercial, wholesale, and industrial activities. For example, the SMC in Wujiang County, outside Suzhou County, which I visited in summer 1988, and which expanded its commercial and industrial activities in 1984, now owns 42 factories and employs 8,000 workers, which according to the director is the result of its open-minded attitude towards business opportunities. Under a freer economy and with more active leadership, the SMC in Jiangpu County may also be able to grow more rapidly.

Conclusion

The dilemmas described here, which have resulted from continued regulatory controls on some sectors of the rural economy, combined with deregulation of other sectors or actors, are part of the distortions that develop in socialist systems undergoing gradual transitions to a market economy. Nevertheless, they do create inequitable conditions for some firms, even while others receive special advantages. Ironically, the firms that are suffering most are those that held monopolistic control over the commercial sector during the Maoist era, and that tried to undermine the reforms in their early stages. Similarly, some units that are losing out on new economic opportunities were advantaged under the planned economy, in that they were allowed to grow vegetables; others, however, were kept in poverty by the irrational demands of a state that enforced excessive levels of grain production.

Even though one major goal of the reform is to get politics out of the economy, the reform's partial nature has ensured that politics remains an important deter-minant of one's position in the marketplace. The price of remaining under state control can be high, making opportunities to get out from under state regulations dependent on political relationships. Politics also determines which units remain under local political control. From the county level down, local governments still intervene in the market and force firms to follow the government's political agenda rather than the dictates of their own economic logic.

China's economists and social scientists recognize these dilemmas, but the question is, what should be done next? Should rural China push forward and further deregulate the rural economy? If it were to do so, would the state be able to ensure that there would be enough grain for urban residents? As it is, the state is pressed to match grain production to population growth. In a nonregulated economy, larger firms are likely to do well, allowing collective and state firms to compete better with the private businesses; but, if their size and power doom the rural private sector to oblivion before it establishes itself firmly, services in the rural areas would suffer again.

Yet, are continued regulations and discriminatory policies not themselves somewhat self-defeating due to the hostility they generate against the reforms? Data suggest that, even as state and collective firms try to reform and compete, continuing regulations and pro-private sector, affirmative action policies create a great deal of local tension. Moreover, under current conditions, these firms are having difficulty reforming internally and competing externally. But, can the state really allow them to go bankrupt, without being certain that the private sector will fill in the employment gaps created?

Notes

1. See Linda Hershkovitz, "The Fruits of Ambivalence: China's Urban Individual Economy," *Pacific Affairs* 58 (1985): 427–450.

2. See Douglass C. North, *Structure and Change in Economic History* (New York: W. W. Norton and Co., 1981).

3. See David Zweig, *Agrarian Radicalism in China, 1968–1981* (Cambridge: Harvard University Press, 1989).

4. Yet, while many rural bureaucrats have lost access to rural resources, some organizations such as local party branches and township (i.e., administrative) governments have maintained significant control over rural resources and, thus, have lost little political power. See Jean C. Oi, "Peasant Grain Marketing and State Procurement: China's Contracting System," *The China Quarterly*, no. 106 (1986): 272–290. Township enterprises run by these administrative organs have boomed as well (see chapter 10 of this book). Finally, some basic rural cadres have abandoned the collectives and struck out on their own as entrepreneurs. See John P. Burns, "Local Cadre Accommodation to the Responsibility System in Rural China," *Pacific Affairs* 58, no. 4 (1985–1986): 607–625.

5. See Dorothy J. Solinger, *Chinese Business Under Socialism* (Berkeley: University of California Press, 1984).

6. See Chinese State Council, "Certain Regulations Governing Individual Industry

and Commerce in Rural Areas," February 27, 1984, in Foreign Broadcast Information Service, *China: Daily Report* (hereafter cited as *FBIS*) (March 13, 1984): K 10–13.

7. See Ellen Salem, "Peddling the Private Road," *Far Eastern Economic Review,* October 8, 1987, p. 106.

8. Ibid.

9. Interview ICAMO, 1986.

10. Marc Blecher, personal communication with the author, 1987.

11. Although state policy prohibits cadres from running private businesses, a school teacher opened a small factory employing over twenty workers registering his 20-year-old daughter as the formal owner. Although everyone knew this was a cover—in fact, some people wrote letters of protest—township officials responsible for private businesses turned a blind eye to this infraction. Officials also helped the families selling pork in the free market to buy a freezer to insure the quality of the meat being sold.

12. Solinger, *Chinese Business Under Socialism,* pp. 202–203.

13. One informant in rural Nanjing admitted that a director of a township SMC had approached the local Commercial and Industrial Bureau official and tried to persuade him to restrict the activities of the private businesses. These kinds of reports appeared frequently in 1983 in *Farmers' News (Nongmin bao).*

14. For a more in-depth discussion of the problems small businesses face, see Hershkovitz, "The Fruits of Ambivalence"; and Marcia Yudkin, *Making Good: Private Business in Socialist China* (Beijing: Foreign Languages Press, 1986).

15. Interview FCD, 1986.

16. Interview NCIB, 1986.

17. Interview LYL, 1986; see also *Nongmin bao,* October 19, 1985.

18. Interview ZTSSMC, 1986.

19. See Han Baocheng, "Farmers Active in Commercial Sector," *Beijing Review,* no. 19 (1987): 17–18.

20. Zhu Weiwen, "The Nature of the Supply and Marketing Coops and Their Reform" (*"Gongxiao hezuoshe de xingzhi jiqi gaige"*), *Problems in Agricultural Economics* (*Nongye jingji wenti*), no. 2 (1986): 14–16.

21. "Ten Policies of the CPC Central Committee and the State Council for Further Invigorating the Rural Economy (January 1, 1985)," *FBIS* (March 25, 1985): K 1–7.

22. By the end of 1984, villagers had invested over fifty-seven million *RMB* in SMCs in Jiangsu Province, increasing the liquid capital from 4.79 to 11.64 percent. See *The Situation of Economic and Social Development in Jiangsu, 1984* (*Jiangsu jingji he shehui fazhan gaikuang, 1984*) (Nanjing: Jiangsu People's Publication House, 1985). In Qingdao's six counties and one suburban district, capital under the control of the SMC coming from the villagers' investments rose from 2 to 3 percent of total capital in 1984 to 20 percent in 1986. Han, "Farmers Active in Commercial Sector."

23. *The Situation of Economic and Social Development in Jiangsu, 1984.*

24. See *Nongmin bao,* August 31, 1985, p. 2; August 1, 1985, p. 2; November 7, 1985, p. 2; and "Fuyang County Supply and Marketing Coop Enthusiastically Serves the Development of Commercialized Agricultural Production," in *Develop the Rural Commodity Economy* (*Fazhan nongcun shangpin jingji*) (Beijing: Agricultural Publishing House, 1984), pp. 268–278, respectively.

25. Han, "Farmers Active in Commercial Sector," p. 17.

26. *Nongmin bao,* August 1, 1985, p. 2.

27. In many parts of rural China, these small collectives were made up of privately owned stores that were collectivized in 1950s. They ran many of the stores in the villages and brigades during the collective era, but today are supervised by the SMC system.

28. See Meng Lijia, "Discussion of the Reform of the Structure of the Supply and

Marketing Cooperatives," *Problems in Agricultural Economics* (*Nongye jingji wenti*), no. 2 (1986): 19–21.

29. Ibid.

30. The state is trying to stop these firms from decreasing their pretax profits and, therefore, their taxable income, through large bonus disbursements.

31. See Zhao Panxing and Zhang Shouzheng, "Impact of Urban and Rural Reforms on Small Town and City Development," in *Small Towns: A New Beginning* (*Xiao chengzhen, xin kai tuo*) (Huaiyang: Jiangsu People's Publishing House, 1986), pp. 315–329.

32. While the press recognizes the problems SMCs face in carrying out internal reforms, it lauds those SMCs that introduce these *systems of responsibility*. See "Take Responsibility for Managing the Wholesale Department and the Retail Shop of the S&M Coop," *Nongmin ribao*, September 12, 1985, p. 2.

33. See Meng, "Discussion of the Reform."

34. Interview LYL, June 26, 1986.

35. See *Economic Daily* (*Jingji ribao*), December 5, 1985, p. 3.

36. According to discussions held with local officials in southern Jiangsu Province, the central government sent down a document stipulating that in every locality at least 5 percent of businesses must be private.

37. Meng, "Discussion of the Reform."

38. Ibid.

39. Interview NRWD, May 30, 1986.

40. Oi, "Peasant Grain Marketing."

41. Interview NRWD, May 30, 1986.

42. Interview MQZ, June 3, 1986.

43. Interview NRWD, May 28, 1986.

9

Urbanizing Rural China
Bureaucratic Authority and Local Autonomy

As with all major shifts in rural policy since 1949, the current Chinese reforms have altered the distribution of power, authority, and resources at the county and subcounty levels. Farmers have been freed from the dependent relations that bound them to their village leaders;[1] this change allows them greater leeway to determine which crops to grow and their avocation. Some farmers can now migrate into other rural or urban settlements. A booming rural industrial sector, legitimized by the central government in 1984, is generating new resources, which have strengthened the power of lower-level officials, who control and tax these new enterprises, vis-à-vis their administrative superiors.[2] And, resurgent markets and market towns have revitalized both the "natural economy" and interregional trade that crosses administrative boundaries, further weakening the influence of administrators who previously had tightly controlled all rural marketing.[3]

However, not all reform policies weaken administrative power as the bureaucracy continues to limit the effect of many reforms on the distribution of resources and authority in the rural areas. One such policy is rural urbanization. Since the early 1980s, the state has called for increased urbanization, with the bulk of growth to occur in small cities, rural towns, and villages. Yet, the process of rural urbanization has shown that authority remains ensconced within the bureaucracy and distributed among the various levels within it, making bureaucratic authority, not the market, the best predictor of the outcome of decisions and the distribution of resources. County and town officials still possess important mechanisms of command and control over resources, production, migration, and economic opportunities. Although market forces are expanding, new pockets of local autonomy are developing, and county officials often must negotiate with

221

subordinates, such that old patterns of authority have not decreased or changed as much as might have been predicted, given the sweeping nature of the reforms.

Rural Urbanization as an Issue Area

Like a blind man studying the elephant, a researcher's perspective on the reforms' impact on the distribution of authority will be determined by which aspect of the rural reforms he or she addresses. A village-level focus may show a major transformation, as a new generation of rich farmers takes control from former production-team leaders.[4] Examination of the privatization of wholesale and long-distance trading would show a dramatic drop in state controls, depending on the location.[5] But, studying rural urbanization demonstrates that a decreasing scope for the national plan need not lead to a total shift to a market economy.

This issue area remains constrained for several reasons. First, unlike marketing reforms that cross administrative boundaries, these expanding settlements overlap with the existing administrative hierarchy, which means prereform authority patterns persist within the reforming rural bureaucracy and community. Second, these settlements and towns remain the locus of party and government committees and political authority at the county and subcounty levels. Towns are the sites of income-enhancing opportunities, are the end points of migration, and have governments that own much of the expanding industrial base, allowing bureaucrats there to influence strongly the flow of people and resources. Furthermore, the central government left responsibility for the rural urbanization process to county and county-town governments (see the appendix to this chapter). However, limited resources for urban infrastructure let the county government influence resource allocations and maintain relations of dependency over lower levels in the hierarchy.

To demonstrate how the rural bureaucracy influences the rural urbanization process, this chapter examines prereform rural settlements and administrative hierarchy and then describes administrative changes that have occurred under the reforms. This is followed by a discussion of how county officials use the process of planning, the imposition of "development labels," and the "nesting" of administrative offices and enterprises within the physical boundaries of the county-towns and townships to maintain significant influence over localities within their domain. A study of the struggle among the county, county-towns, and townships over funds for town development will help clarify this relationship. I also show how county-town and township officials control access to the towns. In conclusion, this chapter makes some generalizations about the relationship among resources, hierarchy, and political authority as they relate to rural urbanization.

Prereform Structure of Authority and Settlements

In 1949, the Chinese Communist Party (CCP) inherited the Guomindang's local administrative hierarchy. Unlike the Qing dynasty, the Guomindang had established the "district" (*qu*) between the "county" (*xian*) and the "administrative villages" (*xiang*) or towns. The *qu* was a supervisory agent by which the *xian* government managed the *xiang*, which, with a fairly well-developed governmental structure, constituted the most basic level of government administration.[6] Large *xiang*, whose locations made them major marketing centers, were classified as "market towns," or *jizhen*.[7]

In their ceaseless efforts to control both the economy and the political administration, leaders of the CCP extended subcounty controls. The *qu*, as the administrative level for organizing land-reform teams, doubled in number by 1955, and became full-scale governments between the *xian* and the *xiang*. But, as collectivization increased the size of each agricultural producer cooperative, the size of the average *xiang* expanded to ensure continued coherence between economic and administrative organizations. As the *xiang* grew, they began to approximate the size of the *qu*; therefore, in December 1955, the disbanding of the *qu* left the *xiang* as the major administrative level below the *xian*.[8] Continuing state efforts to control private marketing throughout the 1950s and 1960s killed the market town (*jizhen*) as a commercial force and seat of autonomous authority.[9] When the 1958 Great Leap Forward amalgamated the agricultural cooperatives and the *xiang* government, and placed the headquarters of the new People's Communes in former *jizhen* or *xiang* government centers,[10] the former bifurcation of the commercial system and administrative control was ended. This left the commune seat as a powerful node in the rural bureaucratic hierarchy, which combined economic, political, and social control.[11]

The reforms following the Great Leap Forward's failure transferred ownership and control over land and most resources to the village or subvillage production team, leaving communes and brigades with weak economic bases. County-controlled market towns, which were not the seat of the commune government (by 1978, there were only 1,100 such market towns in all of China) virtually disappeared from view, having little contact with a collectivized countryside. With commune towns serving supervisory roles for county interests,[12] (county organizations, such as the Agricultural Bank, supply and marketing cooperatives, and the Grain Bureau, had commune-level branches that controlled production and investment decisions, migration, financial exchanges, and labor mobilization) infrastructure in the commune seats did not expand, because most investment went into supporting agricultural production.[13]

One common trend throughout this period saw county, commune, and even brigade officials expropriating bank funds, grain supplies, and villagers' labor to establish rural enterprises, expand administrative capabilities, and build a semiautonomous political-economic base.[14] On the eve of reform, the commune system defined not only a spatial distribution of rural settlements, smaller villages, and fields, but also a governmental and party hierarchy from the county to the commune, through the brigade to the village, with each unit's location and rank or status within that hierarchy determining the economic resources under its political control, its relations to other organizations, and its economic and political power.

Administrative Structures and Changes Since 1983

Since the early 1950s, the People's Republic of China (PRC) has maintained a sharp dichotomy, almost a second Great Wall, between the urban and rural sectors: for individuals, it was their household registration; for settlements it was whether they were "designated towns" (*jianzhi zhen*).[15] For both, the critical issue was whether the state would share with a larger population the benefits urbanites were receiving.[16] Thus, the PRC has established a hierarchy of urban and rural towns that reinforces these differences and structures the distribution of these benefits.

There are four categories of small towns in China: "county-government seats" (*xian zhengfu suozaidi*), "county-towns" (*xianshu zhen*), "township-government seats" (*xiang zhengfu suozaidi*), and "rural market towns" (*nongcun jizhen*). Their characteristics are outlined in the appendix to this chapter. As part of the urban hierarchy of settlements, county-government seats and county-towns are "designated" towns in that their status within the urban hierarchy has been approved by the appropriate provincial authorities according to the guidelines of the State Council.[17] Both are under the direct control of the county government. Of all county-towns, county-government seats are most directly controlled by that government, but before 1984, over 370 of the 2,074 county government seats were not designated towns.[18] County-towns include market towns and former commune headquarters—now sites of township governments—whose populations and employment structures meet the necessary criteria to become towns. These guidelines have varied over the years and today they vary regionally as well.[19] Since 1984, the state has raised the status of rural towns to brake the flow of villagers into larger cities: therefore, the number of designated towns expanded from 2,781 (1983) to 7,956 (1985) and eventually to 10,280.[20] As part of the urban hierarchy, designated towns are eligible for more benefits than their poorer cousins, the township-government seat and small market town, and over time are able to offer rural residents greater amenities.

Township government seats and market towns, which are under administrative control of the township government, are at the top of the rural hierarchy and are treated as part of the rural, not urban, areas. This is a critical break point, for although their populations are increasing as well, they receive little state assistance and must extract funds from their own industries and the surrounding countryside to expand their urban infrastructure.

But being designated has both advantages and disadvantages. Designation increases a county-town's authority vis-à-vis the county government, the township around it, and the county-town's "ability and authority to manage well enterprises and units established at the town over whose affairs they must have administrative authority and responsibility."[21] They can levy more taxes than undesignated towns. In addition, the county helps former commune headquarters that are designated as county-towns before it helps those that remain lower status, township-government seats, because it is obliged to help urban settlements. As a result, some township officials seek ways, such as padding the number of urban residents, to shift into the urban hierarchy. Township leaders in Jiangpu County, Jiangsu Province, argued successfully that, because the residence permits of agricultural workers on the nearby state farm, who ate state-supplied grain, were kept in their town's police station, the town's urban population sufficed to qualify it as a county-town. Since then, the county government has helped build new roads, a drinking-water system, and a new school.

Yet, after towns become part of the urban hierarchy, county penetration can increase. The current policy to expand the county's economic role could place more bureaucrats in the county-towns.[22] Officials in a Guangdong Province township resisted designation because acquiring county-town status would subject their industries to demands from the state industrial sector and stricter tax supervision.[23] In addition, after a town becomes designated, the county can determine its "developmental nature" (*fazhan de xingzhi*) and decide the town's economic plan.[24]

Other administrative changes have had only limited effect. Replacing the commune administration with the township government only affected the size of the area township officials administered.[25] Efforts to separate township party, government, and economic structures had little impact on the real distribution of power; the Party's control still dominates. If these township-government seats do not meet the criteria for becoming county-towns, they remain part of the rural hierarchy with the same control over the countryside that they exercised when they were the commune headquarters. Former brigades have become "administrative villages" (*xingzheng cun*), but they are still run by the party branch, not the village management committee. Only their size may have changed.[26]

Authority and Hierarchy under Rural Urbanization

How does the distribution of power within the local bureaucratic hierarchy affect rural urbanization? Does the bureaucracy still control these outcomes or have market forces and the emerging private sector come to determine the pattern of growth and development of rural urbanization? Reform, by its very nature, creates possibilities for reallocating resources. The extent to which resources for rural urbanization are reallocated, as opposed to following the old distributional pattern, demonstrates the limits to which rural reforms can have an impact on one aspect of the distribution of power within the Chinese bureaucracy and the extent to which that bureaucracy can still affect society at large.[27]

The Special Case of Jiangsu Province

The emergence of vast regional discrepancies complicates efforts to write about local changes in China. Although these were not insignificant under Mao, today, less pressure for uniform policy implementation allows each locality's natural or historical characteristics to affect policy implementation. Therefore, I emphasize the uniqueness of Jiangsu Province and the focal points of this discussion, Jiangpu County, outside Nanjing, where I did most of my interviewing for this chapter, and of southern Jiangsu Province, or *Sunan,* where I also did some interviewing, but which is the locale primarily referred to in many of the secondary sources used for this chapter. Jiangpu County, as a "suburban county" (*shiqu*), may be more tightly controlled than counties in China that are not directly under a city's administration.[28] However, Nanjing has contributed little to its economic development, leaving it with only average per capita income for the nation as a whole. Jiangpu's county-towns and townships are poorer than those in Sunan, and rural industries, although of some importance, are also less developed. Therefore, Jiangpu County reflects national trends more than Sunan. However, unlike private businesses in Guangdong and Fujian Provinces, those in Jiangpu County have been quite restricted. As of 1986, there were few private entrepreneurs in the county-towns and townships, although in 1987–1988, their numbers increased. In addition, there has been little migration to this area from outside the county. In this regard, the impact of marketization and commercialization on urbanization in Jiangpu probably reflects conditions in Sunan more than it does conditions in the Pearl River Delta.

Conditions in Sunan, particularly in counties in Suzhou and Wuxi municipalities, do not reflect national trends. Rural Sunan is more industrialized and urbanized, with a tradition of small towns. For example, Wujiang County, outside Suzhou, where I carried out some interviews in summer 1988, has seven county-towns that have historically been of significant size. As county-towns, they had only two vegetable brigades under their authority. Since 1983, however, six of them have been combined with neighboring townships, increasing their control over the surrounding countryside. The extent to which this has occurred in other parts of China is unclear; moreover, it is unlikely that there were more than a thousand towns like these Wujiang towns in all of China in the early 1980s.

Towns in Sunan also have powerful industrial bases, and these local government-owned factories inhibit private industrial activity. Wujiang County's supply and marketing cooperative simply "swallows" private industrial firms before they become serious competitors.[29] In addition, although rural migration is a major factor in parts of rural China,[30] factories in Wujiang and Wuxi counties employ outsiders mainly as construction, not factory, workers. The townships treat the factories as community resources that should benefit local residents, not outsiders. Only one town in Wujiang County hires outside laborers. Another experimented with moving villagers into town; six hundred villagers moved in, but the policy was not introduced elsewhere in the county.

As owners of most industrial enterprises, Sunan township governments and county-town governments have more leverage with both farmers and the county government than governments elsewhere in China. Private enterprises may resist government demands for investment funds, but county-town governments can draw funds from factories they own far more easily. Also, county-towns in Wuxi County are wealthy, so the new "financial responsibility system" (*caizheng baogan*)—a new form of tax farming in which each level of government has a fixed tax quota to pass up to the next level of government—makes them more independent. Because they have so many factories, they still have enough funds for urban development.[31] On the other hand, county-towns in poorer areas in Jiangsu Province, such as those in Jiangpu County, which rely on county assistance for urban development, remain vulnerable to county control. To this extent, Jiangpu County is more representative of trends elsewhere in China, although the limited development of the private sector and the tighter constraints on migration there strengthen the town's authority vis-à-vis the surrounding farm households.

Indicators of the Persistence of County Control

As a formal level of government, the county has numerous measures for influencing local urbanization. It controls the taxation process, including the income tax for rural industries, a new value-added tax, as well as construction and commercial taxes available for infrastructural development; and, since it can impose its own taxes, it can negotiate tax breaks in return for various concessions. Through its branch offices that are nested in the towns and townships (including the tax office, grain station, supply and marketing cooperative, post office, market management committee, local police station, local branch of the Agricultural Bank of China or credit cooperative, and middle school), it can directly and indirectly influence local development.[32] Similarly, counties own factories, mines, forests, and other productive enterprises located within the spatial domain of county-towns or townships. Because of the shortage of funds for town development and the major role taxes and profits from industrial units play in local development, control over these enterprises gives the county government significant leverage in its dealings with town and township officials. County investments in county-town development also help them control outcomes in their own favor. Other mechanisms include labeling designated towns, drawing up development plans, controlling land usage, making loans, and, particularly in the case of the county-government seat, exercising direct administrative control.

Planning and Bureaucratic Control

Rural urbanization policy authorizes county governments to compose development plans for all county-towns, thereby increasing the county's control. In the case of the county-government seat, county-governmental control is very tight.

The plan for Zhujiang Township, the seat of Jiangpu County, was composed by the county's Urban Planning Office, which asserted that the administrators of the county-government seat cannot evade the plan.[33] While officials from the county government seat had to approve certain aspects of town construction, they complained that they had no decision-making authority: "We want total control of the town, but the county does not want to give it to us, so there is a conflict."[34] Mistrust of town planners in the county-government seat and the large number of county governmental units in the county-government seat require that the county government ensure good conditions for its employees. Therefore, town development is orchestrated to benefit the county, not the town, even though the county-government seat may benefit from better funding and urban planning.

In Wujiang County, planning for the county-government seat is directly under control of a fifteen-person "County Urban Construction Leadership Small Group" (*Xiancheng jianshe lingdao xiaozu*), whose sole task is to develop the county-government seat.[35] Of those fifteen members, fourteen were drawn from various county bureaus,[36] and only one person represents the county-government seat.

A critical planning question concerns land use. Under China's Land Law of April 1987, the amount of land that can shift out of agriculture is fixed at the provincial level, with quotas passed down to counties and towns. Wujiang County can appropriate 144 *mou* each year,[37] the distribution of which is determined by the county Land Management Bureau. Thus, large projects using more than 3 *mou* of land need county authorization, further limiting county-town autonomy. County-towns have officials responsible to the county Urban Development Bureau who monitor land use and housing construction in the town and in the surrounding countryside as well. All farmers must now get permits from the town government before building new homes, even in distant villages.

But informal politics undermines county control. If representatives of the Urban Development Bureau are indigenous to the locality, they will be enmeshed in local politics and will have difficulty denying their colleagues a chance to move onto land near the town.[38] Since towns can expropriate three *mou* of land without county approval, cadres can take land piece by piece for their homes, so long as the local official responsible for monitoring land usage is party to the scheme. In Tangquan Township, between 1985 and 1987, all high-ranking township-government officials, and many of their relatives and friends, moved into villages surrounding the town under the pretext of "town development." Inhabitants in these villages were furious, since each new home shrunk the allotment of land from which farmers made their living, but they could only send letters and photos to the provincial, city, and county governments. Not surprisingly, when county officials asked town officials to investigate, the case died. Thus, although the county may control large projects, town officials can ignore some county directives and expropriate land on the basis of small-town development.

Labeling County Towns

The county government determines the developmental label a county-town receives, which in turn affects its position in the county's overall development scheme, its own budget priorities, the type of outside assistance it receives, and the type of enterprises it can promote.[39] While labels are not part of the formal planning scheme, Fei Xiaotong saw this classification process as "conducive to deciding the direction of future development of small towns."[40]

The five county-towns in Jiangpu County were labeled "industrial," "port," "political," "cultural," and "tourist" towns and received a development plan based on these designations. While county officials in the Urban Planning Bureau claim that the "basic direction" of development comes from the towns, the county looks at the issue from both the county's overall perspective and the needs of Nanjing Municipality, whose Urban Planning Office has ultimate decision-making authority over those issues.

For example, Tangquan Township, a Nanjing test point for small-town planning since 1984, which had been earmarked for tourism (they had a beautiful reservoir and an old temple destroyed during the Cultural Revolution), medicinal development (because of their wonderful hot spring), and tree nurseries, could not get county permission to develop potentially polluting factories.[41] In fact, the county and city governments hoped to establish a tourist circuit that would incorporate a visit to an old temple in neighboring Anhui Province. One driving force behind this plan was the goal of earning foreign exchange.

But, local perceptions diverge from the county's view.[42] Some Tangquan officials felt that the tourist label severely restricted their entrepreneurial efforts; they could seek funds only for hotels, while other towns were developing industry. Efforts to obtain county assistance for industrialization had been rejected; moreover, despite a lack of funds, equipment, and a decent road from the county-government seat, Tangquan officials lamented what they saw as an unrealistic effort by provincial, county, and city officials to attract foreign tourist investment.

> Their plan is empty talk. We can't do it. We have our own plan which fits our reality. We put that plan forward, but the upper levels didn't agree. We want to proceed from the real situation, but they want to do it in a big way, to build a big hotel near the State Tree Farm. We have a contradiction with them, but they want to earn foreign currency. So the province, city, and county all helped draw the plan but it didn't work. There hasn't been any development.[43]

Given that no foreign company appears willing to invest in this project, the local view appears justified. Moreover, the county planning commission is reconsidering its plan. Nevertheless, concern that the hospital and the public school were in the same building, making it easy to pass on diseases, led the county to donate over 300,000 *yuan* for a new school.

The degree of control incorporated in planning and labeling varies across counties. In Wujiang County, outside Suzhou, the wealth generated by township enterprises gave county-towns more autonomy. However, in Jiangpu County, where the county-towns' weak industrial bases strengthen the county's role in the local political economy, labeling and planning were effective forces for county control, especially over county-towns needing development assistance. So long as towns rely on state budgets for construction funds and do not develop their own resources by promoting rural industries, they remain hostage to the decisions of the county government.

Nesting and Bureaucratic Authority

A widespread network of offices and enterprises owned and operated by the county government, but nested within the county-towns or township-government seats, increases the county government's influence. These sub-bureaus or enterprises—such as mines, forests, factories, or shops—support county-government interests if they conflict with those of the town. Enterprises owned by the county government resist the county-towns' request for contributions to development funds in ways factories owned by county-towns cannot. In the cases that follow, local development efforts by county-towns were undermined by the nested county bureaucracy whose interests predominated.

In Tongli Township, a county-town in Wujiang County, the county Grain Bureau wanted to construct two housing units for its staff in an area not designated as residential in the town's master plan. After several months of wrangling, the town government had to concede to county administrators, and the housing construction was allowed.[44] Similarly, a running-water and drainage pipeline, built by Dongliu Township, Dongzhi County, Anhui Province, "crossed the doorway of the dormitory for the county's transportation station workers; the workers did not agree, so there was no choice but to halt the project."[45] We do not know the content of the negotiations process, but in both cases the issue was not one of political equality or negotiations among equals; rather, decisions were made in favor of the more powerful county administration.

County domination harmed development in the pre-1984 county-towns, which have been the clearest losers in the hierarchy of towns. Factories in those towns were often owned by the county government; yet, while they used local facilities and resources, the county invested little in the towns. Because jobs in them were allocated by the County Labor Bureau, county-town youths did not necessarily receive first access. County-owned businesses, such as supply and marketing cooperatives, in these towns were nominally led by both the county-government departments and the county-town administrators, but according to Fei, "they accept only the leadership of departments and ignore town leadership"; thus, stressed Fei, in 1986 county-towns that are not county-government seats experience the sharpest conflicts within the current administrative system.[46] As county employees, these nested county administrators respond to the "hier-

Table 9.1

Urban Population Growth by Town Type, Jiangpu County, Jiangsu Province, 1953 and 1979

Type	1953	%	1979	%	Rate of Increase
County-government seat	4,643	28.4	16,927	37.4	2.65
County-towns	4,061	24.9	4,266	10.5	0.05
Market towns	7,641	46.7	19,480	52.1	1.77
Total	16,345	100.0	40,673	100.0	1.49

Source: Zhang Fubao, "A County under Nanjing Municipality—Preliminary Research on the Development of Small Town Construction in Jiangpu County" (*"Nanjingshi xia xian—Jiangpu xian xiao chengzhen de jianshe fazhan chubu yanjiu"*), *Economic Geography* (*Jingji dili*), no. 2 (1982): 139.

archical system" (*tiao-tiao*) rather than local leaders, whose authority is more "horizontally organized" (*kuai-kuai*).

In Jiangpu County, these county-towns developed poorly before 1979.[47] Of people living in all towns in the county, the proportion living in the county-towns, compared with the county-government seat and commune or market towns, decreased from 24.9 to 10.5 percent from 1953 to 1979, while the increase in these towns' actual population over twenty-six years was almost minimal (Table 9.1). Unlike commune government towns, which became the sites for commune or township enterprises, as well as centers of political administration, these county-towns developed little industry and few administrative jobs, which accounts for their limited population growth. Data from other parts of Jiangsu Province from 1984 show why these towns declined. Of the total industrial output within the older county-towns, the indigenous county-town government owns or controls less industrial output within its own territory (at 12.91 percent) than governments from either surrounding townships (20.74 percent) or the county government (45.15 percent) (see table 9.2). With little outside investment and few resources to draw on, these county-town governments have a weak tax base and little income for investment, making the county's authority dominant.

To resolve the nesting problem, county-owned factories situated outside the county-government seat are expected to shift control to the county-town governments.[48] And nested officials in some towns and townships are to come under greater horizontal administrative control, as county-town governments are empowered to hire, fire, transfer, reward, and penalize them.[49] Still, the nesting problem will persist. First, directors of these nested organizations are to remain outside county-town and township-government control. Second, not only are some factories that are owned by the county government not shifting to county-town control, but some county officials are taking over lucrative former township factories after the townships have become designated towns and suddenly

Table 9.2

Ownership Contribution of Industrial Enterprises in 190 Small Towns in Jiangsu Province, 1984 (by industrial output)

	Location of industrial enterprises (%)		
Level of ownership of industrial enterprise	County-government seats	County-towns	Township seats
County government	50.58	45.15	7.52
County collective	24.87	19.73	4.60
County-town government	11.38	12.91	0.00
Township government	8.60	20.74	76.77
Village	3.91	1.15	8.84
Subvillage entity	0.51	0.16	1.40
Individual	0.05	0.11	0.30
Others	1.16	0.04	0.38
Total	100.00	100.00	100.00

Source: The Research Group on Small Towns in Jiangsu Province, "The Objectives and the Experience of Small Town Construction in Jiangsu Province," *Sociological Research* (*Shehuixue yanjiu*), no. 4 (1986): 16.

come under their control.[50] Finally, because county-government seats have many county-government offices within them, county-government control over town development is imperative. County-level organizations in the county seat will not obey officials of the county-government seat, which has no authority over them. Only a development committee of the county government has the authority to compel these county organizations to contribute to development projects in the county-government seat.

County officials have long been the most powerful administrative actors directing local development. And, although market forces are decreasing the county's control over some aspects of the rural political economy, patterns of authority established over forty years of economic planning continue to play a major role. In fact, as townships become county-towns, the county's formal right to dictate their development pattern increases. No doubt, wealthy towns are more independent, and their ability to invest in their own future may expand under the fiscal responsibility system. But for county-towns seeking to improve their urban infrastructure, county controls embodied in the labeling, nesting, and planning processes remain significant factors in their day-to-day existence.

Control of Resources for Town Development

Small-town growth is critical for successful rural modernization.[51] The almost 100 million rural laborers liberated by the rural reforms need to find work out-

Figure 9.1 **Sources of Funding for Town Construction**

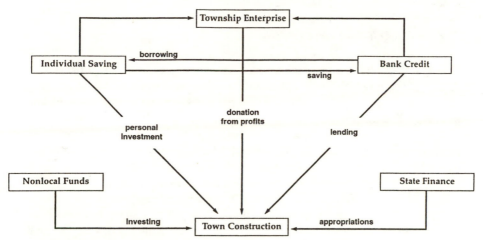

Source: Tang Zhongxun and Ye Nanke, *"Jizhen jianshe zijin laiyuan tansuo"* (Reflections on the sources of capital for town construction), *Xiao chengzhen, xin kai tuo* (Small towns, a new beginning) (Huiyang: Jiangsu Publishing House, 1986), p. 339.

side large urban centers. The commercialization of agriculture has also increased the need for marketing centers.[52] Expanding rural enterprises need public services and infrastructural development such as electricity, water, housing, and entertainment facilities. The decision to expand rural towns has created a public-policy environment within which county and subcounty governments can allocate funds for expanding urban infrastructure and industry. Figure 9.1 shows the sources of that investment. But, does the county government, the county-government seat, the county-town, or the township-government seat control the new funds? Does the county government use its influence over funds to its own benefit? What does the allocation of funds tell us about the distribution of authority in the countryside?

County-towns now receive development assistance from the county. In two county-towns in Jiangpu County, the county government helped build roads, drinking-water pipes, a new school, a new market, and a new housing project. Similar investments are occurring all over Jiangsu Province.[53] Some of these funds, such as those for schools or hospitals, originate from central government ministries, such as education and public health, whose investments in the rural areas improve town life.

Yet, funds for town construction are limited. A vice-minister of construction in Beijing stressed that "people's towns should be built by the people themselves."[54] Others have referred to "using the town to develop the town" (*yi zhen yang zhen*).[55] But although local taxes and state budget assistance allow simply for "subsistence" governmental work,[56] the search for funding has been decentralized, making the struggle over local taxes and funding a meaningful reflection of the distribution of authority in the countryside.

Taxes and Small-town Development

The county receives a variety of taxes that it may use for rural urbanization. Although these taxes change constantly, in 1987 they included "public-facility fees" (*gong yong shiye fei*), villager income taxes, and local real estate or land use taxes. The income tax paid by all rural enterprises could take as much as 55 percent of their industrial income. Five percent of these funds are earmarked for urban construction. Recent findings showed that a sales tax (or value-added tax applied to all goods produced in rural enterprises) supplies county governments with much of their funds.[57] However, it is not known for certain how this tax affects factories owned by county-towns or township governments.

Still, because these funds are usually distributed to county authorities for investment in town construction, the county government can invest the great majority of these funds in the county-government seat, not in county-towns. Although central and provincial governments stipulated that local industrial and commercial surtaxes, public utility surtaxes, and real estate surtaxes should be used for small-town construction, "the funds they provide are too small to be of any help."[58] In Suzhou Municipality, the sum from these three sources amounted to 2 million *yuan,* which was divided among eighteen county-towns. "But the greater part of the sum is spent on construction in county [government] seats, while other towns get only a few tens of thousand *yuan* each. Many leaders of county-towns say their share is not enough even for repairing unsafe buildings in the town."[59] Other cases also show that the county government keeps most funds for its own administrative costs. Factories in Qingyang Township, a county seat, paid the county 13 million *yuan* in 1984 taxes, but between 1981 and 1984, county appropriations to the county seat totaled only 380,000 *yuan,* less than 100,000 *yuan* a year. Although the county government was expected to give the town the "three types of appropriations (*san xiang bokuan*), for many years this has been empty talk."[60] Moreover, because the county government wanted its taxes first, some of the county-government seat's projects could not get off the ground. In one instance, county officials refused to let two enterprises, which as beneficiaries had to contribute 10,000 *yuan* to a town-run bridge building project, draw their contribution out of their pretax profits. The county government wanted its taxes first, even though the entrepreneurs' after-tax profits were insufficient for completing the project. After three years of wrangling, the money had still not been appropriated and the bridge had not been completed.[61] The county is extremely judicious in distributing this most popular of tax breaks.

Similarly, all enterprises owned by the county-government seat in Wujiang County paid the county government an "urban-construction protection fee" (*chengshi jianshe weihu fei*), which is 7 percent of their pretax income. Before

1987, the county government reinvested only 70 percent of these funds in the county-government seat, spending the remaining 30 percent on other towns or projects. In this way the county government used taxes and urban development to redistribute funds within the county. However, after 1987, when the county began a major project to expand the county-government seat, the county stopped investing in building up other towns. Even in Jiangpu County, where the county government supplied the county-government seat with funds for administering the town (in 1985, the county gave 120,000 *yuan* and in 1986 it gave 260,000 *yuan*), much of this money came from taxes imposed on the county-government seat's own factories.

Yet, the new fiscal responsibility system, which is intended to make county-towns and townships collect taxes more aggressively and be fiscally more responsible and autonomous,[62] may increase county-town independence, particularly for wealthy towns that can meet their quotas. But county governments will still try to keep more funds in their own hands. For example, in the case of Tangquan Township, Jiangpu County officials were withholding 5 percent more funds than they should have been. In summer 1988, I observed a Tangquan official complaining to a county cadre that the county government returned only 10 and not 15 percent of anticipated funds. When the county official justified the added withholding by pointing out the county had recently helped build a drinking-water system in the town, the manager of this county-town argued that development assistance must be separated from a policy that gave county-towns more funds for their own use. As we can see, the county government was willing to invest in the town, but it tried to keep surplus funds in its own hands and thereby determine the locus of investment, rather than give the funds directly to the town. This way it could insure that more funds went to develop the county-government seat, where its bureaucrats and their families live and work. The system of financial responsibility should put more taxes directly in the county-town governments' hands and help them invest in their own urban infrastructure. Yet, one can feel confident that the county government will also use its authority to keep in its own hands as much as possible of the surplus taxes collected by the town.

Profits from Rural Industry and Small-town Development

Since township and village enterprises (TVEs) are the major source of new capital in the rural areas, rural governments constantly try to control their fiscal activities.[63] Poorly defined, collective property rights facilitate government interference.[64] Although township governments, reestablished in 1984, were to separate economic and political power, they still control TVEs under their jurisdiction, making them both levels of government administration responsible for a community's development and owners of community-run enterprises.

A major debate has ensued over how much after-tax profits from, TVEs should go or actually do go to county-town and township governments for urban development and how much should be left in the factory. Under one scheme, 20 percent of after-tax profits from TVEs goes to town development, 50 percent to reinvestment in the enterprise, 10 percent to its workers' welfare and 20 percent to supplement agriculture.[65] A potentially inflated figure posits that 20 to 30 percent of the profits of locally controlled rural enterprises is going to develop educational and health services in small towns.[66] Two different townships, one in Wuxi County, Jiangsu Province, and the second in Shangrao County, Jiangxi Province, made dramatically different contributions to rural urbanization. The township in Wuxi County spent 10.7 percent of its total income (1 million *yuan*) on public and social services; the Shangrao County township spent 68.9 percent, or only 285,700 *yuan,* of its total income on public and social services. While 95 percent of the income available to the former township came from enterprise profits, the latter township got only 3.2 percent of its income from enterprise profits and had to rely on a massive budget allocation from Shangrao County, which comprised over 50 percent of its income and over 73 percent of the funds used for public and social services.[67] According to Yok-shiu Lee, the percentage of after-tax profits of TVEs going to "collective welfare" (rural highways, schools, theaters, and market-town infrastructure) tripled from 1978 to 1984, rising from 5.9 percent to 15.7 percent (see Table 9.3).

Before 1985, when county-towns in Wujiang County did not control the surrounding rural areas, county-town leaders had difficulty attaching the profits of township-owned enterprises that existed within their geographic domains, even though they had previously used these funds for repairing streets, roads, and bridges. Unlike the county government's superior status vis-à-vis the county-government seat, the legal status of county-towns and township governments was the same; directors of township-owned enterprises, therefore, could refuse funding requests from the county-town, accusing county-town officials of "levying contributions at random."[68] In fact, poorer towns in northern Jiangsu Province, that took too much money from TVE profits for town development, undermined industrial development.[69] But the 1985 merger of county-towns and townships in Wujiang County has probably helped county-town officials raid township factory profits for urban development projects. As a result, profits from TVEs are a critical source of funding for infrastructural development in county-towns and township-government seats, although the precise level of after-tax profits allocated for this investment remains unclear.

Banking and Small-town Development

While banking flexibility increased in some localities in the 1980s,[70] Jiangsu Province's banks remained strongly influenced by county officials and were unlikely to invest in projects not approved by the county government. Banks also became more responsible for their own profits and losses, and became more independent from township or county-town officials than they had been from

Table 9.3

Distribution of After-Tax Profits of Township and Village Enterprises, 1978–1984 (percentages)

	1978	1979	1980	1981	1982	1983	1984
1. Reinvest in TVEs	45.3	50.4	49.7	43.0	46.0	48.4	61.2
2. Assist agriculture	38.5	33.3	23.9	17.0	13.8	13.0	6.6
Purchase farm machinery	16.9	14.0	9.6	7.0	5.1	3.9	n.a.
Farmland infrastructure	17.1	14.5	9.9	8.0	6.9	6.9	n.a.
Aid to poor teams	4.3	4.8	4.4	2.0	1.8	2.2	n.a.
3. Distribute to team members[a]	—	—	NA	NA	21.7	16.3	6.4
4. Collective welfare[b]	5.9	6.1	7.2	7.0	9.1	10.9	15.7
5. Others	10.0	10.1	NA	NA	9.4	11.4	10.0
Total	99.7	99.9	80.8	57.0	100.0	100.0	99.9

Sources:

1978–1979: *Zhongguo nongye nianjian, 1980*, p. 366.
1980–1981: *Zhongguo nongcun tongji nianjian, 1985*, p. 190.
1982: *Zhongguo nongye nianjian, 1983*, p. 83.
1983: *Zhongguo nongye nianjian, 1984*, p. 84.
1984: *Zhongguo nongye nianjian, 1985*, pp. 181–182.

Notes:

[a] Team members are those who remained in farming and not TVE workers.

[b] Collective welfare includes rural highways, schools, theaters, and market town infrastructure.

This table was compiled by Yok-shiu Lee and appeared in a draft chapter of his dissertation for the Department of Urban Studies and Planning, Massachusetts Institute of Technology.

prereform commune officials who had taken funds without authorization. Consequently, without guarantees or prodding from the county government, banks are
unlikely to invest in such nonprofitable projects as expanding urban infrastructure. Not surprisingly, banks are far more interested in investing in rural industries than in urban construction.[71]

Hierarchy also affected investment in urban infrastructure, because in 1988,
whether a settlement was a county-government seat, a county-town, or a township government center determined which bank it could approach. Township
governments and newly designated county-towns were required to rely primarily
on agricultural bank funds, but if the project called for capital construction, they
could approach the construction bank for help. If the agricultural bank was short
of funds, they could go elsewhere, even though funds were constrained by the
county's overall plan. But, because the county government had much more influence with the construction bank, which funds all large construction projects, than
county-towns have, county projects were more likely to find funding than those
of other towns.[72] In Jiangsu Province, then, the county was likely to come out on
top in the battle for bank loans. County-towns that needed large funds for development projects either needed to have their own funding or needed to rely on the
county government to promote their case with the banks.

Migration Policy and Access to Towns

Town growth creates new opportunities, making access to town a scarce and
valuable resource. As a result, some officials charge fees for access to towns or
for work permits, while others try to limit migration. In towns, villagers increase
their wealth and improve their quality of life and status. For many, work in town
is more lucrative than work in the countryside. According to data from Yueyang
District, Hunan Province, the incomes of thirty specialized households still in
their villages averaged 415 *yuan* per capita and 811 *yuan* per laborer, whereas
incomes of specialized households who had moved to the town averaged 592
yuan per capita and 1,224 *yuan* per laborer.[73]

Since rural-urban migration is a contentious issue, social and legal limitations
exist on villager access to towns. Important social groups pressure cadres to
restrict in-town migration. According to He and Zhang, town cadres fear that too
many private businesses would change the social structure; financial cadres fear
that migrants would hurt the supply and marketing cooperatives and the town's
financial income; public security cadres and those responsible for monitoring the
markets fear the disruption of social order; local businessmen fear that the competition would break their "rice bowls"; and village cadres are afraid that, with
migration, their control of the whole situation would collapse.[74] China's laws
allow officials to redirect rural migrants away from the county-government seat
and into lower-status market towns and county-towns.[75] Migrants must have (1)
a permanent place to live in the town, (2) management skills or longtime jobs in

a town enterprise or unit, (3) a license for their business from the local Industrial and Commercial Bureau, (4) a sublease on their contracted farmland to another farmer (so land is not abandoned), and (5) an independent source of food.[76] To ensure that migrants meet these criteria, local officials in larger towns lacking "public security offices" (*paichusuo*) have been required to set up "registration offices" (*huqi dengji bangongshi*) to control population flows.[77] After migrants get to town, Industrial and Commercial Bureau officials still control the permits needed for access to marketing opportunities.[78] And, in smaller towns, illegal migrants probably find even fewer opportunities for illegal businesses or places to hide.

State officials have willingly used the household registration or *hukou* system to impede farmers' access to the greater benefits and opportunities reserved for urban residents. As a result, many farmers who have applied for permission to move were turned down. In Taishan County, Guangdong Province, over a four-month period in late 1984, 15,000 farmers applied for permission to move to the county-government seat; 9,000 (60 percent) were not allowed to move.[79] In the first half of 1985, of 4,000 prospective migrants to Longgang Town, Jiangsu Province, only 515 (13 percent) were permitted to move.[80] When 580 households applied to leave their villages in Changsanqiao County, Sichuan Province, 369 (64 percent) failed to get permits.[81] In the town Helen Siu studied, only rural residents with immediate family members in town could register, and only as "households who supply their own grain" (*zili liang hu*).[82] In Jiangpu County, as of May 1986, only 268 farmers had moved into the county-government seat, but none had changed their residence status, receiving only "long-term residence permits" (*chang zhu hukou*). Thus, county-town officials still maintained serious controls over migration into town, although restraints on migration were breaking down. By 1987, the major restriction on rural-urban migration in Jiangpu County was economic. According to one official, "most people who want to come in, get in. We turn them down only if they want to work in some field that is already quite full. Anyway, if it's very full, they'll go back on their own." For example, between 1983 and 1986, 50 to 60 migrant families ran sewing businesses; as of 1988, only 20 families remained. In addition, in Xingdian Town, west of Tangquan in Jiangpu County, where only 110 peasant families had moved to town in 1983–1985, the local government began a housing project in 1986 to move another 200 village households into town.[83]

Still, farmer migration can make county-town governments less dependent on county financial assistance. Migrants are a major funding source for new housing and buildings, particularly where rural industry is less developed. In Yueyang District, Hunan Province, migrants built 62.2 percent of the floor space for new housing and shops. In Chenggu County, Shaanxi Province, villagers in 1984 contributed 5.02 million *yuan* toward town construction. And, in Anhui Province, average investment by each migrant household in the towns ranged from 4,700 to 15,500 *yuan* in 1984. Migrants also pay taxes and fees for licenses, market management, land use, and construction.[84] Moreover, cadres charge farmers fees or *rents* for access to income-increasing opportunities in these towns. For example, township and county-town governments charge aspiring factory workers an entrance fee, ranging from 1,000 to 7,500 *yuan,* calling them "workers bringing capital to factories" (*gongren dai zi ru chang*). In another case, Tangquan's government, hungry for funds for industry but unable to secure bank loans, pressured villagers and village leaders to give the factory a loan. Although some villagers resisted, brigade officials persuaded them to agree.

A main impetus for small-town development is to channel rural laborers away from big cities. To date, one critical and successful component of China's development strategy has been its ability to stem long-term rural-urban migration, thereby avoiding the urban slums common to many developing countries. But, because small towns have limited resources and economic opportunities, local officials in the parts of Jiangsu Province covered by this study have continued to control the number of farmers moving to town. Nevertheless, the resulting floating population in cities such as Shanghai has passed one million, making it uncertain if the small-town strategy will alleviate demands for rural-urban migration.

The Politics of Rural Urbanization

Freedom at the lowest levels of rural society has expanded as both state and collective cadres have withdrawn from the daily management of village life. But, at the middle reaches of the rural hierarchy, the relationship between the county government and expanding rural settlements has demonstrated the continuing role of bureaucratic authority as a determinant of resource allocations. Although it might be assumed that increased rural urbanization would weaken the county's control over the local political economy, the distribution of authority has not changed as dramatically as might have been expected. County officials, through their bureaucratic positions, still control resources that either flow into these towns or are created within them. No doubt, modernization's demands for bureaucratic specialization have fragmented power within the county leadership. However, findings here appear to confirm the control image offered by Lieberthal and Oksenberg and the argument that vertical authority remains more powerful than horizontal ties even under the reforms.[85]

Two factors affect the relationship between hierarchy and power. First, disparities in resource bases can increase or decrease the impact of hierarchy. If resource distribution is highly asymmetrical, relations between bureaucratic superiors and inferiors are even more likely to be based on a command model, leaving the inferior actor in the interaction with obedient or supplicant behavior as the only major option (except for the threat of bankruptcy, which an individual's superior cannot accept). In the current policy environment, in which expanding a town's social and economic infrastructure becomes a town official's major responsibility, officials in poorer towns could become more dependent on county officials for development assistance. And, although counties also have political obligations to help towns grow, making county officials reliant on cooperation from town managers, planning, labeling, and investments have kept the county firmly in control of the development process. Even efforts to strengthen county-town and township financial bases may increase a county-town official's dependence on the county, particularly for poor towns. Under the fiscal responsibility system, counties can lend funds to strengthen county-town and township governments, which the recipients must repay through judicious tax collection. Although surpluses benefit the county town, especially wealthy county-towns with strong tax bases, shortages are cumulative, making tax-poor county-towns, as well as state-owned firms, highly dependent on county-government support. And, even for wealthier county-towns, the county government's control over the planning process allows them to set the county-town's development agenda. By financing only a part of the projects and pressuring the county-town to fund the remainder, the county can determine how the county-town invests its own funds. Such "conditional grants" are a powerful mechanism by which administrators can indirectly control lower-level governments.

Second, the nesting process compounds the impact of hierarchy on the distribution of authority by giving county governments a core of allies who have directly penetrated these towns and who participate in government and party meetings in the county-towns and township-seat governments. County-affiliated firms and bureaus make profits and collect taxes and fees in the towns, which revert to the county government, all the while contributing little directly to the town's growth. And, while new policies are trying to expand a town's control over county-level factories and offices within its physical domain, these units' county-level status may keep them beyond the town's political reach. As we have seen with the county-government seat, the new impetus for rural urbanization ensures even tighter control by the county government and undermines any devolution of authority over these nested units to the leaders in the county-government seats.

On the other hand, towns with strong industrial bases can undo some of the power disparity inherent in hierarchy. County-town and township governments that can draw on the profits of their own rural enterprises to strengthen their economic base are better able to negotiate with county officials. As in Wujiang County, unifying county-towns with neighboring townships, particularly if the latter have strong industrial bases, should weaken the county's influence. How different relations must be between county and town officials in poor counties, such as Shangrao County, Jiangxi Province, where the county finances all township-level administration, and wealthy counties, such as Wuxi County, where county-towns fund themselves and have a surplus that the county can tax. Although county-towns or townships in Wuxi are hierarchically subordinate to the county government, their wealth should make them stronger adversaries in the negotiations process.

Power relations among villagers and bureaucrats are affected in a similar way. Farmers who plant their land and market only small surpluses remain relatively free of state intrusions. Unlike lower-level bureaucrats who have no exit option, these farmers can withdraw in the face of abusive or unjust cadre demands. Clearly, independence is relative, since many resources needed for farming, such as seeds, fertilizer, pesticides, and land, remain locally controlled, making farmers dependent on local cadres. But, the asymmetry of power expands dramatically as common villagers, seeking access to new sources of wealth developing in and around the town, become subject to bureaucratic authority vested in town officials. As gatekeepers to the boundaries of income-enhancing opportunities, such as small shops, factories, or factory job, cadres are extremely powerful vis-à-vis China's common citizen. Cadres can take a farmer's land to build their own homes, and there is little villagers can do. No doubt, wealthier rural residents or those with strong family alliances possess resources to confront cadre authority. But atomized individuals, stripped of their collective protection, remain in a highly vulnerable and inferior status in confrontations with formidable bureaucratic forces.[86]

Central control over local investment and development has decreased, but this devolution of central authority has not weakened bureaucratic control at the local level. In some ways, it may have increased it. While forces unleashed by the commercialization of the rural economy, particularly the production and marketing of agricultural produce, no longer are monopolized by local officials, the county's control over development assistance and investment for expanding urban infrastructure at the county-town and township levels has ensured a continuing—in some locations an expanding—role for the local bureaucracy.

No doubt, rural urbanization is in its incipient stage, and what the final distribution of authority derived from this process will be remains unclear. Efforts to reform both the financial relations between the county and the county-towns or townships and the authority relations between county-level nested units and the towns where they reside may weaken the county's authority. New resources, developing at all levels of rural society create opportunities for redistributing authority. The prudent scholar must recognize that leaders in the emerging county-towns and townships, as did their forebears in the communes, will use their political and economic authority over the countryside and their towns' critical locus at the nexus between the rural and the urban economies to expand their financial and political resources. However, a careful reading of past and current trends—tightening local finances in 1989 under the current retrenchment probably increased the county's influence—suggests that county officials through a multiplicity of channels will significantly influence the pattern of growth in the county-towns and townships and will remain the dominant force in the political economy in much of rural China.

APPENDIX

Types and Characteristics of Small Towns in China

Designated Towns (jianzhi zhen)

Administered by county governments, all designated towns are part of the hierarchy of urban settlements.[87] There are two types of designated towns:

1. *County-government seats (xian zhengfu suozaidi)*: These towns are directly controlled by the county government. Larger county-government seats are sometimes designated as cities and are directly under the control of the nearby urban administration. Their main function is administrative, although many have become industrial centers since the late 1970s.

2. *County-towns (xianshu zhen)*: County-towns decreased in the prereform era, but now many township-government seats have been designated as county-towns and have moved up into the hierarchy of urban settlements. Former township-government seats still control most of the countryside they administered as commune or township-government seats, while some county-towns that were not formerly township-government seats control only a few villages, which supply food for town residents. In some instances, county-towns have been unified with the nearby township government and now control much of the rural area administered by the former township.

Undesignated Towns (fei jianzhi zhen)

These towns are administered by the township governments or may be autonomous. All undesignated towns are part of the hierarchy of rural settlements and are part of the countryside. There are two types of undesignated towns:

1. *Township-government seats (xiang zhengfu suozaidi)*: Linked with economic cooperatives in the late 1950s, these settlements served as commune headquarters from the 1960s into the 1970s. In the 1980s, their names were changed to townships. They have urban administrative functions as well as economic ones, given that many township governments own rural enterprises. They are often regional marketing centers. Leading officials may be state cadres who receive state-subsidized grain.

2. *Rural Market Towns (nongcun jizhen)*: These rural settlements, which are major marketing centers, declined under CCP rule and were resurrected under the reforms. They are often centers for service industries linked to marketing. In wealthier areas of the countryside, they are likely to be run by the former brigade committee of the Maoist era, now called "administrative villages" (xing zhen cun).

Notes

1. Jean C. Oi, "Communism and Clientelism: Rural Politics in China," *World Politics* 37 (January 1985): 238–266.
2. See chapters 10 and 12 of this book.

3. See chapter 7 of this book.

4. Gordon White, "The Impact of Economic Reforms in the Chinese Countryside: Towards the Politics of Social Capitalism," *Modern China* 13 (October 1987): 411–440.

5. Andrew Watson, "The Reform of Agricultural Marketing in China since 1978," *The China Quarterly*, no. 113 (1988): 1–28.

6. A. Doak Barnett, with Ezra Vogel, *Cadres, Bureaucracy and Political Power* (New York: Columbia University Press, 1965), pp. 318–338.

7. According to Schurmann, settlements with an urban character of a hundred to a thousand households became *zhen*; those with similar populations and rural character became *xiang*. See Franz Schurmann, *Ideology and Organization in Communist China* (Berkeley: University of California Press, 1968).

8. Schurmann, *Ideology and Organization,* p. 453.

9. See "Jizhen fazhan de quzhe licheng," in Editorial Board of Contemporary China Series, ed., *The Construction of Towns and Villages in Contemporary China (Dangdai Zhongguo xiangcun jianshe)* (Beijing: Shehui kexue chuban she, 1986), pp. 117–121. For example, Songhe Township in Hubei Province, built in the Ming Dynasty, had been a town of 65,000 before the 1946–1949 civil war. The end of grain markets, collectivization, and the Great Leap Forward forced 3,000 shops to close and the population to drop to 3,000 residents. During the Cultural Revolution, the town became a large village. In the 1930s, there were about 45,000 market towns in China; by 1965, only 37,000 remained, and by 1978, there were only 33,000. See Chang Sen-dou and R. Yin-wang Kwok, "The Urbanization of Rural China," in R. Yin-wang Kwok, William Parish, and Anthony Gar-On Yeh, eds., *Chinese Urban Reforms: What Model Next?* (Armonk, N.Y.: M.E. Sharpe, 1990), p. 101.

10. As the size of the agricultural producer cooperatives increased, the number of *xiang* decreased from 220,000 in 1953 to 117,000 in 1956 to only 80,000 by mid-1958. According to Skinner, the original number of communes, 24,000, may have been imposed on the standard marketing communities built around marketing towns. See G. William Skinner, "Marketing and Social Structure in Rural China, Part III," *Journal of Asian Studies* 24, no. 3 (1964): 363–399. However, the shrinking of the size of communes during the rectification movement of the early 1960s, which created 74,000 communes, suggests that commune headquarters were established in the *xiang* that existed in mid-1958. See Barnett, *Cadres,* 1965.

11. Below the people's communes were production brigades, which in many parts of China were established either in large villages or in several villages that were linked together under one bureaucratic and economic authority. Below the brigade lay the production team, composed either of one village or of twenty to thirty families within a large village.

12. See Steven B. Butler, "Conflict and Decision-Making in China's Rural Administration, 1969–1976" (Doctoral Dissertation, Columbia University, 1980).

13. A common characteristic of communist regimes is their refusal to invest in infrastructural development, such as roads and housing, and a major preference towards increasing agricultural or industrial output.

14. See David Zweig, *Agrarian Radicalism in China, 1968–1981* (Cambridge: Harvard University Press, 1989); and Victor Nee, "Between Center and Locality: State, Militia and Village," in Victor Nee and David Mozingo, eds., *State and Society in Contemporary China* (Ithaca, N.Y.: Cornell University Press, 1983), pp. 223–243.

15. For the best discussion of the discrimination toward farmers under state socialism, see Sulamith Heins Potter, "The Position of Peasants in Modern China's Social Order," *Modern China* 9 (October 1983): 465–489. For a discussion of the changing nature of rural-urban relations under the reforms, see chapter 8 of this book, and Edward Friedman, "Deng versus the Peasantry," *Problems of Communism,* vol. 39 (September-October 1990): 30–43.

16. Whereas residents of designated towns were eligible for state-subsidized grain, nonagricultural residents in undesignated towns were counted as rural population and were ineligible for state grain. See Lawrence J.C. Ma and Gonghao Cui, "Administrative Changes and Urban Population in China," *Annals of the Association of American Geographers* 77, no. 3 (1987): 377–378. During the famine of the 1960s, the state cut the number of designated towns and knocked millions of people out of the ranks of state grain eaters. In the late 1980s, the introduction of "households that are self-sufficient in grain" (*zili kouliang*) has meant that more towns can become designated without increasing the demand on the state to supply subsidized grain.

17. Ma and Cui, "Administrative Changes," p. 376.

18. Larger county-seats may be "cities" (*shi*); in addition, some administered towns in city suburbs are directly under the control of cities, not counties. These are not included here. See Ma and Cui "Administrative Changes."

19. According to a 1955 State Council resolution, to be considered urban, a settlement had to have a total population of over two thousand, of which half were not engaged in agricultural pursuits. Smaller locales of between one thousand and two thousand people could be counted as urban if 75 percent of the inhabitants were registered as nonagricultural. See R.J.R. Kirkby, *Urbanization in China: Town and Country in a Developing Economy, 1949–2000 A.D.* (New York: Columbia University Press, 1985), p. 74. In response to the great famine of 1960–1962, the criteria became stricter in 1963: only settlements of 3,000 people with at least 70 percent of inhabitants registered as nonagricultural laborers, or settlements of twenty-five hundred to three thousand people with 85 percent of inhabitants registered as nonagricultural population, could be designated urban.

20. See *Chinese Statistical Yearbook* (*Zhongguo tongji nianjian*) (Beijing: Chinese Statistical Publishing House, 1988), p. 23.

21. Zhang Yuelin, "City-Town-Township Network and Small Towns' Overall Distribution" (*"Cheng-zhen-xiang wanglo he xiaochengzhen de zhengti buzhu"*), in *Small Towns: A New Beginning* (*Xiao chengzhen, xin kai tuo*) (Huiyang: Jiangsu Publishing House, 1986), p. 98.

22. Tyrene White, "Political Reform and Rural Government," in Deborah Davis and Ezra Vogel, eds., *Chinese Society on the Eve of Tiananmen: The Impact of Reform* (Cambridge: Council on East Asian Studies, Harvard University Press, 1990), pp. 29–31. This situation changed somewhat in 1986, with the establishment of the township public finance system, which gave township governments the right to collect an above-quota tax, after the fixed tax quota had been paid to the county government, thereby increasing the township seats' financial resources and tax base.

23. Helen F. Siu, "The Politics of Migration in a Market Town," in Davis and Vogel, eds., *Chinese Society on the Eve of Tiananmen*, pp. 61–84.

24. According to Yok-shiu Lee, counties can make land-use plans for designated and undesignated towns but can make economic plans for only the designated towns. Personal communication, 1988.

25. As communes became townships, many more townships were established, suggesting that, on average, townships were about 65 percent the size of the former communes. While the final number of communes was 56,331 in 1983, by 1984, there were 91,171 township and town governments. See *Chinese Agricultural Yearbook* (*Zhongguo nongye nianjian, 1985*) (Beijing: Chinese Agricultural Publishing House, 1985). Since the number of towns was 7,320 (Ma and Cui, "Administrative Changes," p. 377), the number of townships must have been approximately 85,000, significantly more than the number of communes.

26. The size of these administrative villages increased, given that the number dropped by 10 percent between 1985 and 1986. In 1985, the number of "rural residence committees"

(cunmin weiyuanhui), which are the local governmental committees for managing the administrative villages, dropped from 940,617 to 847,894. See *Chinese Statistical Abstract* (*Zhongguo tongji zhaiyao*) (Beijing: Chinese Statistical Publishing House, 1987).

27. A cautionary note: The situation on the ground is changing rapidly. Chinese articles written in 1984 and published in 1986–1987, may, by 1992, reflect a reality that is no longer current.

28. All counties in Jiangsu Province are under the direct administration of a specified city. This policy was introduced throughout the province in March 1983. Some other provinces have followed suit.

29. Interview with officials at the supply and marketing cooperative, Wujiang County, July 12, 1988.

30. See Ezra Vogel, *One Step Ahead in China: Guangdong Under Reform* (Cambridge: Harvard University Press, 1989); and Siu, "The Politics of Migration."

31. During a January 1989 visit to Wuxi County I was told by the director of Meicun Township that the fiscal responsibility system made his town more independent; after it paid its taxes, the town could determine how to allocate the rest of its funds. Dongting Township, also in Wuxi County, is undergoing a major urban expansion program, and when all current projects are completed, the town will be more modern and bigger than Jiangpu County's county seat.

32. Barnett, *Cadres,* pp. 352–357 and 318–338.

33. Interview with officials from the Planning and Management Office, Department of Urban Development and Environmental Protection, Jiangpu County, Jiangsu Province, May 13, 1986.

34. Interview in Jiangpu County, 1986.

35. Interview with the deputy mayor of Songling Township and the deputy director of the county's "Urban Construction Office" (*Xiao cheng jianshe bangongwei*), July 14, 1988.

36. The units included the Materials Bureau, Public Security Bureau, Communications Bureau, Land Management Bureau, Environmental Protection Bureau, Industrial Electricity Bureau, Post Office and Labor Bureau, among others.

37. One *mou* is a fifteenth of a hectare.

38. Chinese analysts recognize that the main desire of many rural cadres is to move into town. See Zhao Pengxing and Zhang Shouzheng, "Urban-Rural Reforms' Influence on Small Town Development" (*"Chengxiang gaige dai xiaochengzhen fazhan de yingxiang"*), *Xiao chengzhen, xin kai tuo, 1986,* p. 326; and chapter 5 of this book.

39. The county government cannot do this for undesignated towns.

40. See Fei Hsiao Tung, eds., *Small Towns in China: Functions, Problems and Prospects* (Beijing: New World Press, 1986).

41. Restrictions on Tongli Township, Wujiang County, Suzhou Municipality, "one of the best preserved old water county-towns in existence," may limit the town's development, but according to Fei Xiaotong it is necessary to ensure that the concept of "destruction for construction does not destroy the town." See Fei, *Small Towns in China,* p. 340.

42. This information is based on conversations with local officials in Tangquan Township in summer 1986.

43. Ibid.

44. Fei, *Small Towns in China,* p. 338.

45. See Bai Yihua, Song Zhiqiang, and Tang Pusu, "Go a step further in perfecting the functions of town and township governments, reform the system of vertical and horizontal division of administrative management" (*"Jinyibu wanshan xiangzhen zhengfu zhineng gaige de tiaokuai fenge xingzheng guanli"*), *Political Science Studies* (*Zhengzhixue yanjiu*), no. 6 (1987).

46. Fei, *Small Towns in China,* 1986, p. 85.

47. Zhang Fubao, "A County under Nanjing Municipality—Preliminary Research on the Development of Small Town Construction in Jiangpu County (*"Nanjingshi xia xian—Jiangpu xian xiao chengzhen de jianshe fazhan chubu yanjiu"*), *Economic Geography* (*Jingji dili*), no. 2 (1982): 139.

48. Zhao and Zhang, "Urban-Rural Reforms Influence," p. 324.

49. Zhou Fuyuan, "Smooth Vertical and Horizontal Relations; Carry Out Administration According to Levels" (*"Lishun tiaokuai guanxi, shixing fenji guanli"*), *Chinese Agricultural Economics* (*Zhongguo nongcun jingji*), no. 8 (1987): 48–51.

50. Personal communication, Yok-shiu Lee, March 21, 1988. In Zhujiang Township, Jiangpu County, county officials in 1986 took over a lucrative factory owned by the county-government seat, but Jiangpu officials say this type of expropriation, common in the 1960s, is rare today. Recent press reports, however, suggest that this remains a problem.

51. Dennis A. Rondinelli, "Small Towns in Developing Countries: Potential Centers of Growth, Transformation and Integration," in H. Detlef Kammeier and Peter J. Swan, eds., *Equity with Growth: Planning Perspectives for Small Towns in Developing Countries* (Bangkok: Asian Institute of Technology, 1984), pp. 10–48.

52. Tang Zhongxun and Ye Nanke, "Reflections on the Sources of Capital for Town Construction" (*"Jizhenjianshe zijin laiyuan tansuo"*), in *Xiao chengzhen, xin kai tuo, 1986,* pp. 339–347. In Xingdian Township, Jiangpu County, one market was built in 1983, but it was already too small, so the county was helping build a new one.

53. Tang and Ye, "Reflections on the Sources," p. 341.

54. The slogan was *"renmin de chengzhen, renmin jian."* Speech made to the National Meeting to Exchange Experiences among Test Points in Town Construction (*Quanguo jizhen jianshe shidian gongzuo jingyan jiaoliu hui*), February 16–21, 1987, Guangzhou, cited in *City and Town Construction* (*Chengxiang jianshi*), no. 4 (1987).

55. Tang and Ye, "Reflections on the Sources," p. 343.

56. William A. Byrd and Alan Gelb, "Why Industrialize? The Incentives for Rural Community Governments," in William A. Byrd and Lin Qinsong, eds., *China's Rural Industry: Structure, Development and Reform* (New York: Oxford University Press, 1990), pp. 358–388.

57. Andrew Walder, lecture presented at the Fairbank Center for East Asian Research, Harvard University, February 10, 1989.

58. Fei, *Small Towns in China,* pp. 83–84.

59. Fei, *Small Towns in China,* pp. 83–84.

60. Zhao and Zhang, "Urban-Rural Reforms Influence," p. 325.

61. Zhao and Zhang, "Urban-Rural Reforms Influence," p. 325.

62. "Research Report on Dingzhou City Strengthening Xiang (Zhen) Administration by Simplifying and Decentralizing its Administrative Powers" ("Dingzhou shi jian zheng fang chuan jiaqiang xiang [zhen] zheng chuan jianshe de diaocha"), *Chinese Agricultural Economics* (*Zhongguo nongcun jingji*), no. 8 (1987): 54.

63. World Bank estimates for four counties in Jiangsu, Anhui, Jiangxi, and Guangdong Provinces showed that 1986 profits handed over by township-owned enterprises to township governments made up 38 percent of township revenues. See Song Lina and Du He, "The Role of Township Governments in Rural Industrialization," in Byrd and Lin, eds., *China's Rural Industry,* pp. 342–357. See also Jean C. Oi, "Peasant Households Between Plan and Market," *Modern China* 12 (April 1987): 230–251.

64. Byrd and Gelb call this "fiscal predation." See Byrd and Gelb, "Why Industrialize?" pp. 377–380.

65. Tang and Ye, "Reflections on the Sources," p. 346.

66. "Small Town Construction Work Should Proceed Cautiously" ("*Jizhen jianshe yao liangli er xing*"), *Town Construction* (*Chengxiang jianshe*), no. 1 (1987): 34.

67. See Byrd and Gelb, "Why Industrialize?" Table 17–5.

68. Fei, *Small Towns in China,* p. 84.

69. Tang and Ye, "Reflections on the Sources."

70. In Nanhai County, Guangdong Province, where banks were deregulated and acted independently, they played a major role in developing private, as well as collective, enterprises. See Luo Xiaopeng, "Ownership and Status Stratification," in Byrd and Lin, eds., *China's Rural Industry,* p. 160. Many of the statements here about banking reflect policies before the Fifth Plenum of September 1988, after which local bank lending declined dramatically, while rural credit cooperative loans to township industries increased. For a discussion of the ebb and flow of funds for TVEs, see chapter 10 of this book.

71. In Cheqiao Township, northern Jiangsu Province, from 1980 to 1984, banks lent township enterprises 4,455,700 *yuan,* but lent only 220,000 *yuan* for town building, most of which went to private shops, department stores, and theaters that could generate some profits. See Tang and Ye, "Reflections on the Sources," p. 342.

72. Interview with the Party secretary of a county-government seat, July 1988. In this county-government seat, the construction bank was funding a major housing project.

73. He Peijin and Zhang Pingyong, "An Important Phase in Small Town Development" ("*Fazhan xiaochengzhen jingji de zhongyao buzhu*"), *Chinese Agricultural Economics* (*Zhongguo nongcun jingji*), no. 4 (1985): 31–35.

74. He and Zhang, "An Important Phase in Small Town Development," p. 35.

75. He and Zhang, "An Important Phase in Small Town Development," p. 35.

76. Yok-shiu Lee found similar requirements in Taishan County, Guangdong Province.

77. "State Council Directive on the Question of Farmers Investing and Settling in Towns" ("*Guowuyuan guanyu nongmin jinru jizhen luohu wenti de tongzhe*"), *PRC State Council Bulletin* (*Zhonghua Renmin Gongheguo guowuyuan gongbao*), no. 26 (1984): 920.

78. In the 1980s, officials from supply and marketing cooperatives and other government-owned businesses in rural towns tried to persuade Industrial and Commercial Bureau officials to close private enterprises. See chapter 8 of this book. But, the increased legitimacy of the private sector made this type of harassment more difficult.

79. Field notes from Yok-shiu Lee's trip to Guangdong Province, 1985, which he kindly shared with the author.

80. Chapter 5 of an earlier draft of Yok-Shiu Lee's Ph.D. dissertation that was not included in the final dissertation. For the dissertation, see "Rural Nonfarm Activities in China: Growth and Effects of Township Enterprises" (Doctoral Dissertation, Massachusetts Institute of Technology, 1988).

81. *Chinese Agricultural Yearbook,* 1985 (*Zhongguo nongye nianjian*) (Beijing: Chinese Agricultural Publishing House, 1985), p. 101.

82. In Guangdong Province, town officials kept farmers from the surrounding countryside out of enterprises owned by the county-town, which paid higher wages, pressuring them instead to work in township-owned factories. The numbers of outsiders in county-town owned factories was under 3 percent, and farmers had internalized the idea that county-town enterprises were part of a system that was beyond their reach. See Siu, "The Politics of Migration in a Market Town."

83. Interviews in Jiangpu County, 1988.

84. See, respectively, He and Zhang, "An Important Phase;" *People's Daily,* April 30, 1985; An Jian, "Town Development in Longgang Town" ("Longgang zhen de jizhen jianshe"), *Town Construction (Chengxiang jianshe),* no. 6 (1986); and Tang and Ye, "Reflections on the Source," p. 346.

85. See Kenneth Lieberthal and Michel Oksenberg, *Policy Making in China: Leaders, Structures, and Processes* (Princeton: Princeton University Press, 1988).

86. For a forceful, but perhaps overstated, expression of this viewpoint, see Vivienne Shue, *The Reach of the State* (Stanford: Stanford University Press, 1988).

87. The appendix was adapted from Table 5–2 in Lee, "Rural Nonfarm Activities," p. 111.

Part IV

Industrialization
and Internationalization:
Rural China Turns Outward

10

Rural Industry
Weathering the Storms of Central State Policy

Introduction

China's rural industry has been the most vibrant sector of the national economy since the mid-1980s. For several decades after they first emerged from the 1958 Great Leap Forward as a product of self-reliant development, rural factories were seen both within and without China as only an ancillary part of China's economic development. They offered a strategy by which rural surplus labor could effectively use local resources. By the late 1960s, rural industry became a conduit for introducing urban technology to the rural areas. Yet, they remained part of Mao's cellular approach to economic development and his goal of protecting the urban sector from the economic demands of the countryside. Rural, not urban, industry would supply finances and material for agricultural modernization, leaving urban, state-owned enterprises (SOEs) free to fulfill urban demands. In this way, too, profits from the SOEs could be used exclusively to modernize China's cities, strengthen the national economy, and improve the living standards of urban residents.

Since the mid-1980s, the increased interdependence of the urban and rural sectors has transformed the role and status of rural industry. Following the reintroduction of household farming, and the freeing up of tens of millions of surplus rural laborers,[1] promoting rural industry and developing a rural service sector became vital national policy to stem the tide of rural-urban migration.

By 1987, the output value of rural enterprises, including industry and the service sector, surpassed the total output value of agricultural production.[2] The rapid increase in rural living standards following decollectivization created a huge market for home appliances, transportation services, and construction materials, as farmers demanded amenities previously reserved for urban residents. Rural industry produces many light industrial goods needed by Chinese in their everyday lives, for example, electric fans, tools, cooking utensils, and clothing—undermining the state sector's monopoly on light industrial production. As these goods were removed from the state plan, rural industry, with its more flexible production lines, responded rapidly to increased nationwide demand for consumer goods.

By 1988, rural industry, excluding services, produced over 26 percent of total nationwide industrial production. And as the quality of these light industrial products improved, rural industry in the coastal regions moved swiftly into the export sector; in 1989, rural industry directly earned almost 20 percent of China's foreign exchange, and by 1993, rural enterprises earned over 32 percent of China's foreign exchange. Local governments have also used flaws in the banking system to siphon enormous amounts of scarce capital from central coffers into local industry, which has become the local governments' cash cow.

The central government has tried on numerous occasions, most recently in 1988–1990,[*] to limit the growth of the rural industrial sector. Whenever rural factories have expanded rapidly, challenging SOE monopolies or competing with them directly for capital, inputs, or markets, the central government has tried to constrain their development and force them to close down a good percentage of the new firms. Indeed, the central state does possess important mechanisms for limiting rural industrial development. Nevertheless, local resilience has succeeded in weathering these storms, progressing rapidly once the environment improves. Moreover, each time the state has cracked down on rural factories, it has been forced to recognize that these enterprises are critical for enriching the countryside, resolving China's rural surplus labor, and ensuring overall economic and political stability. Thus, although it continues to challenge the state sector in light industry and export earnings, China's leaders have recognized that rural industry has shifted from a supplementary role in China's economy to what Bo Yibo now refers to as "a major pillar of the national economy."[3]

Historical Development

Even before rural industry rose to such prominence in China's economic development, its history showed a remarkable resiliency and a penchant for unsuppressible autonomous development. In 1988–1990, leaders who favored more planned development with greater emphasis on state-owned industry tried to inhibit rural industry's development, but they confronted a sector that had weath-

---

[*]In 1996, the Chinese State Council introduced a new law on township and village enterprises (TVEs) whose purpose was to impose greater legal constraints on their development. See *South China Morning Post,* September 12, 1996.

ered numerous assaults from the central government, emerging from each confrontation better equipped for continued economic growth.

During the Great Leap Forward, rural inhabitants were mobilized to produce steel in backyard furnaces and to set up small workshops as part of the People's Communes. Soviet-built plants, coming on line in 1957–1959, would not affect the countryside, so the state promoted rural industry to address the rural-urban gap. But central plans for guiding and promoting small-scale rural industries, drawn up in 1957–1958, were ignored as local initiatives to set up factories took over. At least 7.5 million new factories and workshops, with the majority processing agricultural produce, were set up in the first nine months of 1958. According to local reports, many had been divorced from the reality and "established blindly" (*magmu xingban*).[4] However, because the famine and economic catastrophe of 1960–1962 dried up material resources, state policy, which called for the closing of all loss-incurring industries, also advocated that 90 percent of China's rural labor force remain in agriculture. In response, local officials shut down many rural factories.

From the mid-1960s through the early 1970s, rural industry grew for two reasons. Responding to the U.S. escalation of the Vietnam War in fall 1964, China moved a third of its industrial base to the hinterlands, creating its Third Front.[5] With almost a third of its national budget going to establish this new industrial heartland, rural areas were left to develop on their own. Second, China's burgeoning "green revolution" called for increased production of chemical fertilizer and cement for both water conservation projects and power plants for pumping water. When the 1970 Northern Districts Agricultural Conference advocated agricultural mechanization[6] and the "five basic industries"—cement, agricultural machinery, power generation, fertilizer, and steel—local enthusiasm for industrialization in many locations led once again to what the government characterized as excessive factory construction or "blind development."[7] The August 1971 National Conference on Rural Mechanization, which decided that rural industry should promote agricultural mechanization, made rural industries eligible for bank loans and fiscal support.[8] These policies led to rapid growth in county-owned rural industry. Between 1965 and 1969, the production capacity of small, nitrogenous fertilizer plants grew five times, and their share of national fertilizer output increased from 12 percent in 1965 to 60 percent in 1971. The number of cement plants increased tenfold between 1965 and 1973, producing almost half of China's cement. Similar growth occurred in pig iron production, small-scale power generators, and farm equipment.[9]

From 1971 to 1978, what became known as "commune and brigade enterprises" (*she dui qiye*) grew rapidly. Urban youths sent to the rural areas in the Cultural Revolution persuaded urban factories to set up workshops in their villages as a way of getting themselves out of fieldwork and into factories.[10] A 1974 policy, implemented in parts of rural Jiangsu Province, called on all communes to promote brigade-level factories, while another policy carried out in suburban Nanjing allowed local officials to demand that state enterprises, which took village land, build workshops in these villages and employ some of their displaced rural laborers.[11] And the 1976 founding of the National Rural Industry Administration formally legalized the position of rural firms.[12]

In the late 1970s and early 1980s, decollectivization, which shifted large amounts of resources from collectives into private hands, decreased funding for rural industry. In 1981 alone, 20,000 commune and 85,000 brigade enterprises nationwide closed, resulting in a loss of 500,000 jobs.[13] However, local capital accumulation in the 1970s through "extra budgetary funds;" a 1979 financial reform allowing local government to retain and invest larger shares of its revenues;[14] a doubling of Agricultural Bank of China (ABC) loans to rural industries in 1979–1980; and three-year tax-free development for new enterprises introduced in the late 1970s and early 1980s all gave many local governments the funds and incentives to promote rural industry. Reforms in agricultural procurement created new opportunities for food processing plants, while the legitimization of private enterprises in the mid-1980s boosted rural industry.[15]

The result in some rural communities was a Chinese version of "the great transformation," whereby agricultural communities industrialized almost over night. If one looks at a community such as Zhangjiagang (formerly Shazhou County) in Suzhou Municipality, the shift from agricultural to industrial labor was breathtaking. As Table 10.1 shows, in 1976, rural industrial workers there comprised 10.5 percent of the total rural labor force. Nine years later, in 1985, TVEs employed 43.5 percent of the total rural labor force. The number of workers increased fourfold from 41,000 to 187,200. Nationwide, however, the 1984 State Council Document No. 4 (1984), which renamed "commune and brigade enterprises" as "township and village enterprises" (xiang cun qiye) (TVEs), triggered a major boom in TVE growth, making rural industry a major factor in the national economy. Loans to TVEs in 1984 were 2.3 times those of 1983.[16] Local data collected by the author in counties around Nanjing show an industrial boom in 1984–1985. In one township, output increased from 4.6 million RMB in 1983 to 7.3 million in 1984 and to 9.97 million in 1985. From 1983 to 1984, in Jiangpu County, outside Nanjing, industrial output increased 24 percent; by 1985, it was up another 26 percent. As Table 10.2 (page 258) demonstrates, from 1983 to 1988, the number of TVE employees increased threefold from 32.3 million to 95.4 million. Weakened central government control over material allocation of producer goods, brought on in part by the dual price system introduced in 1984,[17] and increased local control over investment funds fueled further growth, particularly in areas with strong industrial bases. In Jiangsu and Zhejiang Provinces, rural industrial growth far surpassed overall industrial growth, in that much of the industrial expansion in these provinces was due to growth in TVEs.[18]

Township and village enterprises, particularly in coastal China, took on a critical new function following Chinese Communist Party General Secretary Zhao Ziyang's November 1987 call for China's coastal areas to implement an

Table 10.1

Number of Township and Village Enterprises and Their Laborers, Zhangjiagang, Jiangsu Province, 1970–1990

Year	Number of Township Enterprises	Number of Village Enterprises	TVE Industrial Labor Force	TVE Labor (% of Total Rural Labor)
1970	55	—	—	—
1971	82	—	—	—
1972	108	—	—	—
1973	121	—	22,000	6.0
1974	145	—	25,000	6.6
1975	161	—	32,000	8.6
1976	197	758	41,000	10.5
1977	249	NA	54,000	13.4
1978	301	473	94,400	23.5
1979	311	465	87,300	22.1
1980	346	502	106,300	26.8
1981	380	525	116,800	29.9
1982	408	524	123,200	31.7
1983	405	592	139,000	34.0
1984	464	626	168,400	39.4
1985	472	596	187,200	43.5
1986	520	607	189,100	44.7
1987	528	1,271	189,400	45.2
1988	518	995	183,700	45.8
1989	523	971	169,800	44.5
1990	502	783	167,600	44.7

Source: Zhangjiagang Statistical Bureau, November 1991.

export-led growth strategy.[19] Dissatisfied with the results of his 1984 urban industrial reforms, Zhao argued that rural enterprises, not state-run ones, are the "new impact force" for establishing an export-oriented economy and for earning foreign exchange.[20] After this, the role of rural industry in China's foreign trade expanded rapidly (see Table 11.1, p. 277), adding an important rationale for protecting TVE growth, despite its challenge to the state-owned sector.

The most recent retrenchment targeted at TVE growth began in fall 1988, following the October 1988 Third Plenum's decision to deflate China's overheated economy. With rural industry a major target of that effort, the total number of employees in rural enterprises, and the number of enterprises, decreased for the first time after 1981. Moreover, after the June 4, 1989 People's Liberation Army military assault on Beijing, the new dominant planning faction led by Yao Yilin and Li Peng, whose base of support rested with the state-owned, heavily industrial sector, resurrected the centrality of SOEs and squeezed rural industry mercilessly by closing off most forms of credit. The *Thirty-Nine Points* put forward at the Fifth Plenum in November 1989 called on all rural

Table 10.2

Selected Data on Township and Village Enterprises, 1978–1994

Year	Number of Firms (1,000s)	Number of Employees (1,000s)	Total Output Value (100 million *RMB*)
1978	1,524.2	28,265.6	493.07
1979	1,480.4	29,093.4	548.41
1980	1,424.6	29,996.7	656.90
1981	1,337.5	29,695.6	745.30
1982	1,361.7	31,129.1	853.08
1983	1,346.4	32,346.4	1,016.83
1984	6,065.2	52.081.1	1,709.89
1985	12,224.5	69,790.3	2,728.39
1986	15,153.0	79,371.4	3,540.87
1987	17,502.4	88,051.8	4,764.30
1988	18,881.6	95,454.5	6,495.70
1989	18,686.3	93,667.8	7,428.40
1990	18,504.0	92,647.5	8,461.60
1991	19,078.8	96,091.1	11,621.70
1992	20,792.0	105,811.0	17,975.40
1993	24,529.0	123.453.0	31,540.70
1994	24,945.0	120,175.0	42,588.50

Sources: Number of firms and number of employees come from the *Rural Statistical Yearbook of China, 1995*. Total output value comes from the *Statistical Yearbook of China, 1995* (Beijing: State Statistical Bureau, 1995).

enterprises that wasted energy, produced shoddy goods, polluted, or competed with state enterprises for raw materials to close down, suspend production, merge with other firms, or shift product lines. As had been advocated in previous anti-TVE retrenchments, rural enterprises were now to process only local materials "instead of scrambling with large enterprises for raw materials and energy."[21] Almost two million firms closed or were taken over by other firms, and almost three million workers lost their jobs (Table 10.2). According to estimates by the Ministry of Agriculture's TVE Bureau, as of early 1990, only 30 percent of firms were making a profit, 50 percent lacked inputs or could not sell their products, 10 percent were ready to go bankrupt, and another 10 percent had already gone bankrupt.[22] An extremely hostile environment compelled many private entrepreneurs to close shop in part because local governments, under pressure to close a certain number of firms, targeted private TVEs. Also, those who had contracted collective enterprises returned firms to the collective, causing the firms to stop production. Unofficial estimates at the time suggested that problems in rural industries had forced 15 million farmers back to the land.

By spring 1990, a major lobbying effort to protect TVEs forced the central government to reconsider its hostile policy towards TVEs.[23] China's looming

Table 10.3

**Rural Credit Cooperative Loans to Township and Village
Enterprises, December 1987 to September 1989** (in billion *RMB*)

Month/Year	RCC Loan to TVEs
December 1987	32.9
June 1988	46.3
December 1988	45.6
June 1989	51.2
September 1989	53.7

Source: People's Bank of China, cited in World Bank, *China: Country Economic Memorandum Between Plan and Market,* Report no. 8410–CHA, May 8, 1990, p. 16.

foreign debt crisis made it unwise to restrict a major foreign exchange generating sector. China's state budget was facing an increasing deficit, yet rural industries had supplied over 50 percent of new state taxes since 1980. With almost 100 million rural inhabitants employed in rural enterprises, nationwide plant closings and massive unemployment could lead to further rural-urban migration and both urban and rural unrest. Important party leaders, including a member of the old guard, Bo Yibo, who reemerged with more power as a result of the Tiananmen crackdown, lobbied on behalf of rural industry.[24] According to sources in Jiangsu, Fei Xiaotong had published some articles in Jiangsu newspapers critical of the central policy on TVEs. Further speeches, national conferences, exhibitions, and press reports supporting rural industry, which took on the style of a concerted lobbying effort, forced Premier Li Peng to visit Jiangsu Province in February, where he admitted that "insufficient stress has been laid" on rural industry whose significance must be recognized.[25]

Yet, despite the crisis, growth persisted at a stable rate of 15 to 16 percent (as compared to earlier rates of 45 percent in provinces such as Jiangsu). While the state restricted direct capital flows to TVEs, funding came either from rural credit cooperatives not controlled by the Agricultural Bank (Table 10.3), or from bank loans that were available to rural industries that did not pollute, use local resources, were linked to state firms, or earned foreign exchange. Township and village enterprises also used various local strategies including forcing workers to invest in factories, setting up local savings and loan companies outside the banking system, and imposing local government surcharges.[26] Some local officials felt that the retrenchment had allowed them to close inefficient firms, preparing them again for rapid development once funds become more readily accessible.

Administrative Structure Supervising Rural Industry

In considering China's economy, precise definitions are often problematic. For example, the Chinese have applied the term "township and village enterprise" (*xiang cun qiye*), to a wider category of firms than those run only by these two levels of local government. In addition, since the mid-1980s, they refer more often to "township and town industry" (*xiang zhen qiye*), which includes former townships now incorporated as towns. Finally, township and village enterprises also includes many enterprises that are not industrial factories; in fact, of 125 million rural residents employed in TVEs, only 55 million are employed in factories. For this chapter, however, I define rural enterprise as any factory, enterprise, firm, hotel or shop situated in the rural areas or rural towns and owned cooperatively, privately, or by a local government (village, township, or town) below the county level (Table 10.4).

Unlike most industrial sectors in China, which are defined by product types, rural industry is defined by the level of ownership—township, village, cooperative, or private—and its geographic location. Still, there is a bureaucratic structure which gives some guidance to rural industries.

At the top of this administrative structure is the "Township Enterprise Administrative Bureau" (*Xiangzhen qiye ju*) under the Ministry of Agriculture (MOA), which was established in 1979. According to the 1989 *Name List of Chinese Government Organizations,* its major tasks include researching and directing rural industry's planned development, management, laws, economic structure, technological development, and liaison with other ministries to improve the quality of rural industrial products.[27] The most recent office to be established is the "Office for Promoting External Economic Relations" (*Waixiang jingji kaifa chu*).

Other ministries and commissions have their own offices responsible for rural industry. For example, the State Planning Commission has its own "Division of Township Enterprises" (*Xiangzhen qiye chu*) whose task is to organize the work of different units to support rural industry. According to one official in the MOA, every ministry has an interest in TVEs (which may suggest that several of them have specific offices for dealing with TVEs), and the MOA's responsibility is to work out all the relationships among the different ministries.[28] Given that rural industrial production crosses many product lines and, therefore, challenges the products of many ministries, most industrial ministries need to coordinate with rural industries in some manner.

At the provincial level, the "Township Enterprise Department" (*Xiangzhen qiye ju*) is separate from and reportedly has equal bureaucratic status with the provincial "Department of Agriculture" (*Nongye ting*). Within this department are several bureaus, one of which is now an office for promoting external economic relations. The provincial Planning Commission also has an office for coordinating the relationships among the different industrial bureaucracies related to rural enterprises. Similar structures exist at the municipal level, with the Ministry of Agriculture replaced by a Rural Work Department within the city government. The city's "Industrial and Commercial Bureau" (*Gong shang guanli ju*) and its "Individual Household Department" (*Getihu chu*) are responsible for collective and private commercial endeavors in the suburban counties. While the

Table 10.4

Rural Enterprises by Level of Ownership, 1984, 1985, 1988

Year	No. of Enterprises	No. of Employees	Output Value (billions RMB)
1984			
Collective			
Township	401,513	18,791,661	
	(2.5)[b]	(36.1)	143.3
Village	1,248,128	19,689,332	(86)
	(7.8)	(37.8)	
Private			
Cooperative[a]	1,119,583	6,559,453	15.9
	(6.9)	(12.6)	(9)
Private	13,295,900	7,020,462	11.7
	(82.8)	(13.5)	(7)
Total	16,065,124	52,060,908	170.9
1985			
Collective			
Township	419,476	21,113,565	
	(3.44)	(30.3)	198.78
Village	1,149,595	20,407,813	(72.9)
	(9.4)	(29.2)	
Private			
Cooperative[a]	1,402,012	9,463,290	74.06
	(11.5)	(13.5)	(27.1)
Private	9,253,509	18,805,660	
	(75.6)	(27)	
Total	12,224,592	69,790,328	272.84
1988			
Collective			
Township	420,000	24,900,000	243.9
	(2.2)	(26.1)	(37.5)
Village	1,179,000	24,040,000	192.4
	(6.2)	(25.2)	(29.6)
Private			
Cooperative	1,200,000	9,770,000	56.1
	(6.4)	(10.2)	(8.6)
Private	16,090,000	36,750,000	157.2
	(85.2)	(38.5)	(24.1)
Total	18,880,000	95,450,000	649.6

Sources: Data for 1984 are from Christine P.W. Wong, "Interpreting Rural Industrial Growth in the Post-Mao Period," *Modern China* 14 (January 1988): 13; for 1985 are from *China's Agricultural Yearbook, 1986 (Zhongguo nongye nianjian, 1986)* (Beijing: Nongye chubanshe, 1986), pp. 158, 160; and for 1988 are from Ministry of Agriculture, *A Survey of China Township Enterprises* (August 1989).

Notes:

[a]While data for 1984 and 1985 divided cooperatives into *peasant joint cooperatives* and *other types of cooperatives,* I combined them for simplicity. The ratio between these two types of cooperatives in terms of numbers of firms, employees, or total output value, based on 1984 and 1985, was approximately 4 to 1 or 5 to 1 favoring farmers' joint cooperatives.

[b]Numbers in parenthesis refer to the percentage the number directly above is of the total column for that year.

scale of bureaucratic supervision is vast, these overlapping bureaucracies mean that direct control often lies with the level of government that owns or directly supervises the enterprise.

Thus, real control over rural enterprises lies at the county level and below; in suburban areas, the city's "district government" (*qu*) plays this same role. Here, the most important organization for fostering the expansion of rural enterprises is the county (or district) Planning Commission, which is responsible for determining economic priorities and apportioning local funds. It allocates foreign exchange to different factories in the county and townships. Other important organizations responsible for rural enterprises include the "Bureau of Township and Town Enterprises" (*Xiangzhen qiye ju*), which helps foster township, town, and village enterprises, and the county, which is responsible for licensing, training, and overseeing all commercial enterprises in the county. The ICB's "Individual Household Department" (*Getihu ke*) supervises all private industrial and commercial activities within the county.

However, while these bureaucracies monitor or promote development, large numbers of county-level organizations own rural factories directly. Although these enterprises would not be included in the statistics on rural industry, because they are owned by administrative units at the county level, they form part of the ever-increasing landscape of rural industrialization. For example, county supply and marketing cooperatives, which until the mid-1980s had a monopoly on the purchase and sale of most agricultural inputs and production, control a large number of rural enterprises. As of 1985, the Supply and Marketing Cooperative of Wujiang County in Suzhou Municipality owned 42 factories and employed over 8,000 workers. According to its vice director, there were about five cooperatives like this in all of China. In Zouping County, Shandong Province, Walder found that of twenty-six collective enterprises under county control, eleven were owned by the supply and marketing cooperative, six were run by the light industrial collective, three by the construction commission, two by the Grain Bureau, two by the Bureau of Public Affairs, and one each by the Commerce Bureau and the Agriculture Bureau.[29] At the township level, the most direct control belongs to the "township industrial company" (*gongye gongsi*).[30] Before these companies were established in the mid-1980s, all rural enterprises were controlled by the commune party committee and the commune management committee. In the 1983 reform of the commune structure, the commune administration was split into a township government, a township party committee and an "economic association committee" (*jingji lianhe weiyuanhui*) responsible for supervising all economic activities.[31] Beneath it were four offices responsible for agriculture, industry, sidelines, and economic management. In Zijingshan Township, when the Economic Association Committee was disbanded in February 1986, the industrial, sideline, and agricultural companies remained under the supervision of the "Office of Economic Management" (*jingying guanli bangongshi*). According to interviews in 1986, however, the township industrial company was actually under the direct supervision of the district Planning Commission, and the Office of Economic Management was under the district party committee's Agricultural Work Department.[32] While the sideline company ran a tree farm and a small cattle business, all commercial and sideline endeavors owned by the township were really under the management of the industrial company, and would be included as rural enterprises. Interviews with the township party secretary, however, suggested that he still had great influence over economic decision making in these industrial enterprises.

Finally the "administrative villages" (cun) work within the same broad framework, with the village management committee supervising all industrial enterprises owned by the village, and the village party committee often interfering in local economic management. In some locations, the township may exercise direct control over cun industries, but in regions where the administrative villages are highly industrialized, townships may wield little control.

Establishing the Rural-Urban Linkage

Since 1984, a major reason for rural industrial growth has been the increasing connection between urban and rural factories. After the State Council raised the status of rural enterprises in 1984, city governments and rural officials were called on to establish economic linkages between these two industrial sectors. In some provinces, the new policy of "cities leading the counties" (shi lingdao xian) increased the authority of urban administrators over the rural areas. In 1986, all factories in Nanjing with output of over 3 million RMB had to help rural industry. One Wuhan official in the city planning commission was given the task of establishing economic linkages with rural factories, opening training courses for their new managers, and sending retired workers and technicians to these factories. Much of southern Jiangsu Province's rural industrial boom was due to the out-migration of many technicians from Shanghai factories into rural areas around Wuxi, Suzhou, and Changzhou municipalities.[33]

These linkages benefit urban factories. As the growth of the market economy undermined many urban factories' planned markets, linking with rural factories enlarges the scope of their sales. This connection also allows urban SOEs to escape the physical and administrative constraints of the urban economic environment. Urban factories lack land for expansion, but rural governments can expropriate land for new factories. Piece goods or certain parts of the product cycle can be efficiently farmed out to lower-paid, rural industrial workers who do not receive state-mandated welfare benefits, lowering production costs for the SOEs. For example, many TVEs in Kunshan County, Jiangsu Province, were sub-factories of Shanghai SOEs. Whereas rural governments cherished these contacts, because they allowed people to enter the nonfarm sector without migrating to the cities and brought the benefits of industrialization to the countryside, they made rural industries vulnerable to fluctuations in the planned economy.

Sectoral Breakdown of TVEs

Rural enterprises cover numerous economic sectors. The five basic industries promoted in the 1960s and 1970s, which were designed to make the rural areas self-reliant, linked rural industry with the chemical, cement, agricultural machinery, iron and steel, and energy sectors. Since the 1970s, the sectoral breakdown of rural enterprises has changed significantly. While we do not possess detailed comparative data from before 1980 on output according to products, Table 10.5 shows that, in terms of labor, agriculturally oriented firms declined as did industrial firms with the major exodus of workers from agricultural labor to transportation, construction, and commerce (including small restaurants and food stands).[34] However, while rural labor entered the construction trade before 1984, only after 1984–1985, when the constraints on farmers working in the service sector and transportation were lifted, did significant numbers of rural inhabitants shift into these latter two sectors (Table 10.5). Similarly, the biggest jump in output in the communication and transportation sectors occurred in 1985–1986. Clearly, the pace of deregulation in these various sectors differed.

Similarly, the TVE sector has shifted from low-profit small farm tools to high-profit consumer goods.[35] Table 10.6 (page 266) presents sectoral breakdowns for 1980, 1985, and 1988. Significant changes since 1980 have occurred in textile production, papermaking, mining, and chemical production. While construction boomed between 1978 and 1980, its role in rural industry has steadily declined, even though it has developed significantly in terms of total output.

When these different rural factories are linked with state-owned factories, they fall into different bureaucratic systems or *xitong*. Textile factories fall under the light industrial system; chemical plants fall under the chemical system. Overall, linkages between central ministries and rural enterprises are quite weak. While the State Planning Commission might include output from TVEs in its projected growth data, it does not include transfers of output or inputs to rural industry even in the guidance aspects of the plan. These firms have access to planned goods only if the larger SOEs with which they deal allocate planned commodities to them.

Mechanism of State Controls

While the central government has few direct controls over rural industrial production, Beijing has been able to implement frequent retrenchments of rural industries. As discussed above, in the 1960s, the state closed 20,000 commune enterprises and laid off 500,000 workers. In October 1985, *People's Daily* called for another such retrenchment, and in 1988–1989, especially after the June 4, 1989 crackdown, the state forced over one million inefficient enterprises to close.

The major source of central control is the supply of loans to rural industry. While wealthy counties may have sufficient capital for self-generation, most

Table 10.5

Total Employment in Township and Village Enterprises by Sector, 1978–1994 (in 1,000s)

Year	Agriculture		Industry		Construction		Communication and Transportation		Commerce and Catering	
	Number	%	Number	%	Number	%	Number	%	Number	%
1978	6,084.2	21.5	17,343.6	61.4	2,356.2	8.3	1,038.3	3.7	1,443.3	5.1
1979	5,330.0	18.3	18,143.8	62.4	2,984.5	10.3	1,159.0	4.0	1,466.1	5.0
1980	4,560.7	15.2	19,423.0	64.8	3,346.7	11.1	1,135.6	3.8	1,530.7	5.1
1981	3,799.4	12.8	19,808.0	66.7	3,488.3	11.8	1,073.8	3.6	1,526.1	5.1
1982	3,440.0	11.1	20,728.1	66.6	4,212.9	13.5	1,129.4	3.6	1,618.7	5.2
1983	3,092.2	9.6	21,681.4	67.0	4,827.2	14.9	1,097.1	3.4	1,648.5	5.1
1984	2,839.3	5.5	36,560.7	70.2	6,834.9	13.1	1,293.0	2.5	4,553.1	8.7
1985	2,523.8	3.6	41,367.0	59.3	7,899.5	11.3	1,141.8	1.6	16,858.2	24.2
1986	2,408.0	3.0	47,619.6	60.0	12,703.7	16.0	5,412.6	6.8	11,227.5	14.2
1987	2,441.8	2.8	52,666.9	59.8	13,739.8	15.6	6,231.4	7.1	12,971.9	14.7
1988	2,499.9	2.6	57,033.9	59.7	14,848.1	15.6	6,841.6	7.2	14,231.0	14.9
1989	2,393.0	2.6	56,241.0	60.0	14,037.3	15.0	6,993.7	7.5	14,002.8	14.9
1990	2,360.6	2.6	55,716.9	60.1	13,468.4	14.5	7,112.2	7.7	13,989.4	15.1
1991a	2,430.8	2.7	58,135.5	63.5	13,843.3	15.1	7,323.1	8.0	9,841.0	10.7
1992	2,548.0	2.4	63,364.0	59.9	15,407.0	14.6	7,979.0.	7.5	16,523.0	15.6
1993	2,854.0	2.3	72,596.0	58.8	18,269.0	14.8	9,314.0	7.6	20,420.0	16.5
1994	2,605.0	2.2	69,615.0	57.9	16,220.0	13.5	7,256.0	6.0	24,479.0	20.4

Source: Rural Statistical Yearbook of China, 1995 (Zhongguo nongcun tongji nianjian).

Note:

aThe data in the yearbook for 1991 appear to be incorrect. The unexplainable drop in *Commerce and Catering* is too great. It also makes the total percentage for the year imbalanced. But I simply report it as published.

Table 10.6

Township and Village Enterprise Output by Industrial Sector
(in 100 million *RMB)*

	1980		1985		1988	
	Output	Percent	Output	Percent	Output	Percent
Mining/						
metallurgy	10	2.0	49	3.3	150	4.3
Electric power	2	0.4	5	0.3	8	0.2
Coal	21	4.1	56	3.8	75	2.2
Petroleum	1	0.2	2	0.1	7	0.2
Chemical,						
plastic	42	8.3	122	8.4	361	10.5
Machinery	132	25.9	372	25.5	847	24.6
Building	104	20.4	275	18.8	546	15.9
Forestry	15	2.9	43	2.9	89	2.5
Food	41	8.1	114	7.8	271	7.9
Textile	34	6.7	182	12.5	476	13.8
Sewing	19	3.7	53	3.6	130	3.8
Leather	8	1.6	23	1.6	59	1.7
Papermaking/						
stationery	20	3.9	78	5.3	221	6.4
Other	55	10.8	79	5.4	199	5.8
Total	509	99.8	1,459	99.21	3,438	99.8

Source: For 1980 and 1985, data came from Ministry of Agriculture, *A Survey of China Township Enterprises* (June 1988). For 1988, data came from Ministry of Agriculture, Township Enterprise Bureau, *A Survey of Township Enterprises in China* (August 1989).

counties and townships need loans for industrial growth. Through their control of the ABC, the Ministry of Finance and the People's Bank of China control the flow of funds to rural industry. Constraints imposed on new capital construction can cut the flow of funds to new factories. Simply by insisting that banks call in all outstanding loans, the center can force many cash-short rural industries into bankruptcy. They can also stop them from withdrawing their own funds from the bank.[36]

The effort to promote more technologically advanced products from rural enterprises also increases central government influence. In 1985, to improve the quality of rural enterprises and agricultural production, the State Council approved the Sparks Plan, put forward by the State Science and Technology Commission (SSTC).[37] Under this plan, the SSTC allocates funds, scientific information, management skills, new crops, and technological innovations to rural industry. The SSTC promotes linkages between scientific research institutes and rural industry. If a rural firm becomes part of the Sparks Plan, it receives more loans and is included in the state plan.[38]

The new emphasis on exports from rural areas increased central governmental control over TVEs. Beginning in 1987, the Ministry of Foreign Economic Relations and Trade began passing down export quotas and foreign exchange quotas to the county governments, which divided them among county-run firms and township governments. These, in turn, divided them among township-run firms. Negotiations over these quotas allowed for only minor adjustments at the margin.[39] In 1990, 190 township enterprises whose products were to be promoted overseas were brought more directly under state control by becoming part of the export-oriented manufacturing system.[40]

Finally, in the "Regulations Governing Rural Collective-Owned Enterprises," published in 1990, the leadership declared that township-, town-, and village-owned enterprises—as distinct from cooperatively and privately owned firms—were component parts of China's socialist "public ownership economy."[41] Throughout, the document stressed the state's role in encouraging, promoting, and yet guiding rural enterprises. Firms were warned that they had to produce goods that accorded with the state's industrial policy; those that continued to produce low-quality products were to be shut down.

Local Government Controls

Although rural enterprises are either leased to individuals by contract with the local government or owned privately, they remain tightly controlled by different local government officials. While collectively owned rural enterprises are nominally independent of local political controls, county, township, and village governments wield significant power and in many cases completely determine the decisions of factory managers.[42] Even private firms have shown a propensity to become closely entwined with local governments in many parts of China, although in some cases local entrepreneurs may wield important political influence. Thus, the formal management structure may obscure the locus of real decision-making authority.

The most important reason for government interference is that rural industry has become the local government's main source of revenue. Under the fiscal responsibility system, introduced in the mid-1980s, whereby each level of government contracts with its immediate superior to turn over a fixed sum of funds, with the surplus remaining with the local government, a predatory system of tax farming has been established. As a result, local governments use every method possible, including many which straddle the boundary of legality, to promote rural industry, at the same time milking it to supplement their government budgets.

In some prosperous locations, townships and villages have sufficient funds to generate their own rural enterprises. Red Flag Township, near Wuxi, invested 12 million *RMB* in 1978–1984, 80 percent of which came from profits retained from other enterprises in the county.[43] One newspaper reported thirteen different ways for local governments to raise funds for rural enterprises.[44]

Local banks and local governments have close relations. Even while the state calls for cutbacks on capital investment, the county and township governments can get new funds through the efforts of local branches of the ABC, in particular the rural credit cooperatives. The credit cooperatives rely primarily on villagers' deposits for their investment funds; as a result, the central government has difficulty preventing them from loaning their deposits to rural industries, particularly if local governments apply strong pressures. As mentioned above, rural credit cooperatives expanded the scale of their loans even at the pinnacle of the government's 1988–1990 prohibition on loans to TVEs. Because township industries pay a high rate of tax to the county, county governments have become their active protectors. According to Luo, since TVEs are "the political and economic foundation for Wuxi County as a whole," local banks have consistently come to their rescue.[45] When funds were short in Wuxi in 1986, banks borrowed 100 million *RMB* from other areas which they loaned to rural industries at cost. They also reduced interest rates for loans to the lowest legal level, even though lending rates are subject to central government regulations. Walder's findings show that, rather than compel the banks to give loans, the county assumes the financial risks that the bank would face by promising them that the government will give the enterprises continued tax breaks until the firms repay the loans. In this way, expanding rural industry in the short run costs the county, and probably township governments, short-term tax revenues.[46]

County and township governments aggressively defend their own economic interests, particularly from challenges by private firms. In 1985, when burgeoning private firms and village enterprises drew labor and business away from county- and township-owned firms, Wuxi County's government imposed restrictions on these firms. It thoroughly investigated village-owned firms, and if they were *de facto* private and only nominally collective, they were closed down. Relatives of skilled workers who left collective enterprises to work for private ones were permanently barred from jobs in TVEs. By these methods, Wuxi County drove out the competition, allowing private enterprises to survive only in commerce, transportation, and services.[47] Similarly, Zhangjiagang also reported that the parents of people who left their jobs in the collective factories to open private firms would no longer receive retirement benefits from the collective firms that had employed them; moreover, requests for licenses to open private firms would be similarly rejected and those who tried to open private businesses would be fired from their collective jobs.[48]

After June 4, 1989, and the reemergence of a political atmosphere that was critical of excessive private profits, taxes on privately owned enterprises, as well as new restrictions on how these profits could be used, increased.[49] In addition, if managers who leased collective enterprises were earning salaries that were several times higher than those of their workers, the local government could force them to reinvest more in the collective.[50] When local enterprises, including factories, orchards, and other collective enterprises, were first leased in the early and mid-1980s, local officials grossly underestimated the size of profits that leases could earn. As profits soared, villagers and cadres often demanded renegotiation, triggering a rash of contract disputes. As a result, China has found it necessary to uphold the legality of rural contracts.[51]

To maximize their political and economic security, private firms established ties to collective firms or local governments. Researchers in Jieshou County, Anhui Province, found that an individual villager had opened a firm that was nominally called a township enterprise, but which was under the direct control of the county. This villager got easy loans, tax exemptions, a bank account, and the opportunity to purchase land in the county seat.[52] In the reverse situation, Luo discovered a case in which four individuals opened a food processing plant that nominally belonged to the district, but the district never interfered in the individuals' private business decisions. In Nanhai County, Guangdong Province, local governments established joint private-collective ownership, according to which successful private firms or factories were financially supported by local governments that needed their products.[53] A contractual division of profits was worked out. Similarly, in Wenzhou District, Zhejiang Province, because private businessmen could not do business with the socialist sector, they established formal affiliation with collective or state enterprises for which they paid the firms a fee. Local cadres there helped businessmen become collective or "partnership firms" to protect them; in return they received voluntary donations and assistance for local government projects.[54] Unclear rural property rights allow governments to expropriate firms owned by other levels.[55] In Jiangpu County, Jiangsu Province, the author discovered that a successful export-oriented factory owned by the government of the county seat was taken over by the county government in 1986, whereas in Jieshou County, Anhui Province, Luo found that some private firms were taken over by the county. Factory workers there hoped that, by turning these private firms into county-owned collectives, they would be eligible for benefits similar to those received by state workers. The private owners could also become state cadres and their families could get access to urban household permits.

Problems and Prospects for Rural Industry in the 1990s

Because rural industries have grown at a rather remarkable rate, they constantly generate and confront new problems. Many of these problems will continue to affect state and local policy towards rural industry.

As rural industry has become more capital intensive, it no longer serves as a major repository for excess labor. Yet, it must continue to absorb tens of millions of workers, lest social unrest become far more problematic in the countryside. Estimates in the late 1980s suggested that surplus rural labor was anywhere from 70 to 156 million.[56] To stem the tide of massive rural-urban migration and help resolve rural unemployment, rural industries, including the service sector, must continue to expand.

As rural industries become more complex, they challenge state industries more directly. Their unquenchable need for resources did increase the price of raw materials in 1987–1988. The resultant bidding war prompted localities to keep resources in their own region, decreased profitability in the all-important state sector, and fostered inflation. Yet, if rural industries are prevented from seeking resources outside their local areas, they cannot attain economies of scale or develop the necessary scientific and technical knowledge that will improve their efficiency or the quality of their products.

Rural industry exacerbates interregional inequalities.[57] With expanding ties to urban industries, suburban industries and those in developed areas near state firms should develop much faster. Coastal rural industry's increased access to foreign exchange offers its workers, managers, and local governments benefits unavailable to inland rural areas.[58] Different provinces earn greater amounts of foreign exchange and have higher retention rates than other provinces.[59] Moreover, by selling foreign exchange at the higher market rate, coastal areas like Guangdong, Fujian, and Jiangsu provinces can pay a higher price for raw materials from the hinterland. These areas then process these goods for export generating a cyclical process of "internal colonialism," whereby the inland areas supply raw materials to the coastal areas who earn the "value added."

Yet, despite efforts by the central government to retard the development of the TVE sector, rural industry has remained resilient and a driving force for the ultimate modernization of the Chinese countryside. The Chinese Communist Party, in spite of its rural roots, quickly favored the urban industrial sector in part for political expediency, to stabilize the cities which had been hesitant to accept its rule. In part, too, the communist elite dwelled in the cities and relied on SOEs for the funds to run its government administration. Whenever these urban interests have been threatened, the central state has aggressively used its fiscal and administrative powers to stifle the emergence of an autonomous industrial force in the countryside. But, like a prize fighter who refuses to take a dive and who strives for the right to control his own future, TVEs and the local governments that own or support them have become an autonomous force limiting central state authority, and empowering local rural elites and the farmer/industrial workers of rural China.

Notes

1. According to China's leading analyst of rural development, Du Rensheng, at least 200 million rural inhabitants would have to find work in the rural nonagricultural sector. Du Runsheng, "Second-stage Rural Structural Reform," *Beijing Review,* no. 25 (1985): 15–17, 22.

2. *Farmers' Daily (Nongmin ribao),* February 24, 1988, p. 1.

3. See Bo Yibo, "To Develop Township and Town Enterprises Is a Task of Strategic Significance," speech to the delegates for the inauguration of the Chinese Township and Town Enterprise Association, January 11, 1990, in Foreign Broadcast Information Services (hereafter cited as *FBIS*), no. 9–S (February 9, 1990): 41–43.

4. Carl Riskin, *China's Political Economy: The Quest for Development Since 1949*

(Oxford: Oxford University Press, 1987): 125–126, and Carl Riskin, "Neither Plan nor Market: Mao's Political Economy," in William A. Joseph, Christine Wong, and David Zweig, eds., *New Perspectives on the Cultural Revolution* (Cambridge: Council on East Asian Studies, Harvard University, 1991), pp. 132–152.

5. Barry Naughton, "The Third Front: Defense Industrialization in the Chinese Interior," *The China Quarterly,* no. 115 (September 1988): 351–386.

6. *Major Economic Events in the PRC, 1949–1980 (Zhonghua renmin gongheguo jingji dashiji, 1949–1980)* (Beijing: Zhongguo shehui kexue chubanshe, 1984), p. 463.

7. *Major Economic Events in the PRC, 1949–1980,* p. 472.

8. Luo Xiaopeng, "Ownership and Status Stratification," in William Byrd and Lin Qingsong, eds., *China's Rural Industry: Structure, Development and Reform* (New York: Oxford University Press, 1990), pp. 134–171.

9. Riskin, *China's Political Economy,* pp. 214–215.

10. The important role of rusticated urban youths to the expansion of rural industry that I had observed in 1980–1981 was confirmed by *Kushan County Gazeteer (Kunshan xian zhi)* (Shanghai: Shanghai People's Publishing House, 1990), p. 160.

11. Information collected by the author during various research trips to rural Jiangsu Province.

12. Luo, "Ownership and Status Stratification."

13. Christine P.W. Wong, "Interpreting Rural Industrial Growth in the Post-Mao Period," *Modern China* 14 (January 1988): 8–9.

14. Wang Bingqian, "Report on Financial Work," *Beijing Review,* September 29, 1980, pp. 11–23.

15. Wong, "Interpreting Rural Industrial Growth," pp. 7–9.

16. *Chinese Economic Yearbook, 1985 (Zhongguo jingji nianjian, 1985)* (Beijing: State Statistical Bureau, 1985), pp. v-228.

17. The dual price system introduced as part of the urban industrial reform of 1984, whereby the same good might be sold at a low planned, and a higher market, price, pushed resources onto the market where demand from TVEs was increasing.

18. Robert Delfs, "The Rural Uprising," *Far Eastern Economic Review,* July 11, 1985, p. 56. According to Delfs, between 1978 and 1984, annual growth in rural enterprises of nearly 25 percent in Jiangsu Province increased the province's industrial output value by 19 percent per year.

19. See chapter 11 of this book.

20. "Zhao on Coastal Area's Development Strategy," *Beijing Review,* February 8–14, 1988, pp. 18–23.

21. See "Decision on Further Improving the Economic Environment, Straightening Out the Economic Order, and Deepening the Reforms (Excerpts)," adopted at the Fifth Plenary Session of the Thirteenth Central Committee of the Chinese Communist Party on November 9, 1989, in *Beijing Review* 33 (February 12–19, 1990), pp. i–xvi.

22. Interview by the author at TVE Bureau, Beijing, March 1990.

23. The most important article was a commentary in *Nongmin ribao* on March 15, 1990, entitled "Correctly Appraise the Role of Township and Town Enterprises." See *FBIS-CHI*-90–078 (April 23, 1990): 51–53.

24. In January 1990, Bo Yibo called on his old comrades to deepen their understanding of rural industrialization, reminding them that it was party policy (i.e., not just the reform faction's policy) and the creation of the farmers. Rural industrialization was the "inevitable trend in Chinese economic development," and a "strategic task" for invigorating the rural economy. See Bo, "To Develop Township and Town Enterprises."

25. Li's comments were quoted in "Correctly Appraise the Role of Township and Town Enterprises."

26. Jean Oi, lecture presented at Fairbank Center, Harvard University, August 10, 1990.

27. See *Name List of Chinese Government Organizations, vol. 1, 1989* (*Zhongguo zhengfu jigou minglu, Shang, 1989*) (Beijing: Xinhua chubanshe, 1989), pp. 191–192.

28. One would assume that the TVE Bureau in the MOA calls together all the different offices relating to TVEs in the central bureaucracy to coordinate TVE-related work. On the issue of exports from rural areas, national conferences are always run by both the MOA and the Ministry of Foreign Economic Relations and Trade.

29. Andrew G. Walder, "A Profile of Zouping County Industry and Finance," Shandong Field Research Project, 1988 Field Report, presented at the conference at Wingspread Center, Racine, Wisconsin, November 4–6, 1988.

30. The name of this organization varies in different locations and over time. In some locations, such as Nanhai County, Guangdong Province, the industrial company at the township level is called the Township Industrial and Trading Company. Luo, "Ownership and Status Stratification."

31. This describes the process in Zijingshan Township, in the suburbs of Nanjing.

32. At the county level, this meant that township industrial companies were not under the direct leadership of the county TVE Bureau; rather, they were under the county Planning Commission, which was assumed to be the most powerful economic organization in the county.

33. For a longer discussion of urban-rural industrial linkages, see chapter 7 of this book.

34. By 1986, many urban construction projects were contracted to rural governments that sent labor teams all over the country. For example, in 1986, Qidong County, in Jiangsu Province, one of the most renowned counties in China for doing construction work, was carrying out projects as far away as Guizhou Province. Interviews by the author in Nanjing in summer 1986.

35. *People's Daily,* April 1, 1981, p. 1.

36. *China Daily-Business Weekly,* May 1, 1989, p. 3.

37. *Nongmin ribao,* September 3, 1985.

38. *China Daily-Business Weekly,* January 16, 1989, p. 4.

39. Interview by the author in Beijing in April 1989.

40. *China Daily-Business Weekly,* May 14, 1990, p. 1.

41. *FBIS* (June 15, 1990): 31–35.

42. See, inter alia, Byrd and Lin, eds., *China's Rural Industry;* and Walder, "A Profile of Zouping Industry and Finance"; and Jean C. Oi, "The Fate of the Collective After the Commune," in Deborah Davis and Ezra Vogel, eds., *Chinese Society on the Eve of Tiananmen* (Cambridge: Harvard Contemporary China Series, 1990), pp. 15–36.

43. Delfs, "The Rural Uprising," p. 94.

44. These include, for example, selling stock or dividends; making new workers contribute funds as they join factories; cooperating with state, other collective, or specialized households; private credit loans; cooperating with educational or research institutes; loans from other enterprises; cutbacks on other new projects; and efficiently using capital. See *Nongmin ribao,* August 16, 1985, p. 2.

45. Luo, "Ownership and Status Stratification."

46. This fact explains why some wealthy counties with expanding industrial bases pay farmers with IOUs for the grain they procure; all government and bank funds are tied up in promoting rural industry.

47. Luo, "Ownership and Status Stratification."

48. See "The Office for Zhangjiagang's Local Gazeteer" (*"Zhangjiagang shi difang zhi bangongshi"*), *Zhangjiagang City TVE Industrial Gazeteer (Zhangjiagang shi*

xiangzhen gongye zhi) (Shanghai: Shanghai People's Publishing House, 1990), p. 96.

49. Adi Ignatius, "Beijing Reins in Wenzhou Experiment," *Asian Wall Street Journal,* February 13, 1990, p. 1.

50. Oi, "The Fate of the Collective After the Commune."

51. See chapter 6 of this book.

52. Report by Zhao Yang at the Fairbank Center-State Council Development Institute Joint Seminar, Nanjing, China, January 1989.

53. Byrd and Lin, *Chinese Rural Industry.*

54. Liu Ya-ling, "The Reform from Below: The Private Economy and Local Politics in the Rural Industrialization of Wenzhou," *The China Quarterly,* no. 130 (1992): 293–316.

55. Unclear property rights, or what one scholar called "soft" property rights, are part of China's traditional heritage. Under the communists, such expropriations became common during "leftist" or radical periods. See David Zweig, *Agrarian Radicalism in China, 1968–1981* (Cambridge: Harvard University Press, 1989), pp. 145–168.

56. Jeffrey R. Taylor, "Rural Employment Trends and the Legacy of Surplus Labour," *The China Quarterly,* no. 116 (December 1988): 136–166.

57. See David Denny, "Regional Economic Patterns During the Decade of Reform," in Joint Economic Committee, Congress of the United States, *China's Economic Dilemmas in the 1990s: The Problems of Reforms, Modernization, and Interdependence* (Washington: U.S. Government Printing Office, 1991), pp. 186–208.

58. See chapter 12 of this book.

59. See *Township and Villages Enterprises Yearbook, 1987 (Xiangzhen qiye nianjian, 1987)* (Beijing: Agricultural Publishing House, 1988), p. 616. See also chapter 11 of this book.

11

Internationalizing China's Countryside

The Political Economy of Exports
from Rural Industry

The ten years of the open policy changed China dramatically. Expanding its exports and importing technology, funds, and management skills to bring to fruition the historic goal of modernization opened China to new forces in the international system. Yet, while most studies of China's growing foreign trade sector have emphasized its impact on China's trading partners and the international economy,[1] few studies have addressed the domestic impact of the decision to open up parts of the domestic economy to foreign trade and shift into a more export-led pattern of economic development.[2]

The potential domestic impact of such a massive restructuring of domestic and external economic relations is large. For Gourevitch, the nature of the international system can determine a state's political system, whether it is democratic, authoritarian, or totalitarian; the type of domestic political alliances that exist within the system; and the system's political structure.[3] Thus, the U.S. threat from the south following the 1964 Gulf of Tonkin incident and the increased Soviet threat from the north led China's leaders to introduce the Third Front. Resource allocations, factional alliances, and the country's psychological climate were affected by these decisions, which contributed to the Cultural Revolution.[4] Another study showed how joining the World Bank affected policy, policy process, and institutions in China, as well as many Chinese leaders' perspectives about China's economic performance.[5]

This chapter considers how China's open policy affected the domestic political economy, opportunity structures, and the nature of political conflict and competition within China by focusing on how the decision to promote exports from township and village enterprises (TVEs) generated new opportunities, inequalities, and political competition on rural policy and within rural China.

The Rural Sector in China's Export Economy

The rural sector has played an important role in Chinese foreign trade, particularly in coastal areas.[6] From 1983 to 1989, annual growth rates in agricultural trade were almost 12 percent, and the value of exports increased yearly by 13.4 percent; in both 1986 and 1987 the surplus in agricultural trade of over 4 billion in U.S. dollars subsidized exports in other sectors.[7] In 1987, total foreign exchange earned in the rural areas of Guangdong Province, worth US$2.7 billion, totaled almost half the foreign exchange earned in the province.[8] In the same year, over $1 billion in U.S. dollars was earned in salaries throughout rural China for processing or finishing products in the rural enterprises.

Township and village enterprises have become a key engine of growth for China's overall exports. From 1986 to 1990, growth in Chinese exports was US$33.1 billion, while growth in TVE exports was US$8.0 billion. Thus, growth in TVE exports explains 24 percent of the growth in total exports. However, between 1990 and 1993, total growth in Chinese exports was US$26 billion, while growth in TVE exports was US$17.5 billion. According to this figure, growth in TVE exports explains 67 percent of the growth in China's total exports. Clearly, the role of TVEs in China's export boom has increased significantly.

In fact, since the mid-1980s, TVEs have been the most important sector linking the rural areas to foreign trade.[9] Table 11.1 shows the rapid expansion of TVE exports and their importance to China's foreign trade. Whereas in 1985 state foreign trade companies (FTCs) rarely turned to TVEs in searching for exportable commodities (only 4.8 percent of domestic purchases of export commodities came from TVEs), by 1993, more than half of the exportable products purchased domestically were produced by the TVE sector (see Table 11.1). Similarly, TVEs have played a critical role in China's search for foreign exchange. In 1984 and 1985 combined, TVEs earned only US$2.38 billion, while by 1993, TVEs earned over US$30 billion in foreign exchange and made up over 32 percent of foreign exchange earnings (see Table 11.2, page 277). Moreover, Chinese analysts argue that, if industry owned and administered by the "county" (*xian*) government and the work done by TVEs on goods eventually exported by state enterprises are included, the rural industrial sector's contribution to China's export earnings would be significantly greater.

Foreign Trade's Domestic Impact

China's vast rural areas changed under the opening to the outside world in numerous ways. Linking TVEs with the world market affected the struggle over

Table 11.1

Growth in Export Purchases from Township and Village Enterprises, 1985–1994

Year	Total Purchases of Export Commodities[a]	Total Purchases of TVE Commodities for Export[a]	Purchases of Export Commodities[b]
1985	81,200	3,900	4.80
1988[c]	140,700	26,900	19.10
1989	169,300	37,100	29.94
1990	199,300	48,600	24.40
1991	225,900	67,000	29.66
1992	281,300	119,200	42.40
1993	436,800	235,100	53.82
1994	—	339,830	—

Sources: *TVE Yearbook, 1994*, p. 274; and *China Rural Statistical Yearbook, 1995*, p. 41.
Notes:
[a]Figures are in million *RMB* This column refers to nationwide purchases.
[b]Figures represent purchases from township and village enterprises as a percentage of total export purchases.
[c]Data for 1986 and 1987 were not available.

many resources, including exported and imported goods, raw materials that could be processed for export, foreign exchange, export and import licenses, market information, loans, opportunities for secure jobs, and international business contacts. The opening affected the level of technology in the countryside through imports of new equipment.[10]

Opportunity structures in the rural areas for expanding industry, improving social and political mobility, building social networks, and consolidating local government power changed as well. The decision to decentralize control over foreign trade and foreign exchange earnings shifted the decision-making authority on what goods to produce, with which foreign firms to link, and how to spend foreign exchange, from the Ministry of Foreign Trade and Economic Cooperation (currently MOFTEC) in Beijing and the provincial FTCs to other bureaucratic levels. Units which increased their authority over foreign trade issues could claim a bigger share of the domestic, as well as international, market. Yet, by introducing quotas for the total value of exports, foreign exchange earnings, and the amount of Chinese currency spent to earn the foreign exchange, the central state gave cadres new responsibilities and new indicators of success or failure.

As for the major actors, despite reforms in the foreign trade system, the prereform foreign trade bureaucracy remained strong in much of rural China. Similarly, local governments from the county to the township used their bureaucratic authority to gain or maintain control over export industries and the international goods and opportunities. According to Lardy, decentralization of control

Table 11.2

Foreign Exchange Earnings by Township and Village Enterprises, 1984–1993
(US$ billion)

Year	Total Earnings	China's Total Export Earnings[a]	Percentage of Total Exports
1984–1985	2.4[b]	52.1	5.0
1986	4.5[c]	31.4	14.0
1987	5.1[d]	39.5	13.0
1988	8.04[e]	47.6	17.0
1989	10.1	52.9	19.0
1990	12.5[f]	64.5	19.0
1991	17.0[g]	71.9	24.0
1992	20.0	85.5	23.4
1993	30.0[h]	91.6	32.7

Sources:

[a]The 1984 figure for total export earnings is from *Direction of Trade Statistics Yearbook, 1991* (Washington, D.C.: International Monetary Fund, 1991); 1992 and 1993 data are from *Direction of Trade Statistics Yearbook, 1994* (Washington, D.C.: International Monetary Fund, 1994), p. 151; and all other data are from *Direction of Trade Statistics Yearbook, 1992* (Washington, D.C.: International Monetary Fund, 1992).

[b]Based on *Foreign Broadcast Information Service* (April 13, 1990), which reported that 1984–1989 TVE exports totaled US$35 billion.

[c]*China Daily,* September 25, 1989, p. 1.

[d]Interview by the author with REBDZ in April 1989.

[e]*China Daily,* December 15, 1987, p. 1.

[f]*Beijing Review,* January 28 to February 3, 1991, 29.

[g]Xinhua General News Service, October 4, 1992.

[h]Lin Dinggen, "Speed Up the Development of TVE's Export Oriented Economy," *China TVE Reports* (*Zhongguo xiangzhen qiye bao*), May 25, 1994, in People's University Journal Materials, *Management of TVE's and State Farms,* F 22, no. 6 (1994): 66–69.

over foreign exchange and the contract system for foreign trade led to more powerful local governments.[11] New organizations were established in the central and local bureaucracies to facilitate or control the opening. Decentralized control over foreign trade expanded the pattern of conflict and competition. What had once been solely a central-local conflict, in which local governments resisted turning over produce at low state-controlled prices, became intra-local and intra-regional, as many localities competed to use the new opportunities emerging in a liberalizing economy; for weaker localities, the battle was simply to meet the new quotas. Since coastal areas benefited more from foreign trade than inland areas, the opening may have exacerbated regional inequalities. Finally, competition developed among farmers for access to factory jobs in the more lucrative export sector.

If we define power as control over resources and their allocation, then studying how promoting rural foreign trade led to new forms of competition over resources among organizations, or to the redistribution of resources among units

Table 11.3

Ratio of Exports of Rural Enterprises to Total Exports by Industrial Sector, 1988–1992

	1988	1989	1990	1991	1992
Garments	49.6	65.2	72.0	77.5	89.7
Artwork and handicrafts	39.0	43.1	45.0	52.0	63.7
Light industrial manufactures	19.3	22.8	28.5	38.7	53.9
Chemical products	23.6	36.3	27.3	31.5	53.2
Silk products	21.4	25.1	24.3	33.7	54.0
Textile products	16.4	19.2	21.9	25.0	NA
Machinery products	16.2	19.6	21.8	23.8	NA

Sources: China Rural Enterprise Yearbook (*Zhongguo xiangzhen qiye nianjian*) and others, cited in Yan Shanping, "Export-Oriented Rural Enterprises," *JETRO China Newsletter,* no. 118 (1985): 11.

Note: Exports of rural enterprises are totals of Renminbi-based direct and indirect exports and revenues from consignment processing.

and levels, presents an important mechanism for understanding how the open policy affected the distribution of power in rural China. Moreover, because these major shifts occurred in such a short time, the behavioral changes involved and their impact on rural residents were significant.

Reforming China's Foreign Trade System in the 1980s

Rural industrial exports grew rapidly for several reasons. The first was the increased status of rural industry created by Central Document No. 4 (1984). The number of rural enterprises increased tenfold between 1983 and 1985, and increased by another 50 percent by 1988 (see Table 10.1). The number of employees more than doubled between 1983 and 1985 and had increased by another 27 percent by 1988. Output value increased by 270 percent between 1983 and 1985, and by 1989 was eight times higher than in 1983. Similarly, by the late 1980s, rural industrial output was about 25 percent of total national industrial output. This growth alone might have allowed rural industry to play a significant role in China's export drive. However, a second key factor was that those sectors in which TVEs competed most effectively with the state-owned enterprises (SOES)—mainly primary and light industrial products—were particularly appropriate for export promotion as China sought greater participation in the global economy. Whereas Japan, South Korea, Taiwan, and even Hong Kong dominated highly valued, capital-intensive products, China could compete advantageously with other developing countries for market share in the production of lower-valued, labor intensive goods. But, as China tried to promote these types of export products in the 1980s (and 1990s), the state discovered that TVEs now dominated many of those sectors (Table 11.3).

Third, TVEs had depended on the initiative of local officials who, in the face of several onslaughts against rural industry since the late 1950s, had been able to expand the firms under their control.[12] By the mid-1980s, however, the decentralization of China's foreign trade sector into the hands of local government entrepreneurs created new vibrancy for it. Finally, the central government's decision in 1987–1988 to adopt an export-led growth strategy under the title of the Coastal Development Strategy, with the resultant political pressures that this imposed on the local governments, led to a rapid growth in exports from rural industry.

Before looking at the foreign trade reforms, we must understand the old system. Prereform foreign trade was monopolized by the then Ministry of Foreign Trade (MFT), which purchased resources or finished products for export through centralized FTCs organized along product lines. The MFT had divisions under its direct control at the provincial, municipal, and county levels. Control over foreign exchange was in the hands of the "Foreign Exchange Management Bureau" (*waihui guanli ju*) in the Bank of China, with branch offices at the city and provincial levels.

After 1978, all agricultural products were bought through the procurement system at fixed prices that helped the state extract wealth from the farmers. Local FTCs bought exportable goods whose prices and quantities were fixed in the state plan; however, FTCs often gave farmers slightly higher prices than those paid by domestic state procurement agencies, making procurement easy for the MFT. Fifty percent of exports were agricultural products. During the prereform period, FTCs limited all direct contact among villages, export-orientated TVEs, and foreign importers. Export licenses were unavailable to organizations outside the foreign trade system. Thus, TVEs and communes spent their time building relations with FTCs, rather than foreign importers.[13] As of 1981, there were few export-orientated TVEs outside the 1,500 in Guangdong Province.[14]

Elite Debates and Conflict over Township and Village Enterprise Exports, 1984–1988

The first step towards internationalizing the rural economy in the post-Mao era was made in 1978 in Guangdong Province, when officials began to redirect Guangdong's rural production towards serving Hong Kong's market. The "grain first" policy of the Cultural Revolution decade was replaced by expanding fruit, fish, poultry, and pig production geared at the tastes and living standards in Hong Kong. Soon, compensation agreements were signed with Hong Kong businessmen who supplied equipment to TVEs in return for the factory's output. By 1981, rural Guangdong was so dependent on exports to Hong Kong that, when the American recession harmed Hong Kong's economy, growth in Guangdong Province slowed as well.[15]

The first nationwide effort to link the rural economy with the export sector occurred in 1984 when then premier, Zhao Ziyang, on a visit to Guangdong, raised the slogan of "trade-industry-agriculture" (*mao gong nong*). Zhao wanted to restructure agricultural production "in accordance with the needs of export markets. . . ." The direction of trade policy should be trade-industry-agriculture not agriculture-industry-trade. "It's not a case of you planting what you want, processing what you want, and then making available for export what you can spare; quite the opposite, based on the international market you both plant and process."[16] At that time, Zhao's strategy was limited to rural export bases, and did not encompass the whole of the countryside.

Zhao's slogan met with some response. The Research Center on Rural Development (RCRD), under Zhao's colleague, Du Runsheng, began to study how to reform the foreign trade system and assess the international demand for China's agricultural produce and industrial products from TVEs.[17] This study was part of a larger project to study coastal development. While rural exports did increase, the policy still focused on agricultural exports from rural export bases, not on TVEs. Although some economists in the RCRD suggested in 1985 that TVEs could play a significant role in exports, Du did not pass this view on to Zhao Ziyang.[18]

By 1987, Zhao had become a public advocate of increasing the role of TVEs in China's exports. While state enterprises were hard to invigorate in the short run, argued Zhao, small rural enterprises

> are filled with vigor from the very start. . . . They have a strong sense of competition and survival. They are flexibly managed and able to adapt themselves to market changes. They also offer good services and their delivery time is short. All this makes foreign trade companies happy to deal with them and foreign business people to co-operate with them. . . . They have become the new impact force for the development of labor-intensive industries, the establishment of an export-oriented economy, and the expansion of foreign currency-earning exports in the coastal areas.[19]

Zhao visited the coastal areas in December 1987 to launch this new period in the internationalization of the rural economy and society.

Zhao apparently changed his mind for several reasons. First, according to some Chinese, whether a leader is premier or general secretary affects his view on the role of TVEs versus SOEs in export promotion. When Hu Yaobang as general secretary was responsible for the millions of rural party branches, he supported linking rural industry to exports; Zhao, then premier, preferred to leave that task to state industries. By 1987, Zhao had become less sure of the ability of SOEs to respond flexibly to international demands, and once he became general secretary in autumn 1987, a series of internal documents by Wang Jian of the State Planning Commission finally changed his views.[20]

Wang argued that, due to China's excessive rural population, industry, not agriculture, would have to resolve the looming labor crisis, supply capital formation, and eventually help develop agriculture.[21] Land shortages and labor surpluses meant that rural labor should be used for labor-intensive development of the export sector. Wang also stressed that TVEs were the heart and soul of the labor-intensive export strategy.

Zhao's report triggered debate in the Central Committee.[22] Li Peng opposed making coastal development and increased exports from TVEs key parts of China's developmental strategy. According to Chinese economists, Li, unlike Zhao, had never worked at the local levels, and, therefore, neither understood local party branches nor cared to strengthen them at the risk of weakening the SOEs for which he was responsible. The booming TVE sector seriously challenged the job security of the tens of millions of state industrial workers. Li also did not understand how TVEs had changed by the mid-1980s. As a representative of the planning faction, he could not favor policies which weakened central control of foreign exchange earnings. Both role expectations and personal experience explain the different attitudes of Zhao and Li on TVE exports.

The Impact of Decentralization on TVE Exports

One major readjustment that followed the decision to promote TVE exports was the concomitant choice to decentralize control over the foreign trade system even further.[23] While Cummings asserts that China was forced to open itself to capitalist penetration, because otherwise the world capitalist system would not share its technology with China,[24] the decision to decentralize was following a long tradition of shifts between central and local control. No doubt the structure of the international system dictated that, if China wanted to borrow technology to facilitate rapid growth, it had to earn foreign exchange through loans or export promotion. Yet late modernization in Japan, South Korea, and Taiwan had involved significant planning and import-export controls. However, given the overly centralized nature of the Chinese economy, Zhao and other reformers decided that decentralization was critical if China was to compete internationally. Only if managers of export-orientated firms and the local governments who controlled them had strong incentives, such as greater control over raw materials used for exports, foreign exchange, import and export licenses, new information or new equipment, would they innovate, earn more foreign exchange, and willingly adjust to the rigors of the international market. Thus, decentralization was not so much the result of pressures from the world capitalist system or international forces penetrating the system, as the complex interdependence model might argue, but rather resulted from conscious state policy.[25] One proof of this is the ability the central government has demonstrated to reassert control over foreign trade. Whenever imports have expanded too rapidly, as in 1979–1980, 1984–1985 or 1988–1989, the state has regained control over imports and prevented the ballooning of its debt burden.

Further Reforms in the Foreign Trade System, 1987–1988

The most important foreign trade reform was the "contract managerial responsibility system," based on the *Draft Plan for Restructuring the Foreign Trade System*. Under this system, the then Ministry of Foreign Economic Relations and Trade (MOFERT) contracted with the State Council "to fulfill State Council assigned targets involving export earning in foreign exchange, export costs, and control over total financial losses."[26] Each province signed an annual contract with MOFERT specifying: (1) projected export values, (2) "net export costs,"[27] and (3) amount of foreign exchange they would turn over to the state.

Under the new policies, firms might establish contacts with different FTCs, and some were even able to make direct ties with foreign firms.[28] Suzhou Municipality held a trade show in 1987, where individual firms and county governments displayed their products and set up contacts directly with foreign firms that attended from twenty different countries.[29] While "first category goods" regulated by the plan had to be sold through provincial FTCs, controls on other categories of goods were relaxed. In many cases, township- and county-level firms simply had to report to the Foreign Exchange Management Bureau, which was responsible for controlling foreign exchange.

As firms became freer to choose the FTC to which they wanted to sell, competition among FTCs that were expected to help their province meet its quota increased. According to Ross, "this system begins to shift the FTCs' source of livelihood from MOFERT—which used to control and subsidize their activities—to the enterprises themselves."[30] Yet, while some FTCs courted rural firms enthusiastically, others tried to keep control by limiting information and holding back foreign exchange. Other strategies, described below, were also used.

Still, the reforms strengthened local governments. According to one report, administrative control over most of MOFERT's local trading companies and its bureau-level offices were transferred to local governments.[31] They also became responsible for fulfilling the foreign exchange quotas.

The Impact of the Foreign Exchange Contract System

At the same time that control over licenses, export ports, and production decisions was decentralized, China's leaders agreed to revise the formerly stringent controls placed on foreign exchange. The first tests were carried out in Guangdong Province in 1978–1979, and controls on foreign exchange retention were progressively loosened nationwide throughout the 1980s. However, the excessive importing of foreign consumer goods in late 1984 and 1985, following the Third Plenum's urban reform policy, forced the central government to reimpose controls.[32]

The "foreign exchange contract system" (*wai hui bao gan*) was reinvigorated in 1988 as part of the decentralization of foreign trade. Foreign exchange quotas came down to the province, which sent them to the county, which, in Wujiang County, Jiangsu Province, at least, passed them down to county-owned, township-owned, and village-owned firms. The quotas set for three years in 1988 were based on the previous year's foreign exchange earnings. According to one source, "the quotas came down mostly as commands. There may have been some negotiations at the margin, such as, if the quota was 50 million *RMB*, the local and central governments may have tried to get a deal at forty, with the two parties agreeing on 45."[33]

Firms and local governments suddenly had great incentives to increase their foreign exchange earnings, because they had "use rights" to 80 percent of their above-quota foreign exchange earnings. The surplus could be sold to other governments or factories or firms with export licenses through "foreign exchange redistribution centers" (*waihui tiaoji zhongxin*), established in many cities and provinces in 1988. A shortage of dollars nationwide meant firms could sell their foreign exchange at almost twice the official rate: in 1988, it was almost 6 *RMB* to the dollar. While factories still had to ask permission to use these funds and report any activity to the Foreign Exchange Management Bureau, the use of foreign exchange became much less restrictive. Nevertheless, as of 1989, county governments in Suzhou and Wuxi municipalities, which were very powerful, still controlled the allocation of foreign exchange.

The Impact on Rural China's Domestic Political Economy

Much of the politics that ensued before and after 1987 resulted from the partial nature of reform.[34] With policy in a perhaps never-ending transition stage between plan and market, the foreign trade bureaucracy remained powerful, the central government still imposed immense obligations on local units, and dependency relations existed between the officials who controlled the allocation of resources and entrepreneurs and producers of exportable products who either worked with them or sought to evade their controls. Bureaucrats hoped that, if they resisted the reforms, policy might revert to a more planned economy before they conceded too much control. Moreover, most rural entrepreneurs and local governments, especially those without overseas Chinese relations, lacked access to international marketing information or contacts, leaving them dependent on FTCs or local governments that fought to maintain old patterns of dominance.

But dependency is two-sided. While the planned allocation of goods and the imposition of export quotas made households, villages, TVEs, and local governments dependent on those who controlled resource allocations, many felt comfortable selling to the state when few market alternatives existed. Even after the scale of the market expanded, global market fluctuations and insecurity meant that local producers often preferred the security of contractual agreements with the FTCs.

Nevertheless, new opportunities that emerged in 1987–1988 due to the decentralization of foreign trade and the establishment of the foreign exchange contract system turned the old, secure dependent ties into constraints. The introduction of quotas let FTCs, local governments, and TVEs keep more of the surplus foreign exchange they earned, an immensely valuable commodity in China. It could be swapped at a profit, bartered for other shortage goods, or used to buy foreign products unavailable to most Chinese. Because increased demand for rural products increased the value of exportable goods, rural entrepreneurs and TVEs sought to extricate themselves from contractual obligations when market forces favored such activity. And, while many may not have broken their agreements, they did grow restless at the low prices paid by some local FTCs that tried to maintain their dominant position to extract more foreign exchange for themselves. Press reports and interviews suggest that the conflict between different local actors intensified, which is supported by the fact that the conservatives tried to withdraw these rights after June 1989.

The Strategy of Mobilization

While self-interest encouraged some rural producers to enter the export sector (as discussed below), the importance of government compulsion indicates the degree of central control or direction that accompanied the Coastal Development Strategy and the mercantilist nature of rural export promotion. Surprisingly, China's export promotion strategy relied on many of the mobilization techniques that had been used in the past to gain compliance with elite goals.[35] These included using quotas, test points which receive favorable treatment, and models in the press that were to be emulated, all of which politicized economic decisions and gave rise to policy winds. Many localities which tried out the policy or received quotas should never have been involved in export production. As a result, the shift to an export-led growth strategy generated waste and social unrest.

Using test points meant that certain areas were given preferential treatment which, when the policy was generalized, was unavailable to much of the country. Without the same state support, some of these non-test point locations simply could not compete. The favoritism given to Guangdong Province generated nationwide resentment, because Guangdong in the early 1980s accumulated more foreign exchange than any other province. And, while Guangdong's success was necessary if the policy was to be adopted nationwide, FTCs in Guangdong used their foreign exchange and special marketing opportunities to profit at the expense of other parts of the country by paying producers higher prices for resources and finished goods that the FTCs themselves would then export.

Propagating models in the press and reporting how some towns went from rags to riches overnight because they found an export niche created false expectations, resulted in frustration for localities that were unsuccessful, and led some local governments and farmers to enter the export market blindly only to have their hopes come crashing down when their goods did not sell. While such risks are inherent in market systems, transitions always prove problematic, and the use of models to encourage others to climb on board aggravated the trauma.

China returned to a quota system, rather than taxing profits, both to compel policy implementation and generate foreign exchange for the state. Local governments, local MOFERT bureaus, and even local offices of the Foreign Exchange Management Bureau[36] were all under great pressure from higher levels to fulfill the quotas under their jurisdiction. As the drive for exports intensified, local governments put pressure on enterprises and bureaus under their control to enter the international market. As a result, the expansion of exports took on all the characteristics of a political movement, with compulsion and quotas coming down level by level, forcing localities to comply. In such circumstances, one Chinese analyst has argued, localities appear enthusiastic, but the policy fails to attain its real goals.[37] Negative results proliferated: localities that could not meet their quotas bought foreign exchange, pushing up its value on the domestic market. Also, evidence of problems were ignored, such as when one top leader denied that the Coastal Development Strategy could lead to "internal colonialism," or when the policy confronted serious opposition which threatened to overturn it entirely.

The Politics of Dependency

In this changing environment, MOFERT, its local FTCs, and local governments all tried to maintain the dependent relations they had established with other units, with farmers, and with TVEs during the prereform era. In Table 11.4, "Direct Exports Not Through MOFERT," is a measure I built to reflect empirically the level of provincial autonomy from MOFERT. These data demonstrate that, in 1987, MOFERT had tight control over TVE exports in most provinces other than Guangdong, Fujian, and Hunan provinces.[38]

To ensure its exports can compete internationally, MOFERT must suppress the export procurement prices of the exportable goods it buys. Its ally is the State Pricing Bureau in Beijing, which controls domestic prices for exportable goods. Until the late 1970s, therefore, the prices of exportable goods in Guangdong Province had not gone up for over 10 years.[39] As a result, MOFERT's purchase price for export goods, such as prawns, could be as much as 30 percent below the domestic market price.[40]

The result has often been devastating for TVEs. According to one report, many enterprises "grit their teeth" in order to use domestic sales of other products to supplement the export goods, but because they cannot bear the loss caused by the demands to earn foreign exchange, they resist getting involved in the export market.[41]

Foreign trade companies had numerous levers to use over TVEs in much of rural China, including control over market information, product samples or patterns,

Table 11.4

Provincial Exports of Township and Village Enterprises, 1987 (1,000 *RMB*)

Location	Total Exports	Direct Exports	Direct Export Through MOFERT	Direct Exports Not Through MOFERT		Indirect Exports
				Absolute	Percentage	
Total	16,195,770	11,902,670	10,204,530	1,698,140	14.27	4,293,100
Beijing	496,860	330,590	317,490	13,100	3.96	166,270
Tianjin	789,630	789,630	736,430	53,200	6.73	—
Hebei	770,620	352,240	339,630	12,610	3.58	418,380
Shanxi	120,980	86,830	83,170	3,660	4.22	34,150
I. Mongolia	24,050	16,150	16,150	—		7,900
Liaoning	600,020	442,920	434,440	8,570	1.93	157,050
Jilin	46,400	39,260	34,400	4,860	12.38	7,140
Heilongjiang	74,620	53,840	52,220	1,620	3.00	20,780
Shanghai	2,190,510	1,526,630	1,526,630	—		663,880
Jiangsu	3,253,220	2,296,370	2,150,990	145,380	6.33	956,850
Zhejiang	1,647,990	1,019,460	912,230	107,130	10.52	628,530
Anhui	102,710	67,580	64,710	2,870	4.25	35,130
Fujian	652,190	561,870	440,310	119,560	21.28	90,320
Jiangxi	158,660	95,140	87,690	7,450	7.83	63,520
Shandong	1,090,320	910,010	910,010	00		180,310
Henan	225,800	157,710	138,270	19,440	12.33	98,090
Hubei	289,220	211,370	203,370	8,000	3.78	66,850
Hunan	371,980	251,470	186,240	65,230	25.94	120,510
Guangdong	2,489,500	2,112,960	1,022,240	1,090,720	51.62	376,540
Guangxi	161,460	129,030	123,530	5,500	4.26	32,430
Sichuan	412,590	297,230	282,570	14,660	4.93	115,360
Guizhou	47,180	39,680	33,950	5,730	14.44	7,500
Yunnan	60,210	35,670	34,780	890	2.50	24,540
Tibet	—	—	—	—	—	—
Shaanxi	36,750	30,080	24,720	5,360	17.82	6,670
Gansu	30,090	21,550	20,800	750	3.48	8,540
Oinghai	9,320	9,030	9,030	10	—	290
Ningxia	15,530	12,520	11,320	1,200	9.58	3,010
Xinjiang	8,360	5,800	5,250	550	9.48	2,560

Source: Township and Village Enterprises Yearbook, 1978–1987 (Beijing: Agricultural Publishing House, 1989), pp. 616–617.

Note: While the Chinese table did not make clear what indirect exports were, they are likely to be products produced in conjunction with SOEs, which are then exported as the product of the SOE. I assume that direct exports refers to goods produced in the province that leave directly through provincial ports. These would include sales to the foreign purchaser through local FTCs not under MOFERT's control and through MOFERT and its local representatives. Of these direct exports, the amount not controlled by MOFERT (columns 5 and 6) indicates the extent to which the official foreign trade system did not control the exports in the provinces.

new equipment, scarce natural resources that had to be imported or bought elsewhere in China, and the foreign exchange or domestic currency loans needed to buy these resources.[42] Because FTCs often did not disclose the end user of the product or the price at which the goods were sold, rural firms were not able to challenge the price paid by the FTC.[43] Foreign trade companies were often accused of not paying the TVEs a fair share of the foreign exchange earnings. In fact, in 1988, the minister of agriculture chastised MOFERT for not sharing market information with rural producers.[44] In Wuxi County in 1989, when I tried to distribute subscription forms for an East Asian marketing magazine, I discovered that city officials preferred to keep TVEs in the dark and limit their direct global contacts. In return for supplying information about their products, firms would get a subscription to the marketing magazine and access to international marketing information. However, foreign affairs officials in Wuxi City quickly took the forms away from me, saying they would distribute them.

Nevertheless, the responsibility system weakened MOFERT's controls over foreign trade. Agricultural products are now produced by families that want the best price. They sell where conditions are best, often on the domestic market. In one survey done in Weifang City, Shandong Province, by the State Council's RCRD, over 40 percent of 300 rural entrepreneurs cited problems with the "export procurement prices" (*shou gou jiage wenti*) as the main obstacle to developing agricultural exports further.[45] Also, in the late 1980s supply and marketing cooperatives had lost their monopoly, so in some locations they closed roads to prevent farmers from marketing their agricultural produce in other regions.

As a result, relations among MOFERT, local FTCs, and farmers were sometimes troubled. In the RCRD survey in Weifang, some farmers openly criticized MOFERT. While 72 percent of the rural entrepreneurs said that relations with MOFERT were good, 19 percent said that relations were just "okay" (*yi ban*), and 9 percent admitted to a "contradiction" (*maodun*) or serious conflict. Given the caution of farmers in this type of survey, that 28 percent would admit to disagreements is significant. Yet, some individual entrepreneurs still want MOFERT to facilitate foreign trade. When asked for the most important blocks to developing exports from TVEs, 12 percent complained that the foreign trade bureau had not made the necessary arrangements.[46]

Problems between MOFERT and local entrepreneurs were the subject of a meeting in the summer of 1988. Some of the 100 representatives from exporting TVEs who attended this meeting convened by the Ministry of Agriculture and MOFERT raised many of the issues outlined above. They included complaints that, (1) MOFERT did not pay them for their goods until a year after the initial sale (MOFERT probably waited until it got paid by the foreign buyer); (2) MOFERT had cut the foreign exchange retention level in Sichuan Province by 4 percent; (3) Jiangsu Province had been forced to buy foreign exchange domestically at a high price to meet its quota (probably because its quota was high);

(4) the price of inputs had gone up 150 to 200 percent since 1979, but the price MOFERT paid for finished goods had not changed since that year; and (5) export-oriented TVEs wanted to repay their loans with pretax, not post-tax, income, in essence making loan repayments tax deductible.[47]

Some higher-level FTCs ended their relations with lower-level FTCs if it was in their interest. After the export responsibility system was introduced in 1988, the provincial FTC took back clients it had previously introduced to Wuxi City, closing TVEs' local export channels. Export quotas made international channels or contacts very valuable commodities that provincial FTCs wanted to exploit.[48] Similarly, some city-owned enterprises refused to renew their contracts with TVEs, preferring to produce and export the goods themselves. The TVEs could not then fulfill their foreign trade production quotas or receive the surplus foreign exchange. Yet, when TVEs tried to evade controls, the FTCs were upset. The FTCs force TVEs to export through their offices, so they can fulfill their quotas, but TVEs prefer exporting from ports that pay the best price, no matter what province they are in. As a result, conflict emerges.

The Search for New Opportunities

As recently as 1986, many rural industries eschewed exports. According to one county official, "some people thought that it was too difficult to meet the quality demands, and the styles kept changing all the time."[49] TVE managers in Wuxi County interviewed in 1985 were uninterested in the international market, preferring to strengthen ties with state firms.[50]

By 1988, the view of county officials had changed for a number of reasons. Greater domestic competition, lower profit margins, and a scarcity of planned resources made other countries an important market for some TVE goods. Chinese refer to the risk-avoidance strategy of "walking on two markets"; when either market slows, one can shift one's focus. Similarly, during a domestic recession or period of tight credit policy, some firms may see export promotion as the only means of expanding production. Second, foreign sales offer a new strategy for improving a firm's domestic competitiveness, since firms that have earned foreign exchange can import new machinery. Between 1985 and 1988, 5,000 TVEs in nine coastal provinces and cities imported over 11,000 different pieces of machinery.[51] Such machinery increases both international and domestic competitiveness. Some TVEs use the new equipment, skills, and product lines to challenge state firms. For example, a township factory in Shunde County, Guangdong Province, controls half the national market for bicycle lights.[52] Third, foreign exchange facilitates economic development and political stability, because it allows local leaders to buy foreign goods that are scarce in China. Wujiang County's supply and marketing cooperative, which has ample foreign reserves, imported Japanese fertilizer in 1986, when a domestic shortage developed, keeping the county economy stable.

State subsidies for export production create incentives for local governments to promote export-oriented TVEs, because inputs and loans are easier to get if the plant exports. These incentives were particularly important after autumn 1988, when loans for TVEs tightened. Thus, local officials who want to expand their industrial base may shift into export-orientated production. One township official in Wuxi County saw exports from TVEs as a stabilizing force for ending the seasonal nature of labor and raising workers' skills. And, international market fluctuations were not a problem because of subsidies from the local government.[53] Some FTCs cover the risk of introducing new products in TVEs. In Shandong Province, an FTC bought Italian equipment for making blue jeans and sent it to a factory in Zouping County. If the products did not sell, however, the FTC, not the rural factory, would suffer the loss.[54] No wonder FTCs get angry if rural enterprises that begin to produce good quality products seek their own markets.

Access to foreign exchange offers many benefits. Under the fiscal responsibility system (*caizheng baogan*), local governments must turn over a fixed sum of money to their bureaucratic superiors in a form of tax farming.[55] Exports become a way to increase government income in that governments can sell the foreign exchange to meet these financial obligations. Local officials can use the foreign exchange and foreign contacts for their own benefit. Foreign guests bring gifts, new information, prestige, opportunities for banquets, and invitations to travel overseas. Foreign currency buys cigarettes and other resources useful for establishing relationships. In addition, exporting a product proves its quality, increasing the likelihood of it becoming a "brand name" (*ming pai*). Local governments can expand the posts under their control through export promotion. In Wuxi County, several townships established foreign trade offices. After 1987, some county officials set up local foreign trade companies, giving jobs to friends and allies. Even if the counties lost funds through exporting, some local governments squeezed bonuses from local banks for earning more foreign exchange.[56]

Finally, a ready market in Hong Kong and the arrival of Hong Kong businessmen who wished to base their products in China pushed TVEs into exports. Contacts built on family ties decrease the risk, unless the Hong Kong relative reneges on the deal. This fact highlights the importance of overseas Chinese in the internationalization of TVEs. Sometimes, however, domestic competitors challenge Hong Kong businessmen and try to stop them from exporting into Hong Kong. For example, when Hong Kong firms raised pigs in Guangdong Province for export to Hong Kong, domestic producers fought them for export licenses, arguing that, although the joint venture was legally a domestic firm, its interests were foreign.[57] Only MOFERT intervention at the request of the Hong Kong government settled this issue.

Regional Conflicts and Product Wars

Using test points for this policy and allowing such favored localities to enjoy these advantages over the long run has had deleterious results for interregional relations. While Guangdong and Fujian provinces were allotted special privileges in exports in the late 1970s,[58] most of the favorable opportunities came to the rest of the coastal areas much later. Thus, after the 1986–1987 foreign trade reforms, county FTCs in Guangdong, called local "tigers," used their long experience in export marketing to find exportable commodities in provinces near Guangdong.[59] The most inequitable policy allowed Special Economic Zones and parts of Guangdong more favorable foreign exchange retention rates. Shenzhen could keep 100 percent of its foreign exchange, while Guangdong Province could keep from 30 to 100 percent, depending on the product and the province's total export earnings.[60] Yet as mentioned above, Sichuan's retention rate was cut in 1988 from 25 to 21 percent.[61]

Table 11.4 shows the wide discrepancy in export volumes by TVEs in different provinces in 1987, and also suggests possible regional inequalities that may have expanded due to the internationalization of the rural economy.[62] Because of favorable policies, which earn Guangdong Province more domestic currency for the same volume of exports, Guangdong's rural foreign trade enterprises have prospered at the expense of Hunan and Guangxi provinces, which are outbid for exportable commodities produced in their own provinces. For example, Shenzhen, which kept 100 percent of its foreign exchange, could use the foreign exchange to buy domestic *RMB* at a discounted rate because of the domestic shortage of foreign exchange. With more *RMB*, it could pay higher prices for food, grain, and pigs to FTCs in Hunan and Guangxi provinces. In 1987, an FTC in a Guangxi provincial county sold exportable goods worth over US$100 million to Guangdong Province because of better prices.[63] As a result of these policies, trade between Hunan and Guangdong provinces in 1988 was up 50 percent, whereas in the first half of the year, Hunan's direct exports were the same as sales to Guangdong. With extra foreign exchange earnings, Guangdong firms can keep ahead of FTCs in Hunan and Guangxi provinces and continue to outbid them even for exportable commodities in their own provinces. The cycle continues as the inland provinces then fail to meet their foreign exchange and export quotas. And, because of sales of about US$100 million to Guangdong, Guangxi's direct exports dropped by over 20 percent in 1988. Provincial officials in the inland provinces objected both directly and indirectly. At the peak of this trade war, Hunan and Guangxi provinces erected trade barriers to interprovincial trade.

Some Western analysts have challenged the characterization of this relationship as a form of internal colonialism, in which the entrepôt, through links to the global economy, exploits the hinterland for its own benefit and that of the international market.[64] They correctly point out that Shenzhen and Guangdong provincial FTCs pay market value for these goods and help undermine the dependent relations inland provincial FTCs established over producers of exportable commodities, who are compelled to sell their goods at low, state-controlled prices. In this freer climate of competition, farmers, local governments, and local TVEs can exercise their free-market rights to seek the best price.

Yet, the partial nature of the reform allowed some foreign trade firms greater freedom to work within a market context than those in other provinces—local tigers in Guangdong no doubt work under fewer constraints than inland provinces.[65] Guangdong FTCs had more opportunities than other actors (because of their greater experience and links to the international market) and more domestic currency to pay higher prices (because of preferred treatment as well as their own business acumen). And, once the cycle—by which they bought inland products, exported them, sold the foreign exchange for more local currency, and then returned to the hinterland to buy more exportable resources—was established, only outside government intervention or efforts to disrupt the market could end it. After all, FTCs in inland provinces still had quotas to fulfill, and failure to do so no doubt harmed their incomes. Thus, the director of Hunan's Foreign Economic and Relations Trade Commission complained in 1990 that "the playing field is not level" in foreign trade.[66] And while geography already gives Guangdong Province a comparative advantage, other provinces should be given the same rights to retain foreign exchange as Guangdong. And, while one Chinese author warned against letting coastal areas exploit inland natural resources by doing processing or finishing work on the coast, his call for the coast to pass on new equipment and technology and establish new relations between coastal and inland areas did not trigger much response from the coastal areas.[67]

Conflict among Export and Nonexport Factories

Within localities, conflict could develop between export-orientated and nonexport factories and their workers. Because exporting factories get subsidies from local governments and MOFERT, and better access to resources, electricity, and loans, they may have more stable outputs and better profits than nonexporting firms. If they can sell their foreign exchange, their profits will also increase. With the improved conditions in export factories, farmers prefer to work there.

In Wujiang County, Jiangsu Province, workers recognize these differences. Workers in joint venture firms have their own uniforms. Export factories have better working conditions, and workers there have higher salaries, greater status, and feel better about their work because their products are exported. But, according to one county official, "you can't see the differences in their day-to-day behavior because some domestic-orientated TVEs, such as the shoe factory, are better factories."[68]

In some county-towns, where TVEs may sit beside state-owned plants, these differences are sometimes even more significant. State workers feel superior to TVE employees, but if TVE workers make more money or get more benefits, the state workers are unhappy. In Changzhou, Jiangsu Province, when a state firm contracted with a Canadian firm to build a joint venture, the state firm made the joint venture a TVE to increase its flexibility. However, since salaries in the TVE would be higher than in the state firm, they set up the joint venture in a separate building.[69]

In fact, the internationalization of rural industry has created a new salary gradation. At the bottom are often TVE workers who produce for the domestic market; next are employees in TVEs that produce export products; and at the top are employees in joint-venture TVEs.[70] One can only imagine how officials trade access to these opportunities to build networks or reward friends and family members.

On the other hand, a researcher familiar with Guangdong asserts that farmer-workers there do not mind that export factories pay higher salaries. "That's not a big problem. In Guangdong Province workers have tests when people hire them, so if they work well they stay on. The reforms in the rural areas were so early that farmers are used to competition and the fact that more skilled ones will do better."[71]

Rural Exports After Tiananmen

After June 4, 1989, conservative leaders in charge of the economy attacked rural enterprises as part of their broad strategy to restrengthen their own base of political support, that is, the state sector and state-owned industries. The *Decision on Improving the Economic Order,* also called the *Thirty-Nine Points,* said that TVEs that consume lots of energy, produce shoddy goods, pollute, or compete in a major way with state enterprises for material should be closed down, suspended, merged, or forced to shift to other production lines. This, of course, is not the first time that state leaders have tried to close down TVEs that compete with SOEs.[72] The *Thirty-Nine Points* also called for recentralization of the foreign trade sector. Preferential treatment for some localities would "in principle be abolished." The incentives for localities based on foreign exchange retentions were to be withdrawn, as local retention was to be cut. Loans for local economic development were also cut dramatically. Li Peng continued this line in April 1990, calling for continued cutbacks in the excessive number of local FTCs, the recentralization of foreign exchange controls, and continued rectification of TVEs to keep their development in line with "the actual requirements of state industrial policies," that is, the state plan.[73]

Nevertheless, exports from TVEs reached US$10 billion in 1989, and in 1990 rose another 25 percent, to over US$12.5 billion.[74] Thus, the attack on TVEs in general did not affect their exports. In the wake of a looming debt-burden crunch, brought on by the end of multilateral and bilateral loans, China's leaders decided to expand exports and decrease imports, making it foolhardy to undermine the fastest-growing export sector in the economy. The Coastal Development Strategy which so boosted TVE exports was reaffirmed by the general secretary, Jiang Zemin, during his trip to Fujian Province in December 1989.[75] Even Li Peng advocated continuing the open policy during his Shenzhen visit in

March 1990. Under the terms of the *Thirty-Nine Points*, TVEs could expand if they (1) produced labor-intensive exportable handicrafts; (2) served as adjuncts to SOEs, which still allowed SOEs to develop joint ventures with TVEs as a way to get land and resources; and (3) introduced more flexible labor policies.

The economic retrenchment stimulated the expansion of rural exports. In fact, in early 1990 the central government formulated eight preferential policies to encourage TVE exports.[76] Since loans became available only for export-orientated TVEs, local governments seeking to expand their local industrial base had to make their new enterprises at least appear to be export oriented. With the closing of many nonproductive TVEs, those that remained had access to more funds. Strengthening the bureaucracy's control over rural industrial exports also increased the mercantilist forces in China, a pattern of export-led growth that was successful in other parts of East Asia.

The limited impact the retrenchment has had on Guangdong Province's FTCs suggests that the extent of the retrenchment in foreign trade may be less than a reading of documents would suggest. The trade war between Guangdong and Hunan Provinces has lessened but not ended,[77] suggesting that the independent, county-level FTCs remain active in Guangdong. The continuing call for reasserting control over local trading companies shows that such control has yet to be completed, and preliminary figures suggest that, by spring 1990, only 800 of approximately 6,000 FTCs had been closed or amalgamated.[78] Second, most pressure has been on independent FTCs that import goods for resale domestically at a profit, and not on ones that compete for goods for export, which China still wants to promote. Given the stress on import substitution and export promotion, any firm that expands exports, regardless of how it does so, is likely to gain support in this climate.

Conclusion

How can the impact of the internationalization of the Chinese countryside be evaluated? Did the opening to the outside world affect the distribution of power in China? How is this policy likely to develop in the future?

Looking at its impact on state power, we find a mixed picture. Local governments initially promoted exports under state pressure and quotas imposed by the state bureaucracy. Local initiative was not the initial driving force. From Migdal's perspective, the result was a weaker state, with the growth of local bosses who manipulate national policy in their own interests.[79] Yet, Migdal's dichotomy between state and society does not apply well to China, for the key rival to central authority in the export sector is not society but local public institutions that wield the authority of the state.

Decentralizing foreign trade to the county and township has strengthened the nexus of local political and economic power by giving it new resources—foreign exchange, foreign machinery, control over external access in general—for its continuing pursuit of local power.[80] As with many other policies in China, the center faced the classic Maoist dilemma: how to give people the freedom to behave exactly as the center wants them to. While campaign techniques vitalize the localities, quotas are the state's preferred institution to ensure compliance with its guidelines.

But, once the center discovered that too little money was entering its coffers and too many independent trading firms were behaving in ways that did not promote national goals, it chose to restrict foreign trade. Through its control over licenses, the center stopped the flow of imports and prevented the drain of foreign currency, again demonstrating its ability to control the localities when it marshals its forces to do so. Yet each time it decentralizes, it leaves some power behind. Even if the foreign trade bureaucracy takes back control of the international channels of exchange from local governments, the center may find that "wealth and power" (fu qiang) come by ceding domestic power to regional and local officials. While the center may abhor this loss of power, it cannot reassert total control without giving up its current strategy of modernization. Yet in some ways this policy has created a stronger state in that economic growth has been rapid, living standards for coastal farmers have gone up, more people have left farming, and the state can still reassert its authority over the openings to the outside that it had allowed.

While the opening invigorated the coastal economy, it also brought to the surface conflicting interests that had been suppressed or dormant under the more centrally controlled system. As often happens in China, when decentralization brings new local opportunities, people's mistrust of the continuity of policy makes them grab these benefits in a massive wave, undermining the stable development of any new policy and triggering a reaction that brings the worst fears to fruition. In the case of foreign trade, the conflict between FTCs and local governments reappeared as the latter fought for control over the import-export process. The social instability that characterizes the quick search for profits, which is often followed by a few successes and many failures as actors try to follow the models propagated in the press, also characterized this process of openings.[81]

Old regional rivalries reappeared, as central policies favoring certain localities allowed these areas to work the system to their maximum benefit; other areas watched with anger as the regional gap seemed to grow. In China's egalitarian ideological context, some Chinese scholars use words such as *exploitation* to describe the terms of trade between the coastal and inland areas.[82] These social conflicts explain part of the decision to restrict local freedoms. Yet, with instability and inequality came growth and a better life for many coastal residents who competed successfully in this new economic sector.

Again, we see a part of the system under reform, but many emerging problems are due to the transition between plan and market. As a provincial foreign trade official remarked as his province's resources flowed into Guangdong, "Our basic problem is being stuck between the market and the planned economy."[83] One sympathizes with local firms that want freedom from MOFERT and its local agents, but these agents also find the transition difficult. While FTCs made many of the original international contacts that brought foreign trade to rural China, their quotas have become onerous as local firms and governments gain direct access to foreign traders and refuse to sell to the FTCs. Yet, as MOFERT and its agents fight to reassert control, they increase the probability that the transition process will become the final stage, that is, an everlasting transition, as China's reforms get stuck between an administered and a market economy, with the bureaucracy remaining powerful.[84]

Yet while party Secretary Zhao Ziyang did not see his plan for a decentralized, invigorated, and wealthy China through to the end, the rapid response of farmers and local officials to the opportunities to mesh with the international system has given meat to the bones of his vision and locked China into his strategy for modernization. Internationalizing TVEs and modernization through export promotion have created a new rural lobby which can bring prosperity to the countryside, but at the price of increased local power. As long as China remains committed to economic modernization by borrowing from the outside, Zhao's policies will be hard to replace.

Various dilemmas loom. Protectionism is expanding worldwide, as the percentage increase of world trade subsides. China is a latecomer to export-orientated development, a problem Zhao recognized when he argued that "China has in the past missed a few good chances for development, we must not miss this one. We must have a sense of urgency."[85] The free market, Atlantic vision of the world is being replaced by the Pacific Basin's more mercantilist idea of development.[86] No doubt this may be the kind of world in which China's coastal entrepreneurs will best succeed, with their state subsidies, their reliance on personal ties, and the center's effort to promote import substitution. Yet limiting TVEs to low-quality, labor-intensive goods and preventing local governments from accumulating sufficient capital for significant technical innovation, in the name of modernizing state industries, fly in the face of the product cycle theory and the pattern of Taiwan's modernization. Too much centralized control could slow the modernization of the coastal areas and the technological innovation of TVEs. In addition, internationalizing the countryside increases China's vulnerability to global trends and pressures, the cost of ending Most Favored Nation status being an excellent case in point. For a government that prides itself on its autonomy, China has moved into the realm of interdependence in which growth can only come about with the potential loss of sovereignty. Whether China's leaders are able to adapt to this global status will affect the continuing internationalization of rural China.

Notes

1. For a discussion of the impact of China's foreign trade sector on Northeast Asia, see Nicholas R. Lardy, *China's Entry into the World Economy* (Lanham, Md.: University Press of America, 1987).

2. For a discussion of how the faction tied to the oil industry pushed for the opening to the outside, see Kenneth Lieberthal and Michel Oksenberg, *Policy Making in China: Leaders, Structures and Process* (Princeton: Princeton University Press, 1989). For a discussion of how the open policy led to new coalitions, see Susan Shirk, "The Domestic Political Dimensions of China's Foreign Relations," in Samuel Kim, ed., *China and the World* (Boulder, Colo.: Westview Press, 1984), pp. 57–81. For an economic analysis of the linkage between domestic economic reform and foreign trade reform, see Nicholas R. Lardy, *Foreign Trade and Economic Reform in China* (New York: Cambridge University Press, 1992).

3. Peter Gourevitch, "The Second Image Reversed: The International Sources of Domestic Politics," *International Organisation* 32 (Autumn 1978): 881–911.

4. See Barry Naughton, "Industrial Policy During the Cultural Revolution: Military Preparation, Decentralisation, and Leaps Forward," in William A. Joseph, Christine Wong, and David Zweig, eds., *New Perspectives on the Cultural Revolution* (Cambridge: Harvard Contemporary China Series, 1991), pp. 153–182, and Barry Naughton, "The Third Front: Defense Industrialization in the Chinese Interior," *The China Quarterly*, no. 115 (1988): 351–386.

5. See Harold K. Jacobson and Michel Oksenberg, *China's Participation in the IMF, The World Bank, and GATT: Towards a Global Economic Order* (Ann Arbor: The University of Michigan Press, 1990).

6. See Andrew Watson, "Agricultural Reform and China's Foreign Trade," *Australian Journal of Chinese Affairs*, no. 14 (1985): 39–63.

7. Francis C. Tuan, "Performance of China's Agricultural Trade in the 1980s," in *CPE Agriculture Report* (March-April 1990): 2–5.

8. See *Farmer's Daily* (*Nongmin ribao*), March 15, 1988, p. 1.

9. Unless otherwise stated, TVEs include enterprises owned privately, by the village or township governments, or by the village or township that are leased to individuals.

10. By 1988, rural China had imported over 800,000 pieces of machinery reportedly used for export processing. Interview REBDHZ, April 1989.

11. Lardy, *Foreign Trade and Economic Reform in China.*

12. See chapter 10 of this book; and Christine P.W. Wong, "Interpreting Rural Industrial Growth in the Post-Mao Period," *Modern China* 14 (January 1988): 3–29.

13. Interview SNBDI, January 1989.

14. Interview DRCRWW, April 1989.

15. John Kamm, "Foreign Trade," in Ezra Vogel, ed., *One Step Ahead in China* (Cambridge: Harvard University Press, 1989), p. 362.

16. *People's Daily* (*Renmin ribao*), December 26, 1984, cited in Kamm, "Foreign Trade," pp. 384–385.

17. Interview DRCRWW, April 1989.

18. Interview in 1990 with a former member of the RCRD.

19. See "Zhao on Coastal Area's Development Strategy," *Beijing Review*, February 8–14, 1988, pp. 18–23.

20. See Wang Jian, "Pursue the Possibility and Demands of the Economic Development Strategy of Large-Scale International Circulation" (*"Zou guoji daxunhuan jingji fazhan zhanlue de kenengxing ji qi yaoqiu"*), in Rong Wenzuo and Liu Huiming, eds., *On Large-Scale International Circulation* (*Lun guoji da xunhuan*) (Beijing: Economic Daily Publication House, 1988), pp. 265–269.

21. Wang, "Pursue the Possibility," p. 168.

22. Information in this paragraph came from interview DRCRWW, April 1989.

23. For the most comprehensive study of reforms in the foreign trade sector and the debates that surrounded these decisions, see Lardy, *Foreign Trade and Economic Reform in China.*

24. Bruce Cummings, "The Political Economy of China's Turn Outward," in Samuel Kim, ed., *China and the World: New Directions in Chinese Relations* (Boulder, Colo.: Westview Press, 1989), pp. 203–236.

25. Robert Gilpin, *U.S. Power and the Multinational Corporation* (New York: Basic Books, 1975), argues that some states are able to exert more control over these outcomes than others.

26. Thelen, Marrin, Johnson, and Bridges, *China Business: Current Regulation and Practice* (New York: Thelen, Marrin, Johnson, and Bridges Law Firm), May 1988, p. 13.

27. This concept refers to the total magnitude of domestic currency subsidies provided by the center to subsidize exports. Thanks to Nicholas R. Lardy who clarified the three quotas in personal correspondence with the author, 1991.

28. According to an official in the Ministry of Agriculture, by April 1989 all TVEs could legally talk to foreign businessmen and did not need to go through FTCs. However, the decision to control exports in a planned economy meant that FTCs still had important responsibilities to pass up foreign exchange to the state and then distribute the excess foreign exchange back to the firms. Interview REBDHZ, April 1989. Guangdong factories with annual export sales of over one million U.S. dollars could get export licenses and trade directly with foreign firms. See Kamm, "Foreign Trade," p. 376.

29. Interview MHXWJ, July 1988.

30. See Madelyn C. Ross, "Changing the Foreign Trade System," *The China Business Review* (May–June 1988): 34.

31. Thelen et al., *China Business*, p. 13.

32. The dramatic rise in imports in 1985 was due in part to a central decision to use foreign exchange to import consumer durables to soak up the excess capital brought about by the drastic wage and bank loan expansions in late 1984. This was one issue for which Hu Yaobang was later criticized.

33. Interview DRCRWW, April 1989.

34. For a discussion of the problems in the transitional period see chapter 8 of this book and Jean C. Oi, "Peasant Households Between Plan and Market," *Modern China* 12 (April 1986): 230–251; Christine Wong, "Between Plan and Market: The Role of the Local Sector in Post-Mao China," *Journal of Comparative Economics*, no. 11 (1987): 385–398; and Y.Y. Kueh, "Growth Imperatives, Economic Recentralisation, and China's Open-door Policy," *The Australian Journal of Chinese Affairs*, no. 24 (1990): 93–119. Kueh argues that the plan always remained dominant.

35. For a discussion of these mobilization strategies and the generation of "policy winds," see David Zweig, *Agrarian Radicalism in China, 1968–1981* (Cambridge: Harvard University Press. 1989), pp. 38–48.

36. Here is another case in which the opening to the outside changed the task of a bureaucratic organization. Before the reform, the Foreign Exchange Management Bureau's task was simply to certify the use of foreign exchange; now, it must aggressively check that local firms turn in their share of foreign exchange. Interview MHXWJ, July 1988.

37. Hong Jingxing, Pei Ping, and Yan Qiang, *Develop the Competitive Tactics and Strategic Reflections for the Development of an Export-oriented Economy (Fazhan waixiangxing jingji de zhanlue sikao he jingzheng celue* (Changzhou: Jiangsu People's Publishing House, 1989), pp. 76–77.

38. Chinese scholars base the greater independence in Shanxi on the export of coal mined in collectively owned coal mines.

39. Kamm, "Foreign Trade," p. 360. While Western firms complain about subsidies for China's exports, domestic firms that must sell their goods to MOFERT at less than domestic costs suffer as well.

40. *Nongmin ribao,* July 8, 1987, p. 1.

41. *Nongmin ribao,* August 11, 1988, p. 1.

42. See Chen Daojin, "A Model for Rural Enterprise Exports—The Pearl River Model" (*"Waixiangxing xiangzhen qiye moshi—Zhujiang moshi"*), in Chen Jiyuan, ed., *Research on Models of Township and Village Enterprises* (*Xiangzhen qiye moshi yanjiu*) (Beijing: Chinese Academy of Social Sciences Publishers, 1989), pp. 166–196.

43. Foreign trade companies in Guangdong Province were forced as early as 1978 to disclose their selling prices to the factories from whom they were procuring equipment for export. See Kamm, "Foreign Trade," p. 357. But, in their dealings with the rural areas, FTCs tried to keep control through this mechanism.

44. *Nongmin ribao,* July 18, 1988, p. 1.

45. *Nongmin ribao,* August 26, 1988, p. 1.

46. *Nongmin ribao,* August 26, 1988, p. 1.

47. *Nongmin ribao,* July 19, 1988, p. 1.

48. *Nongmin ribao,* August 11, 1988, p. 1.

49. Interview MHXWJ, July 1988.

50. Luo Xiaopeng, "Ownership and Status Stratification," in William Byrd and Lin Qingsong, eds., *China's Rural Industry: Structure, Development and Reform* (Oxford: Oxford University Press, 1990), pp. 134–171.

51. *Nongmin ribao,* July 23, 1988, p. 1.

52. Chen, "A Model for Rural Enterprise Exports," p. 177.

53. Interview WXMCTM, January 1989.

54. Personal communication between the author and Andrew Walder, 1989.

55. For the reasons local officials support TVEs, see Jean C. Oi, "The 'State' and the Economy in Rural China: The Impact of Fiscal Reform in the 1980s," presented at the Association for Asian Studies Annual Meeting, Chicago, April 3–5, 1990.

56. For how local governments squeeze loans from banks to promote rural enterprises, see Andrew G. Walder, "A Profile of Zouping County Industry and Finance," presented at the conference on the Shandong Field Research Project at the Wingspread Center, Racine, Wis., November 1988.

57. Interview XLZIL, April 1990.

58. A 1979 ruling let Guangdong keep 70 percent of foreign exchange earned above the quota of US$1.4 billion, which was based on the 1978 level.

59. Kamm, "Foreign Trade," p. 377.

60. Rules established in 1985 gave special retention rights of 70 to 100 percent for garments, arts and crafts, light industrial goods, and others. Kamm, "Foreign Trade," p. 376.

61. *Renmin ribao,* July 19, 1988, p. 2.

62. There has been extensive debate on whether the ten years of reform and open policy expanded interprovincial or interregional inequality. For the case against expanding provincial inequalities, see David L. Denny, "Provincial Economic Differences Diminished in the Decade of Reform," in Joint Economic Committee, *China's Economic Dilemmas in the 1990s: The Problems of Reforms, Modernization, and Interdependence* (Washington: U.S. Government Printing Office, 1991), pp. 180–208. The case for expanding regional inequality is in Dali Yang, "Patterns of China's Regional Development Strategy," *The China Quarterly,* no. 122 (1990): 230–257.

63. Elizabeth Cheng, "Beggar Thy Neighbour," *Far Eastern Economic Review,* January 12, 1989, pp. 45–46.

64. Personal communications from Edward Friedman and Terry Sicular, 1990.

65. A similar situation occurred in 1986–1987, as private firms in the countryside challenged the supply and marketing cooperatives and service companies in county-

towns, because they had fewer welfare obligations to retired workers. See chapter 8 of this book.

66. Seth Faison, "Hunan-Guangdong Trade 'Border War' Continues," *South China Morning Post,* March 5, 1990, p. 11.

67. Hong, Pei, and Yan, eds., *Develop the Competitive Tactics,* p. 79. When I presented an earlier version of chapter 11 at the Sociology Institute at the Chinese Academy of Social Sciences in Beijing in July 1990, several scholars expressed concern about how the coast was exploiting the inland provinces.

68. Interview MHXWJ, July 1988.

69. Interview MEMCY, April 1989.

70. Interview CHZIBJ, July 1990.

71. Interview DRCRWW, April 1989

72. See Chapter 10 of this book.

73. "Li Peng's Government Work Report, March 20, 1990," in *Foreign Broadcast Information Service* (hereafter cited as *FBIS*) (April 6, 1990): 24.

74. "Customs Imports, Exports Figures," *Beijing Review,* January 28–February 3, 1991, 29.

75. "Party Chief on Coastal Development," *China Daily,* December 12, 1989, p. 1.

76. See *Wen wei po,* February 26, 1990, p. 1, in *FBIS* (February 27, 1990): 32–33.

77. Faison, "Hunan-Guangdong Trade," p. 11.

78. "Pay Close Attention to the Work of Rectifying Various Kinds of Foreign Trade Corporations," *International Business (Guoji shangbao)*, March 20, 1990, p. 1, cited in an unpublished paper by Nicholas R. Lardy.

79. Joel Migdal, "Strong States, Weak States: Power and Accommodation," in Samuel Huntington and Myron Weiner, ed., *Understanding Political Development* (Boston: Little, Brown and Co., 1988), pp. 391–436.

80. For an evaluation of how Maoist policies strengthened local governments, see Vivienne Shue, *The Reach of the State* (Stanford: Stanford University Press, 1988); Jean C. Oi, *State and Peasant in Contemporary China* (Berkeley: University of California Press, 1990); and Zweig, *Agrarian Radicalism.* Although Shue believes that the reforms weakened the local government's ability to protect farmers from the state, I disagree with this evaluation.

81. In 1985–1987, excessive shifts in the acreage of certain exportable crops led to overproduction and price collapses, which harmed many farmers. See *Farmers' News (Nongmin bao)*, July 8, 1987, p. 1. When a retired county official made US$350,000 carving jade, many technicians and experts in the region tried to match his success, but most went bankrupt. See *Nongmin ribao,* June 15, 1988, p. 1.

82. Comments made by a reportedly liberal professor when I presented an earlier version of this chapter at the Sociology Institute of the Chinese Academy of Sciences, July 1990.

83. Faison, "Hunan-Guangdong Trade," p. 11.

84. Here, regional variations are important as the growth of private networks in Guangdong and the shift of foreign trade authority to private traders may differ significantly from that in areas of Jiangsu Province where the local bureaucracy competes with the central one.

85. "Zhao on Coastal Areas' Development Strategy," p. 18.

86. James R. Kurth, "The Pacific Basin Versus the Atlantic Alliance: Two Paradigms of International Relations," *The Annals of the American Academy of Political and Social Sciences* (September 1989): 34–45.

12

"Developmental Communities" on China's Coast

The Impact of Trade, Investment, and Transnational Alliances

Most China observers would have predicted that China's externally oriented development strategy, especially the growth of foreign trade, private foreign investment, the reliance on international financial institutions, and an overall opening of global communications to the outside world, would weaken the redistributive and allocative power of the institutions of state socialism and undermine the strength and legitimacy of the Chinese Communist Party. This chapter addresses that assumption by looking at the impact of foreign investment and foreign trade on rural communities in coastal China. Overall, it seeks answers to the following key questions. First, what institutions have emerged linking domestic China and the international system? Who controls these institutions? How do the incentives these institutions and their linkages create influence domestic behavior? Second, have these linkages affected growth and inequality? Third, has the emergence of new transnational ties strengthened state power at the national or local level? Finally, has growth in China's foreign trade affected the relative strength of different industrial sectors, as well as national policy on industrial development?

Three general approaches offer different predictions about the expected impact of China's open policy. The dependency school would argue that socialist states can better protect their national interests as they undergo incorporation into the international capitalist system,[1] but this model would also predict that China's opening to international market forces would increase social unrest, in that, under pressure from the international financial institutions, the state would scale back its welfare functions.[2] Since authoritarianism results from concerted export promotion, an export-oriented China should continue to suppress its working class.[3] With the exception of growth in a small urban core, a shift from planning to comparative advantage could expand poverty and inequality, especially in the rural hinterland.[4] And, directing these changes might be a new alliance among international capital, the dependent state, and a new domestic class, taking China on a more "dependent development" trajectory.[5]

The literature on East Asian development would counter that openness is good for a state's economic development, while autarky retards it. But, success needs good leaders, efficient bureaucrats, and an important role for the state in the early stages of development to create comparative advantage in exportable products. Through a combination of import controls and foreign investment, China could expand by employing an export-led growth strategy.[6] However, because China lacks a capitalist class and a freer domestic market, growth might be more limited than in other, more capitalist economies.[7] In addition, without an autonomous bureaucracy, which helped East Asia avoid the nepotism and protectionism that undermined Latin America's export strategy,[8] China would be hard pressed to end the subsidies which harm competitiveness. To borrow an idea from positive political economy, continued tariffs, quotas, and government intervention in the foreign trade regime should have many negative consequences for a rent-seeking society, by creating incentives for domestic actors to pursue those rents.[9] Nevertheless, successful growth, as in Taiwan and Korea, might lead to greater democratization without expanding rural-urban inequalities.[10]

Finally, the International Political Economy (IPE) literature might have predicted that expanding foreign trade would alter China's industrial structure, as low-end products find a market niche vacated by the increasingly advanced Asian economies.[11] Greater openness might alter the power distribution among government organizations within the domestic regime and the government's policies,[12] leading to a more pluralistic society, with domestic coalitions that support foreign trade[13] and oppose protectionism[14] pushing their programs onto the national agenda.

Somewhat surprisingly the view from the grass roots both supports and challenges all three models. Unlike any other communist system, China has proven remarkably adept at following an export-led development strategy.[15] Foreign trade has grown 16 percent a year since the late 1970s, and is a key force behind China's remarkable economic boom. And despite massive amounts of foreign investment and international borrowing, China has maintained control of its domestic economic policies. Yet, that same involvement in foreign trade, which has remained primarily a coastal phenomenon, has exacerbated regional inequalities and the urban-rural gap in areas outside coastal China. Second, living standards for tens of millions of farmers have increased due to the growth of rural industries in coastal areas and their increasing involvement in international trade. Third, despite expectations to the contrary, areas of deepest foreign penetration are also the areas of highest growth and the most stable local, communist party systems.[16] Finally, the incorporation of the countryside into the international market has strengthened its industrial base, improving its ability to compete with urban state-owned factories, thereby affecting China's overall industrial structure.

As the dependency model might predict, driving this development is an alliance between local communist party officials and foreign investors. Their shared interests in expanding foreign trade and using rural joint ventures to reap large profits in China's domestic market have allowed local party officials to use their relationship with foreign investors to increase their authoritarian power over local communities. Together, they have captured and shared domestic rents that emerged due to the mixed market/plan, foreign trade system. And, by undermining the center's institutional framework for monitoring foreign investment and trade, party officials and foreign investors have weakened the central state's ability to control its own foreign trade regime. This chapter is chiefly concerned with the emergence of Communist Party–dominated, export-oriented "developmental communities," which use foreign trade and links with private investors to enrich the peasantry, strengthen Party authority, improve the industrial structure, and challenge the central state's control over China's external boundaries.[17] In addition, the increased authority of the local party/state and its bureaucratic appendages, even with internationalization, suggests that the future path of China's development may differ significantly from that of other authoritarian states, such as Taiwan and Korea, whose export-oriented path to prosperity ended in political liberalization and democratization.

Consequences of Export-Led Growth and Transnational Alliances for China

The transnational alliance between local ruling authorities and foreign investors, as well as the emergence of export-oriented developmental communities in rural coastal China, has affected China's growth, industrial structure, regional inequality, central-local relations, and local political power.

First, rural communities that have aggressively and successfully entered the international market have witnessed remarkable growth. In rural areas along China's coast, exports have brought new markets, more jobs, and new wealth. The foreign exchange earned from these exports is used to import new technologies, and this has altered the comparative advantage of township and village enterprises (TVEs), allowing them to compete more effectively with the heavily subsidized, state-owned enterprises (SOEs).[18] And, because access to technology alters China's industrial structure, strong support for global interactions has emerged among local elites, factory managers, and even some TVE workers, consolidating China's open policy.

Second, the demands of foreign partners have increased the leverage of local party officials over the industrial workforce. The result is a new, stricter management regime within rural enterprises and increased power for the local party/state over the local population. The foreign trade bureaucracy, part of the local state structure, has also expanded quickly in response to increased local demand for linkages to the outside world, increasing the number of agents for the local state government.

Third, joint ventures undermine central efforts to control the boundaries between the domestic and international economies. Under the former foreign trade regime, the central state had managed China's foreign exchange reserves, reaped tax benefits, and kept foreign producers out of China's domestic market, thereby protecting SOEs. By offering local producers channels to export directly to foreign vendors, joint ventures help domestic producers evade the state middlemen and their controls and fees. At the same time, elites in developmental communities serve as linkage agents[19] for foreign investors who want access to China's domestic market and the enormous rents available within China to those with more advanced technology, greater efficiency, and better products.[20]

Fourth, while expanded TVE exports have made the urban-rural gap in coastal China less meaningful, TVE exports and the growth of rural joint ventures have made the inland-coastal gap within rural China more salient. Preliminary data from the late 1980s show that TVE exports are a predominantly coastal phenomenon, and that the gap was growing at that time. Similarly, most rural joint ventures are in coastal regions as well. A kind of political dualism has even emerged among the two regions: while exports, joint ventures, and rural industrialization are strengthening the local state in coastal China, slower growth and the pull of the coast are leaving a power vacuum in the rural parts of internal China.

Central State Policy Towards Township and Village Enterprise Exports

After taking power, China's communist leaders adopted the Soviet strategy of centrally planned foreign trade, according to which imports were primarily to supplement insufficient domestic production. China exported only to earn the foreign exchange needed to buy those imports. Specialized foreign trade corporations under the Ministry of Foreign Trade controlled all international commerce, including the purchase of technology. To insure that domestic allocations followed the central plan and were not diverted by market scarcity, prices for exports were set by plan with a disregard for world prices. Overall, China's mix of exports did not reflect China's comparative advantage.[21]

However, initially China's communist leaders did not eschew foreign transactions. Development in the first decade depended largely on one of the biggest cases of technology transfer in world history, delivered by the Soviet Union and the Eastern bloc, and financed through Chinese exports.[22] But, as Maoist predilections towards self-reliance emerged during the Sino-Soviet split, foreign trade in the 1960s and most of the 1970s played a minimal role in China's overall economic development.

In 1978, China started to dismantle the wall Mao had built around China's economy and society. Its outward-oriented development strategy emerged in 1978, and in early 1979, China invited foreign direct investment.[23] Enclaves, called special economic zones, were opened on China's southern coast as a locus for this investment, and a new joint ventures law codified the opening. In 1984, fourteen coastal cities were opened for direct foreign investment, and in 1985, three river deltas, with over 100 million people, were opened as well. By 1991, at the time the research for this chapter was carried out, foreign trade surpassed US$134 billion, with an annual growth rate in 1985–1991 of 17.5 percent. Committed foreign investment was US$47.9 billion.[24]

China's open policy involved a shift to an export-led growth strategy, combined with vestiges of an import substitution industrialization regime. Trade was decentralized to a growing number of local trade companies, and regular currency devaluations helped export prices mirror international prices. However, China also introduced export and import licenses to control the volume and composition of trade.[25] The result was a partially reformed, mixed system,[26] which, like other late industrializers in East Asia, combines import substitution and exports to generate rapid economic growth. Thus, throughout the 1980s, many new goods and resources entered and left China, not through free and open markets, but through bureaucratically controlled channels. Many export factories interacted with foreign traders only through specialized foreign trade companies. But, to promote exports, China allowed exporting enterprises preferred access to foreign exchange, foreign technology, and domestic energy and resources, and instituted bonuses for managers of enterprises earning foreign exchange. These incentives helped trigger China's current export boom.

Export-Led Growth in Rural China: The Role of National Policy

Both national policy, which targeted the countryside for export promotion, and the rural areas' industrial structure made the countryside in coastal China one of the key actors and beneficiaries of the open policy. From 1979 to 1985, central leaders had ignored much of rural China as they opened coastal cities and zones to foreign trade.[27] Township and village enterprise exports were controlled by county and provincial foreign trade departments and companies,[28] as was the ability of TVEs to import technology with foreign exchange they themselves had earned. However, as chapter 10 describes, after the mid-1980s, rural industry became a key component of China's economy, supplanting the state sector in areas such as consumer goods, textiles, and building materials.[29] By 1991 rural industry, excluding the rural service sector, accounted for over 26.6 percent of China's industrial production. By 1991, TVEs, including their service sectors, employed 96 million workers, outstripping SOEs, which employed 60 million workers.[30]

While rural areas have been marginalized in many developing countries, China's rural coastal communities have been incorporated into the state-directed, export-led growth strategy. Why? First, as trade theory suggests, the abundance of skilled, cheap rural labor offered China a comparative advantage. But contrary to the expectations of the IPE literature, central planners, not rural or provincial elites, lobbied for expanding the countryside's role in export promotion to solve rural China's surplus labor problem.[31] In addition, SOEs were not responding to the demands of the foreign market, whereas TVEs were far more market oriented.[32] Thus, in late 1987, when former party secretary, Zhao Ziyang, enunciated his Coastal Development Strategy, the purpose of which was to help China make up for missing the high-growth stage in East Asia in the 1960s and 1970s,[33] the rural areas became a key focus of China's export-led growth strategy.[34] In 1988, the central government opened more of China's coastal rural areas to foreign investment and promised local governments and their exporting TVEs access to new technology on the same tax-free terms that SOEs were given. State regulations stressed the right of TVEs to use their retained foreign exchange for imports of technology, equipment, and raw materials, without bureaucratic interference.[35]

Initially, most leaders in industrialized rural localities resisted pressures to export; many had strong ties with SOEs, and foreign trade was risky.[36] In response, the center employed policy instruments borrowed from Maoist political campaigns to push local governments to export.[37] These national pressures and local interests led to dramatic increases in the role of TVEs in China's exports. Although TVE exports were only 4.5 percent of total exports in 1984–1985, by 1991, they comprised almost 26 percent of total exports (Table 11.2). In 1990, TVEs produced nearly 75 percent of China's exported garments. Their role in foreign direct investment has also been significant, especially in coastal China. By the end of 1991, TVEs had attracted US$5.85 billion in overseas funds, or about 12 percent of total committed foreign direct investment.[38] By 1991, there were over 7,000 rural joint ventures, about 1/4 of the joint ventures in China.

The Emergence of Developmental Communities

While national policy affects incentives and opportunities for communities to adopt developmental strategies, local factors, such as industrial structure, leadership, and location, affect local perceptions of emerging opportunities and determine how localities link with the international market. China's export drive has unleashed natural energies extant in the TVE sector. Township and village enterprises have worked primarily under market conditions, outside the formal, hierarchically planned economy imposed by the central or provincial administration. Compared to SOEs, which are tightly administered by industrial bureaus at different levels of the administrative hierarchy, TVEs confronted fewer "supralocal" bureaucratic constraints as export opportunities emerged.[39] State-owned enterprises must meet a production plan before they can redirect their commercial interactions and restructure their production in line with foreign needs. Bureaus that monitor their behavior can constrain them through control over resources, capital, and marketing channels. Thus, the level of concentration of TVEs versus SOEs within a community can affect whether or not it can respond to emerging foreign trade opportunities.

Second, strategic positions, such as location on a river or the coast, which decrease the transaction costs of exporting; or control over harbors, which serve as channels for the flow of goods inland and overseas, can increase the impact of export-led growth on a community. Harbors need service industries and links to other cities through roads and rail, which under a planned economy increases state investment.[40] It may be hypothesized that, particularly in China, where the transport sector grew so slowly until the late 1980s, the open policy's stress on global linkages has redirected a significant proportion of state infrastructure investment into areas directly related to the export economy.

That even within coastal rural China some localities opted for greater levels of global interdependence suggests that local leadership plays a critical role in determining which areas respond more rapidly to the opening. In these localities, which I label "developmental communities," entrepreneurial state officials at the village, township, and county levels recognized the potential for community growth and personal wealth in global economic linkages and, therefore, mobilized the community to seek those benefits.[41]

Drawing on both their control over TVEs and the taxes derived from them to establish what Oi calls "local state corporatism,"[42] as well as the organizational and coercive power inherent in their roles as communist party officials, leaders of developmental communities mobilize factory workers, local officials, and other members of the local bureaucratic elite for a massive shift into the foreign trade realm. In some cases, almost half of their gross national product (GNP) may go into exports. They centralize the foreign trade plan based on local, not national, interests, and dramatically promote joint ventures throughout the rural community. The leaders of developmental communities also mobilize townships to prepare their best TVEs for joint venture partnerships. Work regimens in factories, which reward productive workers and sanction laggards, are strengthened, in part to entice the foreign investor. Because they are aware that technological innovation and moving up the product cycle are critical if they are to compete with heavily subsidized SOEs, as well as with other rural communities, officials push firms to increase exports and joint venture partnerships to import new technologies. To increase exports, these local governments subsidize their key exporting TVEs, offering lower taxes, easier access to cheap loans, raw materials at lower planned prices, foreign exchange, and technology. Those township and village leaders who do not respond risk their jobs.

Township officials and TVE managers also support this export fever. Why? Technologies that can be imported only by export-oriented TVEs enhance a firm's domestic competitiveness, and, because foreigners buy them, the prestige of export products increases in the domestic market, especially if they receive special provincial or national product awards. Also, frequent domestic recessions cause TVE managers to seek alternative (export) markets. Joint ventures resolve many of these problems by creating new markets and supplying both new technology, which can be imported at low tariffs if used for exports, and much needed capital. Joint ventures allow TVEs direct access to international markets. According to one TVE manager who had established two joint ventures, "the Chinese government doesn't allow us to do business directly with the outside world, so we must find foreign partners. . . . I must have the right to send people out of China for business."[43] Joint ventures receive important tax breaks, including the right to import cars duty free.[44] Having joint ventures in their township is a status symbol for local cadres, a sign that they are progressive and that foreigners appreciate their management skills. In some localities, cadres are given quotas for establishing joint ventures. The increased opportunity for foreign travel and access to foreign exchange are additional benefits. Finally, some factories and local governments see joint ventures as a way to get access to rents that exist due to the partial nature of the foreign trade reforms.

Yet, a sharp line divides insiders and outsiders in these communities. Although, nationwide, controls on land sales and labor mobility are weakening, strictures left over from the Maoist era on exchanges of land, labor, and capital limit welfare benefits, high salaries, and public goods (such as access to schools) in these communities to members of the internal community. Whereas in a market economy, domestic workers who relocate and pay local taxes have equal rights to welfare benefits in their new community, internal migrants in China remain outsiders under law, unless they are given (or purchase, often on the black market) local residence permits. Without such permits, and most county governments do not sell them officially, local governments can expel outside workers after they serve their economic purpose. Thus, while these communities import labor from China's hinterland to perform menial work that the local community's farmer/factory workers no longer want to do, to date they do not have to fear that these outsiders will buy their way in. Building on what Shue calls the "honeycomb" nature of Chinese society, which first emerged during the Maoist era,[45] these developmental communities remain relatively impenetrable and resist pressures from outside authorities in a way that reflects international boundaries more than domestic regions.[46]

Zhangjiagang and the Making of a Developmental Community

Zhangjiagang, which is situated on the south shore of the Yangzi River, a half day upstream from Shanghai, was particularly qualified to respond to the state's call for export-led growth, because of its leadership, position in China's administrative hierarchy, geographic location, and industrial structure. First, it has a tight knit, local elite, which, based on its unity, common purpose, and control over resources, manifests the "corporate coherence" necessary for successful development.[47] Because Zhangjiagang is surrounded by other counties in southern Jiangsu which began to industrialize in the mid-1970s, its farmers and leaders have taken many risks since the early 1980s to enrich their locality. Zhangjiagang officials are known throughout southern Jiangsu as tough and crafty businessmen. Throughout the 1980s, members of the community who had left in the 1960s during hard times returned home. In the early 1980s, 1,000 people returned yearly, but after 1986, Zhangjiagang limited returnees to managers, engineers, skilled workers, and other talented people, as well as the spouses of urban residents, thereby strengthening the meritocratic nature of its bureaucracy.

Second, Zhangjiagang's administrative qualities have made it an effective export community. Zhangjiagang was formerly Shazhou County, under Suzhou Municipality. In 1986, due to the internationalization of its harbor, it was promoted within the urban hierarchical ranks to a "county-level" or third-level city. Because Zhangjiagang had been a county, there remains only one administrative level between the current city government and township leaders who directly administer the rural community and own its TVEs. Even before 1986, all township officials had been directly appointed by the county organizational bureau, which today is Zhangjiagang City's organizational bureau; therefore, township officials owe their loyalty directly to today's city leaders. Moreover, city officials often rotate posts with township leaders and go to work at the basic units, strengthening links between city and township leaders. Unlike second-level cities, such as Suzhou, which have counties or district governments between themselves and the local townships, the close links between city and township elites in third-level cities make it easier for city leaders to mobilize the populace for export-led growth.

Third, Zhangjiagang's economy depends heavily on TVEs. In 1991, almost 60 percent of the total labor force (including officials and bureaucrats) worked in TVEs, and they accounted for 87 percent of industrial firms in the region. From 1974 to 1986, over two-thirds of rural labor left agriculture, 80 percent of which moved into the expanding TVE sector (Table 10.1). But, because of its reliance on TVEs, which were not part of the formal economic plan, there has been little municipal involvement in determining its products or the direction of its trade. For various political reasons, few factories owned by Suzhou Municipality have branch plants in this area, furthering Zhangjiagang's autonomy from supraregional administrative interference. But because TVEs are critical to the local government, when the economic retrenchment of 1988–1989 dropped local GNP growth from 25 percent per annum to only 5.5 percent, and industrial employment dropped 7.6 percent, the local government grabbed the new opportunities for growth emerging in export promotion and joint venture development. From

1990 to 1991, industrial employment increased by 19.8 percent due primarily to growth in exports.

Fourth, the regional policy environment is conducive to export-led growth. Suzhou Municipality, where Zhangjiagang is located, responded more rapidly to the Coastal Developmenet Strategy than any part of Jiangsu Province, and far quicker than almost any part of China. Much of Suzhou's industrial production comes from TVEs in its surrounding counties, so what is good for TVEs is good for Suzhou's total industrial output.[48] In addition, Zhangjiagang has excellent ties to the provincial leadership. The current provincial vice governor responsible for external economic relations was the party secretary of Suzhou in 1988 and had been party boss of Zhangjiagang in the 1960s. When some provincial officials criticized Zhangjiagang for establishing too many joint ventures in 1988, he made them a provincial model for others to follow. Table 12.1 shows that Suzhou had outstripped the entire province in establishing joint ventures, and by 1992 had surpassed Nanjing (the provincial capital) in terms of total foreign direct investment.

Finally, Zhangjiagang's location on the south side of the lower reaches of the Yangzi River helped its infrastructure. The city has expanded its harbor since the mid-1980s; as of 1991, it possessed the seventh busiest container harbor in China. As the harbor for the booming cities of southern Jiangsu—Wuxi, Suzhou, and Changzhou—it has received significant provincial and central financial support.

Mobilizing for Export-led Growth

Under the prereform trade regime, Zhangjiagang had limited contact with the outside world. All exports passed through Jiangsu Province's foreign trade corporations, or those in Shanghai or Suzhou, making officials in Zhangjiagang dependent on foreign trade officials for information about export markets. As Table 12.2 (page 311) shows, the role of exports in the locality's economic development was not significant through the mid-1980s.

Zhangjiagang officials feared global interdependence. As of 1987, when foreign trade first expanded, 90 percent of local leaders feared the international market.[49] Several TVEs had been cheated by Hong Kong businessmen, and in 1988, a sudden shift away from Chinese sources by American purchasers of latex gloves caught Zhangjiagang with containers full of unmarketable products.[50] Thereafter, they diversified, and by 1991, only 10 percent of local officials disliked foreign direct investment.

The domestic climate for export promotion changed in summer 1988. Party meetings in Suzhou empowered localities to approve foreign investment projects of less than US$15 million without higher level approval. Subsequently, Zhangjiagang's first economic meeting in January of each year no longer focused on agricultural development; instead, the January meeting's main goal was

Table 12.1

Direct Foreign Investment in Jiangsu Province, 1988–1993

Location	Joint Ventures and Foreign-Funded Enterprises[a]				Contracted Foreign Direct Investment (US$ millions)[b]			
	1988*	1991[†]	1992	1993[‡]	1988*	1991[#]	1992	1993[¶]
Nanjing	29	146[b]	865[‡]	1,340	173.0[c]	113.06	732.5[‡]	316.98
Wuxi	22	109	—	1,301	18.6	59.75	—	476.31
Suzhou	100	313	2,893[§]	2,532	65.8	95.99	835.87[§]	1,508.74
Changzhou	26	92	—	810	9.1	23.15	—	119.91
Nantong	21	68[b]	585[‡]	1,151	18.4	41.74	306.42[‡]	140.74
Xuzhou	8	22	—	421	4.7	11.24	—	37.28
Lianyungang	9	24[b]	237[‡]	386	4.0	6.82	293.24[‡]	64.88
Huaiyin	1	12	—	219	0.4	2.98	—	21.44
Yancheng	6	33	—	508	2.3	14.85	—	28.29
Yangzhou	13	60	—	731	5.8	16.87	—	152.08
Zhenjiang	12	33	—	560	7.9	18.22	—	133.60
Jiangsu Province	0	4	—	76	NA	70.31	—	7,055.60[c]
Total	247	916[b]	7,856[‡]	10,032	310.0	474.98[b]	7,161.96[‡]	10,055.90

Sources: Data for 1988 (*) are from Richard Pomfret, *Equity Joint Ventures in Jiangsu Province* (Hong Kong: Longman Professional Intelligence Reports, 1989), p. 11; ([†]) data for September 1991 from an interview, Jiangsu Commission on Foreign Economic Relations and Trade, 1992; ([‡])data from *Almanac of China's Foreign Economic Relations and Trade, 1993/1994*, pp. 287–289, 292, 295; ([§])data from *Suzhou Statistical Yearbook, 1993*, p. 240; ([¶])data from *Jiangsu Statistical Yearbook* (*Jiangsu tongji nianjian, 1994*), pp. 225, 321–323; ([#]) data from *Jiangsu tongji nianjian, 1992*, p. 270.

Notes:

[a]Included are both equity and cooperative joint ventures.

[b]According to the *Almanac of China's Foreign Economic Relations and Trade, 1992/1993*, pp. 316, 319, 321, and 324, all of Jiangsu Province ended 1991 with 1,138 projects, valued at US$737.02 million. Nanjing finished the year with 167 projects; Lianyungang with 20 foreign direct investment projects and 7 more "other foreign investment" projects; and Nantong with 86 projects. These results differ from *Jiangsu tongji nianjian, 1992*, p. 270.

[c]The figure for Nanjing foreign direct investment projects probably includes foreign loans that I excluded from all my data. The same is probably true for FDI for Jiangsu Province in 1993.

to promote export-led growth. Between 1989 and 1991, this meeting distributed 200,000 *RMB* to those TVEs that earned the most foreign exchange. In 1990, Zhangjiagang's foreign trade bureau gave firms earning over US$10 million from exports 2 million *RMB* in subsidies for electricity, and supplied cotton and silk at the low planned price. In 1989, township leaders who met their quotas for exports and joint ventures were awarded 1,500 to 2,000 *RMB*, ten months salary for an average TVE worker,[51] while those who failed to meet these quotas were to be passed over for promotions. The number of joint ventures in Zhangjiagang

Table 12.2

The Role of Exports in the Zhangjiagang Economy, 1978–1992

Year	Value of Exports (millions *RMB*)	GNP[a] (millions RMB)	Exports as % of GNP	TVE Industrial Labor Force (1,000s)
1978	18.12	324.43	5.5	94.4
1979	23.53	350.84	6.7	87.3
1980	35.22	432.43	8.1	106.3
1981	46.53	454.42	10.2	116.8
1982	49.41	517.66	9.5	123.2
1983	40.57	611.91	6.6	139.0
1984	59.98	890.02	6.7	168.4
1985	71.79	1,281.46	5.6	187.2
1986	125.18	1,436.75	8.7	189.1
1987	283.92	1,770.18	16.0	189.4
1988	504.70[b]	2,262.28	22.3	183.7
1989	637.43[c]	2,385.60	26.7	169.8
1990	920.63[d]	2,782.07	33.1	167.6
1991	1,181.20[e]	3,200.10	34.9	200.6
1992	3,705.00	6,317.02	58.7	N.A.

Sources: Data for 1978–1991 supplied by Zhangjiagang Statistical Bureau, 1991 and 1992; and for 1992 from *Suzhou Statistical Yearbook, 1993,* pp. 47 and 238. Thanks to Bruce Jacobs who supplied me with a copy of this yearbook.

Notes:

[a]Data in various provincial (Jiangsu) and municipal yearbooks presents GNP in current *RMB*.

[b]According to the *1989 Suzhou Statistical Yearbook,* Zhangjiagang's exports in 1988 in "planned prices" (*jihua jia*) were 479.42 million *RMB*, while its reported GNP matches data supplied locally. If we use the *1989 Yearbook* data, the figure for exports as a percentage of GNP for 1988 is 21.2 percent.

[c]According to the *1990 Suzhou Statistical Yearbook,* export sales in Zhangjiagang for 1989 were 709.86 million *RMB*, which would make 1989 exports as a percentage of GNP 29.7 percent.

[d]According to the *Jiangsu Statistical Yearbook, 1991,* p. 445, 1990 export purchases in Zhangjiagang at *planned prices* were 793.28 million *RMB*, 14 percent less than reported by the local Statistical Bureau in October 1991. Using that figure, exports as a percentage of GNP dropped in 1990 to 24.7 percent. Based on other data received in Zhangjiagang, and the big push in 1990 to promote exports, I question the *Jiangsu Statistical Yearbook* data.

[e]According to the *Suzhou Statistical Yearbook, 1993,* Zhangjiagang's export purchases for 1991 were 1,049.6 million *RMB*, or 11.2 percent lower. Using this data, the figure for exports as a percentage of GNP was 32.8 percent.

increased dramatically. From only two in 1987, Zhangjiagang established twenty-nine in 1988, nineteen in 1989, sixteen in 1990, and forty-eight through October 1991. By mid-1992 more than 300 joint venture contracts had been signed, more than any other county in China.

Although labor-intensive products are the TVEs' comparative advantage, Zhangjiagang officials believe that higher value-added products bring prosperity even faster. As TVEs move up the technology ladder, and their need for labor decreases, officials look to the day when they send back the "guest workers" who currently build the roads and perform menial labor. As officials expel outsiders, only the local population will share the spoils of economic development. No doubt, if labor-intensive exports shift inland, the hinterland will also benefit. But, in the words of one official, "We want to be the Second World; internal China can be the Third World."

The Impact of Export-Led Growth on Zhangjiagang

As Zhangjiagang's links to the outside world deepened, significant changes followed. Exports became the engine of local growth. Whereas in 1986, exports were only 8.7 percent of GNP, by 1990, they had jumped to 33.1 percent. According to local data, by 1992, one out of every two *RMB* produced in Zhangjiagang was exported, for an annual growth rate from 1984 to 1992 of 58.1 percent (Table 12.2).[52] Given that in 1984–1992, GNP increased yearly by 24.3 percent, exports were clearly promoting local economic growth.

Exports and joint ventures strengthened the power of the local state over society. Some local party bosses used joint ventures and the challenges of international competition to tighten workforce discipline. By attributing the tougher rules to the foreign partner, one township party secretary stopped rural industrial workers from resisting his new, harsher work regimen. The emergence of the export economy allowed Communist Party secretaries the legal right to intervene in management and meet directly with foreigners in their role as chairman of the board of the township economic committee. Moreover, some managers in these joint ventures are members of the township management committee. Rather than emerging as an autonomous force undermining party control, they are reinforcing the ruling power hierarchy.[53]

Export growth has expanded the local state bureaucracy involved in trade. The city's foreign trade company, an agent of the provincial Foreign Economic Relations and Trade Bureau, was set up in 1987 with 74 employees. It purchases goods in Zhangjiagang for the provincial foreign trade companies, which must meet the provincial foreign trade plan. In 1989, the city's foreign trade company began seeking unfilled export contracts allocated to other regions in China. As a result, the number of sales agents in the city company doubled to 144 (Table 12.3).

In 1988, Zhangjiagang also established a "local" foreign trade company with twenty-two employees, the main purpose of which was to find export contracts outside Jiangsu Province and Shanghai for Zhangjiagang factories. Sales representatives from this local foreign trade company travelled all over China looking for export quota, particularly in textiles, that was not being used. Only by buying this quota could they expand exports. Whereas in 1988 they purchased 22 million

Table 12.3

Growth of Foreign Affairs and Trade Bureaucracy, Zhangjiagang, 1985–1991

Department	1985	1986	1987	1988	1989	1990	1991
China International Travel Service	—	—	17 EST	17	17	17	17
Foreign Affairs Bureau	EST	3–4	4	4	7	7	7
City Foreign Trade Company	—	—	74	(91)	(108)	(125)	144
Foreign Economic Relations Department	—	EST	(7)	(14)	21	27	32
Local Foreign Trade Company	—	—		22 EST	41	53	64
Total	—	—	81	127	170	205	240
Increase over previous year	—	—	—	37%	26%	17%	15%

Source: Interviews by the author in Zhangjiagang, 1991.

Note: Numbers in parentheses are the best guess of the number of positions based on a perfectly average percentage increase in years when the information was not available.

EST, indicates the year the organization was established.

RMB of exported commodities, in 1989 they bought 36 million, in 1990 they bought 89 million, and for 1991 their projection was 150 million *RMB.*

Numerous functional bureaucracies, not initially established to promote trade and investment, caught the joint venture fever. After the former director of the Township and Village Enterprise Bureau became head of the Foreign Affairs Office, the office no longer kept foreigners at bay, but it aggressively sought their investments. The Taiwan Office, formerly involved in political struggles with Taiwan, now began to promote Taiwanese investment. Similarly, the local branch of the China Travel Service became a trade promotion organization.

The internationalization of the harbor in 1982 led to a major inflow of state investment. As an international port under the administration of the Ministry of Transportation, its amenities for local citizens improved significantly. By 1991, the central government had spent over 100 million *RMB* in the harbor area. According to the director of the Harbor Commission, the state built a middle school especially for the harbor, whose materials, facilities, and teachers were all better than other schools in this area. They built a new hospital for the sailors, directed by the best doctor in the region, and people from all over Zhangjiagang went for operations there.[54]

The harbor brought 4,000 new jobs to the region, many of which went to farmers from nearby villages. High school graduates in the county seat also got jobs here. Plans were to turn the former small, rural community of 12,000 people into a thriving harbor city of 200,000 with a "bonded" duty-free zone full of new factories funded by units from all over China seeking cheap land, low local taxes, and other exemptions available in a bonded zone. A four-lane highway was built from the harbor to the county seat to facilitate communications, and a new highway linked Zhangjiagang to Suzhou, replacing a narrow, winding rural road.

Foreign trade and foreign investment have increased the level of technology in Zhangjiagang's factories. One township, whose exports grew from 1.38 million *RMB* in 1987 to over 137 million *RMB* by 1990, imported 30 to 40 million *RMB* of equipment in both 1989 and 1990, and 64 million *RMB* in 1991. Zhangjiagang imported equipment for a small steel plant and received export quota for steel in 1991 worth US$8 million, a major accomplishment for a rural community. Joint ventures were bringing in more medium-level technology, while in 1991, local meetings promoted a high level of technology in the TVE sector.

The shift to export production was popular because it expanded and stabilized the TVE sector. However, attitudes did vary based on a person's position in the division of labor.[55] The sales director for a joint venture knew that strict management and better products strengthened his market position; and, since he worked on commission, increased sales meant more money in his pocket. He also favored domestic sales by joint ventures—a policy which threatened the domestic monopoly of SOEs—because the foreign manager promised him a new motorcycle if his sales department reached its quota. A technician in another factory reported that, under the old system, his factory could not produce high-quality goods, and salaries, therefore, were unstable. Clear lines of authority under the new management system eased his work. For most managers, the salary increases that come with directing a joint venture are strong incentives. However, one Chinese co-manager of a joint venture complained that the township Communist Party committee, which he referred to as his "boss" (*laoban*), took most of the high salary he received from his foreign partner.

Although a worker in an export factory admitted that it had taken him two years to adjust to stricter management, he applauded these innovations because they had ensured factory jobs for himself and his wife, and had increased his monthly salary from seventy to eighty *RMB* in 1988 to almost 300 *RMB* in 1991. On the other hand, in one village which planned to turn all four of its TVEs into joint ventures, party leaders did not want workers who feared the stricter regimen to withdraw from the new joint ventures. Therefore, workers in the first TVE that became a joint venture were not allowed to change jobs even though the new management system was much tougher. A dissatisfied worker admitted that, despite his anger at having his salary cut even as his workload increased, he could do nothing; all jobs in the village were controlled by the party secretary, and he could not work elsewhere.

Export-led growth affected relations between Zhangjiagang and more distant communities. Guest workers from northern Jiangsu live on boats along the northern coast of the community and reclaim river beds for Zhangjiagang farmers to plant. In export factories, cheap laborers from Anhui, Sichuan, and Jiangxi prov-

Table 12.4

Per Capita Exports for Zhangjiagang and Nantong Municipality, 1984–1992

Year	Zhangjiagang[a]	Nantong Municipality[b]	Zhangjiagang Per Capita Exports as a Percent of Nantong Per Capita Exports
1984	79.34	105.42	75
1985	94.46	120.27	78
1986	162.99	146.82	110
1987	364.48	178.11	204
1988	639.67	216.62	295
1989	796.79	220.98	360
1990	1,135.45	259.88	439
1991	1,399.29	393.75	356
1992	4,389.09[c]	977.86	448

Sources:

[a]Calculated from data supplied in Zhangjiagang by the Zhangjiagang Statistical Bureau, 1991, 1992.

[b]Calculated from data supplied by the Nantong Office of Foreign Affairs, from the Nantong Statistical Bureau, 1992.

[c]Calculated from data from the *Suzhou Statistical Yearbook, 1993* (*Suzhou tongji nianjian, 1993*), p. 238.

inces live in dormitories and work for the local community. Income gaps between these outsiders and community insiders living in two- and three-story homes remain points of tension.

Income disparities within the province have grown as well. If one compares exports in Zhangjiagang with those in Nantong Municipality, or those of its main county, Nantong County, situated on the north side of the Yangzi River directly across from Zhangjiagang, the pace of growth, while strong, has been dwarfed by the growth in Zhangjiagang. In 1984, Zhangjiagang was exporting only 7.6 percent of the value of goods of Nantong Municipality; by 1990 Zhangjiagang was exporting over 45 percent of the value of goods exported by its much larger competitor across the river. Similarly, while per capita exports may be a better measure, given that Nantong Municipality is six times more populated than Zhangjiagang, a comparison of per capita exports shows the same pattern (Table 12.4). While in 1984 per capita exports from Zhangjiagang were 75 percent of those in Nantong Municipality, by 1988, they were three times those of Nantong and by 1990, 4.4 times greater. The problem was not that exports from Nantong had slowed. From 1984 to 1991, annual growth in foreign trade for Nantong Municipality was 21.5 percent; however, for Zhangjiagang, it was an amazing 58.1 percent.[56] Nantong's GNP, however, was less closely integrated into the international market. Even after it was named an "open" coastal city in 1985, Nantong's exports as a percentage of GNP remained approximately 15 percent; only in 1991 did that figure increase to 21 percent.

Similarly, while Nantong County's exports jumped in 1984, and boomed again in 1988, the pace of growth, although impressive, has been dwarfed by the pace of change in Zhangjiagang. While annual growth in exports in Nantong County from 1984 to 1991 was 24.6 percent and from 1988 to 1991 was 28.9 percent, in Zhangjiagang, annual growth in exports from 1984 to 1991 was 45 percent, whereas from 1988 to 1991, it was 23.7 percent.

Joint Ventures, Rent Seeking, and the Alliance with Foreign Capital

Because channels to the international system are critical for community development, Zhangjiagang has become a "linkage community" through which foreigners gain access to China's domestic market on more favorable terms than the central state would prefer.[57] According to national policy, joint ventures get special tax privileges (three years tax free, followed by two years at half taxes) only if they export 70 percent of production. However, of eleven joint ventures visited in Zhangjiagang, five offered foreign partners the chance to sell 50 percent or more of their products domestically. And, when challenged about the joint venture law, some local factory managers suggested they would find ways around it, insuring the joint venture both tax breaks and access to the domestic market.

Zhangjiagang officials are chasing two types of rents. The first is the rent that the provincial foreign trade company earns through its monopsony on foreign trade. The second involves selling joint venture products which are in high demand in the domestic economy but whose imports are restricted by tariff barriers. Producers of these goods earn large profits because the limited domestic competition, due to import constraints, inflates the prices of these goods in the Chinese market.

Rent Seeking in the Export Sector

Despite the decentralization of central controls over foreign trade, most TVEs must export through state-run foreign trade companies, which keep TVEs in the dark as to the international price of their product.[58] The rent the foreign trade company earns is the difference between the domestic price, which they may force down, and the international price, to which only they have access due to the limited market in export licenses.[59]

Local elites in Zhangjiagang try to bypass the foreign trade companies by establishing direct export channels through joint ventures. Some are simply nominal joint ventures. In the case of one joint venture with overseas Chinese from the United States, the foreign partner played no role. He was a front for the joint venture, for which service he received a salary; however, this joint venture allowed the Chinese director to export through his own contacts. In another case,

Figure 12.1 **Rent Capturing Opportunities in Chinese Foreign Trade System**

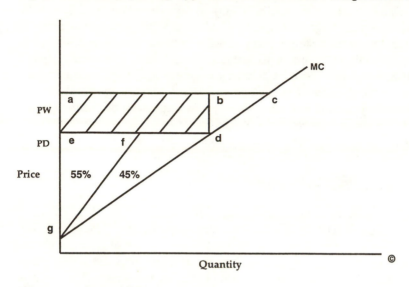

PD	=	Domestic Price
PW	=	World Price
abd	=	Profits collected by **FTC** when **TVE** produces **d**; profits transferred to JV when **TVE** forms JV. In <u>worst case</u> all could be transferred to foreign partner.
bcd	=	Loss to society because **TVE** does not produce at **c** when FTC takes **abde**
gef	=	Tax taken by state from **TVE**; can be recaptured by **TVE** through forming a JV.

© Ed Tower and David Zweig

a foreign businesswoman was invited to set up a joint venture with a tablecloth factory. The Chinese partner admitted that they wanted to circumvent the foreign trade corporation's controls, believing that their own prices were more competitive than those offered for their products by the trading company.

According to Figure 12.1, the rent earned by the foreign trade company—assuming of course that the world price (PW) is above the domestic price (PD)—is represented by the rectangle ABDE.[60] The enterprise produces at point D rather than C, because the domestic price, PD, is below the world price, PW. Therefore, by taking the rent, the foreign trade company leads to the creation of less social welfare, triangle BDC. The state also takes 55 percent of the profits as tax, triangle EFG.

The advantages to the TVE of the joint venture and the loss incurred by the central state are evident. First, because it now receives the world price, PW, the TVE produces at C on the marginal costs curve and shares ACDE with its joint venture partner. In addition, because of the tax break given to joint ventures, the TVE, which previously only got 45% (DFG), now keeps the tax triangle of 55% (EFG), which it previously gave to the central state. While in the short term the enterprise and the foreign partner share whatever rent the foreign trade company was taking, the big loser due to the establishment of the joint venture is the central state, which loses both the foreign exchange the foreign trade company would have earned and the 55 percent tax owed to it, because joint ventures pay no tax for three years and half tax for two years. Depending on the division of profits, the foreign partner could get 50 percent of ACG, while before the joint venture was established, more than half of the factory's production (EDG) was going to various bureaus in the Chinese state administration.

Rent Seeking in the Domestic Market

A second form of rent seeking occurs because of the mixed market/plan nature of the foreign trade system. In its efforts to limit imports, the Chinese state has imposed tariffs or import licenses to prevent the importation of producer goods, such as high conductivity copper wire, valves, or similar products which are in high demand as China tries to produce export-quality machinery. The result is scarcity in the domestic market, making the domestic price higher than the international price.[61] But, the central government's desire for foreign direct investment creates channels for foreigners and TVEs to access these rents. With foreign technology and foreign management, workers in TVE joint ventures can produce high-quality products. And, while production costs may be too high for the international market, import restrictions make the quality and price of these goods so competitive in the domestic market that some Chinese believe that, even if they export 70 percent of their production at a loss, they can still make a profit by selling 30 percent of their product domestically.

This rent seeking is part of Zhangjiagang's overall development strategy, for while trade restrictions prevent other regions of China from importing these products, joint ventures let Zhangjiagang make these high profits. According to one joint venture Chinese manager:

> Next year we will begin to sell about 20–30 percent of our product domestically. The foreign partner raised this and we agreed. If we sell domestically, Chinese factories will know that their domestic costs are too high. When we began this business, we saw from our own firm's perspective there was a domestic market, so we decided to import to do the domestic market. . . . The state gets burned but it is good for our firm.[62]

Domestic Impact of Trade and Foreign Investment

Our three models addressed several core issues and generated competing hypotheses about them. Focusing on the forces favoring collective action, the IPE literature suggests that foreign trade, with its diverse impact on industrial sectors, will generate domestic alliances that lobby for preferred policy outcomes. Our study, however, shows that, at the macro-level, this collective action did not occur. The state had to mobilize the rural areas, even though their labor surplus gave them an important comparative advantage in foreign trade. Why? First, when markets are comprised of many small producers, those firms are ill equipped to promote their collective interests.[63] Individual costs are too high, and in the case of China farmers are poorly represented in Beijing by one weak functional ministry, the Ministry of Agriculture, that confronts dozens of well-placed functional and line ministries lobbying for urban and industrial interests. However, once the state changed the countryside's incentive structure, allowing them access to foreign exchange and technology, rural leaders responded to these new international opportunities.

Community leaders then displayed the capacity for collective action, including forming an alliance with foreign capital, as they sought to promote community interests. Perhaps the rents themselves, and the high costs of market entry, galvanized this collective behavior;[64] thus, only the combined efforts of the county government; its trading companies, which must find foreign investors, export quotas, domestic markets, and foreign technology; and local enterprises controlled by township officials could generate the products, relationships, administrative protection, and information necessary to access the rents and implement successfully local export-led growth. While the IPE literature asserts that private firms or the central state are the critical actors in successful development, intermediate levels below the central or provincial administration and above the firm, such as the community, may provide an equally, if not more, useful subject of analysis for understanding how foreign trade generates collective action and how a large state successfully employs an export-led growth strategy. These communities may be China's autonomous centers of economic power that suppress social demand, increase savings, and promote growth.[65] Thus, late developers need not rely solely on the central state or greater centralization of resources to grow and compete in foreign trade; export-led growth combined with decentralization may propel local communities, which control their own enterprises, to promote their own interests and, in turn, increase national wealth. Despite Migdal's concerns, local "bosses" may not be counterproductive to economic development;[66] in fact, given the right incentives and organizational skills, local governments can be the driving force for export-led growth.

Second, totally different hypotheses about the impact of foreign trade and investment on growth and equality emerge from the dependency and East Asian models; the former predicted rural poverty and urban-rural inequality, while the latter predicted growth and perhaps greater equality. Our case shows that foreign trade can be of enormous benefit to rural areas, particularly those possessing a basic industrial structure or the capability of building one. Nonindustrial hinterlands simply ship out their resources, but an industrialized countryside passes the value-added onto the community (and its leaders); with this comes the possibility of technologically improving the locality's industrial structure. In this way, the alliance with foreign capital strengthens the countryside in its battle with urban workers and increases urban-rural equality.

Nevertheless, foreign trade and foreign investment can exacerbate regional inequalities. Spatial factors or endowments, such as good harbors or proximity to industrialized neighbors, which bring only limited financial benefits under a policy of economic autarky, become enormously valuable under export-led growth. In addition, the pattern by which new foreign resources, technology, foreign investment, and information enter the country affects development and equality, especially if the state first allocates these resources to certain sectors or localities.[67] The granting of legal exemptions from restrictive domestic laws, such as tax breaks or subsidized cheap land prices for joint ventures, to special localities, for example, special economic zones or development zones, endows these localities with enormous powers of attraction, making them not only the locus of foreign investment but also the end point of investment by domestic enterprises seeking tax relief.[68] Imbued with all these benefits, as well as family networks to overseas investors,[69] the coastal areas in China are far better situated for export-led growth than inland China.

But, whether local economies in China's rural hinterland are growing more slowly or are regressing is crucial information. As Hirschman's tunnel metaphor suggests, people will tolerate being in a slower lane, but their situation becomes intolerable if the lane stops.[70] Most data suggest that inland areas are growing, but more slowly, and if estimates of the 60 to 100 million people in China's floating population are correct, their remittances may be an important source of investment for the rural hinterland. No doubt, this migrant labor creates a cash nexus between inland and coastal communities that allows coastal communities to reap the benefits of cheap labor. As controllers of export channels, they also benefit from the new imported technology that produces higher value-added goods. However, internal regions of a country can also be opened. The current phase of China's open policy, that is, the expansion of roads and harbors up and down the Yangzi River, which runs through the heartland of China much like the Mississippi and Ohio rivers in the United States, should decrease the transaction costs of foreign trade for several hundred million people. They, too, may benefit from export-led growth. But, even if only the coastal areas grow dramatically, we are still talking about export-led growth improving the lives of another 200 to 300 million people in East Asia, more than the population of Indonesia and perhaps double the population of Japan.

Finally, what is the relationship between foreign trade and foreign investment and democracy? Both the IPE literature and the East Asian model suggest that foreign trade and growth can generate political liberalization, whereas the dependency model sees bureaucratic authoritarianism as a part of export-led growth. In the Chinese case, both processes may be at work, albeit at different levels. While foreign investment may strengthen village or community authoritarianism, these strengthened communities become more powerful vis-à-vis the central state's own institutions.

Thus, while farmers' autonomy from the local party/state expanded under China's decollectivization, the export economy strengthens local party control over rural society. Moreover, few foreign investors are demanding increased rural democracy. Nor has industrialization triggered the growth of a private sector demanding greater pluralism. In 1989–1990, local governments responded to central demands to constrain the growth of TVEs by closing private firms and protecting local state-owned ones.[71] Our findings, too, show that local controls over the inflow of new resources and the outflow of new products insure that most new opportunities created by the open policy are captured by the local state, not the private sector. Thus, it is no surprise to find that efforts by the Ministry of Civil Affairs in China to introduce democratic procedures in the countryside confront stiffest opposition from wealthy, industrialized rural communities in coastal China.[72]

And, even though developmental communities, with their economic power and international alliances, are undermining the central state's authority and its ability to mediate between the domestic and global economies,[73] the weakening of the central state does not necessarily create democracy. The strengthening of local community power creates a weaker center, struggling with increasingly ineffective tools to reign in powerful, local party/state institutions, which now draw more of their influence from global ties. No doubt, the lessons that implementing an export-led strategy has taught China's rural elites about collective action may generate a more vocal and demanding populace, as the IPE literature would predict. Perhaps the populace will be a driving force for institutionalizing local representation at the center. But, as long as formal access to central decision-making channels remains closed to subnational elites, developmental communities will pursue their interests in more parochial and economic ways, making the center increasingly superfluous.

Notes

1. Fernando H. Cardoso and Enzo Faletto, *Dependency and Development in Latin America* (Berkeley: University of California Press, 1978).

2. See Norman Girvan, "Swallowing the IMF Medicine in the Seventies," in Charles K. Wilber, ed., *The Political Economy of Development and Underdevelopment*, 3d ed. (New York: Random House, 1983), pp. 169–181.

3. Thomas E. Skidmore, "Politics and Economic Policy Making in Authoritarian Brazil, 1937–1971," in Alfred Stepan, ed., *Authoritarian Brazil: Origins, Policies, and Future* (New Haven: Yale University Press, 1973), pp. 24–25.

4. See Andre Gunder Frank, "The Development of Underdevelopment," *Monthly Review* 18 (September 1966): 17–31.

5. Peter Evans, *Dependent Development: The Alliance of Multinational, State, and Local Capital in Brazil* (Princeton: Princeton University Press, 1979).

6. These are the arguments of Alice Amsden, *Asia's Next Giant: South Korea and*

Late Industrialization (New York: Oxford University Press, 1989); Robert Wade, *Governing the Market: Economic Theory and the Role of Government in East Asian Industrialization* (Princeton: Princeton University Press, 1990); and Chalmers Johnson, *MITI and the Japanese Miracle* (Stanford: Stanford University Press, 1982).

7. For the argument that growth depends on the private sector, see Ziya Onis, "The Logic of the Developmental State," *Comparative Politics* 24 (October 1991): 109–126.

8. Stephan Haggard, *Pathways from the Periphery* (Ithaca: Cornell University Press, 1990).

9. Defined as "payments to owners of resources above what value would be in a market situation," rents are excess profits generated in a nonmarket situation, because administrative controls prevent market entry by numerous firms whose competition would otherwise force down the price of the good. See Anne O. Krueger, "The Political Economy of the Rent-Seeking Society," *American Economic Review,* vol. 64 (June 1974): 291–303.

10. Speare sees improvement in both rural and urban areas, although the countryside still lags behind the cities. Alden Speare, Jr., "Taiwan's Rural Populace: Brought In or Left Out of the Economic Miracle," in Denis Fred Simon and Michael Y.M. Kau, eds., *Taiwan: Beyond the Economic Miracle* (Armonk, N.Y.: M. E. Sharpe, 1992), pp. 211–33.

11. For the impact of external forces on economic structural change, see articles by Miles Kahler, Peter Evans, and John Waterbury, in Stephan Haggard and Robert R. Kaufman, eds., *The Politics of Economic Adjustment* (Princeton: Princeton University Press, 1993). The seminal works on this are James R. Kurth, "The Political Consequences of the Product Cycle: Industrial History and Political Outcomes," *International Organization* 33 (Winter 1979): 1–34; and Raymond Vernon, *Sovereignty at Bay* (New York: Basic Books, 1971).

12. Peter Gourevitch, "The Second Image Reversed: The International Sources of Domestic Politics," *International Organization* 32 (Autumn 1978): 881–911.

13. Ronald Rogowski, *Commerce and Coalitions: How Trade Affects Domestic Political Alignments* (Princeton: Princeton University Press, 1989).

14. Helen. V. Milner, *Resisting Protectionism: Global Industries and the Politics of International Trade* (Princeton: Princeton University Press, 1988).

15. The most ardent advocate of this perspective is Yun-Wing Sung, "Explaining China's Export Drive: The Only Success Among Command Economies," Hong Kong Institute of Asia-Pacific Studies, Occasional Paper No. 5, May 1991. While Sung attributed China's success to the role Hong Kong played, similar successes in central coastal China, such as in the provinces of Zhejiang and Jiangsu, suggest that something intrinsic to China and more generic than Hong Kong participation must form part of a more complete explanation.

16. This finding mirrors the argument of Peter Evans, "Transnational Linkages and the Economic Role of the State: An Analysis of Developing and Industrialized Nations in the Post-World War II Period," in Peter B. Evans, Dietrich Rueschemeyer, and Theda Skocpol, eds., *Bringing the State Back In* (New York: Cambridge University Press, 1990), pp. 192–226.

17. I borrow the concept "developmental community" from Chalmers Johnson, who first characterized Japan as a "developmental state." See Johnson, *MITI and the Japanese Miracle,* p. 10.

18. Townships are the current name for the former people's communes established in 1958 during the Great Leap Forward, whereas in today's parlance, villages refer primarily to multivillage units, the former Maoist production brigades. For an analysis of these enterprises, see William A. Byrd and Lin Qingsong, eds., *China's Rural Industry: Structure, Development, and Reform* (Oxford: Oxford University Press, 1990). Despite central

state efforts since the early 1960s to suppress TVEs, they have flourished. See chapter 10 of this book.

19. The classic study on modes or "linkages" between the external and internal world is Karl Deutsch, "External Influences on the Internal Behavior of States," in Barry R. Farrell, ed., *Approaches to Comparative and International Politics* (Evanston, Ill.: Northwestern University Press, 1966), pp. 5–26. For a more contemporary analysis, see Barbara Stallings, "International Influence on Economic Policy: Debt, Stabilization, and Structural Reform," in Haggard and Kaufman, eds., *The Politics of Economic Adjustment,* pp. 41–88.

20. Using foreign technology, joint ventures create producer goods (or high-quality consumer goods) necessary for China's modernization. But, because China limits imports of many of these goods, keeping domestic prices artificially high, manufacturers of these products have short-term monopolies in the domestic market and benefit from the higher prices that monopolies create.

21. For a detailed discussion of the prereform foreign trade system, see Nicholas R. Lardy, *Foreign Trade and Economic Reform in China, 1978–1990* (New York: Cambridge University Press, 1992), chapter 2.

22. Barry Naughton, "The Pattern and Legacy of Economic Growth in the Mao Era," in Kenneth Lieberthal, Joyce Kallgren, Roderick MacFarquhar, and Fredrick Wakeman, eds., *Perspectives on Modern China: Four Anniversaries* (Armonk, N.Y.: M.E. Sharpe, 1991), pp. 233–234.

23. For an excellent discussion of China's process of opening, see Jude Howell, *China Opens Its Doors: The Politics of Economic Transition* (Boulder, Colo.: Lynne Rienner Publishers, 1993).

24. See Foreign Broadcast Information Service, *China Daily Report* (March 9, 1992): 42.

25. This discussion of foreign trade reforms draws heavily on Lardy, *Foreign Trade,* p. 44.

26. Partial reforms in communist systems involve the coexistence of planning and market mechanisms, continued bureaucratic interference, mixed property rights, and "soft budget constraints" for firms. Decentralization often shifts controls to lower levels of the bureaucracy rather than to the production units. See, inter alia, Janos Kornai, "Hard and Soft Budget Constraints," in Janos Kornai, *Contradictions and Dilemmas: Studies on the Socialist Economy and Society* (Cambridge: Massachusetts Institute of Technology Press, 1986), pp. 33–51; Christine P.W. Wong, "Between Plan and Market: The Role of the Local Sector in Post-Mao China," *Journal of Comparative Economics,* 11 (1987): 385–398; and chapter 8 of this book. Vestiges of the planned system increase the value of personal relations as a grease for facilitating transactions and exchanges. See Dorothy J. Solinger, *China's Transition from Socialism* (Armonk, N.Y.: M.E. Sharpe, 1993), pp. 107–126.

27. In 1985, then premier Zhao Ziyang, had called on rural China to turn its agricultural produce into exportable industrial products. But, outside Guangdong Province near Hong Kong, the effort was minimal at both the national and local levels. See chapter 11 of this book for a more detailed discussion of the political economy of TVE exports.

28. In 1987, only 14.3 percent of all direct exports by TVEs throughout China did *not* pass through channels controlled by the Ministry of Foreign Economic Relations and Trade. Data were calculated from *Township and Town Enterprises Yearbook, 1978–1987* (*Xiangzhen qiye nianjian, 1978–1987*) (Beijing: Nongye chubanshe, 1989), pp. 616–617.

29. See also Byrd and Lin, eds., *China's Rural Industry.*

30. Xinhua Overseas News Service (Beijing), October 4, 1992. For more current data, see the tables in chapter 10 of this book.

31. Joseph Fewsmith, *Dilemmas of Reform in China: Political Conflict and Economic Debate* (Armonk, N.Y.: M.E. Sharpe, 1994), pp. 214–217. Shirk argues that provincial leaders or domestic interests have been the key to reform, whereas Solinger argues that central leaders are. See Susan Shirk, *The Political Logic of Economic Reform in China* (Berkeley: University of California Press, 1993), pp. 111–115; and Dorothy J. Solinger, *From Lathes to Looms: China's Industrial Policy in Comparative Perspective, 1979–1982* (Stanford: Stanford University Press, 1991).

32. According to Rawski, growth in China's exports since 1985 was due more to TVEs and foreign-funded enterprises than to state-owned industries. Thomas Rawski, "Export Performance of China's State Industries," unpublished paper.

33. Zhang Bolin and Tao Pengde, "Several Questions on Developing Outward-Oriented TVEs" (*"Fazhan waixiangxing xiangzhen qiye de jige wenti"*), *Theory and Practice in China's TVEs* (*Zhongguo xiangzhen qiye lilun yu shijian*), no. 1–2 (1990): 30.

34. Dali Yang, "China Adjusts to the World Economy: The Political Economy of China's Coastal Development Strategy," *Pacific Affairs* 64 (Spring 1991): 42–64.

35. "Notification about the Rules on Some Policies to Promote Township and Village Enterprises to Export and Earn Foreign Exchange" (*"Yinfa 'guanyu tuidong xiangzhen qiye chukou chuanhui rougan zhengce de guiding' de tongzhi"*) in *Township and Town Enterprise Yearbook, 1989* (*Xiangzhen qiye nianjian, 1989*) (Beijing: Nongye chubanshe, 1989), pp. 140–141.

36. Luo Xiaopeng, "Ownership and Status Stratification," in Byrd and Lin, eds., *China's Rural Industry*, pp. 134–171.

37. See chapter 11 of this book. Even under Deng, campaign-like mobilization remains the tried and true method for obtaining economic policy compliance. See Tyrene White, "Postrevolutionary Mobilization in China: The One-Child Policy Reconsidered," *World Politics* 43 (October 1990): 53–76.

38. *Foreign Broadcast Information Service* (March 9, 1992): 42.

39. See Anthony Leeds, "Locality Power in Relation to Supralocal Power Institutions," in Aidan Southall, ed., *Urban Anthropology: Cross-Cultural Studies of Urbanization* (New York: Oxford University Press, 1973), pp. 15–41. For an application of this model to China see Solinger, *China's Transition from Socialism*, p. 206. For a description of supralocal power institutions that affect TVEs, see chapter 10 of this book.

40. See Zheng Hongyi, *An Analysis of Harbor Cities* (*Gangkou chengshi tansuo*) (Nanjing: Hehai daxue chuban she, 1991).

41. Wade and White see the emergence of developmental states as "a process in which states have played a strategic role in taming domestic and international market forces and harnessing them to a national economic interest." In this case the local state harnesses domestic and international forces, both market and planned, to advance community economic interests. See Gordon White and Robert Wade, "Developmental States and Markets in East Asia: An Introduction," in Gordon White, ed., *Developmental States in East Asia* (London: Macmillan, 1988), pp. 1–29.

42. See Jean C. Oi, "Fiscal Reform and the Economic Foundations of Local State Corporatism in China," *World Politics* 45 (October 1992): 99–126.

43. Interview by the author with BBXG in 1992.

44. According to researchers in the Ministry of Agriculture, 50 percent of rural joint ventures were fronts whose sole purpose was to gain the right to import cars. Interview by the author, December 1991. New policies ended car import benefits to joint ventures in July 1994.

45. Vivienne Shue, *The Reach of the State* (Stanford: Stanford University Press, 1988).

46. For a similar phenomenon in southern China, see Anita Chan, Jonathan Unger,

and Richard Madsen, *Chen Village* (Berkeley: University of California Press, 1993); and Helen Siu, "The Politics of Migration in a Market Town," in Deborah Davis and Ezra Vogel, eds., *Chinese Society on the Eve of Tiananmen* (Cambridge: Harvard Contemporary China Series, 1990), pp. 61–84.

47. See Peter Evans, "The State as Problem and Solution: Predation, Embedded Autonomy, and Structural Change," in Haggard and Kaufman, eds., *The Politics of Economic Adjustment,* p. 163.

48. In Deng's China, a locality's GNP is the key success indicator determining its leader's worth and promotions.

49. Interview by the author with the local Bureau of Foreign Economic Relations and Trade, Zhangjiagang, November 1991.

50. Zhangjiagang officials warned that, if foreign partners had too much control over imported equipment or materials, they could earn unfair profits. By investigations and consulting with foreign trade officials, these officials cut prices by 20 percent and saved US$100,000. See Zhangjiagang City, Xizhang Town Economic Committee, "Run Joint Ventures Well, Develop the Foreign-Oriented Economy" (*"Ban hao hezi qiye, gao hao waixiangxing jingji "*), *Jiangsu TVEs (Jiangsu xiangzhen qiye)*, no. 3 (1991): 43–44.

51. The guidelines stipulated that, in townships that exported fifty million *RMB* of goods, increased exports by 30 percent, had one joint venture, and had per capita exports of 4,500 *RMB,* the township head and the person making the contribution would receive a bonus of 2,000 *RMB.* See *Jiangsu xiangzhen qiye,* no. 5 (1989).

52. The ratio of exports to GNP is probably inflated as local exports in *RMB* are usually calculated in current prices while GNP is usually calculated in fixed prices, which are often based on 1980–1981 prices. Personal communication from Nicholas P. Lardy, January 21, 1993. Whatever the exact ratio, exports had become the engine of growth in Zhangjiagang.

53. For a comparison of township managers with managers in joint ventures in the urban sector, see Margaret Pearson, "Breaking the Bonds of 'Organized Dependence': Managers in China's Foreign Sector," *Studies in Comparative Communism,* no. 25 (1992): 55–57.

54. Interview by the author, November 1991.

55. I was able to interview only two factory workers in private; one supported joint ventures, and one opposed them.

56. These data mirror Rawski's findings that, after 1985, exports from SOEs grew at an average annual rate of 20 percent, a good record for developing countries. But, this pace was dwarfed by the growth in TVE exports. See Rawski, "Export Performance."

57. Development zones in the fourteen coastal cities also became linkage communities. One zone director admitted that he encouraged foreign investors in his zone to sell domestically, even though by doing so they should have lost their tax-free status. Because he needed their investments to pay for the zone's capital construction, he traded access to the domestic market for their investment. Other counties, particularly in southern Jiangsu Province, also tried to attract foreign investment by becoming linkage communities.

58. In 1987, only 6.3 percent of direct TVE exports from Jiangsu Province passed through channels *not* controlled by the Ministry of Foreign Economic Relations, compared with a national average of 14.3 percent. And, while in 1989 decentralization in foreign trade allowed 19.2 percent of TVE exports nationwide to leave the country through channels not controlled by the ministry, only 8.7 percent of TVE exports from Jiangsu Province passed through such channels, less than any other major TVE exporting province.

59. According to David Dapice (Tufts University), "normal" trade companies charge competitive margins of 2 to 4 percent; anything more is rent. Personal conversation with

the author. However, Chinese foreign trade companies are supposed to charge only 1.0 to 1.5 percent.

60. Figure 12.1 and some of the analysis of rent seeking were the result of detailed discussions between the author and Edward Tower of Duke University.

61. A similar problem emerged under Egypt's "open policy" (*infiteh*). The joint venture law allowed foreigners to establish import substitution firms, which earned high profits in a highly protected domestic market. See John Waterbury, "The 'Soft State' and the Open Door: Egypt's Experience with Economic Liberalization, 1974–1984," *Comparative Politics* 18 (October 1985): 76.

62. Interview by the author in November 1991.

63. Robert H. Bates, "Macropolitical Economy in the Field of Development," in James E. Alt and Kenneth Shepsle, eds., *Perspectives on Positive Political Economy* (New York: Cambridge University Press, 1990), pp. 41–43.

64. While I focused on the search for rents, Andrew Walder suggested that high entry costs into these new markets for the TVEs may have contributed to this collective action. Personal communication with the author, 1996.

65. Onis, "The Logic of the Developmental State."

66. See Joel Migdal, "Strong States, Weak States: Power and Accommodation," in Myron Weiner and Samuel Huntington, eds., *Understanding Political Development* (Boston: Little, Brown and Co., 1987), pp. 391–434. While local governments may promote exports efficiently, weakened central control over imports and foreign loans complicates a state's balance of payments.

67. Universities that got World Bank loans developed much more quickly than those that did not. See Chen Changgui and David Zweig, "China's Higher Education and the Open Policy," presented at the Asian Studies Association National Meeting, Los Angeles, Calif., March 1993.

68. Under Egypt's *infiteh,* special "open zones," with tax-free status changed incentives for domestic investors who demanded similar exemptions. Jeswald W. Salacuse, "Foreign Investment and Legislative Exemptions in Egypt: Needed Stimulus or New Capitulations," in Laurence O. Michalak and Jeswald W. Salacuse, eds., *Social Legislation in the Contemporary Middle East* (Berkeley: Institute of International Studies, University of California, 1986), pp. 241–261.

69. Overseas ties, a terrible liability in the Mao era, have become an important source of capital, status, and access to overseas travel. Yuen-fong Woon, "International Links and the Socioeconomic Development of Rural China: An Emigrant Community in Guangdong," *Modern China* 16 (April 1990): 139–172.

70. Albert O. Hirschman, *The Strategy of Economic Development* (New Haven: Yale University Press, 1958).

71. See Susan H. Whiting, "The Comfort of the Collective: The Political Economy of Rural Enterprise in Shanghai," presented at the Annual Meeting of the Association for Asian Studies, Los Angeles, Calif., March 1993.

72. Lecture by Wang Zhenyao, Harvard University, March 3, 1994.

73. Thus, even without a capitalist class, foreign investors can find allies in a socialist system to help them undermine central efforts to control their activities. See Margaret Pearson, *Joint Ventures in the People's Republic of China* (Princeton: Princeton University Press, 1991).

Part V

Reviewing the Record

13

Development, Freedom, and the Future of Rural China

Introduction

Rural reform has been under way for almost 20 years, undermining most institutional constraints imposed during the Maoist era. Labor mobilization into factories, migration into cities and town, the restructuring of rural production, the reemergence of household-dominated farming, rural-urban interdependence on terms far more equitable to villagers than under Mao, an increased inflow of new technologies, and integration of the rural economy via foreign investment and export promotion, have all brought enormous benefits to China's farmers and rural inhabitants. Within these sectors that have benefited from the reforms, household incomes and living standards are up, as is total rural output; villagers' opportunities for self-actualization—such as the freedom to own a business or choose what crops to grow—have all increased. Political freedom and social mobility, as well as farmers' level of awareness of the world outside their villages, has expanded due to an explosion of communication and transportation. Rural China has been transformed, undergoing an intense phase of what Karl Deutsch would call "social mobilization."

Yet change has costs, externalities and unintended consequences. Rapid growth, accompanied by expanded interpersonal and interregional inequality, has been politically destabilizing, as privatization and the redistribution of property create social stress. While some new institutions, such as markets, have grown quickly, laws and norms governing them have taken root slowly, making uncertainty a powerful force affecting economic decisions. A hunger for rapid growth and short-sighted unsatiable demands for natural resources, as well as polluting TVEs which, along with expanded housing, eat up China's precious agricultural

farmland, is stripping China of its long-term potential for sustainable development. Weakened collective institutions and a fiscal crisis in Beijing also threaten
public welfare, such as health care delivery, irrigation systems, rural education,
and the state's capacity to deliver new roads, infrastructure, and communications
and transportation systems.

An Overview and Periodization of
Rural Reform Since 1978

Still, the data presented below and the discussion that follows show remarkable
success along several dimensions. The quality of rural life, levels of economic
development, and the emergence of a more autonomous countryside, embedded
in a more mutually interdependent relationship with China's cities, are clear
successes of the reforms. Similarly, farmers' economic and social autonomy
have grown substantially. Villagers are freer today to speak out, and new village
committees with electoral laws allow farmers in some locations to "throw the
bums out" through established electoral procedures. Political rights, nevertheless,
remain highly restricted, and cadre-farmer relations in many parts of rural China
remain quite tense. Moreover, growing inequality and the damage to the rural
environment of unrestrained growth have become significant problems facing
farmers, cadres, and central policy makers.

The data also show that the trajectory of rural reform has not been linear. For
example, rapid growth in agricultural production in the years 1978–1984 proved
unsustainable. The urban-rural gap, while initially narrowed, reemerged by the
late-1980s. As a result, the reform era can be broken down into four periods:
1978–84, 1985–88, 1989–91, and post-1992 (although since 1994 and the reemergence of more conservative leadership, policy has again begun to shift).

From 1978 to 1984, as the state liberated farmers from collective controls and
household autonomy reemerged, rural output and income boomed in what now
must be seen as the "golden era of rural reform." While the state significantly
increased procurement prices, providing a bonanza for farmers in surplus producing areas, state investment in agriculture, when controlled for inflation, actually declined (figure 13.3). From 1985, through the middle of 1988, the focus of
reform shifted from the countryside to the cities. Yet rural privatization and
commercialization continued, and with it the intensity of urban-rural transactions. This "second stage of rural reform," combined with a jump in rural industrial production—the result of a central decision to promote rural industry—kept
rural incomes buoyant, particularly in coastal areas. But by 1988, rapid growth in
urban incomes, urban inflation, a drop in grain output—due primarily to a drop
in the relative price of grain—and a growing price scissors between the value of
urban and rural products, generated the first spate of rural disturbances of the
reform era.[1]

The post-1988 period is less easy to categorize. On the one hand, it is the era of rural internationalization—coastal TVEs began exporting in earnest and, as the state opened rural coastal China to FDI, foreign investors flocked in. In that sense, the entire period marks a "third phase of rural reform." However, important policy differences across different dimensions within this period triggered striking variations in policy outcomes. The rise of the conservative faction under Chen Yun, Yao Yilin, and Li Peng from the summer of 1988, and the economic retrenchment that ran from fall 1988 through early 1992, slowed growth in rural industry and non-grain agricultural production. But central expenditures on agricultural production and rural capital construction picked up; conservative leaders, it seems, more than liberal-minded officials such as Deng Xiaoping and Zhao Ziyang, supported the more traditional sectors. Also, tight monetary policy and a drop in urban incomes slowed the rate of expansion of the urban-rural gap.

Deng's 1992 "southern trip" (*nan xun*) and the economic boom that followed had a generally negative impact on the countryside. The construction explosion in coastal cities did pull tens of millions of villagers out of the hinterland in search of higher-paying jobs as day laborers, and their remittances have promoted incomes and industry in once non-industrialized areas. Similarly, FDI in the countryside rose dramatically after 1992. And while rural per capita income in 1992–1994 increased significantly (4.94 percent), the pro-city, pro-coastal bias of Deng's post-1992 policies increased the urban-rural gap, undermined grain production, and led rural cadres to ship funds from inland areas to coastal regions in search of higher returns. Rural instability in 1993–1994, Deng's failing health, and Jiang Zemin's search for an alternative, more balanced, growth strategy turned policy around once again. As of early 1997, issues such as resolving rural poverty, narrowing the urban-rural and inland-coastal gaps, increasing the relative price of grain, and demands to reduce the unofficial tax burdens imposed on villagers by local governments have again moved to the foreground.

Criteria for Evaluation

To assess the record of the rural reforms we need categories for evaluation and yardsticks for evaluating these categories. But on what aspects of China's rural development should we focus, and against what should we compare the current situation? In a classic article, Huntington outlined five integrated components of successful political development: economic growth, decreased inequality, autonomy (lessened dependence on external forces), expanded democracy, and stability.[2] These five goals were not necessarily compatible, in that they may not be attainable at the same time. Some might come first; others later. Stability may not always be positive; as Hirschman pointed out, rapid economic growth may be highly destabilizing, so if a premium is set on stability, growth, innovation and change may suffer.[3]

Borrowing from Huntington's typology, I propose my own framework: (1) quality of life; (2) economic development; (3) rural dependency vs. autonomy or interdependence; (4) economic and political freedom; (5) equality; and (6) sustainable development.

The Clear Successes

Quality of Rural Life

If one compares the mid-1990s to 1978, the record of the reforms has been quite remarkable. Per capita income has improved dramatically for most of China's farmers, consumption of food and household goods is way up, as is the quality of their diet, and so is investment in rural housing. In this respect, the golden years were from 1978 to 1984 when rural incomes grew at an annual rate of 15 percent.[4] Table 13.1a shows that net income of rural households, after being adjusted for inflation, has increased from 133.6 *RMB* in 1978 to 442.23 *RMB* by 1995, at an average annual growth rate of 6.9 percent. As a result, consumption of household goods has shot up as well.[5] Table 13.4 shows the dramatic increase in the consumption of consumer durables by rural residents, a clear indicator of an increased quality of life.[6]

Villagers work fewer hours today than under the collective system, allowing more leisure time to enjoy the higher standard of living.[7] The number of people facing poverty has also decreased significantly. First, decollectivization pushed hundreds of millions out of poverty, while the state, after 1986, began a more concerted effort to resolve deep-seated poverty in the northwest and old revolutionary base areas. And although severe poverty remains a focus of current rural policy, compared to India, China's record on issues such as life expectancy at birth remains quite impressive (70 years versus 58 years).[8]

On the issue of housing, the following calculation suggests the remarkable impact of rural reform. In 1978, over 90 percent of farmers probably lived in homes with straw roofs, earthen walls, and dirt floors. Since then, perhaps 80 percent of farmers introduced tile roofs, brick walls, and concrete floors—even in rural Anhui Province I saw very few earthen homes in 1993. Given that Chinese farmers comprise 18 percent of the world's population, decollectivization and the subsequent reforms significantly improved the quality of housing for 16 percent of the world's people, generating the single largest housing boom in world history.[9]

Finally, the reforms disrupted one of the major contributions of the Maoist era, the rural health system. Initially, great concern was expressed that weakening the rural health-care delivery system would significantly undermine the health of China's rural residents. However, because of the overall improved economic conditions and diet in most areas, expected declines in rural health status have not been observed, no matter how hard analysts look.[10] Still, according to some data, improvements in the health-care delivery system introduced in the late Mao era that bore fruit in the late 1970s have lost a little of their impact

Table 13.1a

Rural and Urban Per Capita Income, 1978–1994 (in adjusted *RMB*)[1]

Year	Rural household income	Urban household income	Urban/rural income gap
1978	133.6	316.0	2.36
1980	177.0	401.3	2.27
1984	301.9	506.7	1.68
1985	310.4	510.6	1.65
1988	339.5	593.8	1.75
1989	323.4	575.1	1.78
1991	359.7	661.9	1.84
1992	382.6	720.6	1.88
1994	442.2	864.4	1.95

Source: Zhongguo tongji nianjian, 1996 (China Statistical Yearbook), p. 281.
Note:
[1]To deflate rural incomes for 1978–1985, I used '*shangpin lingshou jiage zong zhi shu*' (index of retail commodity prices) and for 1985–1994 I used '*nongcun jumin xiaofei jiage zong zhi shu*' (index of prices of consumer durables for rural residents). However, since prices of consumer goods, based on the "index of retail commodity prices," had already risen by 28.1% by 1985, I added 28.1% to each year's inflation level for rural residents (now based on the "index of prices of consumer durables for rural residents") before I calculated the real prices. The *Zhongguo wujia nianjian 1995* (*China Price Yearbook*), p. 343, only began its index of prices for rural residents in 1985. It did, however, give a deflator for consumer durables for *urban* residents beginning in 1978, so I used that to calculate urban household income.

due to the reforms.[11] Nevertheless (and somewhat surprisingly), the number of rural hospital beds, while stagnating between 1979 and 1984, increased somewhat between 1984 and 1988, while the number of urban hospital beds declined between 1983 and 1989.[12]

Still there are reasons for both concern and optimism. First, the pace of growth in rural incomes has slackened dramatically since the boom of the early 1980s. While official data controlled for inflation show that growth of farmers' per capita income slowed in 1985–88 to an annual rate of 2.3 percent and then picked up in 1989–91 and 1992–94 (Table 13.1b),[13] some reports suggest that rural incomes began to stagnate around 1985 and that from 1989 to 1992 the increase was only 1.8 percent.[14] No doubt, enormous unofficial tax burdens imposed on farmers (*san luan*), that would not be reported in the national level data, significantly decreased real disposable incomes in areas where fees were imposed.[15] According to one survey of 1,000 villagers in Sichuan Province, the number of burdens had increased from 64 items in 1985 to 107 in 1991.[16] Still, despite predictions that "the sluggish growth in peasant incomes in recent years will probably become a long-term tendency,"[17] data from the *Chinese Statistical Yearbook* show that rural incomes grew faster in 1992–94 than in

Table 13.1b

Rural and Urban Per Capita Income, 1978–1994 (average annual growth rates)

	Rural households	Urban households
1978–1984	12.4	6.8
1985–1988	2.3	3.8
1989–1991	3.6	4.8
1992–1994	4.9	6.3

Source: Zhongguo tongji nianjian, 1996 (China Statistical Yearbook), p. 281.
Note: Calculations are based on adjusted values as reported in Table 13.1a.

1989–91, at an average annual rate of 4.9 percent, albeit at a much slower pace than urban ones (see Table 13.1b).

Economic Development

Broad indicators of economic development demonstrate many successes for the reforms. In 1978, 28 million rural residents worked off-farm; by 1994 over 120 million former farmers now worked in industrial and service sector jobs, a transformation of historic proportions (see Table 10.2). Gross measures of output demonstrate this success as well. For example, the Gross Value of Agricultural Output (GVAO) increased at an annual rate of 9.87 percent per year from 1979 to 1984, and maintained a more rapid rate of growth throughout most of the reform period than during any comparable period before 1978 (Table 13.2). In fact, GVAO during the reforms grew more than twice as fast (8.84 percent) as during the entire pre-reform era (4.19 percent). Most impressive has been the growth of the rural industrial sector and the entire rural non-agricultural sector, which includes construction, transport, and services.[18] Even grain output has kept pace with the population increase, growing at an annual rate of 2.0 percent (1979–1995), despite rapid industrialization and the dramatic decline in arable farmland (see Table 13.3 on page 336). A major restructuring of the rural economy has also improved the quality of rural China's service sector, including restaurants and repairs (Chapter 7).

The initial rural reforms of 1978–1984 probably helped generate China's economic boom of the 1980s. Increased output under the "household responsibility system" (HRS) and higher procurement prices paid for those crops, by increasing rural incomes, dramatically transformed rural demand for urban consumer and industrial goods. Between 1978 and 1985, rural per capita consumption increased 94.4 percent, more than double the pace of urban residents (47.5 percent).[19] Consumption of household goods such as bicycles, sewing machines, wristwatches, and radios all jumped dramatically between 1978

Table 13.2

Rural Agricultural and Nonagricultural Production, 1952–1994 (average annual growth rates)[1]

Years	Gross value of agricultural output[a]	Rural nonagricultural production[b]	
		Total[3]	Industrial[2]
1952–1957	2.58	—	—
1958–1965	4.95	—	—
1966–1978	3.35	—	—
1979–1984	9.87[1]	15.2[4]	15.4
1985–1988	10.4	18.4	21.7
1989–1991	5.0	8.2	9.2
1992–1994	9.78	28.8	29.1
1952–1978	4.19		
1979–1994	8.84	22.1	23.8
1952–1994	6.38		

Source:
[a]*Zhongguo gongye jingji tongji nianjian, 1995 (China Industrial Economics Statistical Yearbook;* Beijing: China Statistical Publishing House, 1996), p. 13.
[b]*Zhongguo nongcun jingji nianjian, 1995 (China Rural Statistical Yearbook;* Beijing: China Statistical Publishing House, 1996), p. 163.
Notes:
[1]Values after 1978 were deflated using the "index of rural industrial products" (*nongcun gongye pin lingshou jiage zong zhishu*), which was quite similar to the consumer price index for rural residents. *Zhongguo wujia nianjian, 1995 (China Price Yearbook),* p. 343.
[2]Industrial production is lower than the values on TVEs reported in Table 10.2 because the former excludes all non-industrial production, such as construction or transport, which is included in the latter broader category of TVEs.
[3]The reported value of "total rural non-agricultural production" was greater than the gross value of agricultural production. Perhaps TVEs were included in the "industrial production" (*gong ye*) and not included in the gross value of agricultural production.
[4]As data for 1979 were not available, values in 1978 were used to calculate the annual growth rates of rural nonagricultural production in the periods 1978–1984 and 1978–1994.

and 1985 (see Table 13.4 on page 337), with consumption on some of these items plateauing in the early 1990s. However, beginning in the mid-1980s, demand for bigger ticket items, such as televisions (black and white and as well as color), sofas, washing machines, and refrigerators increased as well. Moreover, if one recalls that there are approximately 200 million rural households, then increased consumption as documented in Table 13.4 shows that, for example, between 1978 and 1985, farmers purchased 100 million new bicycles, 46 million new sewing machines, and 200 million new wristwatches. Between 1990 and 1995, villagers bought 24.2 million color TV sets and 8.3 million motorcycles. Rather than favor the urban sector and depress the rural economy as has occurred in much of

Table 13.3

Grain Production, 1949–1995 (average annual growth rates)

Pre-Reform Era[1]		Reform Era	
Year	Average annual growth rate	Year	Average annual growth rate
1949–1952	9.70	1979–1984	3.46
1952–1957	2.94	1985–1988	0.97
1957–1965	0.00	1989–1991	2.20
1965–1978	3.20	1992–1995	1.30
1952–1978	2.32	1979–1995	2.00

Source: Zhongguo nongye nianjian, 1995 (China Agricultural Yearbook), p. 314.
Note:
[1]As grain production in successive years—1953, 1958, and 1966—was not available in the pre-reform era, I calculated annual growth rates using overlapping years for these periods.

Africa and the Third World,[20] China's dismantling of its collectives, the substantial boost in state procurement prices, and sharply rising rural incomes in 1978–1984, followed by continued growth through the whole reform era, triggered growth throughout the entire economy.

The reforms also initially greatly benefited grain output (Table 13.3). In 1979–1984, production rose at an annual rate of 3.46 percent, 50 percent faster than the pre-reform rate. But growth rates decreased significantly after that, with a major slump in grain output in both 1985 and 1988 and only 1.1 percent growth per year between 1984 and 1995. If one compares annual growth in grain production for 1952–1978 and 1979–95—2.32 percent versus 2.00 percent—there is little initial reason to say that the reform era outperformed the collective years in terms of increased annual output. Nevertheless, slower population growth in the latter period, a major restructuring of agricultural production into higher value-added crops, a major leap in off-farm labor, and a dramatic increase in the value of non-agricultural rural production demonstrates the success of the more recent period.

Autonomy and Independence

Before 1978, the countryside was totally controlled by China's cities. Rural resources, sucked out of the countryside, developed the urban economy and sustained a higher quality of life for urban residents. The countryside paid "tribute" to the urban areas, through an invisible price scissors of more than 600 *billion RMB* between 1957 and 1987,[21] equivalent to China's total industrial output between 1954 and 1960 or, more importantly, the total value of agricul-

Table 13.4

Rural Household Year-End Possession of Durable Consumer Goods, 1978–1995 (per 100 households)

Item	1978	1980	1985	1990	1995
Bicycles	30.73	36.87	80.64	118.33	147.02
Sewing machines	19.80	23.31	43.21	55.19	65.74
Clocks	24.33	30.95	37.32	49.01	67.94
Wristwatches	27.42	37.58	126.32	172.22	169.09
Electronic watches				23.21	40.44
Electric fans			9.66	41.36	88.96
Washing machines			1.90	9.12	16.90
Refrigerators			0.06	1.22	5.15
Motorcycles				0.89	4.91
Sofas			13.07	36.98	65.41
Wardrobes			53.37	75.67	84.88
Writing desks			38.21	56.08	79.00
Radio sets	17.44	33.54	54.19	45.15	31.05
Black and white TVs			10.94	39.2	63.81
Color TV sets		0.39	0.80	4.72	16.92
Recorders			4.33	17.83	28.25
Cameras				0.70	1.42

Source: Zhongguo tongji nianjian, 1996 (China Statistical Yearbook), p. 309.

tural output between 1952 and 1962. Yet to maximize the center's extractive capacity, the rural economy was isolated from the cities, its consumption levels frozen, and its economy was forced to develop on its own, in a unique mix of state-inflicted autonomy and dependence.

After 1978, if the countryside was to develop successfully, it had to establish a more equitable, two-way relationship with the cities, under which it maintained both relative autonomy and interdependence without exploitation. Rural reform has allowed the countryside to do this by giving farmers greater decision-making authority over crop selection, by allowing them to diversify their agricultural and industrial structure, and by letting rural industry compete with the city on more equal terms. Thus urbanites ate better only because farmers after 1978 diversified their production. Suddenly urban food markets were full of fish, vegetables, and fruits, which improved urban living standards, even as it increased rural incomes. Increased rural demand for consumer durables, the result of fairer procurement prices yielding higher rural output and incomes, also propelled urban industrial growth. Even the current urban construction boom could not occur without the surfeit of rural labor generated by decollectivization.

The clearest measure of the countryside's increased autonomy and economic power is the TVE sector's ability to take over the production of many consumer goods from the ossifying state-owned enterprises (SOEs). While the level of interdependence between these two sectors is far greater than often acknowledged—the suburban nature of rural industry shows its reliance on SOE "outsourcing"—TVE development underpins the farmers' escape from the constraints imposed on their living standard by the urban industrial sector. It also challenges urban views of the countryside as backward and feudal. For years, SOEs and their allies in the central ministries undermined autonomous industrial growth in the countryside, fearing competition for resources and market share. Efforts in 1988–90 to rein in inflation by restricting TVEs, decreased rural industrial employment by 3 percent. But by 1990, central leaders recognized that TVEs had become a pillar of the *national* industrial economy *and* China's export-led growth strategy. From that time forward they have promoted rural industry, which along with foreign invested firms, has been the fastest growing sector of China's domestic and export economy.

Transnational linkages under China's "open policy," the product of the "third phase of reform," while potentially breeding rural dependence on global forces, have contributed positively to rural development. Through exports and foreign direct investment (FDI), TVEs gained access to advanced technologies, improving their ability to compete with SOEs for domestic and international market share. Linkages between Hong Kong and the Pearl River Delta have turned some rural cadres and farmers of the 1970s into the managers of the 1990s, as they now supervise rural employees from inland provinces. Foreign aid has improved the quality of life for villagers in parts of China's hinterland, as the World Bank, The Ford Foundation, and the UNDP/World Bank Water Supply and Sanitation Campaign, as well as aid projects run by Western embassies, have all helped China in its battle against entrenched rural poverty.

Nevertheless, FDI has not always increased rural incomes as dramatically as one might expect. The enormous reservoir of rural labor in inland China has allowed foreign investors in south China to cap wages in rural joint ventures at approximately 300–400 *RMB* per month for the past several years. The flood of inlanders from places such as Sichuan Province, who are willing to be exploited in the short-run in sweat shops in the coastal areas, keeps wages down at the lower ends of the labor market.[22] Also rural communities, competing for foreign markets and technology, allow foreign partners access to the domestic market on more preferable terms than the central government would prefer, undermining Beijing's efforts to keep foreign investors at bay. In this way, rural interests make domestic China more vulnerable to international markets.

More Problematic Sectors

While most of the aforementioned aspects of rural reform must be seen in a quite positive light, the record on equality, democracy, stability, and sustainable development, however, is more mixed.

Figure 13.1 **Rural and Urban Per Capita Income Annual Growth Rates, 1978-1994**

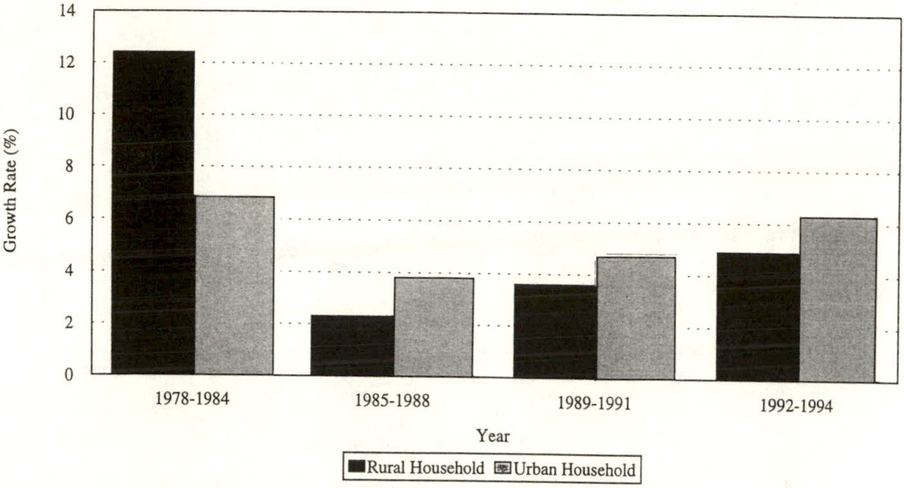

Source: *Zhongguo tongji nianjian, 1996* (*China Statistical Yearbook*), p. 281.
Note: Calculations are based on adjusted values as reported in Table 13.1a.

Equality

Equality has four components: rural-urban, interpersonal, inter-regional, and gender. While increased output following decollectivization and the 1978–1980 jump in procurement prices dramatically narrowed the rural-urban income gap through 1984, in general it continued to expand thereafter, such that the gap in the early mid-1990s was threatening to return to pre-reform levels. According to one report, a gap of 1:2.37 in 1978, dropped to 1:1.71 by 1984, only to return to 1:2.33 by 1992, while Zhao, whose data does not appear to have been adjusted for inflation, found that by 1990, the gap had surpassed what it had been in 1978 (Figure 13.2).[23] My own calculations (figures 13.1 and 13.2) also reflect an initial significant narrowing followed by a reemerging income gap, albeit one constrained by urban inflation which suppressed real average annual growth rates of urban incomes (Table 13.1b).[24] Thus my own findings, which are adjusted for inflation, show that despite a steady increase in the gap from 1985 through 1994, the gap was still significantly lower in 1994 than in 1978 at the end of the Maoist era. Nevertheless, Davis found that average rural per capita income, which in 1988 had been 45 percent of mean urban per capita income, fell further by 1993 to 39 percent.[25] Moreover, according to Davis, the rural-urban gap is growing in all areas of social welfare spending as well.[26]

Other than income, a key measure of urban-rural inequality is the price scissors between industrial goods and agricultural products, and data on this variable

Figure 13.2 **Urban and Rural Income Gap, 1978-1994**

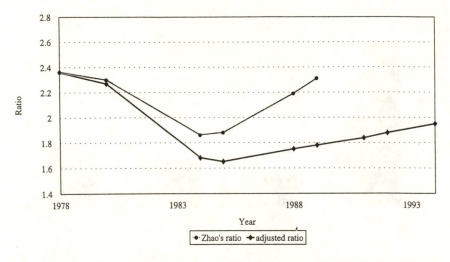

Source: Zhao's ratio is from Zhao Renwei, "Three Features of the Distribution of Income during the Transition to Reform," in Keith Griffin and Zhao Renwei, eds., *The Distribution of Income in China* (New York: St. Martin's Press, 1993), p. 82. The adjusted ratios are from Table 13.1a.

again show trends favorable to the countryside between 1978 and 1984 which were reversed after 1985. According to Xiao, the price ratio of industrial versus agricultural products decreased from 173.1 in 1978 to 137.4 in 1979, reaching a nadir of 106.8 in 1985.[27] Under the Seventh Five Year Plan (1986–1991), however, the price scissors expanded to 133.1 in 1990. And while that imbalance was significantly less than that which existed in 1978, the scissors continued to expand in the early 1990s. Between 1988 and 1992, the price of farm products rose 10.87 percent, while the price of capital goods needed for agriculture rose by 33.59 percent.[28] Similarly, Huang found that between 1989 and 1993, the scissors expanded 83.1 percent, at an annual rate of 12.9 percent.[29] After 1993, however, the scissors appears to have narrowed again.[30]

The urban-rural cultural gap, however, may have narrowed. The glorification of farmers during the Maoist era was primarily rhetorical; extolling the virtues of rural self-reliance paved the way for depressing rural incomes and isolating the rural economy so its surplus could be extracted to supplement urban modernization. Calling on people nationwide to "Learn from Dazhai," and Maoist policies which rusticated over 17 million young people to learn from the "poor and lower-middle peasants," did little to narrow the urban-rural cultural gap.[31] And while the decrease in the uniformed strait jacket of Maoist culture since 1978 has allowed traditional cultural forms to reemerge in the countryside, even as Westernized cultural forms take over the cities,[32] as chapter 7 argued, increased

Table 13.5

TVE Exports by Region, 1987, 1989, 1992 (as percent of total TVE exports)

	1987	1989	1992
Coast[1]	84.3	85.0	89.90
West[2]	0.9	0.7	0.55
Central[3]	14.2	14.3	9.54
Total	99.4	100.1	99.99

Sources:
1987 data from *Township and Village Enterprises Yearbook, 1978–1987*, p. 616.
1989 data from *Township and Village Enterprises Yearbook 1990*, p. 168.
1992 data from *Zhongguo xiangzhen qiye* (Chinese TVEs), no. 5 (1993): 38, in *Renda baokan fuyin ziliao* (People's University Journal Materials), no. 6 (1993).
Notes:
[1]Coastal provinces include: Guangxi, Guangdong, Fujian, Zhejiang, Jiangsu, Shandong, Hainan, Liaoning, Hebei, and the cities of Shanghai and Tianjin.
[2]Western provinces include: Gansu, Ningxia, Qinghai, Xinjiang, Guizhou, and Shaanxi. There were no data for Tibet.
[3]Central provinces include: Beijing, Anhui, Shanxi, Inner Mongolia, Jilin, Heilongjing, Jiangxi, Henan, Hunan, Hubei, Sichuan, and Yunnan.

interactions across what was once a "Second Great Wall" between town and country, and the expansion of rural urbanization has probably narrowed the once sharp divide between urban and rural residents.

Intra-rural, regionally based inequality has emerged as a new problem under the reforms. Rural areas with developed TVE sectors, rural joint ventures, and export enterprises grow far more rapidly than regions still dependent on agriculture. TVEs are primarily a suburban\coastal phenomenon; as a result, in coastal and suburban rural areas GNP is much higher. Also, the gap among regions has been growing. In 1983, the ratio among farmers in the West, Central, and Eastern regions was 100:126:144 and farmers in the highest income province (Shanghai) earned incomes that were 2.69 times higher than farmers in the lowest income province (Gansu).[33] By 1992, that interregional gap had changed to 100:115:166, while farmers in Shanghai now had incomes that were 4.49 times higher than farmers in Gansu Province. Table 13.5 shows that international trade contributes to this inequality, as the gap in TVE exports between coastal and inland provinces continued to expand between 1987 and 1992, as coastal regions got the lion's share of the benefits of foreign commerce. To narrow the interregional, urban/rural gap the central government has called on coastal areas to share their technology with the inland's countryside.[34] But market forces are far more powerful than state exhortations on coastal regions to help develop TVEs in the inland regions.

While interpersonal inequality narrowed under initial decollectivization,[35] in-equality expanded by the mid-1980s due probably to the emergence of the pri-vate sector.[36] Inequitable incomes translate into power differentials, as wealthier farmers have greater opportunity to become local leaders or the economic capital to influence local political outcomes. Many local entrepreneurs are being re-cruited into the CCP in the hopes of coopting them, while some are transferring economic power into political authority through local elections.[37] The end result is that economic power is breeding political power, the reverse of what had been occurring in socialist society, but the more common pattern under a market economy.

Still, despite expanded interregional inequality, the massive shift of rural laborers into coastal cities (and rural factories in the coastal areas) increases the incomes of inland farmers, resolves local unemployment, and helps them send capital and coastal technologies back to the rural hinterland.[38] According to one report, remittances from Sichuanese working outside the province in 1995 amounted to an estimated 20 billion *RMB* (or US$2.4 billion), equivalent to 7 percent of the province's GNP.[39] Sichuan officials also report that 300,000 re-turnees have started businesses expanding the economy of this inland province.[40] Reports tell of farmers travailing in the coastal cities, who transplant the produc-tion process on which they worked into the inland areas.[41] And while these migrants to the coastal areas may work the land for former farmers who have now moved into factories, or even management positions, the returns on their labor are higher in the coastal regions than back in their home villages. Thus, focusing solely on expanding interpersonal or interregional inequalities ignores the growing incomes of migrant farmers.

The impact of reform on the gender gap remains a somewhat mixed picture, although many analysts suggest that rural reform has exacerbated, rather than ameliorated, gender inequality. On the positive side, employment in rural indus-try, reemergence of rural marketing, and the growth of sideline industry all allow women to earn larger incomes than under the collective system. According to Gao, rural women employed in factories occupy a new status, "a middle ground" between urban women and women still employed in agriculture.[42] Today 25 percent of "individual household" enterprises or *geti hu*—i.e., private businesses that employ less than eight employees—are run by women.[43] One need only recall that the collective tied women to the land and paid women on average 60 percent of the work point values given to men to see the significant upside of rural reform for women. Similarly, men totally dominated the ranks of rural cadres; women leaders were an exception. According to Kate Zhou, sexual dis-crimination may also have less of an impact on income-earning potential in industrial jobs than under the collective system, which always assigned lower work point values to women laborers.[44] In this way, gender inequality under Mao had been institutionalized and systematic.

However, according to Ho, the actual number of women directly affected by new opportunities in rural industry is quite small.[45] As of 1990, only 8 percent of rural labor was employed in rural industry (55 million), of which only 30 percent were women. However, while the percent of women in rural industry varies by region, if over a ten-year period 20 million women moved into higher income-earning factory jobs, then even if gender inequality has expanded, the situation for women has clearly improved. Still, the large flow of male laborers to construction sites all over China has increased the share of women among agricultural laborers, and even when rural families run businesses, men are more likely than women to work in it.[46] Women involved in local politics inevitably still do "women's work," serving as heads of township women's federation committees or as family planning cadres.[47] Rural women factory workers in export processing zones, such as Shenzhen, earn much smaller salaries than men and are more likely to be temporary workers, as managers appreciate the ease with which they can hire and fire "working sisters."[48]

Therefore, as Ho argues, "it is simplistic to assume that increased employment leads automatically to improved status." In support of this assertion that "the status of peasant women in China has changed little since the early 1980s,"[49] we can cite the rise of female infanticide, less schooling for girls than boys under reform, and higher rates of female illiteracy.[50] Reports of kidnapping and wife selling suggest that traditional sexist norms have reemerged and life for many rural women remains quite precarious. Still, females are becoming private entrepreneurs, increasing their self-confidence through factory employment, and are considerably more independent than they were under Mao.

Democracy, Freedom, and Order

Freedom is a difficult variable to measure. If one focuses on the ability of an individual to control his own actions, particularly within the economic realm, great freedom has come to China's rural inhabitants. With the collapse of the collective system, mobility has expanded and control of land, labor, and consumption have shifted dramatically from the hands of cadres, state bureaucrats and planners into the realm of the household and the market. The enormity of China's internal migration, while problematic for social order, demonstrates the partial breakdown of the highly totalitarian *hukou* system.[51] Realistic estimates are that 80–100 million farmers have left their home villages, moving into nearby towns, counties, cities within their own provinces, or to the large, booming coastal cities. Farmers are much freer to open their own businesses, too, though as chapter 7 showed, bureaucratic interference remains a serious constraint. Thus, overall the freedom to choose, both politically and economically, for rural inhabitants has increased exponentially since the end of the Maoist era.

Still, economic reform generates political problems. In 1992–93, different growth rates between urban and rural China, and between coastal and inland regions, triggered a political crisis in rural China. Capital accumulated in parts of the countryside is not being invested in rural development; instead in many parts of inland China funds are used for official functions other non-economic endeavors, or to invest in coastal China (including its stock markets) by local cadres who do not want to miss out on the rapidly growing income opportunities in the coast. With little investment capital of their own, these rural cadres resorted to giving farmers IOUs, rather than the capital to pay for their expenses. The political ramifications of expanding urban-rural inequality thereby challenge our perception of the rural reforms as a long-term success.

Thus, politically the rural reforms have been less than successful. First, dismantling the commune's collective system without replacing it with any effective, legitimate, and popular political institutions weakened political order in the countryside. Numerous indicators show that beginning in the early 1980s, village leadership and party power in significant parts of rural China crumbled. A 1989 survey of 413 villages in 17 provinces by the Ministry of Civil Affairs found that 20 percent of rural villages had "paralyzed" leadership organizations, and that in some poorer districts, 30–50 percent of villages had paralyzed leadership.[52] Given the authoritarian bent of rural political culture, and the ability of local officials to utilize formal institutions to suppress the farmers' legitimate concerns and rights, this weakening of authority may not be a bad thing. But it is problematic if the old order is not replaced by one which creates legitimate political authority. "Civil society" needs both legitimate authority that is not dictatorial *and* a citizenry that abides by the rules of that legitimate authority;[53] without both, rural life remains unstable and economic development more difficult.

On the other hand, the growth of "policy based resistance," which rests its legitimacy on the moral and legal responsibility of local cadres to abide by state rules and norms, suggests an expanded role for open political activity and protests which are not automatically declared illegal by the state.[54] The increased reliance on contracts and the courts as a mechanism for establishing commercial exchange and limiting cadre misbehavior also bodes well for a more legally based rural order,[55] although the role of such legal remedies may have declined since the 1980s. Finally, efforts by the Ministry of Civil Affairs to establish "villager committees" and an electoral system to replace local officials suggest as well the inchoate inculcation of a new concept of representativeness which bodes well for democratization and the establishment of a new moral and political authority in the countryside. Recent findings by Manion suggest that elections may be a mechanism for creating greater congruence between the views of farmers and the local leaders who govern them.[56] Even Communist Party secretaries in some villages are now elected by all the villagers.[57]

But these institutions are in an embryonic stage and, despite the enormous international attention reaped on these elections, there is reason to doubt whether any real transfer of authority out of the hands of the Communist Party and into the hand of society has really occurred. Perhaps one could argue that if local CCP officials had the political power to prevent local elections and the transfer of authority to villager committees, without being overthrown by local resistance, then the political vacuum so frequently cited may be less of a problem than we think. However, while some cadres may be able to prevent the emergence of effective popular political representation, those who do so may still lack popular support, leaving only coercive authority as their mainstay of rural order. Greater reliance on strong-arming villagers, the further breakdown of moral authority, and increased lawlessness by both rapacious officials and underground social forces could place parts of rural China on the precipice of social chaos. Moreover, if new political institutions do not emerge, but rural reforms and cadre misbehavior generate greater social mobilization, rural China will face a "participation crisis." And until new and effective participatory institutions emerge, rural reform will not be the midwife of increased rural stability.

Sustainable Development and Investing in the Future

Finally, rural China's future depends on its ability to follow a strategy of sustainable development, growing enough food for its expanding population and increasing per capita income quickly enough to avoid social unrest, all the while doing so in a way that will preserve China's long-term resource endowment and environment.

When one looks at investment in agriculture, the CCP, particularly the more liberal reform wing under Deng, appears guilty of parental neglect.[58] Controlled for inflation, total government expenditure on agriculture drops after 1978 and does not reach the level of 1978 until 1986 (table 13.6b). As a percent of total financial expenditure, state investment peaks in 1979, just as Deng and his allies take total control of agricultural policy, decreases continually through 1988, and then stays around 8–9 percent of total investment through 1994 (Table 13.6a). Finally, as Table 13.6c shows, when controlled for inflation, the central government took a free ride on decollectivization and cut its expenditures on agriculture by 4.6 percent a year between 1979 and 1984. At the same time, the state slashed investment in rural capital construction by 10.9 percent a year, which has a long-term impact on future agricultural output. And while China's conservative leadership of 1989–91 increased investment in agriculture, rural capital construction, and rural relief, even as it cut investments in other sectors of the economy, post-1992 policies again cut back the funds to be allocated to China's traditional sector (Figure 13.3). In fact, investment in rural capital construction and rural science and technology (S&T, as indicated by New Product Development in Table 13.6b) have done poorly under liberal economic regimes.

The amount of land available for farming and the quality of the soil has been declining as well. For too many years, weak enforcement of the Land Law has failed to halt the rapid consumption of rich arable land by urban and industrial expansion.[59] Reports in the late-1980s suggested that China was losing the equivalent of one county a year to urban and industrial sprawl (China has about

Figure 13.3 **Average Annual Increases in Government Expenditure on Agriculture, 1970-1994**

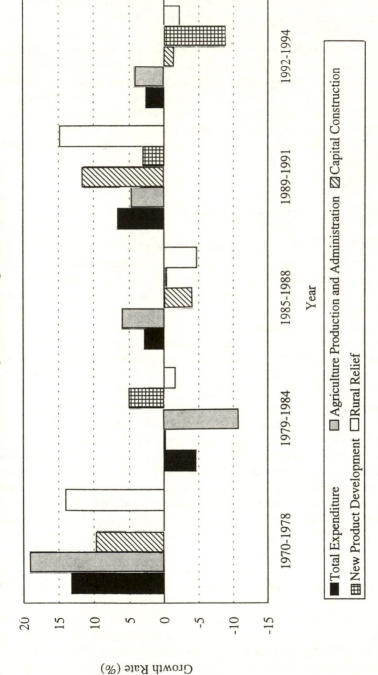

Source: Zhongguo tongji nianjian, 1996 (China Statistical Yearbook), p. 233
Note: These values are based on adjusted prices as calculated in Table 13.6b, using 1978 as the base year. Values for 1970-1978 were not adjusted for inflation, but then, there was not very much inflation in that period.

Table 13.6a

Government Financial Expenditures on Agriculture, 1952–1994
(100 million *RMB*, in current prices)

Year	Total[1]	Expenditures on agricultural production	Appropriations for capital construction	New product promotion	Rural relief	Other[2]	Agricultural expenditures as a percent of total financial expenditure[3]
1952	9.04	2.69	3.84	—	—	2.51	5.10
1957	23.50	7.99	10.93	—	—	4.58	7.70
1962	38.23	19.29	8.67	—	—	10.27	12.50
1965	54.98	17.29	23.51	1.05	—	13.13	11.80
1970	49.40	15.91	22.52	—	3.14	7.83	7.60
1975	98.96	42.53	35.56	0.10	7.42	13.35	12.10
1978	150.66	76.95	51.14	0.93	6.88	14.63	13.60
1979	174.33	90.11	62.41	1.52	9.80	10.49	13.68
1980	149.95	82.12	48.59	1.31	7.26	10.67	12.40
1981	110.21	73.68	24.15	1.18	9.08	4.96	9.88
1982	120.49	79.88	28.81	1.13	8.60	2.12	10.45
1983	132.49	86.66	34.25	1.81	9.38	2.07	10.28
1984	114.29	95.93	33.63	2.18	9.55	0.77	9.13
1985	153.62	101.04	37.73	1.95	12.90	—	8.33
1986	184.20	124.30	43.87	2.70	13.33	—	7.90
1987	195.72	134.16	46.81	2.28	12.47	—	8.00
1988	214.07	158.74	39.67	2.39	13.27	—	7.90
1989	265.94	197.12	50.64	2.48	15.70	—	8.60
1990	307.84	221.76	66.71	3.11	16.26	—	8.90
1991	347.57	243.55	75.49	2.93	25.60	—	9.10
1992	376.02	269.04	85.00	3.00	18.98	—	8.60
1993	440.45	323.42	95.00	3.00	19.03	—	8.30
1994	532.98	399.70	107.00	3.00	23.28	—	9.20

Sources:

For 1952–1965: *Zhongguo nongcun tongji nianjian, 1995 (China Rural Statistical Yearbook)* (Beijing: China Statistical Publishing House, 1996).

For 1970–1994: *Zhongguo tongji nianjian, 1996 (China Statistical Yearbook)*, p. 233.

Notes:

[1]The total of the values in the sub-categories for 1952–1965 as printed in the *China Rural Statistical Yearbook* did not balance with the value given for total investment. The data for 1970 on from the *Statistical Yearbook* did because it included the category of rural relief. Therefore, I increased the values in the "other" category for 1952–1965 to make it balance with "total."

[2]After 1984, *China Statistical Yearbook* divided the "other" category among the other columns.

[3]1979 and 1981–84 "Agricultural Expenditures as Percent of Total Expenditure" was based on "Total Expenditure" as reported in *Zhongguo caizheng nianjian, 1995 (China Financial Yearbook)* (Beijing: China Financial Journal Publishing House, 1995), p. 403.

Table 13.6b

Government Financial Expenditures on Agriculture, 1978–1994
(100 million *RMB*, in adjusted prices, 1978 = 100)[1]

	Total	Expenditure on agriculture	Capital construction	New products	Rural relief
1978	150.66	76.95	51.14	1.06	6.88
1980	148.61	81.39	48.16	1.30	7.20
1981	108.15	72.31	23.70	1.16	8.91
1982	116.42	77.18	27.84	1.09	8.31
1983	127.15	82.93	32.78	1.73	8.98
1984	131.19	89.07	31.23	2.02	8.87
1985	138.27	90.94	33.96	1.76	11.61
1986	165.25	108.37	38.24	2.35	11.62
1987	162.83	111.61	38.94	1.90	10.37
1988	154.56	114.61	28.64	1.73	9.58
1989	161.76	119.90	30.80	1.51	9.55
1990	178.98	128.93	38.78	1.81	9.45
1991	196.14	137.44	42.60	1.65	14.45
1992	205.81	147.26	46.52	1.64	10.39
1993	215.59	158.31	46.50	1.47	9.31
1994	222.63	166.96	44.69	1.25	9.72

Source: Zhongguo tongji nianjian, 1996 (China Statistical Yearbook), p. 233.
Note:
[1]The values presented were deflated from 1978 on (with 1978 as 100) in order to show the real level of expenditure after adjusting for inflation which was quite high in the mid- and late-1980s. The deflator was based on an index of retail prices of rural industrial products (which was lower than the index for urban industrial products), from the *Zhongguo wujia nianjian, 1995 (China Prices Yearbook)*, p. 343.

Table 13.6c

Average Annual Increases in Government Expenditure on Agriculture, 1970–1994[1]

	Total expenditure	Expenditures on agricultural production and administration	Rural capital construction	New product development	Rural relief
1970–1978	13.19	19.1	9.54	n.a.	13.96
1979–1984	−4.6	−0.2	−10.9	4.9	−1.6
1985–1988	2.8	6.0	−4.2	−0.4	−4.7
1989–1991	6.6	4.7	11.4	3.0	14.8
1992–1994	2.6	4.3	−1.3	−8.7	−2.2

Source: Zhongguo tongji nianjian, 1996 (China Statistical Yearbook), p. 233.
Note:
[1]These values are based on adjusted prices as calculated in Table 13.6b, using 1978 as the base year. Values for 1970–78 were not adjusted for inflation, as inflation in those years was quite minimal.

2,000 counties overall). The "zone fever" of 1992–93 is just one more example of a large rural land grab by urban interests.[60] Rural industry has been polluting China's rivers and soil at a much more rapid rate than urban SOEs.[61] Education levels in the countryside, the seedbed of future agro-technicians, has suffered under a policy that has favored the cities over the countryside, as fewer and fewer of China's middle school students actually come from the countryside.[62] Here short-term household calculations which push their children into low skill jobs—which pay more than agriculture—are undermining the long-term development of human capital.[63] Similarly, some Western analysts argue that the lack of secure property rights causes farmers to employ a short-term horizon and eschew investments in land, irrigation, drainage, terracing, wells, and other infrastructure that would promote longer-term development.[64] Others, however, find that farmers are little concerned about securing their property rights, in part because little redistribution of land occurs.[65] Moreover, since 1992, the state has instituted 30-year land contracts for farmers, though Kung found that many localities still ignored this policy. Nevertheless, with the collapse of the communes, the farmers' need for agricultural service and marketing organizations has not been met, as villages play an important service role in only a few localities, leaving farmers in most locations completely on their own, with few cooperative institutions to help them with seeds, pesticides, irrigation and other key inputs.[66]

Will China be able to feed itself? While Lester Brown's malthusian predictions appear to be overstated,[67] his report touched a raw nerve within a Chinese leadership that for almost two decades has underinvested in agriculture. Most rural specialists both in and outside of China believe that China's future demand for grain imports will not affect world prices significantly.[68] One model, which employed high and low rates of growth for production, population, investment, income and economic development, efficient use of feed grains, and land reclamation versus land loss, found that if current trends continue, demand for imports would increase considerably.[69] But, according to Lin, the central government's sensitivity to this issue—their view is "no grain, no stability"—will compel it to introduce more policies, similar to the increased investment in rural capital construction and agricultural science which he observed in 1994–95.[70] Paarlberg, too, believes along with Lin that China and the world would be better served if China produced more higher-value added crops and imported more grain.[71] This is China's best strategy for "sustainable development." Also, by buying more grain, China could stabilize world food prices and agricultural production in rural regions of Europe and North America, helping these government cut the enormous subsidies they give to their own agricultural economies. In any case, Figure 13.4 shows that China has successfully increased grain production quite remarkably since 1978, and many analysts argue that new seed strains soon to hit the market will boost output by as much as 25 percent.

This need to restructure domestic investment led the CCP's General Secretary, Jiang Zemin, in November 1996 to call on central and local officials "to

350

Figure 13.4 Grain Production Output, 1949–1995

Source: Zhongguo nongye nianjian, 1995 (China Agricultural Yearbook), p. 314.

strike a balance between industrial and agricultural development."[72] Agricultural policy makers, speaking at the Harvard conference on "Feeding China," described major plans to improve irrigation, and fall 1996 has witnessed a major upsurge in rural capital construction.[73] Similarly, pollution caused by TVEs has become an issue of major concern in China and a target of national policy. Nevertheless, despite decisions at the Sixth Plenum in fall 1996 to increase agricultural investment, a central government facing its own fiscal crisis, and committed to propping up its ailing urban state enterprises, will remain very hard-pressed to increase significantly its investments in agriculture. Still, if the past 19 years is our guide, this group of more conservative leaders may indeed be willing and able to increase expenditures on the rural areas.

Conclusion

Viewed overall from the perspective of output, growth, autonomy and consumption, the achievements of the past 19 years have been remarkable. Dismantling the collectives freed China's farmers to find more remunerative employment, an important factor in containing the urban-rural gap. Even FDI has found its way into rural coastal China, increasing incomes in the rural coastal regions and strengthening the TVE sector's competitive edge. Little wonder the choruses of supporters of rural reform remain so powerful.

But too little investment in agriculture, particularly in capital construction and rural S&T, as well as the externalities of this growth on gender and inter-regional inequality, social and political order, environmental degradation, and loss of educational opportunities, creates concern for its long-term sustainability. As I have shown, the trends of the last decade are more mixed and the Chinese government, like all governments in developing countries, has serious bottlenecks to overcome before it can feel confident about the future.

In fact, outside of the TVE sector, which are largely limited to coastal and suburban areas, China has failed to replant the seeds of success in rural reform in any meaningful form of capital investment. If China, in the medium term, is forced to pay the price of this short-sightedness, either in terms of increased rural unrest or a major entry into the global food markets, current sanguine views of the rural reform could change. One can only hope that the Chinese state will be able to implement its recently enunciated goals, and through a newly invigorated, pro-rural policy, guide China's countryside on the road to long-term sustainable development.

Notes:

1. See David Zweig, "Peasants and Politics," *World Policy Journal* (Fall 1989): 633–45.

2. Samuel P. Huntington, "The Goals of Development," in Samuel P. Huntington and Myron Weiner, eds., *Understanding Political Development* (Boston, MA: Little, Brown and Co., 1987), pp. 3–32.

3. Albert O. Hirschman, "Rapid Economic Growth as a Destabilizing Force," in Albert O. Hirschman, *The Strategy of Economic Development* (New Haven: Yale University Press, 1958).

4. See Lin Li, "Problems and Strategic Changes in China's Rural Economic Development," *Jingji yanjiu* (Economic Research), no. 1 (January 20, 1994): 31–39, in *Foreign Broadcast Information Service*, No. 93 (May 13, 1994): 48–56.

5. According to Nolan and Sender, the average annual growth rate of per capita real consumption was 7.2 percent for 1978–1989, while for 1952–78 it had been only 1.8 percent. Peter Nolan and John Sender, "Death Rates, Life Expectancy and China's Economic Reforms: A Critique of A.K. Sen," *World Development*, vol. 20, no. 9 (1992): 1281. According to the State Statistical Bureau, per capita consumption by agricultural residents rose from 138 *RMB* in 1978 to 1,479 *RMB* in 1995, at an average annual rate of 13.9 percent. This value, however, was not adjusted for inflation. *Zhongguo tongji nianjian, 1996*, p. 280.

6. I remember vividly when friends of mine in suburban Nanjing first purchased a stereo system. I was quickly corralled into giving them all dancing lessons. Their joy at an improving standard of living was both obvious and infectious.

7. In interviews in China, Prosterman, Hanstad, and Li found that farmers were spending 60–90 days a year on their individual land holdings, while they had spent 250–320 days a year working the land during the collective era. As one farmer told them, he had spent a lot of time "leaning on his hoe." See Roy L. Prosterman, Tim Hanstad, and Li Ping, "Can China Feed Itself?" *Scientific American*, November 1996, p. 92.

8. Nolan and Sender, "Death Rates," p. 1300. Banister, among others, asserts that China's life expectancy data is inflated because China undercounts infant mortality. See Judith Banister, *China's Changing Population* (Stanford, CA: Stanford University Press, 1987). She therefore argues that life expectancy as of 1984 was only 64.6 percent, almost five years lower than state estimates. See Table 4.18. By 1990 life expectancy had risen to 67.3 years, and in 1995 to 68 years. Judith Banister, "Perspectives on China's Mortality Trends," unpublished paper, and personal communication with the author. According to Croll, over 27 percent of rural Chinese (or 218 million people) were in absolute poverty in 1980, but by 1990, the number had dropped to 97 million, or 11.5 percent of the rural population. See Elizabeth Croll, *From Heaven to Earth* (London: Routledge, 1994), p. 282. Recent reports by the World Bank, however, which have raised the poverty line, suggest 300 million rural Chinese still face poverty.

9. According to *Chinese Statistical Yearbook, 1990*, housing space per rural inhabitant doubled between 1978 and 1989 from 8.1 sq mts. to 17.2 sq. mts.

10. Personal communication from Gail Henderson, January 1997.

11. See the sharp critique of Nolan and Sender by Sen, who accuses them of ignoring their own data (which shows the rising death rate between 1978 and 1989) and of historical distortion when they asserted that changes in China's rural institutions "were initiated the moment the 'Gang of Four' was arrested in October 1976" (Nolan and Sender, p. 1280). Sen is clearly correct that Hua Guofeng was responsible for rural policy until late 1978 or 1979 and that serious institutional changes did not occur until 1978–79. See Amartya Sen, "Life and Death in China: A Reply," *World Development*, vol. 20, no. 9 (1992): 1305–12. While China's death rate reached its nadir of 6.4 per 1000 in 1978, well below the rates of 7.4 and 7.1 per 1000 in 1976 and 1977 respectively, the rate increased to 6.7 percent per 1000 by 1989. See Nolan and Sender, "Death Rates."

12. China Statistical Bureau, ed., *Kua jin de sishi nian, 1949–1989* (40 Years of Great Progress, 1949–1989) (Beijing: China Statistical Publishing House, 1990), p. 447. Whyte's own calculations challenge official data as reported in the above cited yearbook and show the rural percentage of the total number of hospital beds continuing to

decline. See Martin K. Whyte, "City Versus Countryside in China's Development," *Problems of Post-Communism* (January/February 1996): 9–22.

13. Rural income dropped because after the jump in grain production in 1984, the state cut procurement prices, which cut rural incomes. See Terry Sicular, "Grain Pricing: A Key Link in Chinese Economic Policy," *Modern China*, vol. 14, no. 4 (October 1988): 470–78.

14. Lin, "Problems and Strategic Changes." According to Lin, growth in rural incomes in 1989–91 was only 0.7%, but rebounded in 1992, placing growth for the entire period of 1989–1992 at 1.8%.

15. See Thomas P. Bernstein, "Incorporating Group Interests into the Policy Process: The Case of Farmers During the Reform Era," paper prepared for the conference on "The Non-Economic Impact of China's Economic Reforms," Harvard University, September 20–22, 1996, p. 20. This and other papers by Tom Bernstein have been singularly helpful to me as I wrote this paper.

16. Sung Kuo-cheng, "Peasant Unrest in Szechwan and Mainland China's Rural Problems," *Issues and Studies*, vol. 29, no. 7 (1993): 129–32.

17. Lin, "Problems and Strategic Changes."

18. One should note that while the economic retrenchment of 1989–91 severely depressed growth rates in both agricultural and rural nonagricultural production, rates rebounded after 1992.

19. *Zhongguo tongji nianjian, 1996*, p. 280.

20. Robert Bates, *Markets and States in Tropical Africa* (Berkeley: University of California Press, 1981).

21. See "Peasants, the Market and Innovation in the Institution," *Jingji yanjiu*, no. 1 (January 20, 1987): 3–16.

22. Kathy Chen, "Boom-Town Bound: A Teenager's Journey Mirrors Inner Migration That's Changing China," *Wall Street Journal*, October 29, 1996.

23. According to Lin, "the gap has returned to the pre-reform level." Lin, "Problems and Strategic Changes." For Zhao's analysis see Zhao Renwei, "Three Features of the Distribution of Income during the Transition to Reform," in Keith Griffin and Zhao Renwei, eds., *The Distribution of Income in China* (New York: St. Martin's Press, 1993), Table 2.5, p. 82.

24. Nevertheless, urban income data in the *China Price Yearbook* reflects only per capita disposable income and excludes subsidies available only to urban residents.

25. *People's Daily*, February 23, 1991, p. 2, and March 1, 1994, p. 2, cited in Deborah S. Davis, "Inequality and Stratification in the Nineties," in Lo Chi Kin, Suzanne Pepper and Tsui, *China Review 1995* (Hong Kong: Chinese University Press, 1994), p. 11.2.

26. Davis, "Inequality and Stratification," pp. 11.3–4. Yet as Davis notes, due to the growth of non-state enterprises, the incomes of the top 15–20 percent of rural (suburban) inhabitants now surpassed the incomes of those on the lower rungs of the urban income scale. A once sharp dichotomy between urban and rural incomes is now characterized by overlapping strata. See Davis, p. 11.17.

27. See Xiao He, "*Gong nong 'jiandao cha' you zai kuoda*" ("The industrial and agricultural price scissors is again expanding"), *Dangdai yuekan* (Current Monthly), no. 28 (July 15, 1993): 38.

28. Lin, "Problems and Strategic Changes."

29. Huang Chingming, "*Gong nong chanpin jiandao cha wenti chu tan*" (Beginning discussion on the problem of the price scissors for industrial and agricultural products), *Jingji yanjiu cankao* (Reference on Economic Research), no. 24 (1996): 4.

30. "*Gong nong san da jiandao cha ji qi xianzhuang fenxi*" ("The three big industrial and agricultural scissors and an analysis of the current situation"), *Jingji yanjiu* (Economic Research), no. 10 (1996): 60.

31. Thomas P. Bernstein, *Up to the Mountains, Down to the Villages* (New Haven: Yale University Press, 1977).

32. See Martin King Whyte, "The Rural-Urban Gap in China's Development," paper prepared for the conference on "Rural China: Emerging Issues in Development," East Asian Institute, Columbia University, March 31–April 1, 1995.

33. Lin, "Problems and Strategic Changes."

34. *Renmin ribao*, April 25, 1995, p. 1.

35. For indicators of the narrowing of inequality in the early years of the rural reform, see Table 2.4 above.

36. Among villagers in Changzhou City, in southern Jiangsu, interpersonal inequality, measured in terms of gini coefficients, doubled between 1978 and 1987, while estimates by the World Bank suggest that after narrowing from .32 in 1978 to .22 by 1982, the gini coefficient of interpersonal inequality in rural China grew to .31 by 1986. See Xu Caiming, et. al., "A Sociological Investigation of 'Relatively Well-Off' in the Countryside," *Nongye jingji wenti* (Problems of Agricultural Economics), no. 9 (1990), and Azzur Rahman Khan, Keith Griffin, Carl Riskin, and Zhao Renwei, "Household Income and Its Distribution in China," *China Quarterly*, no. 132 (1992): 1029–61, respectively.

37. Yang Liping, "*Nongcun jieji bianhua he dang de jianshe*" ("Rural Class Change and Party Construction"), *Dangjian yanjiu* (Research on Party Construction) (Jing), no. 1 (1992): 43–6.

38. In Anhui, by 1993, 20.66 percent of the rural labor force was going outside the province for work. See "*Guanyu Anhui sheng 'min gong chao' de diaocha yu duice jianyi*" (Some Policy Recommendations and Research on Anhui Province's "Wave of Labor Exports"), *Zhongguo nongcun jingji* (China's Rural Economy), no. 1 (1994): 53–7.

39. Bruce Gilley, "Irresistible Force: Migrant Workers Are Part of a Solution, not a Problem," *Far Eastern Economic Review*, April 4, 1996, pp. 18–21.

40. Gilley, "Irresistible Force," p. 19.

41. In Fuyang District, Anhui Province, there are over 700 factories established by returned workers. See Zhang Shanyu and Yang Shaoyong, "*Mingong chao jiang dailai 'huixiang chuanye chao*'," (The Wave of Labor Export Creates a Wave of Returning Entrepreneurship), *Renkou yu jingji* (Population and Economics), no. 1 (1996): 43–7.

42. These women are financially independent and less dependent on their husbands. See Gao Xiaoxian, "China's Modernization and Changes in Social Status of Rural Women," in Christina K. Gilmartin, et al., eds., *Engendering China* (Cambridge: Harvard University Press, 1994), p. 85.

43. Huang Xiyi, "*Zhongguo dangdai shehui bianqian funu jingji shenfen de zhuanhuan*" (The Transformation of the Economic Status of Rural Women in the Midst of Social Changes in Contemporary China), in Li Xiaojiang and Tan Shan, eds., *Zhongguo funu fencheng yanjiu* (*Research on Chinese Women by Stratum*) (Zhengzhou: Henan renmin chubanshe, 1991), cited in Samuel P. S. Ho, "Rural Non-Agricultural Development in Post-Reform China: Growth, Development Patterns, and Issues," *Pacific Affairs*, vol. 68, no. 3 (Fall 1995): 379.

44. Kate Xiao Zhou, *How the Farmers Changed China: Power of the People* (Boulder, CO: Westview Press, 1996), p. 217.

45. Ho, "Rural Non-Agricultural Development."

46. See Barbara Entwisle, et. al., "Gender and Family Businesses in Rural China," *American Sociological Review*, vol. 60, no.1 (February 1995): 52.

47. See Stanley Rosen, "Women and Political Participation in China," *Pacific Affairs*, vol. 68, no. 3 (Fall 1995): 326.

48. According to Gao, processing zones are not a means of improving women's status, particularly that of young rural women. "Exactly the opposite: it is proof of the

disadvantaged position of rural women in the labor market." Gao, "China's Modernization," p. 93.

49. Ho, "Rural Non-Agricultural Development," p. 385.

50. Gao reported that in 1988, 83 percent of school-age children not enrolled in school, and 70 percent of three million who left school, were female. Gao, "China's Modernization," p. 95.

51. Still, much internal migration is arranged by local governments who attach a certain percentage of the migrant laborers' earned income.

52. Tang Pusu, *"Nongcun zhong qian you de weiji bu ke digu"* (We Cannot Underestimate the Depth of the Crisis in Rural China), in China Basic Power Construction Research Association, ed., *Shijian yu sikao* (Practice and Theorizing) (Shenyang: Liaoning University Publishing House, 1989), p. 78. Thanks to Li Lianjiang, who brought this article to my attention.

53. Heath B. Chamberlain, "On the Search for Civil Society in China," *Modern China*, vol. 19, no. 2 (1993): 199–215.

54. Li Lianjiang and Kevin J. O'Brien, "Villagers and Popular Resistance in Contemporary China," *Modern China*, vol. 22, no. 1 (January 1996): 28–61, and Kevin J. O'Brien and Lianjiang Li, "The Politics of Lodging Complaints in Rural China," *The China Quarterly*, no. 143 (September 1995): 756–83.

55. See chapter 6.

56. See Melanie Manion, "The Electoral Connection in the Chinese Countryside," *American Political Science Review*, vol. 90, no. 4 (December 1996): 736–48.

57. *Nongmin ribao*, December 20, 1988, p. 3, and April 4, 1989. For recent reports, see "Yancheng Openly Selects Village Party Secretaries," *Baokan wenzhai*, August 14, 1995, p. 1.

58. For a trenchant critique of agricultural policy, particularly the neglect of farmers' interests by reformers such as Deng, Zhao, and Wan Li, see Bernstein, "Incorporating Group Interests into the Policy Process."

59. Leo A. Orleans, "Loss and Misuse of China's Cultivated Land," in Joint Economic Committee, U.S. Congress, *China's Economic Dilemmas in the 1990s: The Problems of Reforms, Modernization and Interdependence* (Washington, D.C.: Government Printing Office, 1991), pp. 403–17.

60. David Zweig, "China's New Economic Warlords," *Asian Wall Street Journal*, August 3, 1992.

61. When enterprises in the same industry were compared, TVEs emitted 10–20 times more pollutants than SOEs. See Xia Zifen, ed., *Shanghai xiangzhen qiye jingji keji fazhan zhanlue he zhengce wenti yuanjiu* (Research on Problems Concerning the Strategy and Policy for the Economic and Technological Development of Township and Village Enterprises in Shanghai) (Shanghai: Shanghai shehui kexue yuan chubanshe, 1988), p. 52, cited in Ho, "Rural Non-Agricultural Development," p. 375.

62. See the table on urban-rural inequality in Whyte, "The Rural-Urban Gap in China's Development."

63. I have never forgotten a conversation with a 10-year-old boy in Jinjiang County, near Quanzhou in Fujian Province. The boy was hawking goods on the street, and saw no need for school as he was earning a lot of money. His father, who was nearby, supported the boy's decision to quit school.

64. See Prosterman, Hanstad and Li, "Can China Feed Itself?"

65. While Prosterman, et. al., see land redistribution undermining farmer investment, Kung and Liu argue that since 1978, land has not been redistributed very often and redistribution is more likely in poor villages than in rich ones. Also, the vast majority of villagers made only partial readjustments, in order to respond to population changes. See

James Kai-sing Kung and Shouying Liu, "Property Rights and Land Tenure Organizations in Rural China: An Empirical Study of Institutions and Institutional Change in Transitional Economies," unpublished paper. Moreover, Kung's finding that most farmers favored land redistribution challenges Prosterman, et. al. See J. K. Kung, "Equal Entitlement Versus Tenure Security under a Regime of Collective Property Rights: Peasants' Preference for Institutions in Post-Reform Chinese Agriculture," *Journal of Comparative Economies*, vol. 21, no. 1 (1995): 82–111.

66. See Zhao Yang and Xue Yiming, "International Comparison Study on Community Agro-Service Organizations in China," Department of Rural Development, Development Research Center of the State Council, August, 1996 Beijing.

67. Lester Brown, *Who Will Feed China?* For a tough critique of Brown, see Robert L. Paarlberg, "Rice Bowls and Dust Bowls," *Foreign Affairs*, vol. 75, no. 3 (May/June 1996): 127–32.

68. At a seminar in Hong Kong in November 1996, outspoken conservative economist Hu Angang stated that China will probably need to import significant amounts of food in the coming years. Moreover, he supported the idea that China should import food from the U.S. to improve the balance of trade, while China could move to more higher value-added crops. *South China Morning Post*, November 1996. But a conference at Harvard in March 1996, entitled "Feeding China: Today and into the 21st Century," challenged Brown's data. Also, significant underreporting of rural land suggests that China still has more room to expand per-hectare yields.

69. Lin Yifu, "*Zhongguo ren you nengli shihuo ziji*" (Chinese People Have the Ability to Feed Themselves), *Ming bao*, October 9, 1996.

70. Data in Table 13.6c challenges that optimism.

71. Paarlburg, "Rice Bowls and Dust Bowls."

72. Vivien Pik-Kwan Chan, "Jiang Drive to Strike Right Balance," *South China Morning Post*, November 28, 1996, p. 10.

73. See the summary notes from the conference, "Feeding China: Today and into the 21st Century," Center for International Affairs, Harvard University, March 1–2, 1996, Cambridge, MA.

Index

David Zweig is Associate Professor, Division of Social Science, Hong Kong University of Science and Technology. He received his Ph.D. in political science form The University of Michigan and held a postdoctoral fellowship from the Fairbank Center for East Asian Research, Harvard University. He taught for ten years at The Fletcher School of Law and Diplomacy, Tufts University. He is also author of *China's Brain Drain to the United States: Views of Overseas Chinese Students and Scholars in the 1990s*, with Chen Changgui (1995) and *Agrarian Radicalism in China, 1968–1981* (1989). He is coeditor of *China's Search for Democracy: The Student and Mass Movement of 1989* (1992) and *New Perspectives on China's Cultural Revolution* (1991). He is currently writing a book entitled *Linking China to the World.*